AMPHIGOREY ALSO

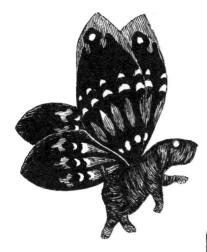

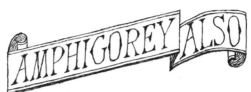

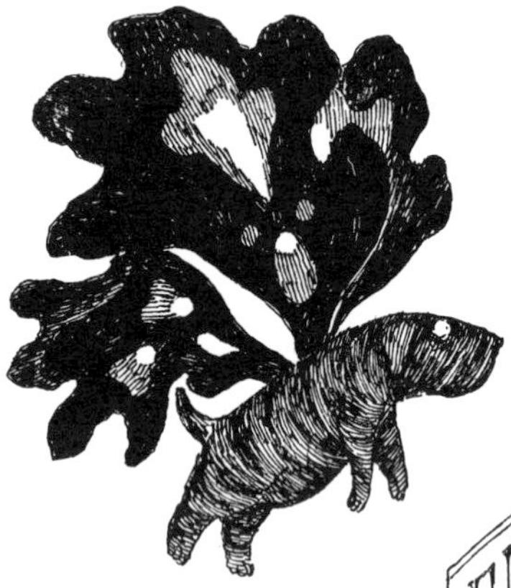

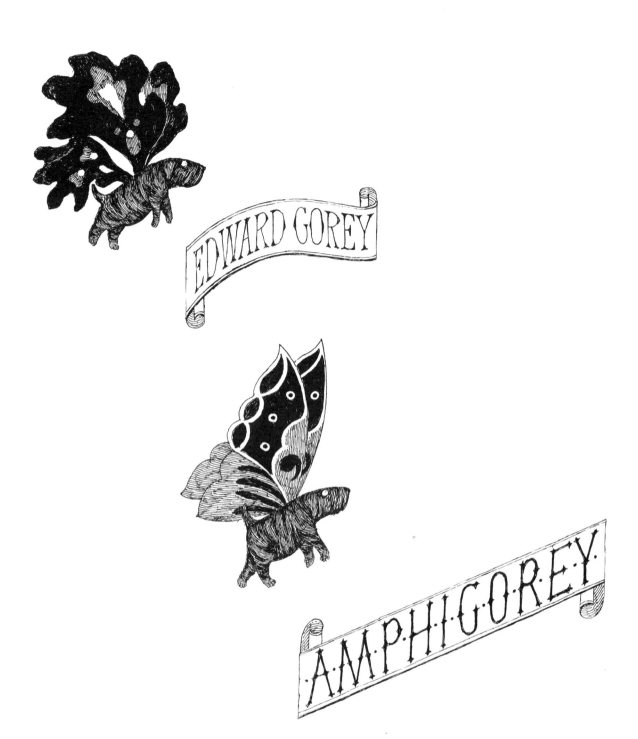

EDWARD GOREY

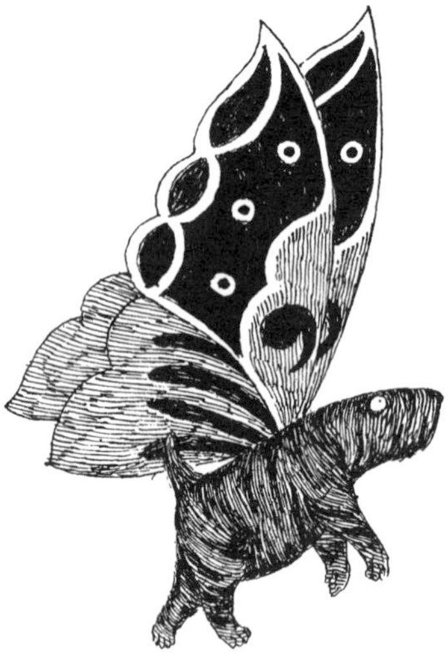

AMPHIGOREY

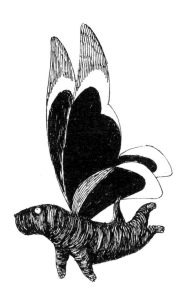

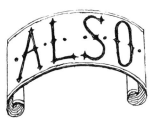

·A·L·S·O·

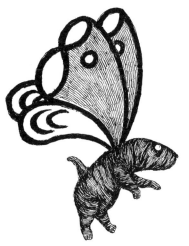

A HARVEST/HBJ BOOK
Harcourt Brace Jovanovich, Publishers
San Diego   New York   London

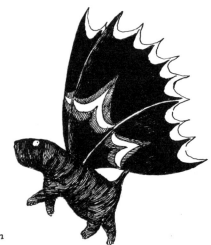

Copyright © 1983 by Edward Gorey

First published 1983 by Congdon & Weed, Inc. and
simultaneously with Methuen Publications
in Canada.

ISBN 0-15-605672-0
Printed in the United States of America
First Harvest/HBJ edition 1993
A B C D E

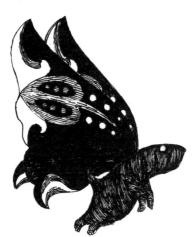

For the dog at Gay Head, 27.iv.83

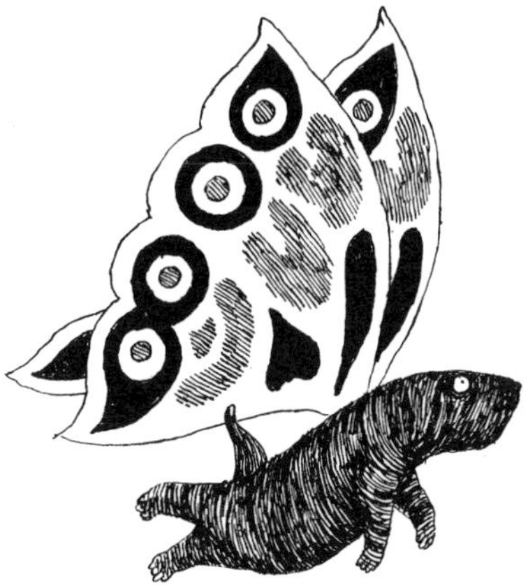

CONTENTS

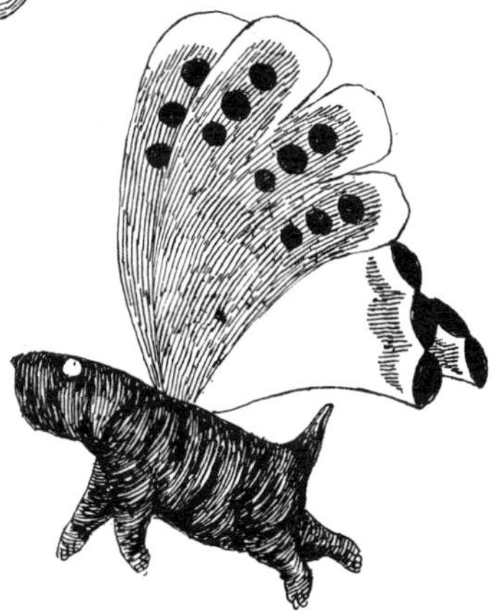

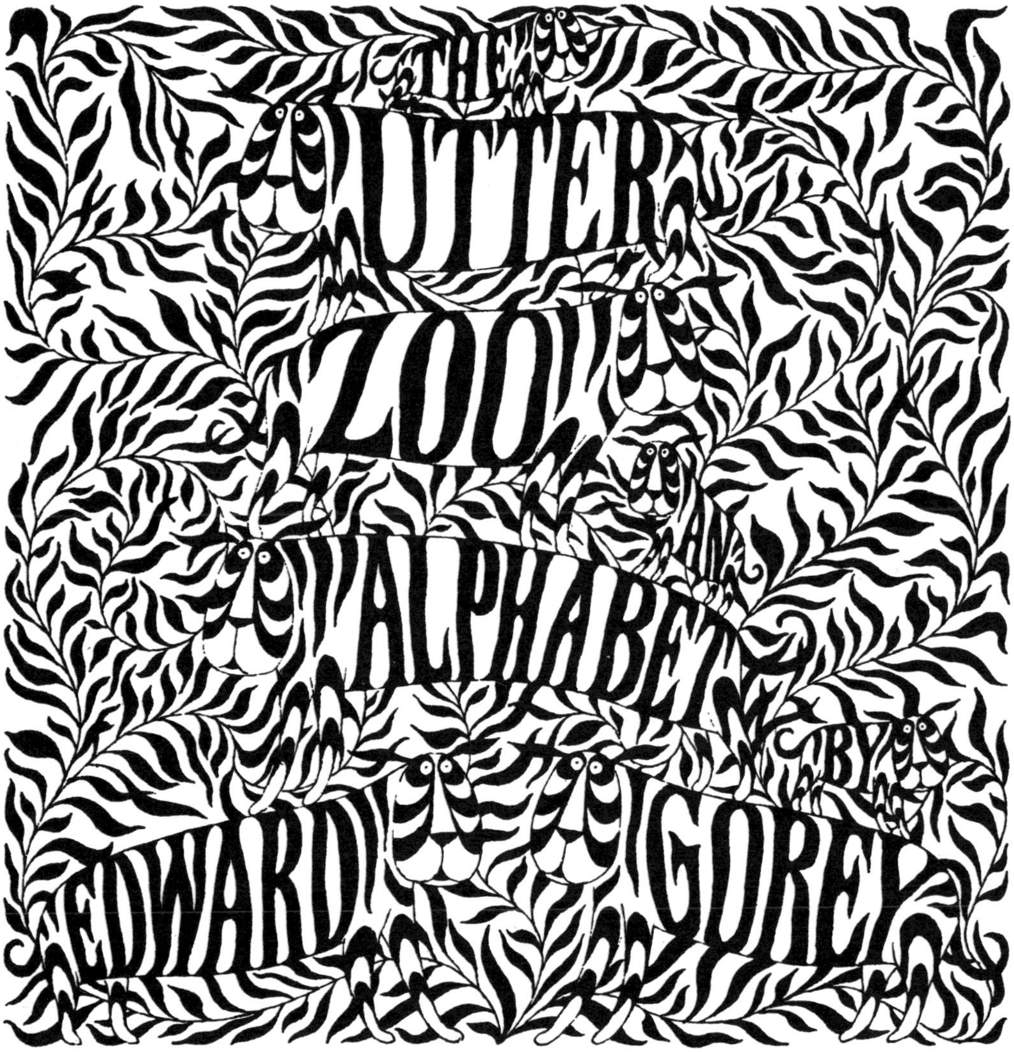
THE
UTTER
ZOO
AN
ALPHABET
BY
EDWARD GOREY

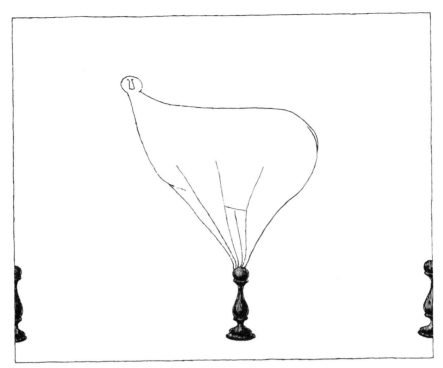

The Ampoo is intensely neat;
Its head is small, likewise its feet.

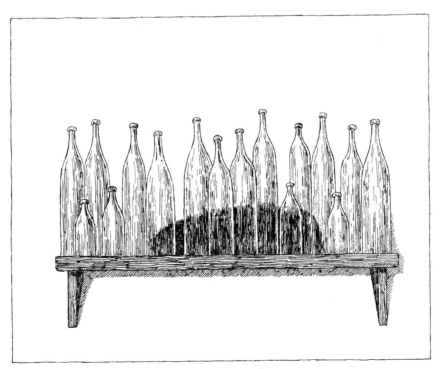

The Boggerslosh conceals itself
In back of bottles on a shelf.

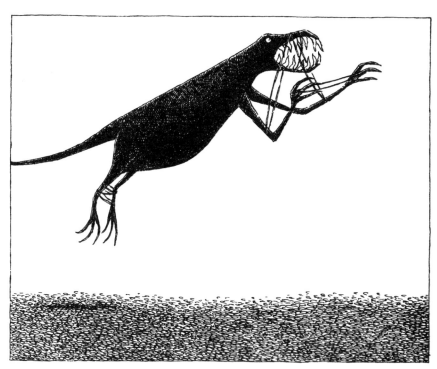

The Crunk is not unseldom drastic
And must be hindered by elastic.

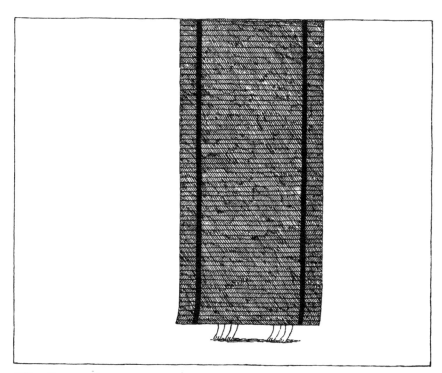

The Dawbis is remote and shy;
It shuns the gaze of passers-by.

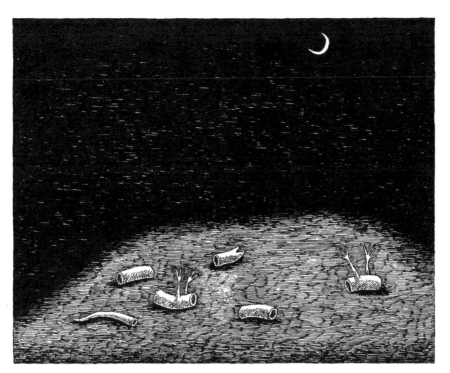

The Epitwee's inclined to fits
Until at last it falls to bits.

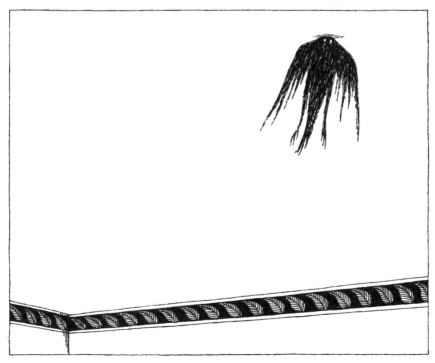

The Fidknop is devoid of feeling;
It drifts about beneath the ceiling.

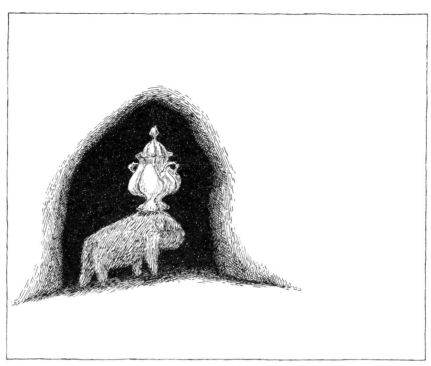

The Gawdge is understood to save
All sorts of objects in its cave.

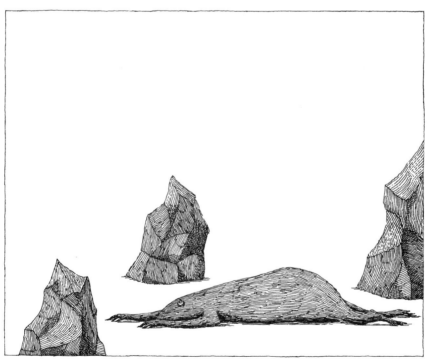

The Humglum crawls along the ground,
And never makes the slightest sound.

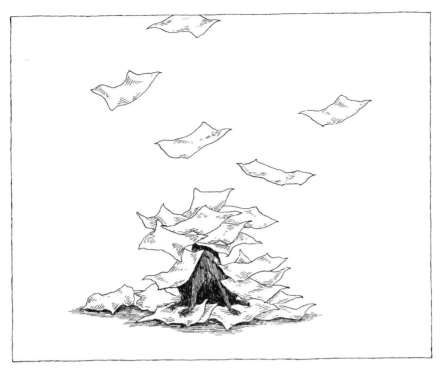

The Ippagoggy has a taste
For every kind of glue and paste.

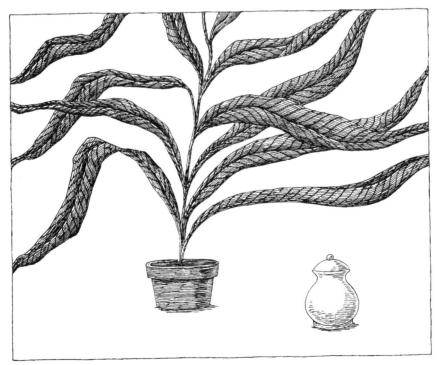

The Jelbislup cannot get far
Because it's kept inside a jar.

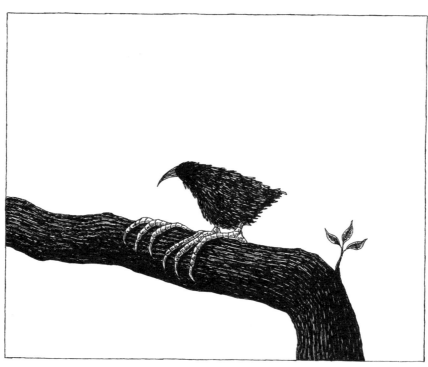

The Kwongdzu has enormous claws;
Its character is full of flaws.

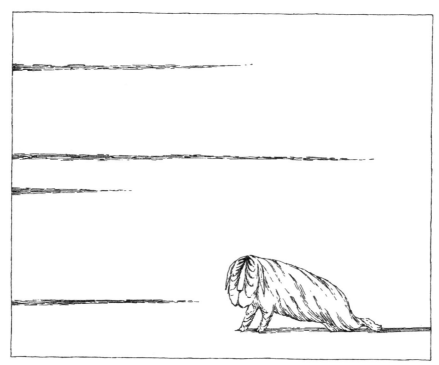

The Limpflig finds it hard to keep
From spending all its life asleep.

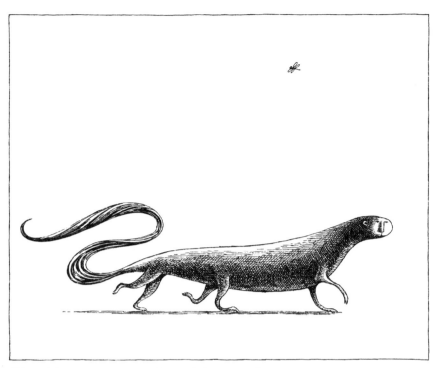

The Mork proceeds with pensive grace
And no expression on its face.

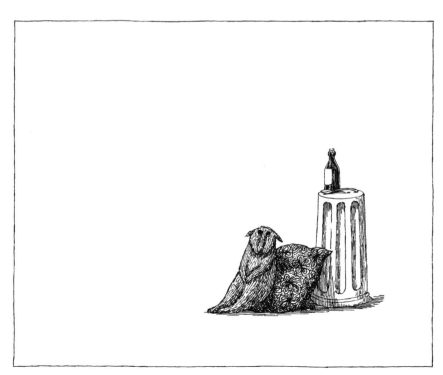

The Neapse's sufferings are chronic;
It lives exclusively on tonic.

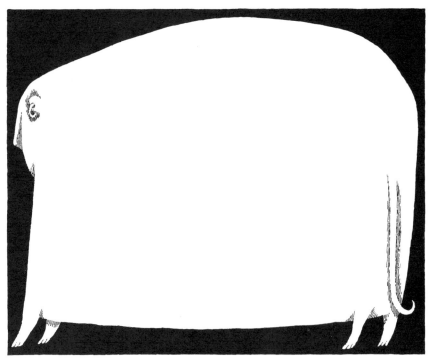

The Ombledroom is vast and white,
And therefore visible by night.

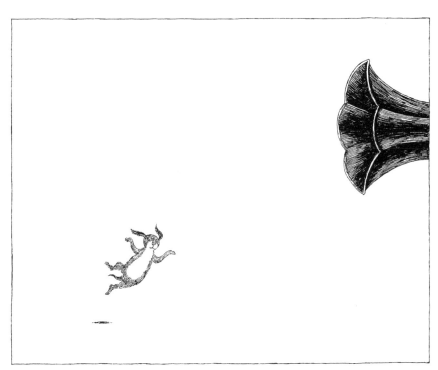

The Posby goes into a trance
In which it does a little dance.

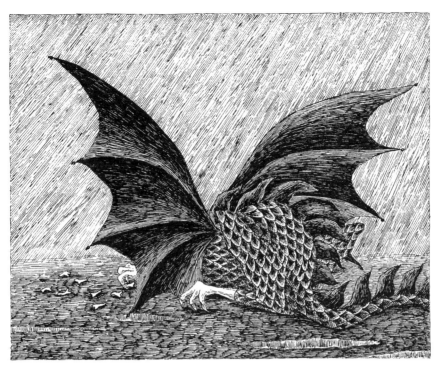

The Quingawaga squeaks and moans
While dining off of ankle bones.

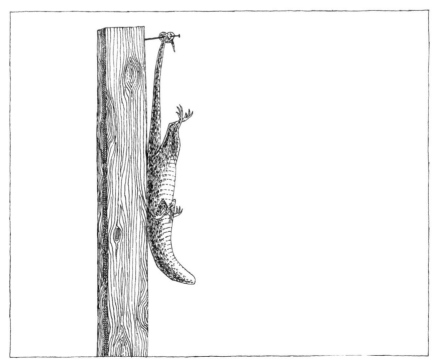

The Raitch hangs downward from its tail
By knotting it around a nail.

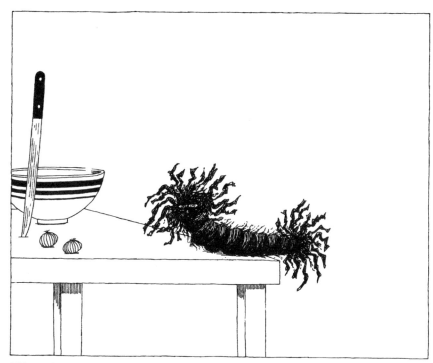

The Scrug's extremely nasty-looking,
And is unusable for cooking.

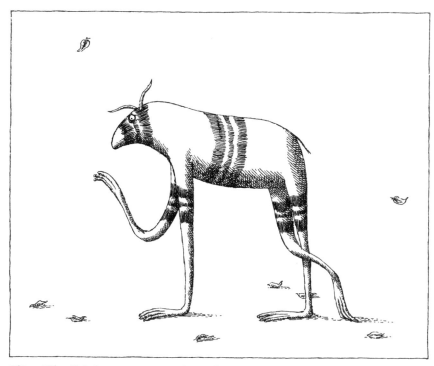

The Twibbit on occasion knows
A difficulty with its toes.

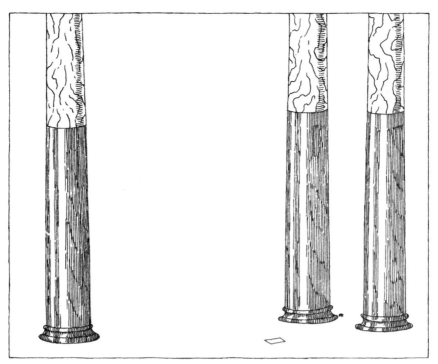

The Ulp is very, very small;
It hardly can be seen at all.

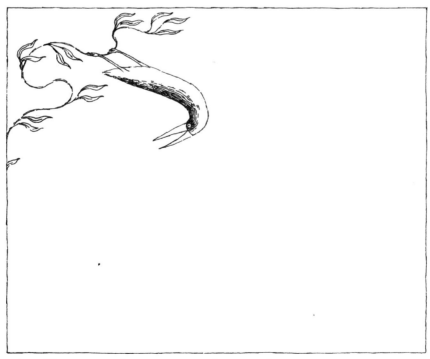

The Veazy makes a creaking noise;
It has no dignity or poise.

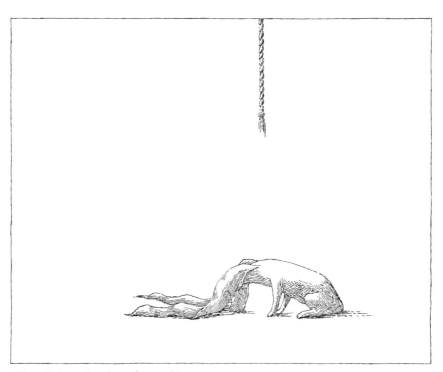

The Wambulus has floppy ears
With which to wipe away its tears.

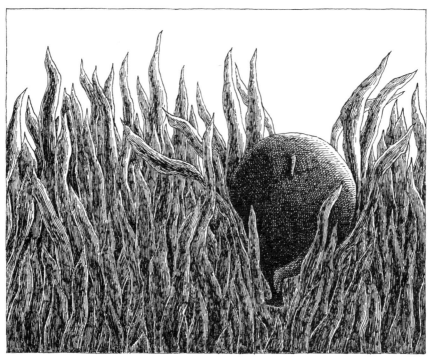

The Xyke stands up at close of day,
And then it slowly walks away.

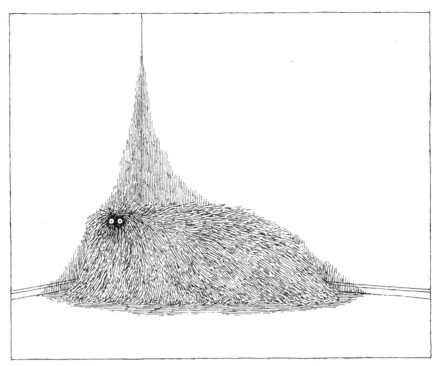

The Yawfle stares, and stares, and stares,
And stares, and stares, and stares, and stares.

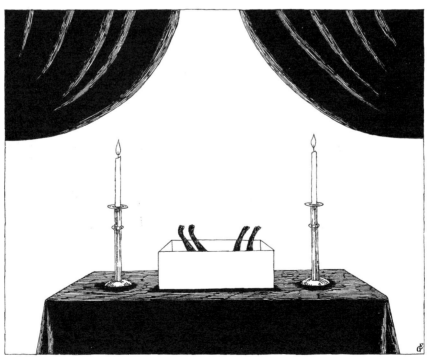

About the Zote what can be said?
There was just one, and now it's dead.

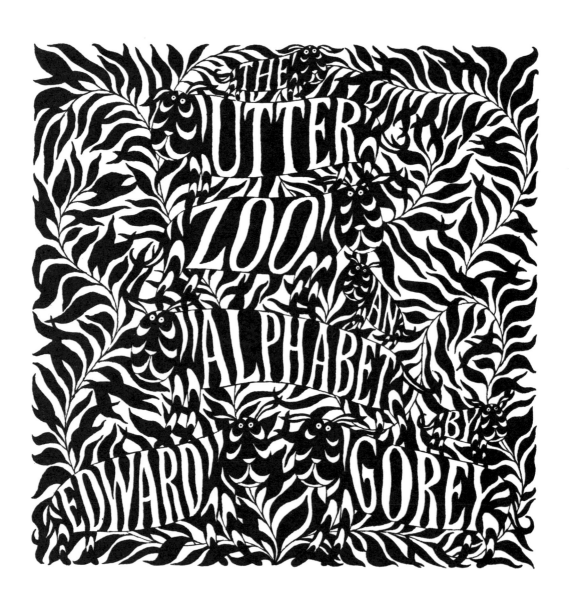

THE UTTER ZOO AN ALPHABET BY EDWARD GOREY

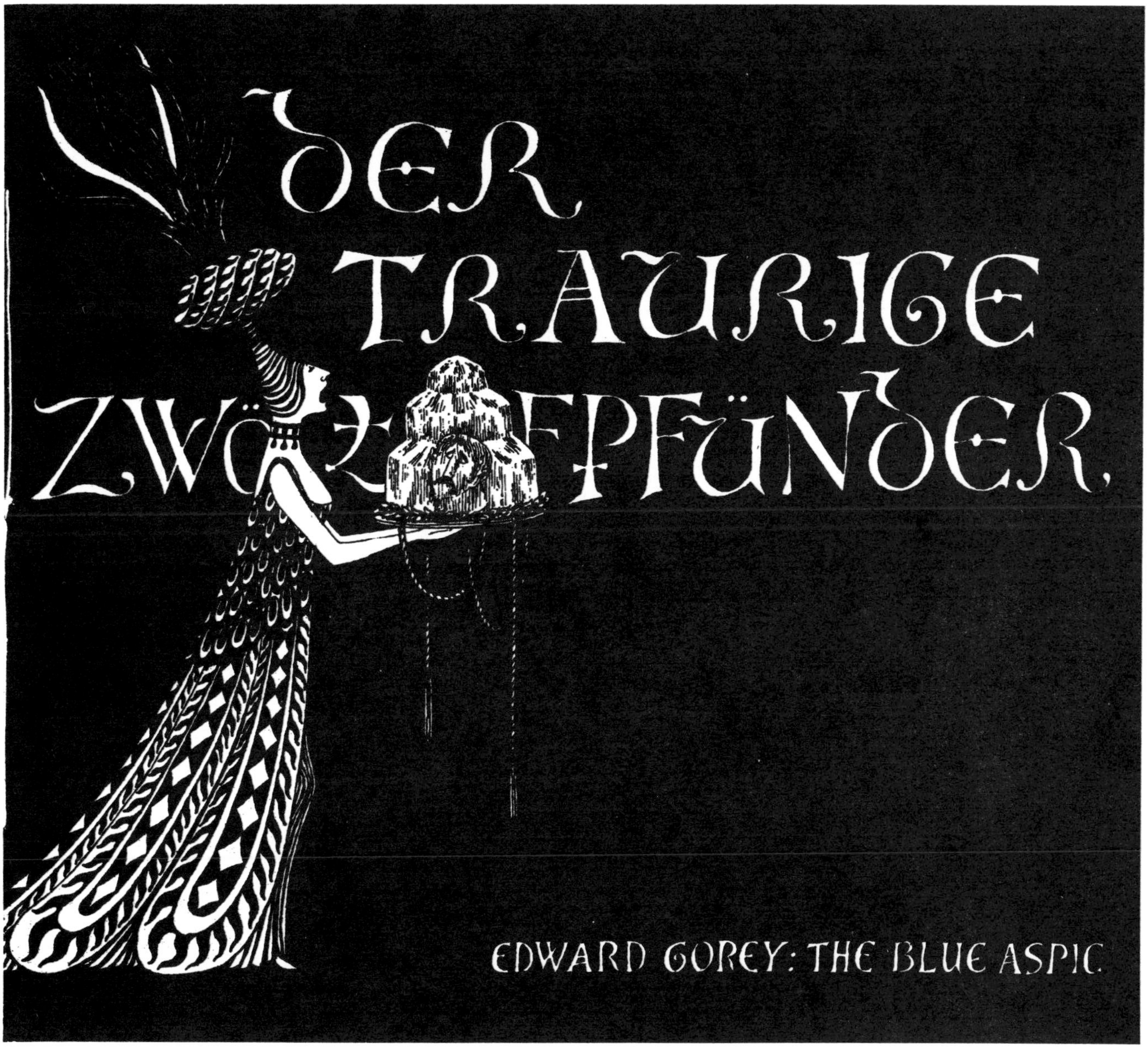
DER TRAURIGE ZWÖLFPFÜNDER.
EDWARD GOREY: THE BLUE ASPIC

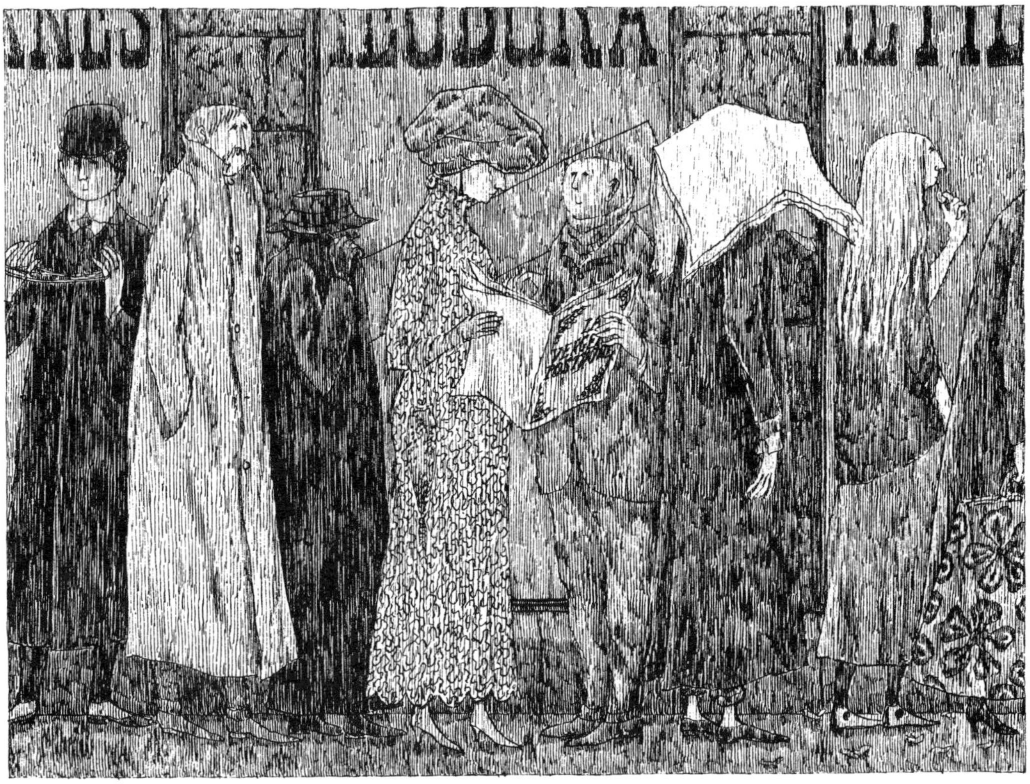

Jasper Ankle stood all night in a drizzle to buy a third-gallery ticket for *La vengeance posthume.*

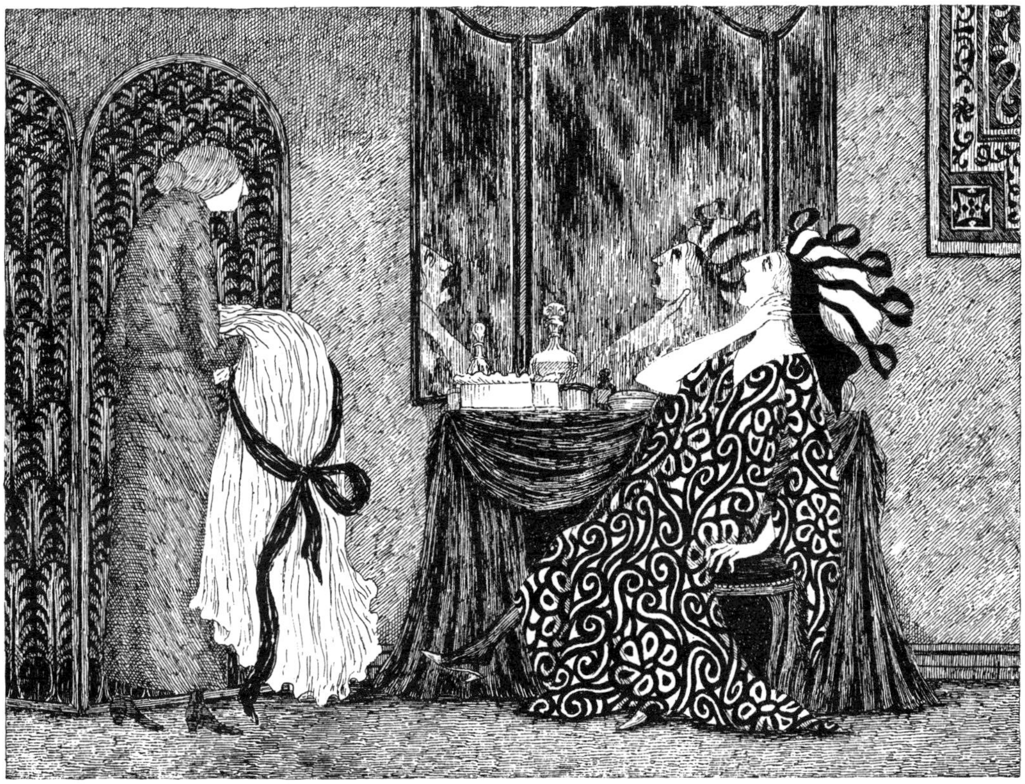

While dressing, Gertrúdis Callosidad dipped into a box of candied violets from an unknown admirer.

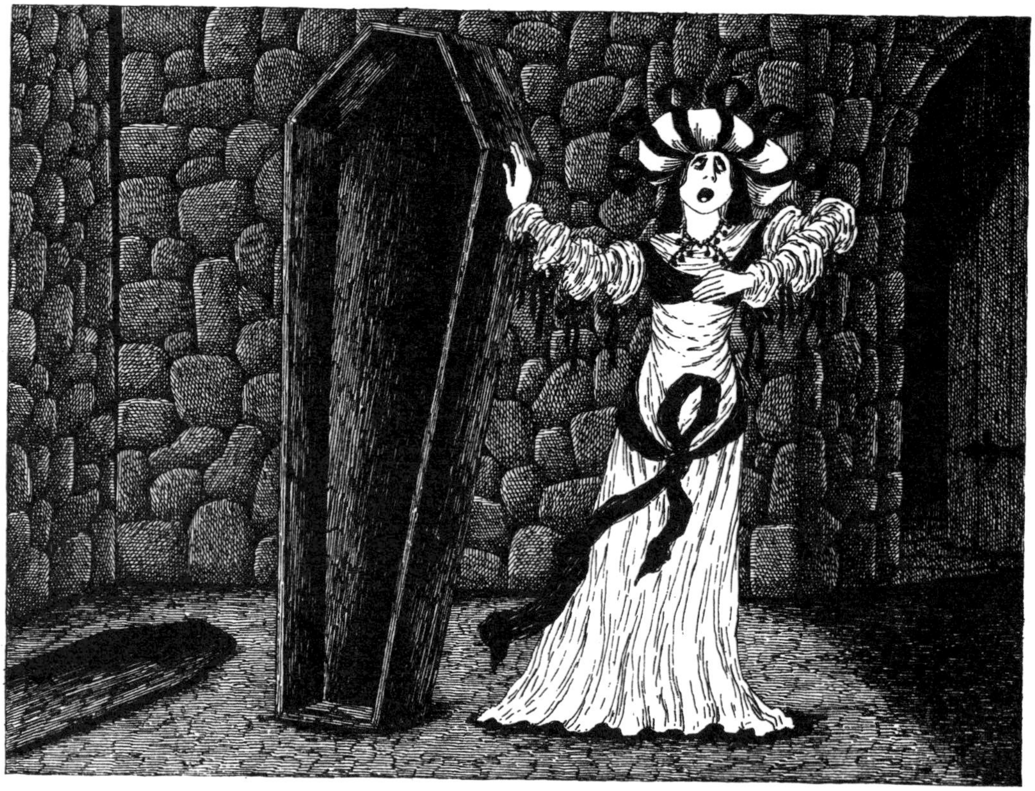

Ortenzia Caviglia, hitherto unheard, went on instead; her 'Vide le cerceuil, vide mon coeur' put the audience into raptures.

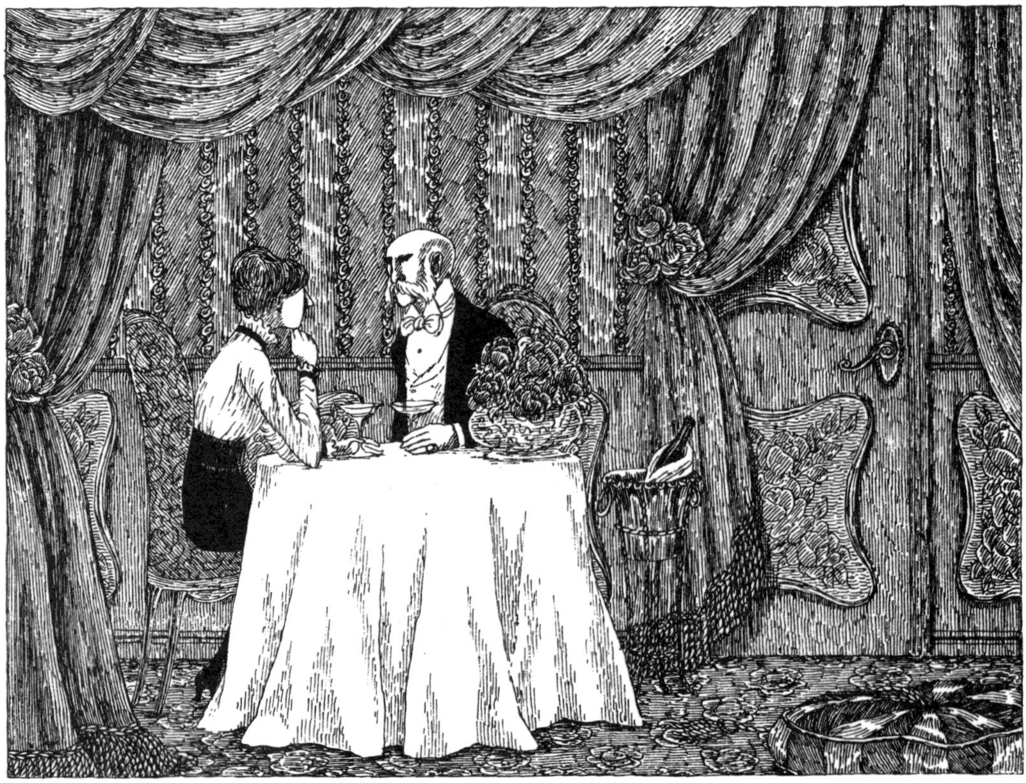

After the performance she was invited to supper by the head of the opera, Baron von Knöchel.

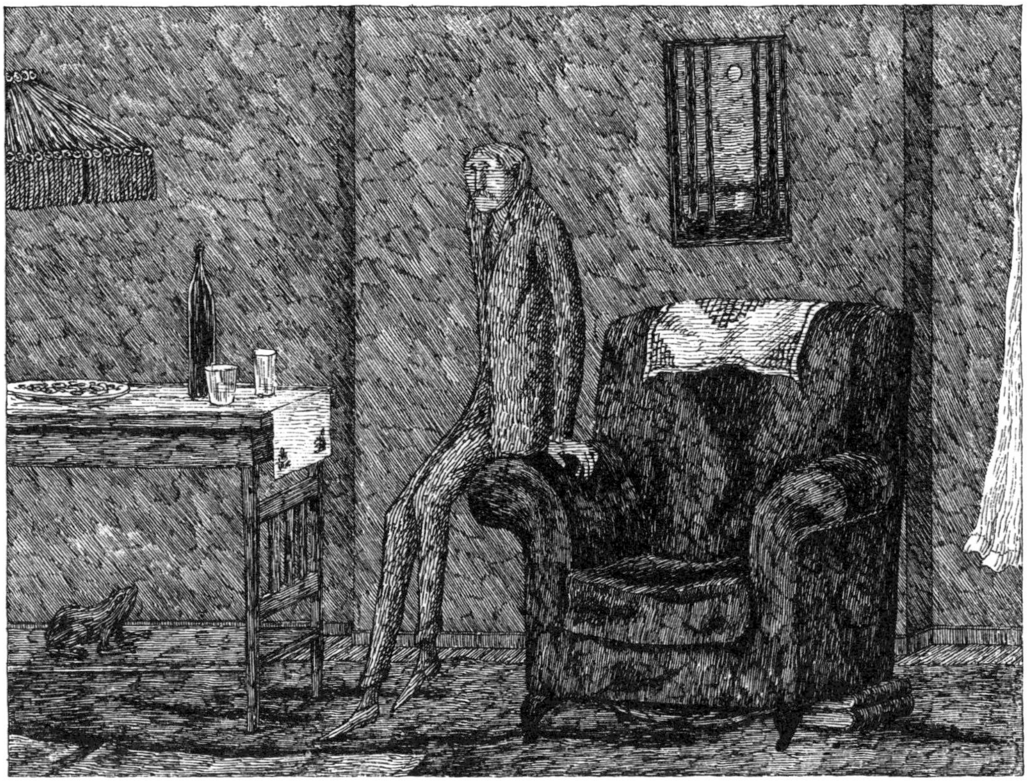

Jasper sat up until dawn by himself.

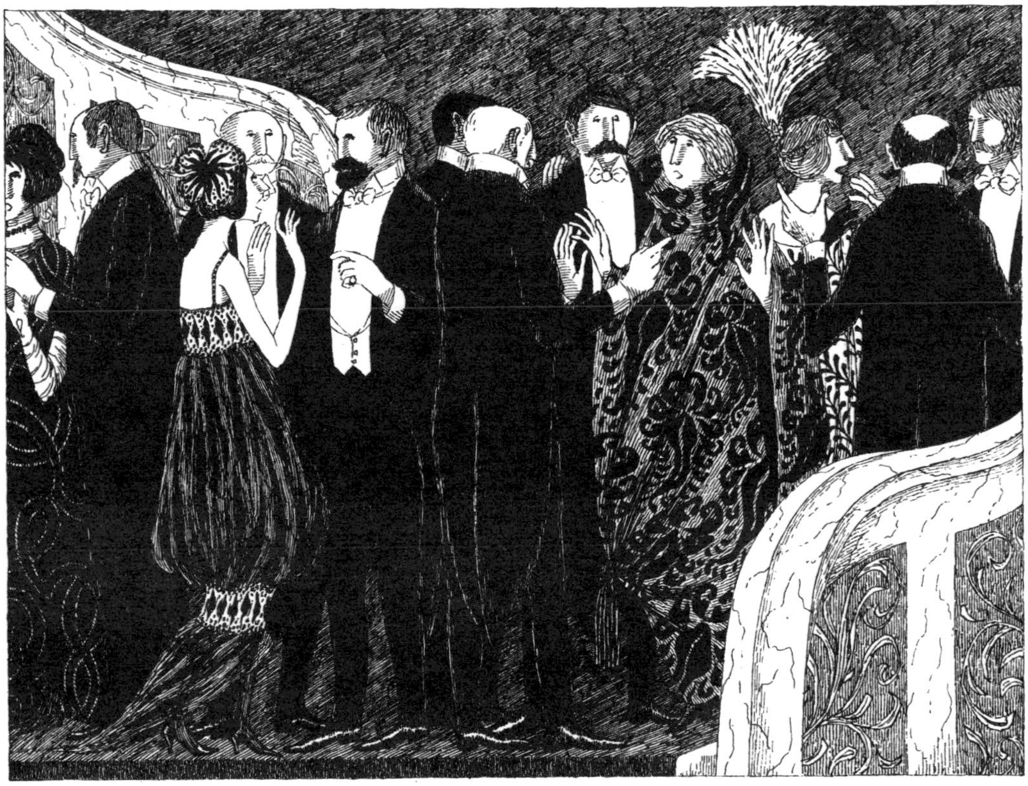

By the end of the season Caviglia had sung *Gli occhielli*, *Lizzia Bordena*, *La reine des iguanes*, *Julietta di Lavenza*, and was talked about everywhere.

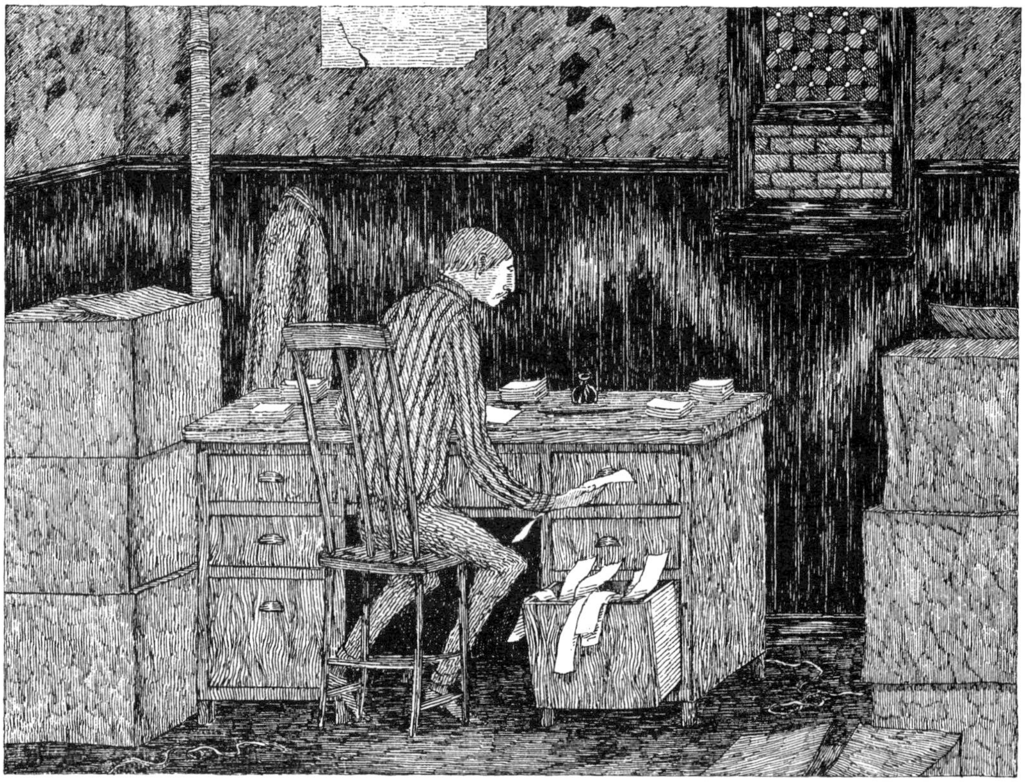

Instead of writing labels, Jasper read and reread the clippings about Caviglia hidden in his desk.

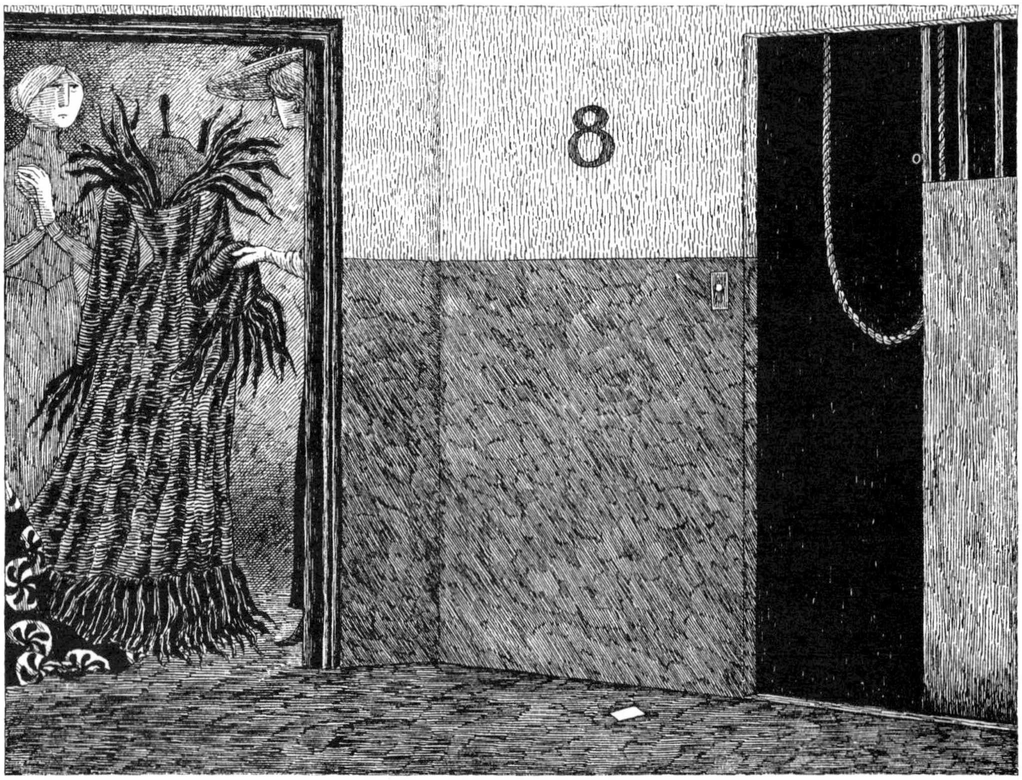
8

Ortenzia's manager, Ambrogio Rigaglie, fell down the elevator shaft at a costumer's, but Herakleitos Vithilogos took his place.

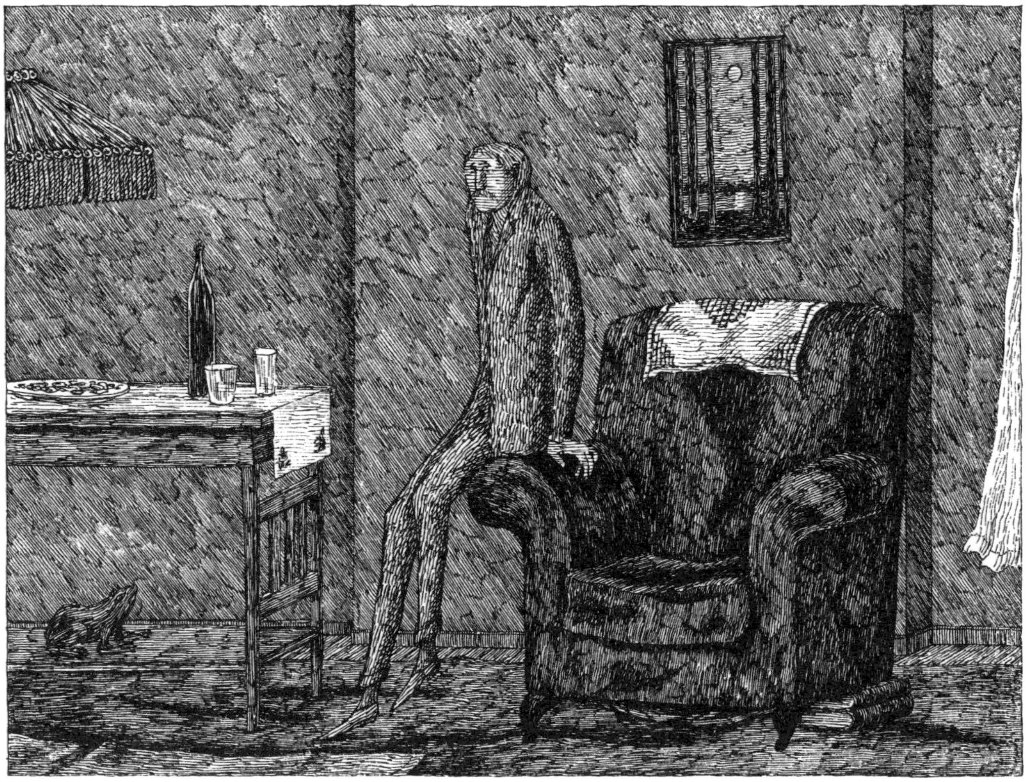

Jasper sat up until dawn by himself.

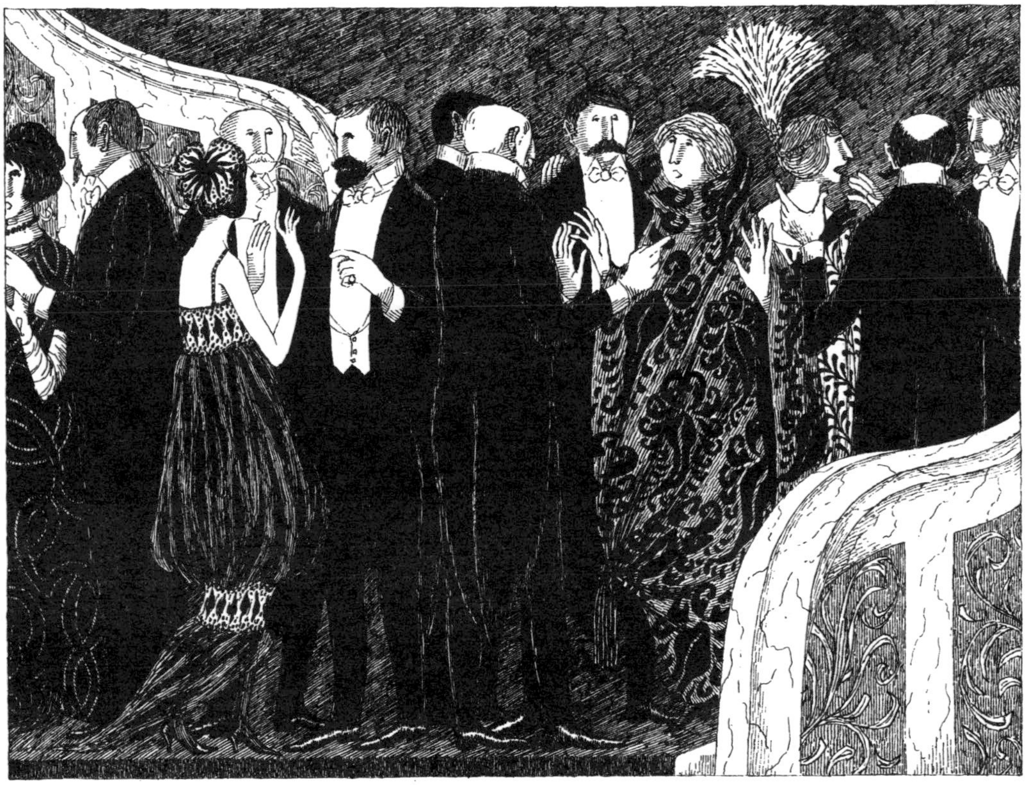

By the end of the season Caviglia had sung *Gli occhielli*, *Lizzia Bordena*, *La reine des iguanes*, *Julietta di Lavenza*, and was talked about everywhere.

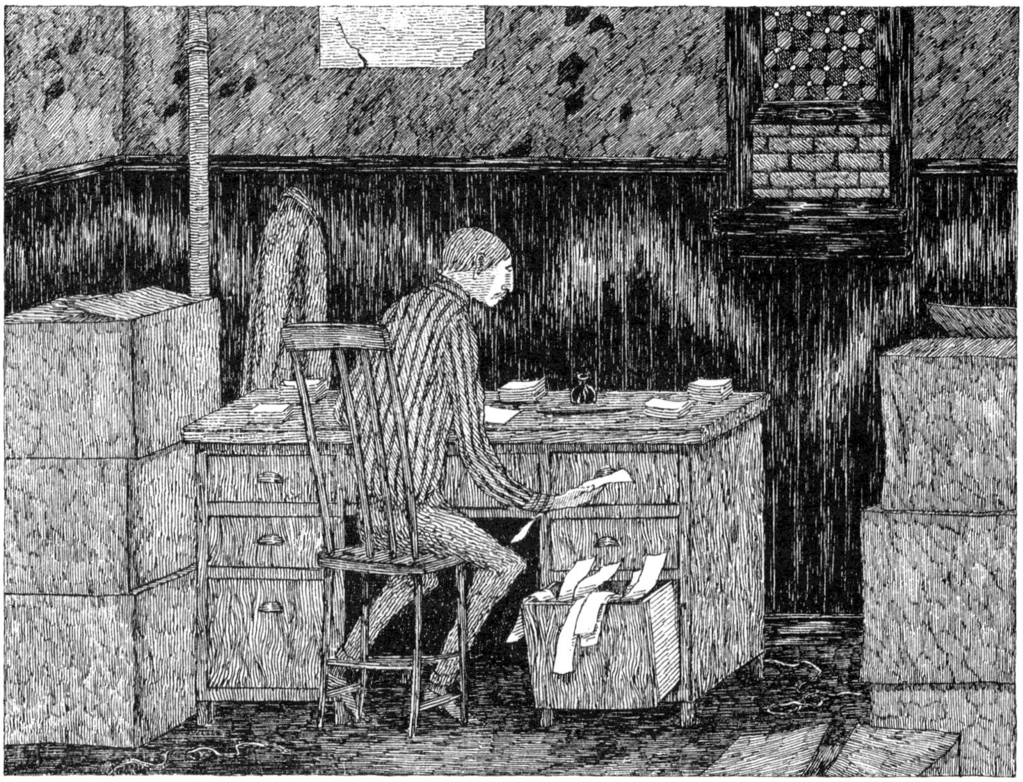

Instead of writing labels, Jasper read and reread the clippings about Caviglia hidden in his desk.

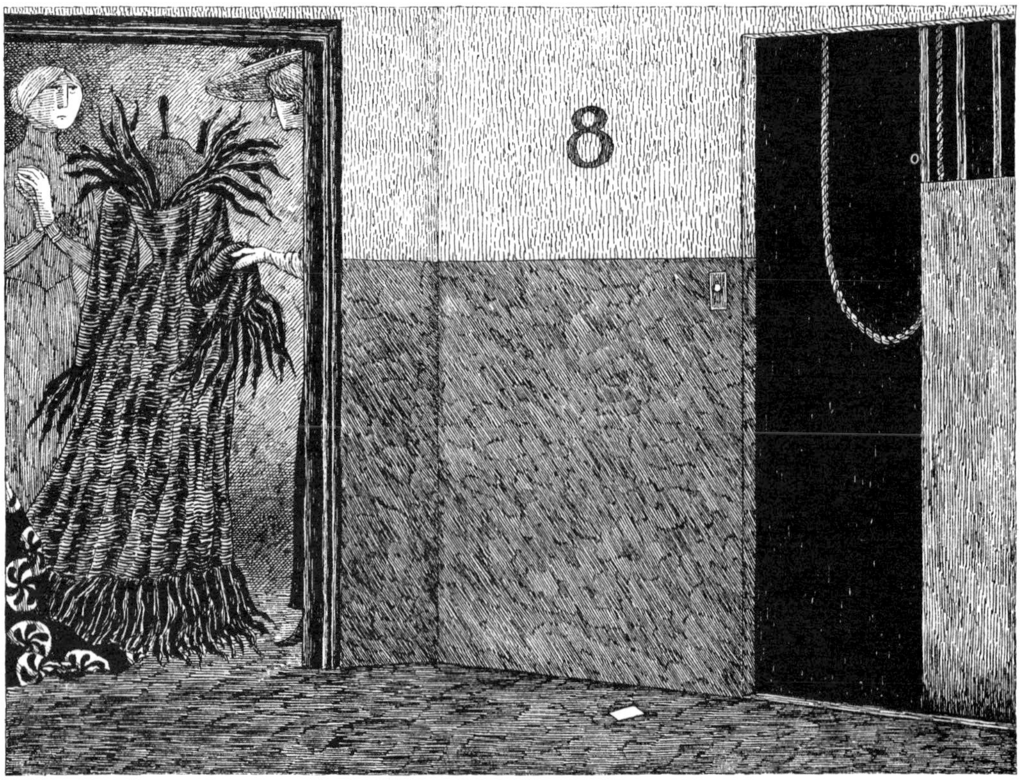
8

Ortenzia's manager, Ambrogio Rigaglie, fell down the elevator shaft at a costumer's, but Herakleitos Vithilogos took his place.

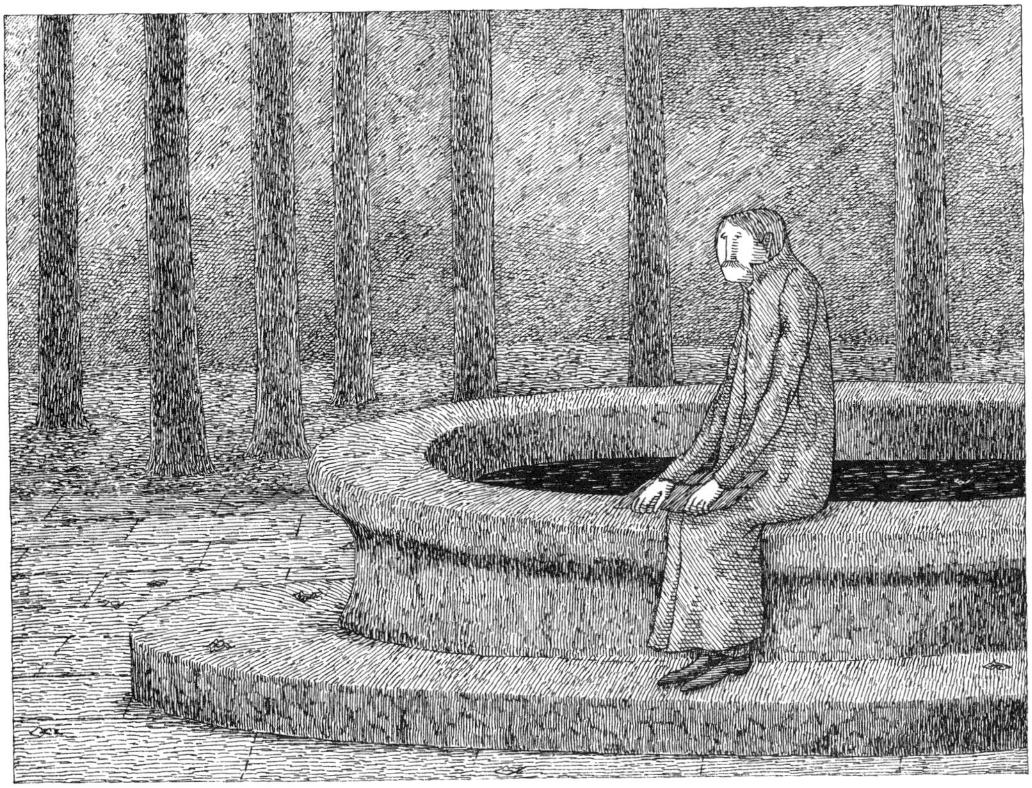

Jasper went without lunch three days running to buy Caviglia's recording of 'Vivi con una mira' from *Il fiore sotto il piede*.

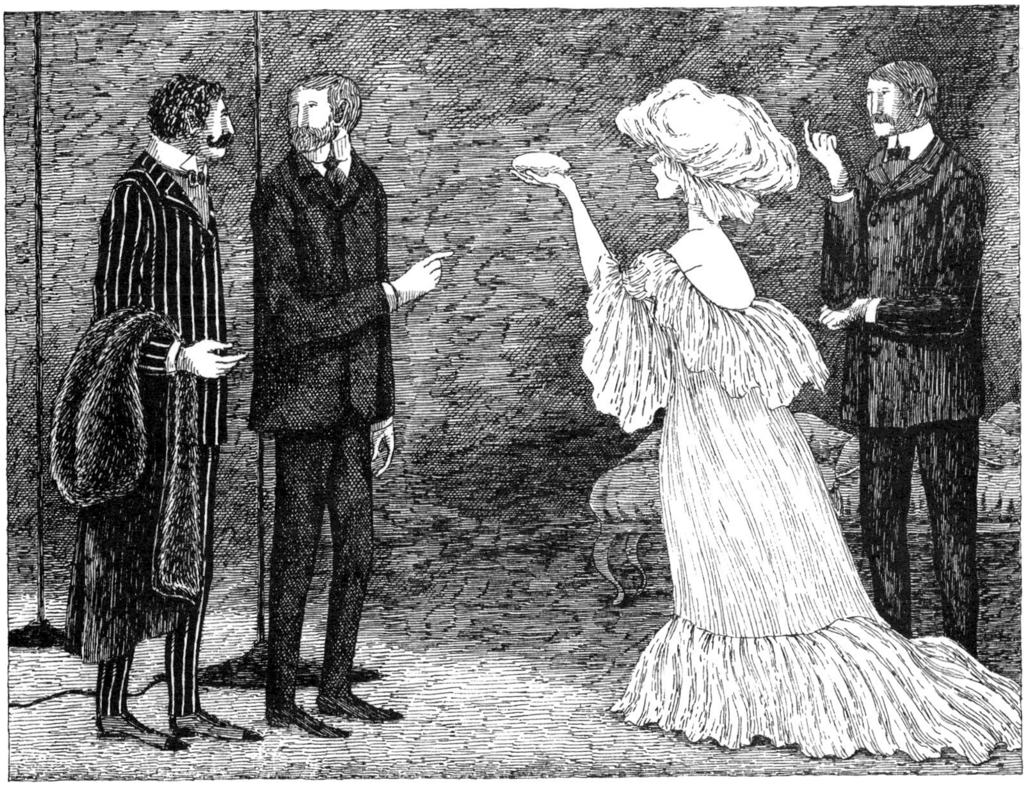

Caviglia appeared in a series of advertisements for Grudge's Cucumber Soap.

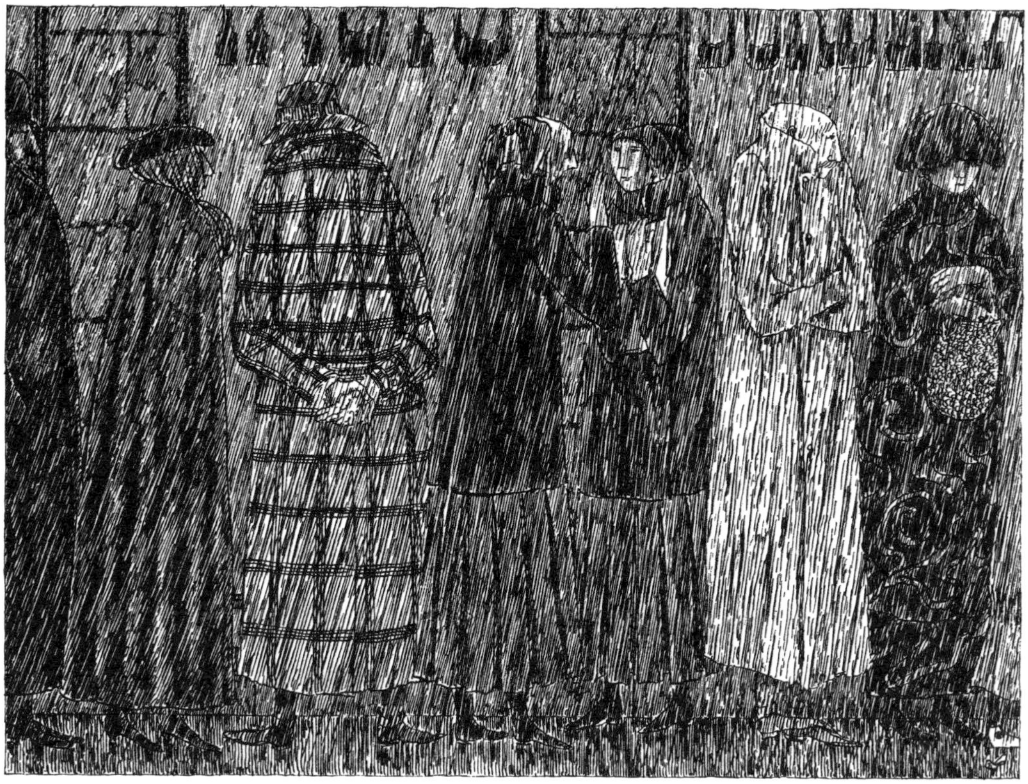

Jasper stood all night in a freezing rain to buy a third-gallery ticket for *Die Chinesische Brille*.

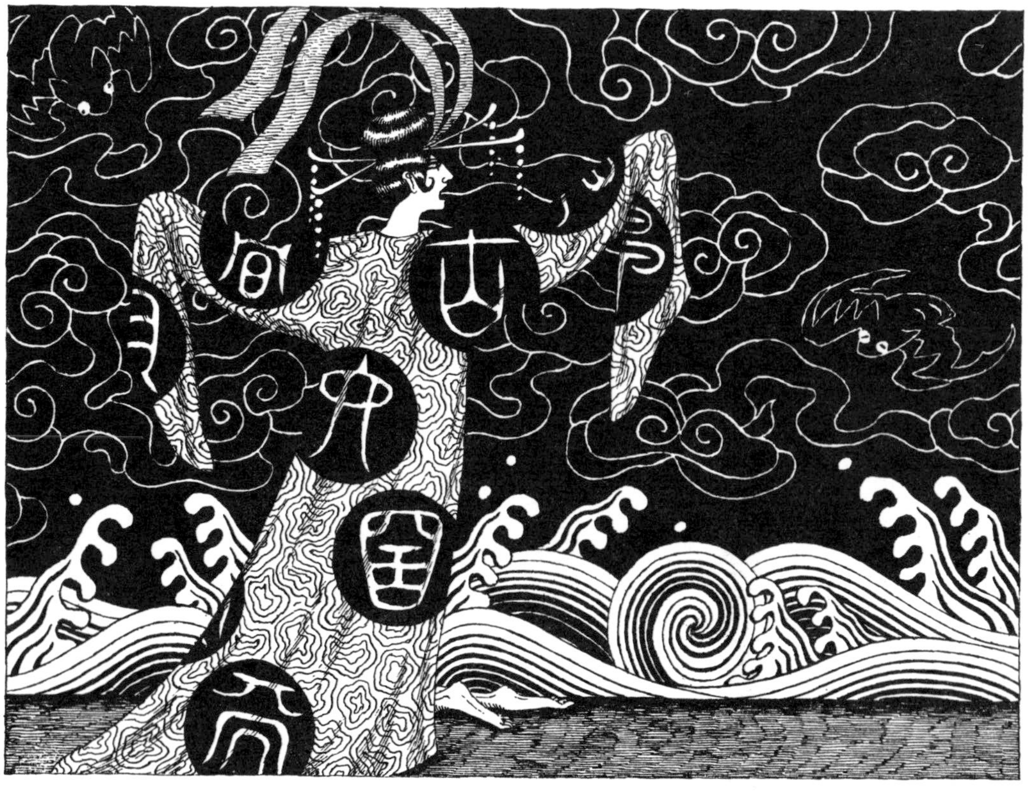

As Tsi-Nan-Fu Caviglia had her greatest triumph to date.

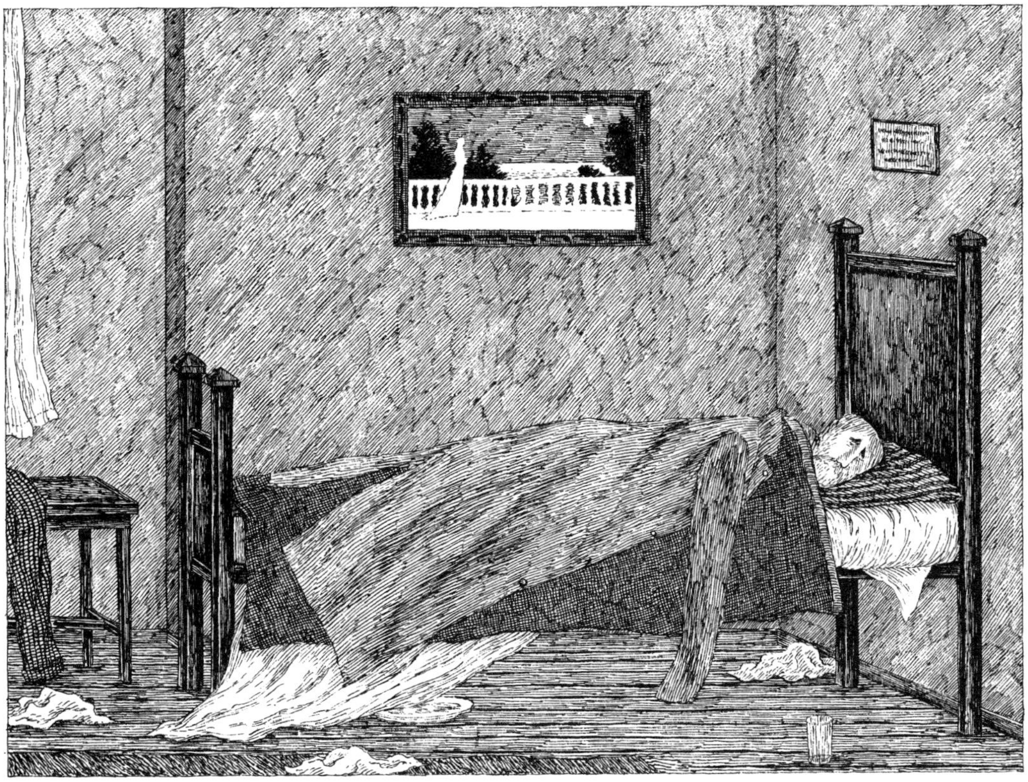

Jasper got pneumonia, and was dismissed from his job.

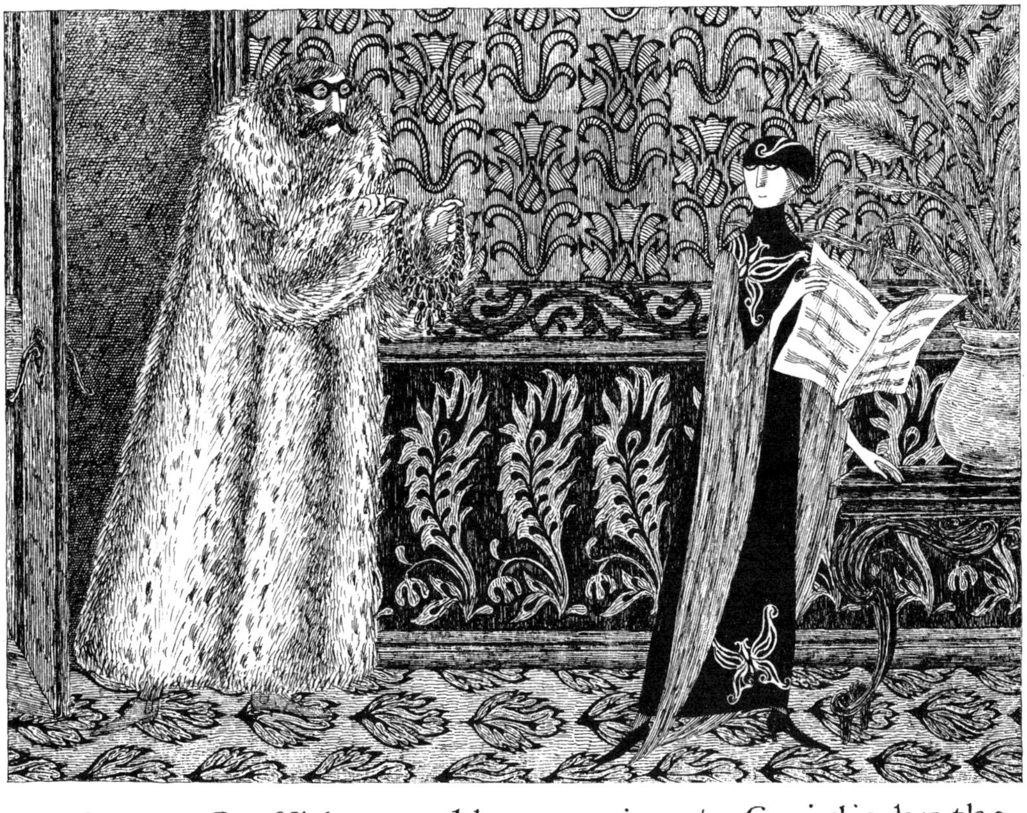

The famous Spoffish emeralds were given to Caviglia by the Duke of Whaup.

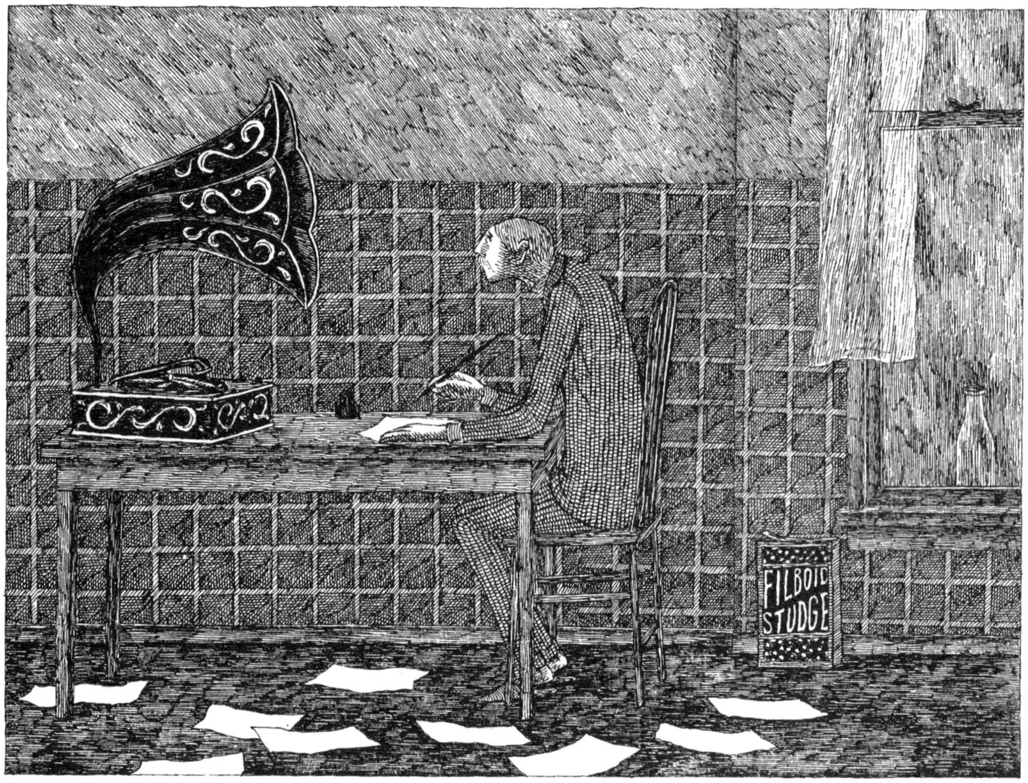
FILBOID
STUDGE

Without his clippings, Jasper now wrote long letters to Ortenzia, which went unanswered.

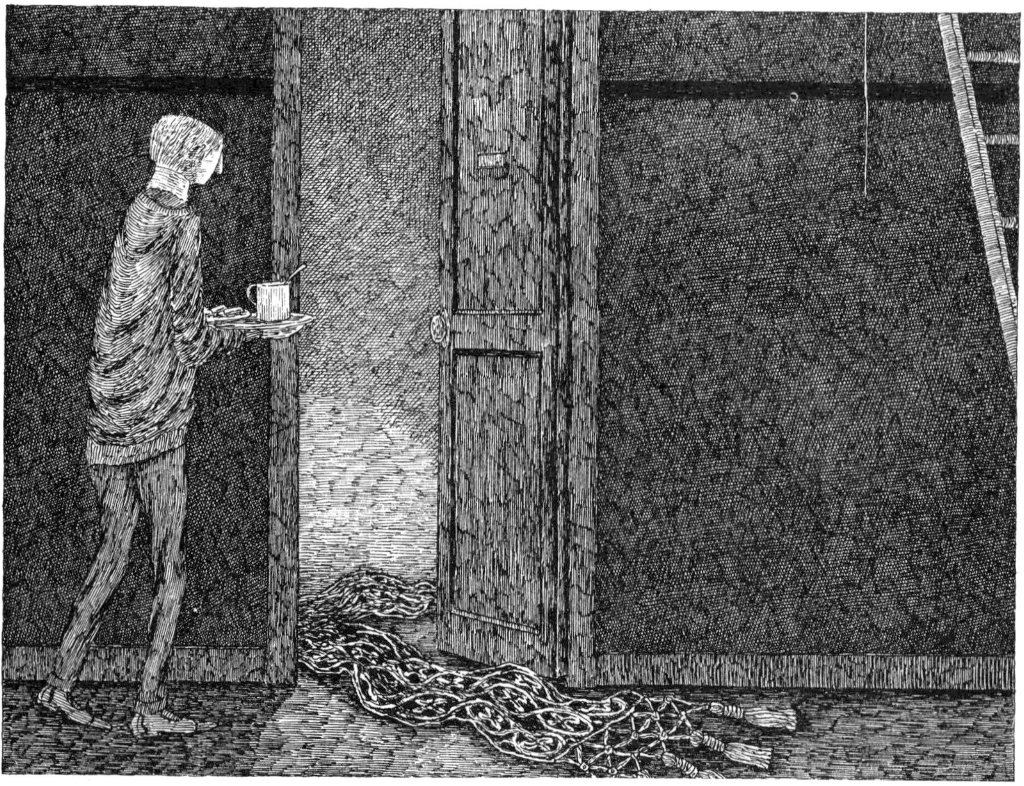

Agnes Alice Popover, Ortenzia's nearest rival, was discovered strangled with a scarf she wore in *Teodora*.

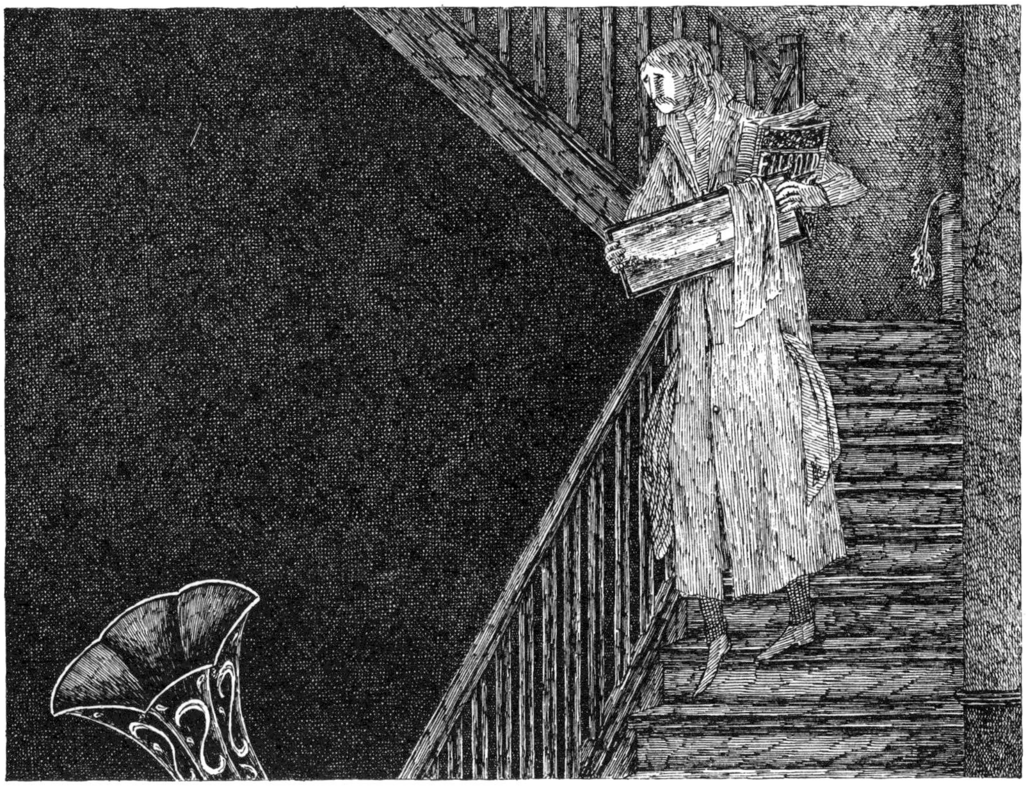

Jasper's gramophone got smashed as he was being evicted from his rooms.

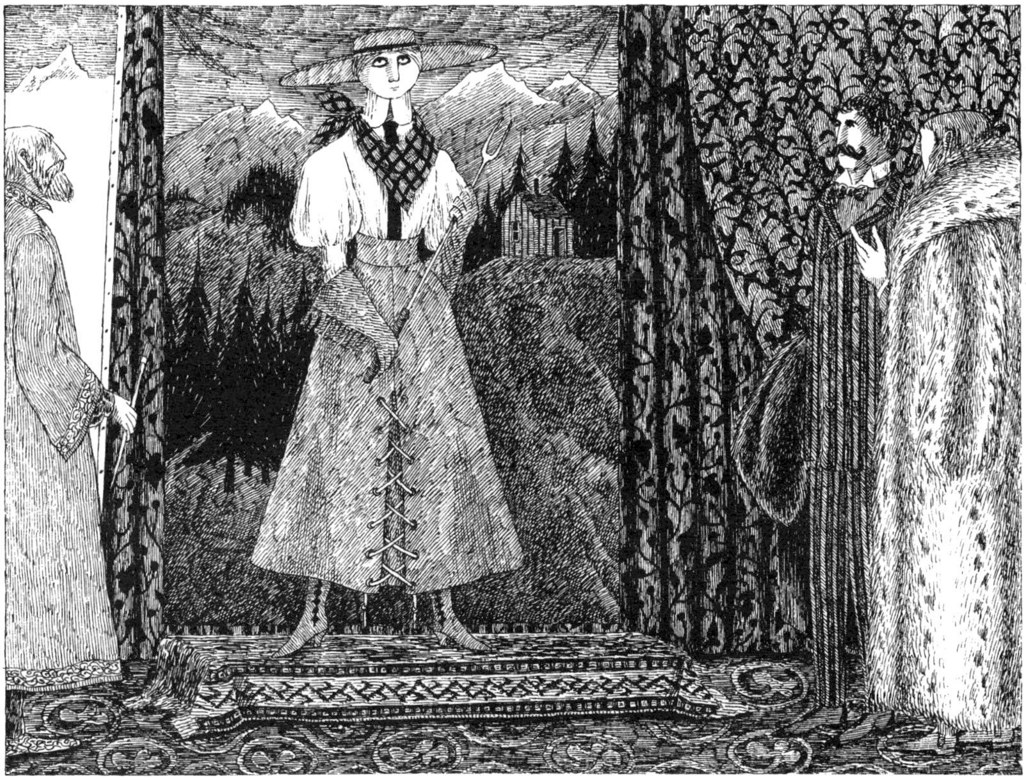

Caviglia was painted by Sergissopov as Mae in *The Dubious Errand*.

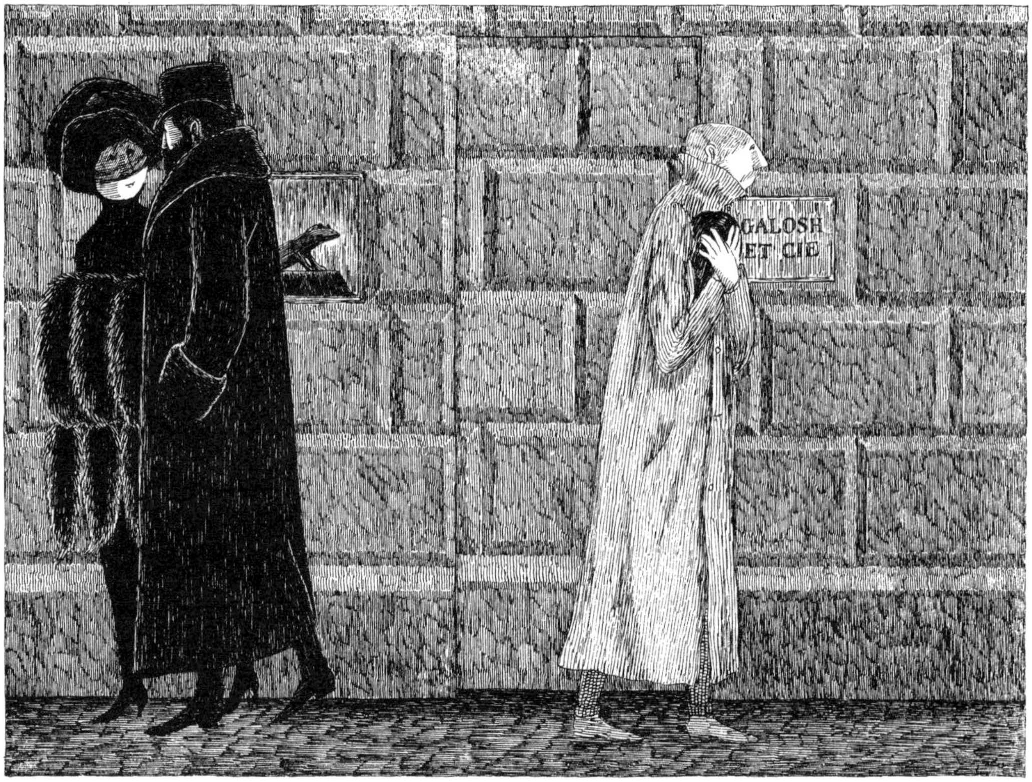
GALOSH
ET CIE

Jasper wandered the streets, his warping records clutched to his chest.

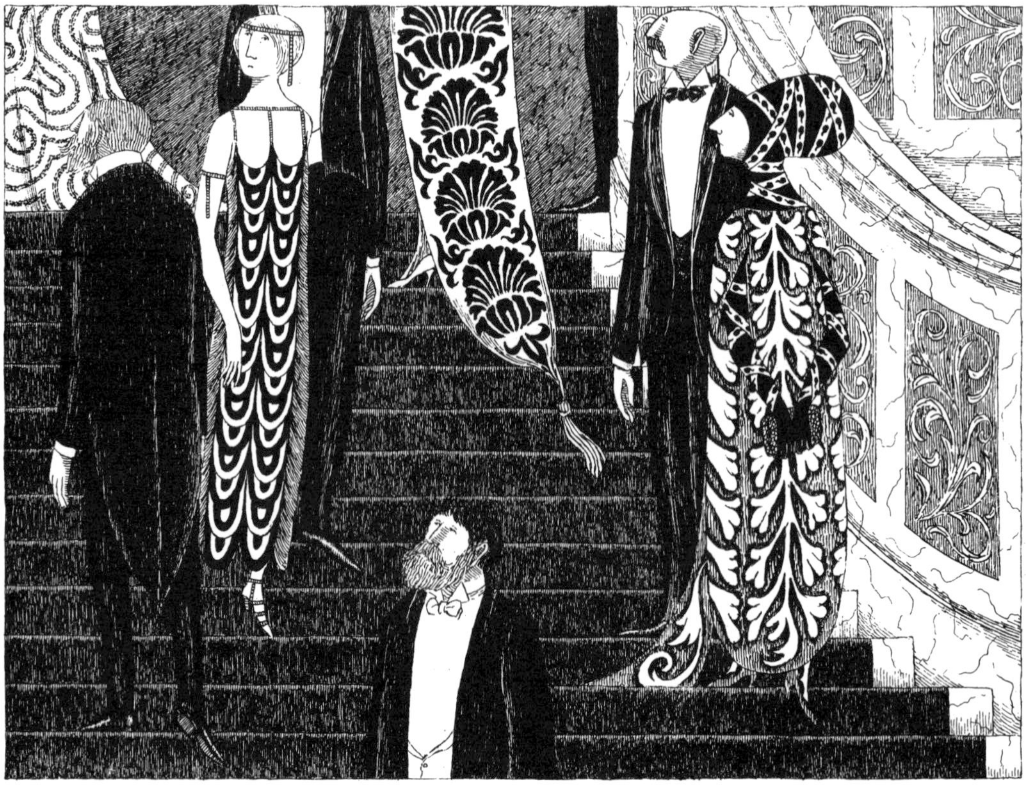

A statue fell on the Duke of Whaup during the second interval of *Amable Tastu*.

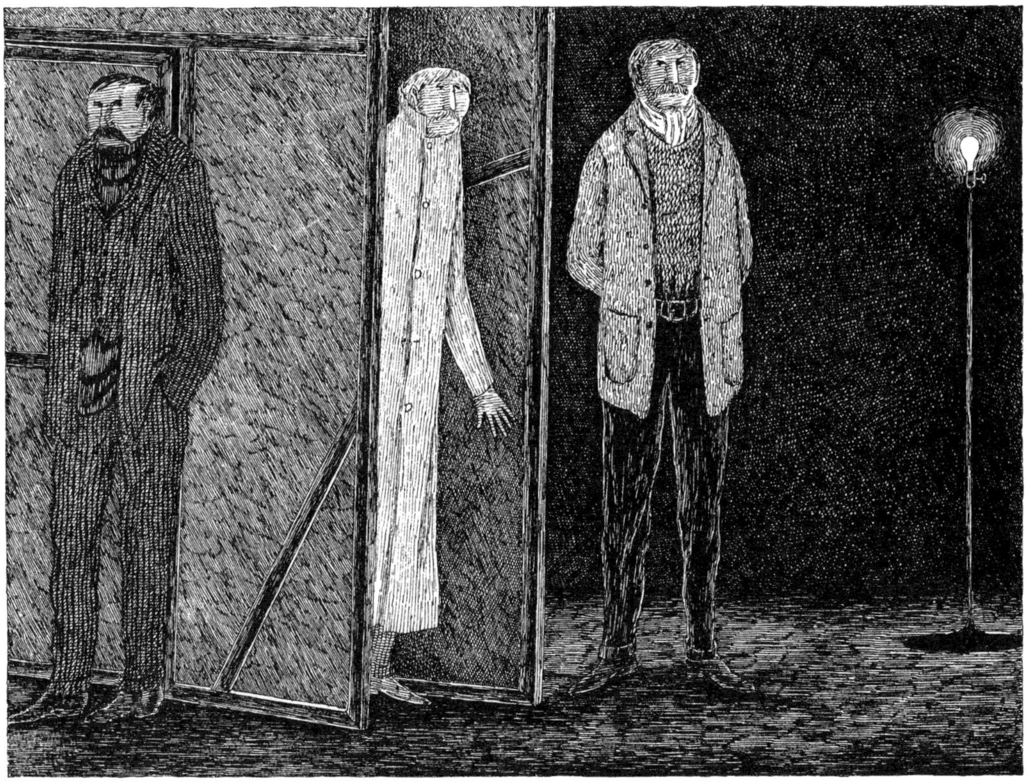

Jasper was apprehended in the wings as Caviglia sang 'Una tazza di cacao' at a rehearsal of *L'avvelenatrice di Glasgovia*.

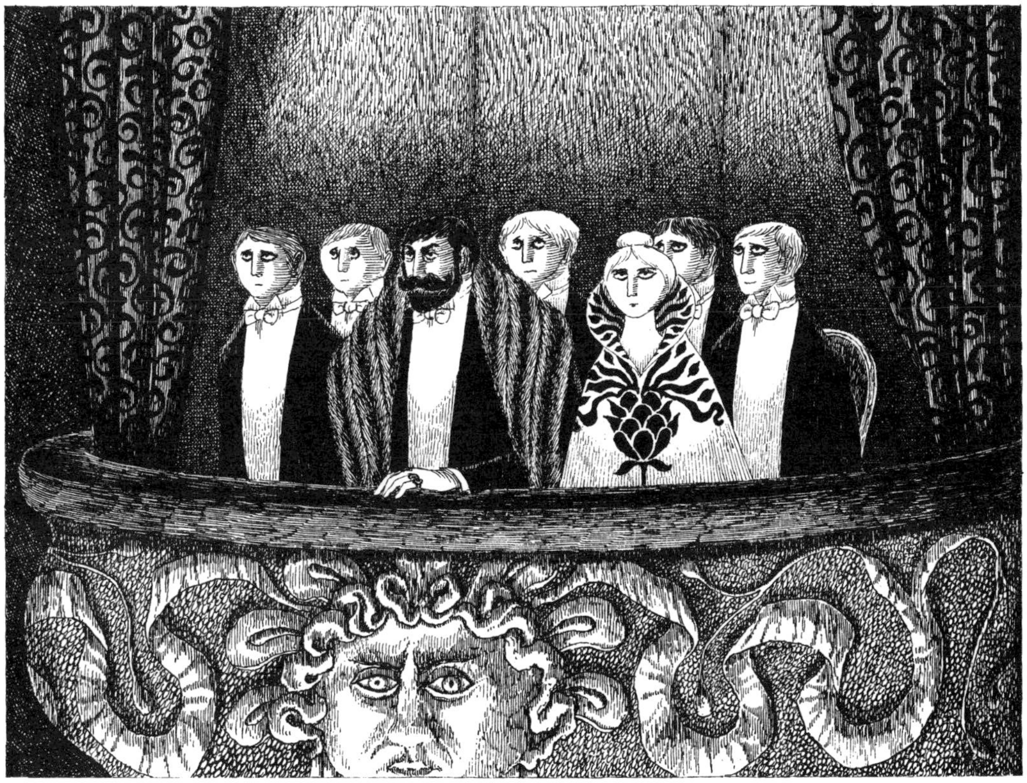

Caviglia's revival of *Elagabalo* was cut short when the authorities had the curtain rung down on the triple-wedding scene.

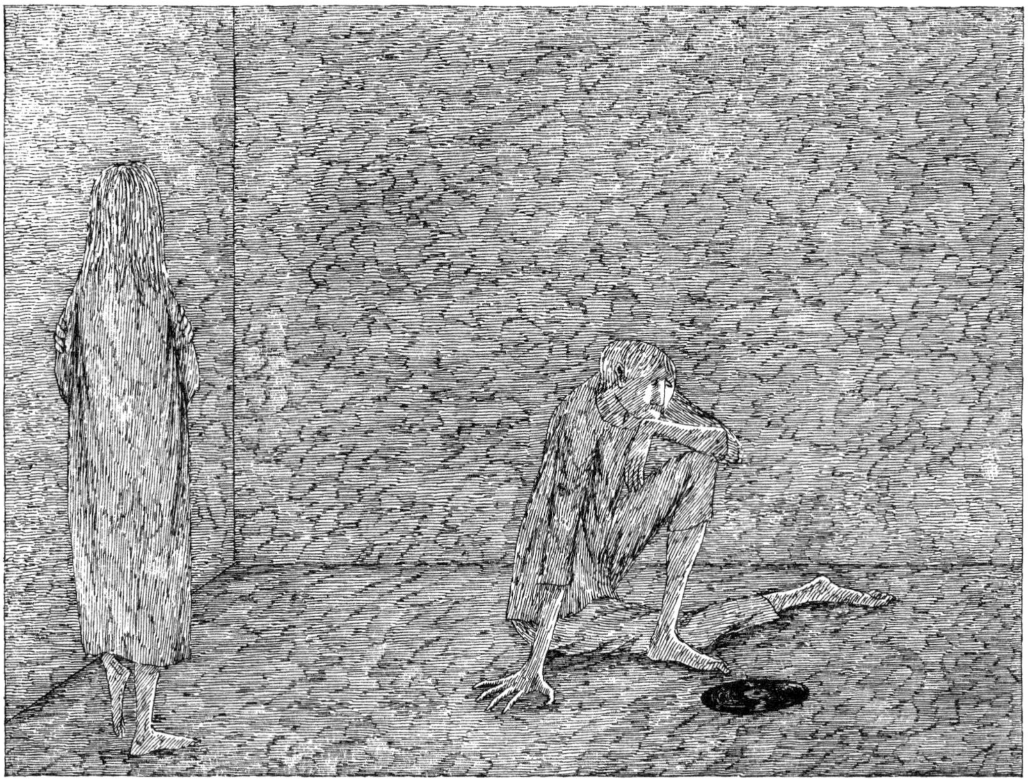

Jasper was committed to an asylum where no gramophone was available to the inmates.

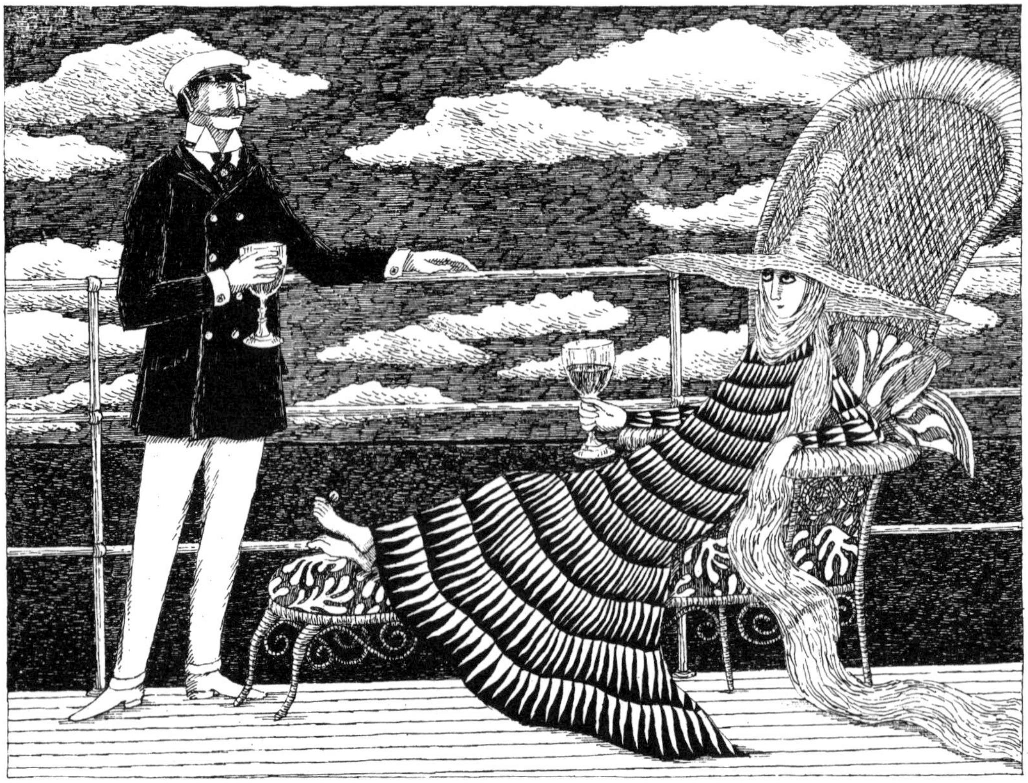

Caviglia cruised the Adriatic with Basil Zaribaydjian, the financier, on his yacht, the *Maud*.

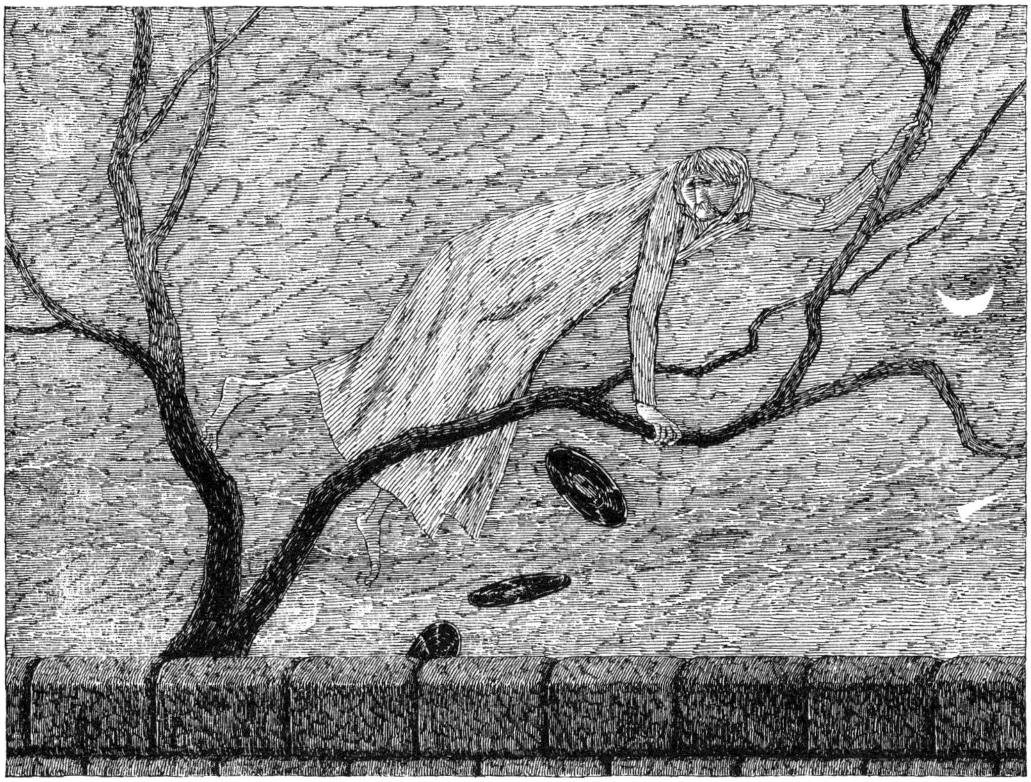

Jasper's records got broken as he was escaping from the asylum.

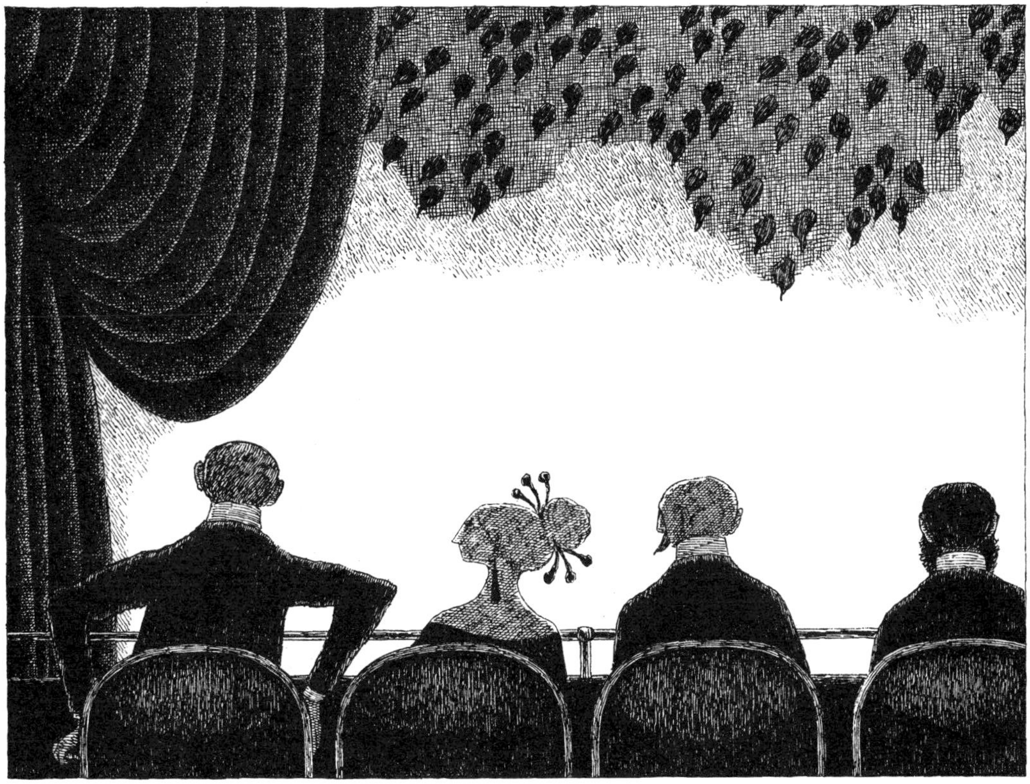

M. Gazogène, the leader of Mme Pince-Oreille's claque, impaled himself on a skewer affixed to his seat during *Gomiti di rammarico*.

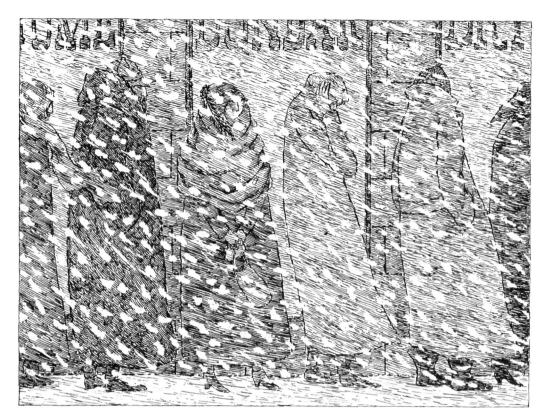

Jasper stood all night in a blizzard to buy a third-gallery ticket for the premiere of *Nera Agnese di Dunbar*.

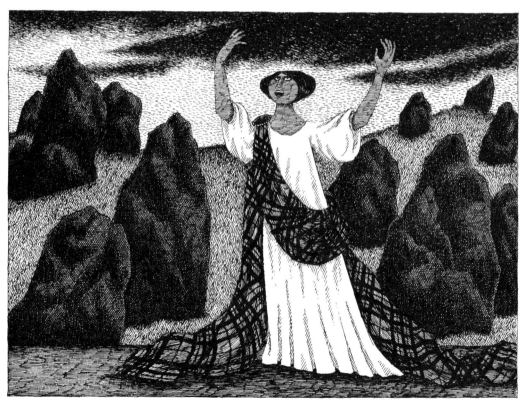

Ortenzia had a premonition while holding the A above high C at the climax of 'Ah, paese dei bovini hispidi!'.

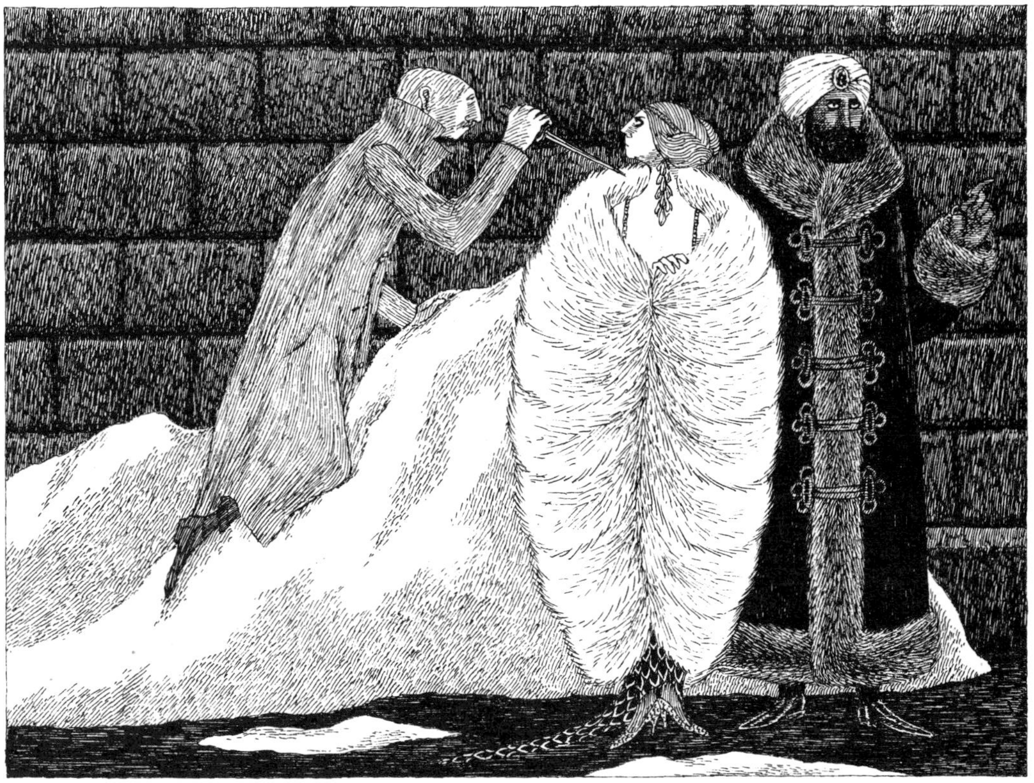

As she left the opera house with the Maharajah of Eschnapur, Jasper rose up from behind a snowdrift and stabbed her in the throat.

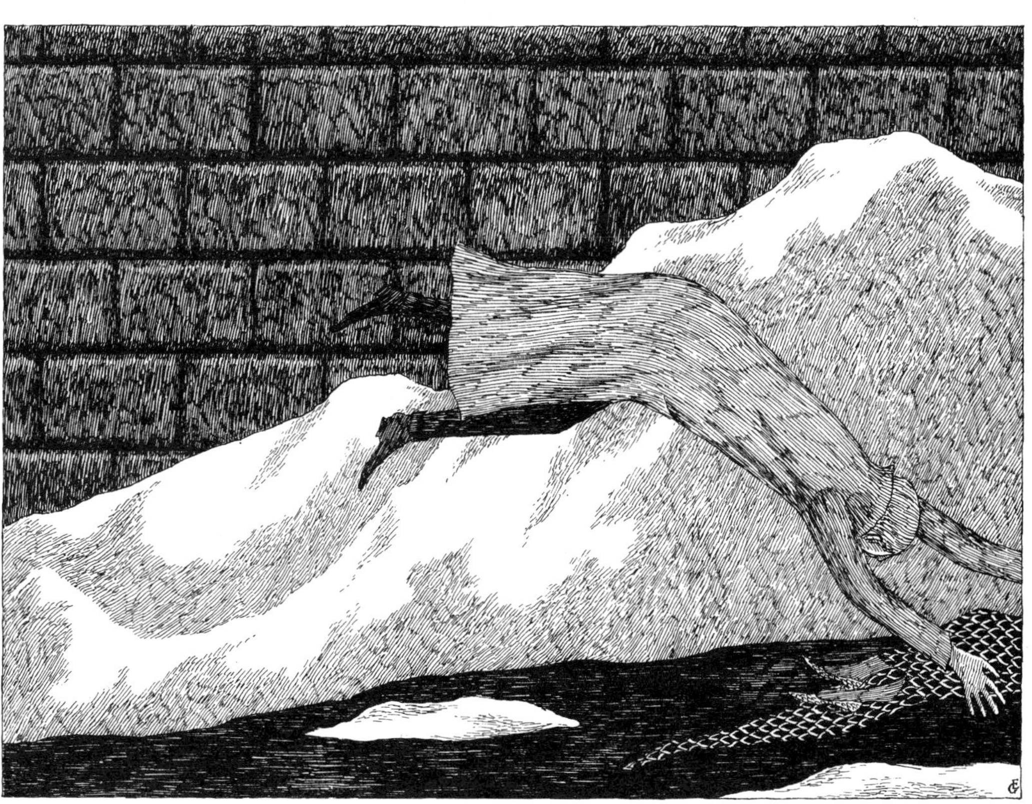

He then stabbed himself and crying 'J'ai trouvé Hortense!', fell dead on her corpse.

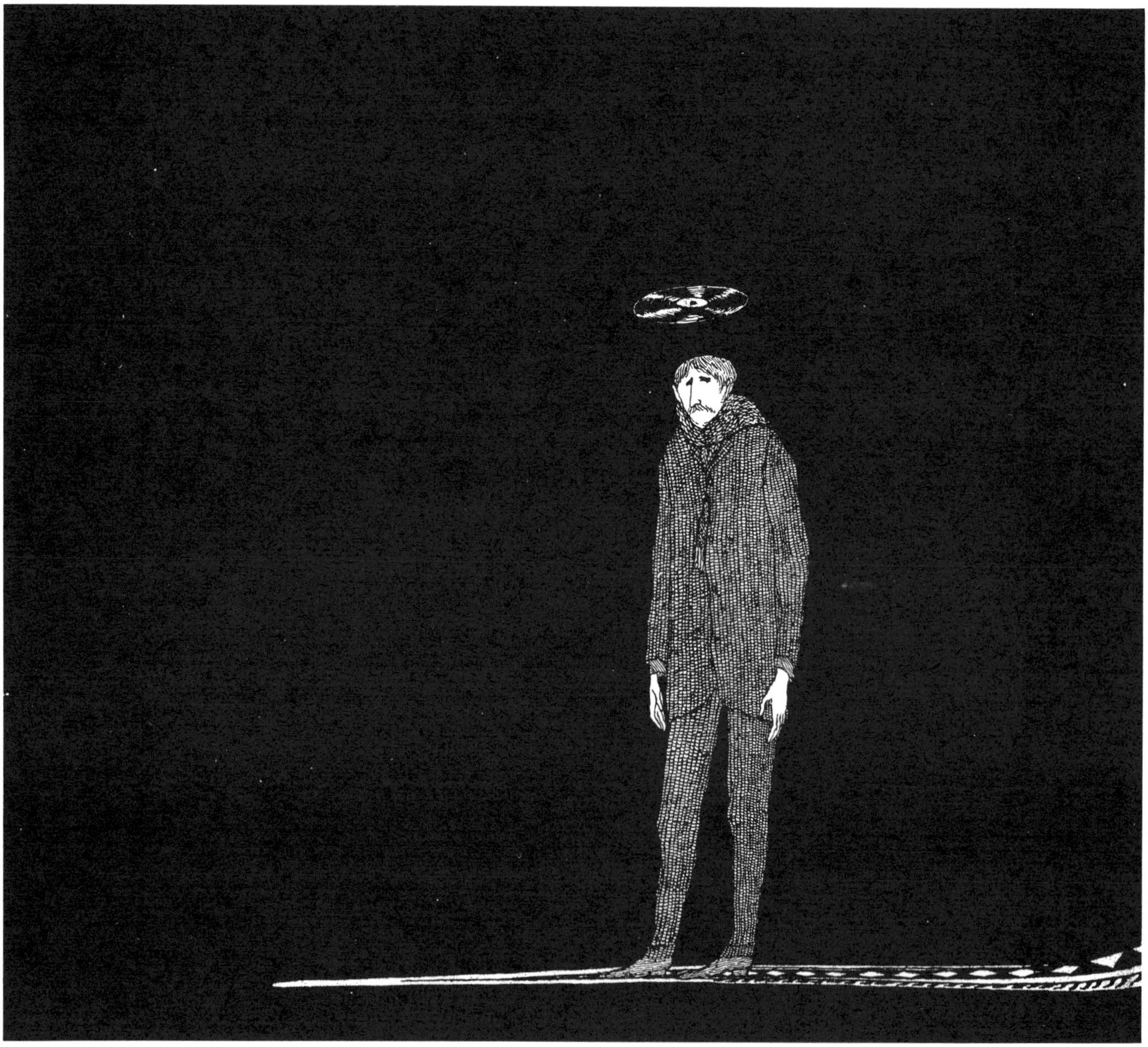

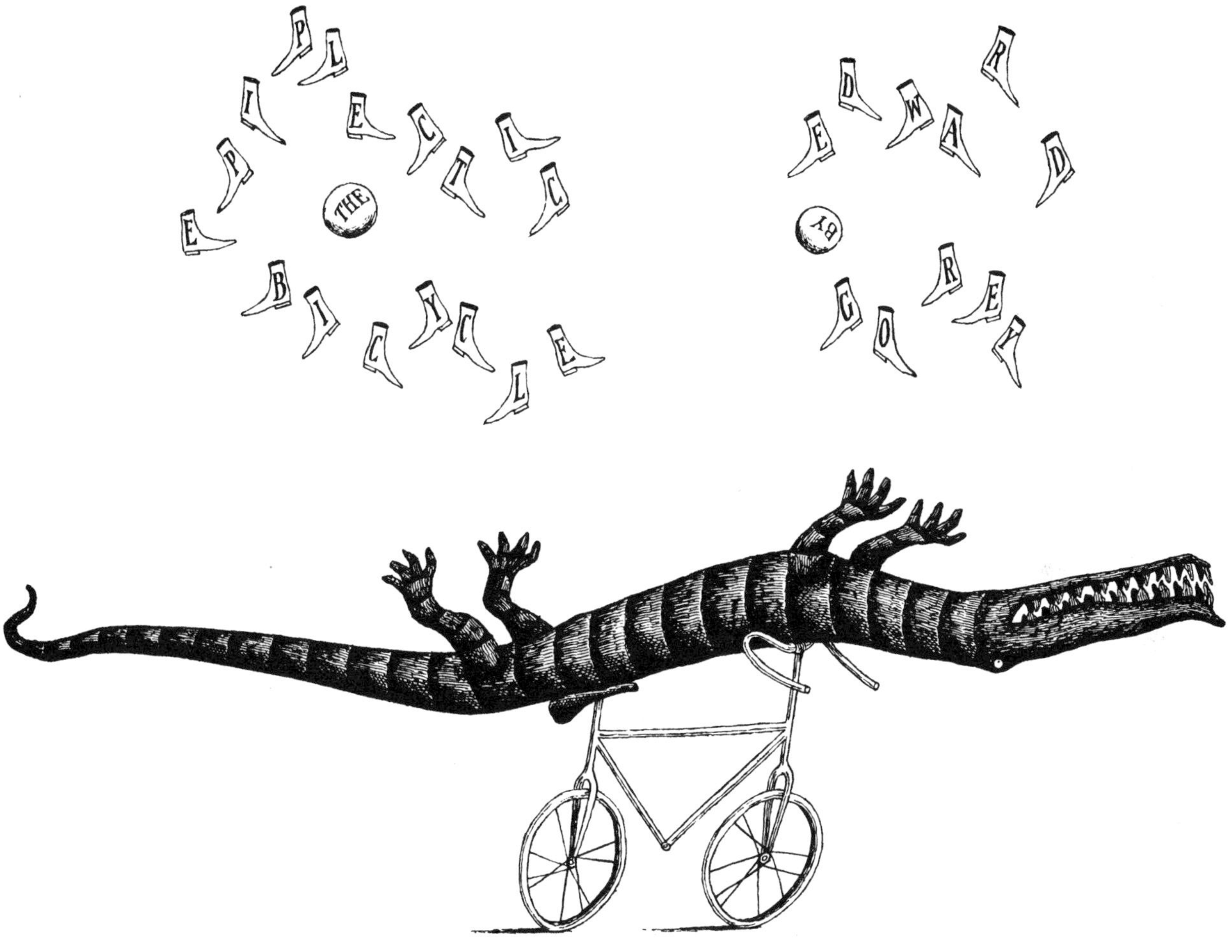
THE EPIPLECTIC BICYCLE
BY EDWARD GOREY

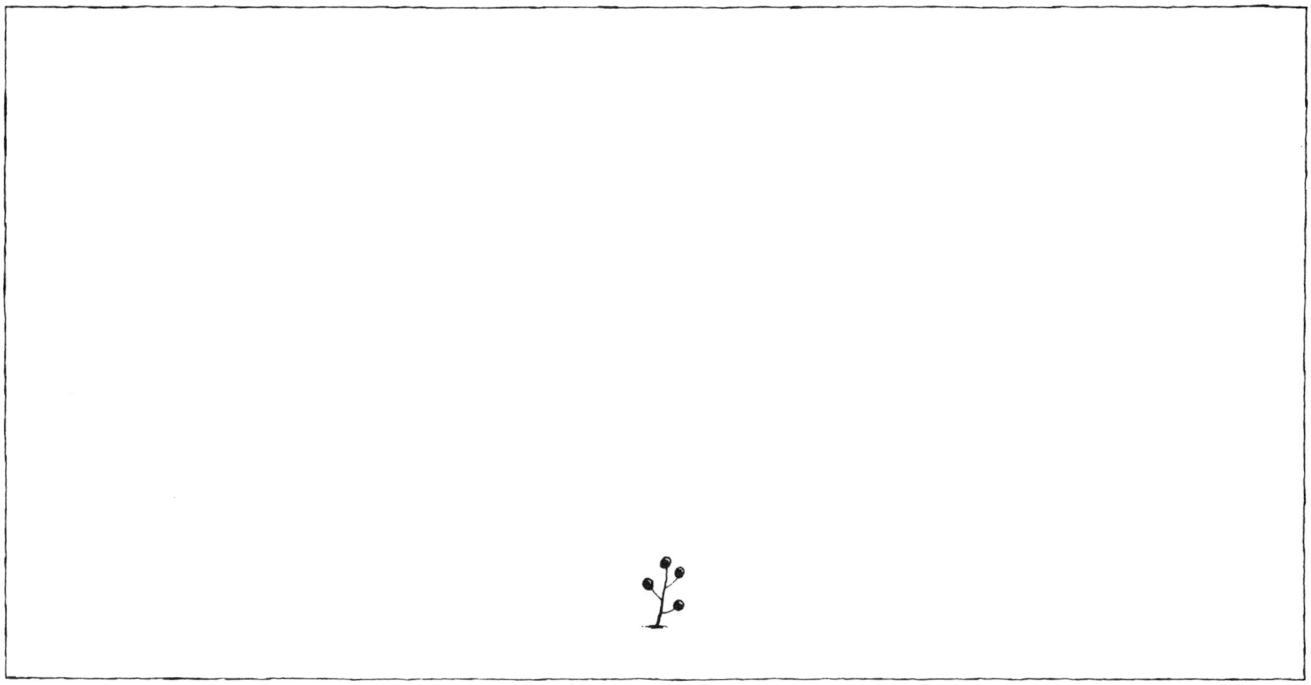

PROLOGUE

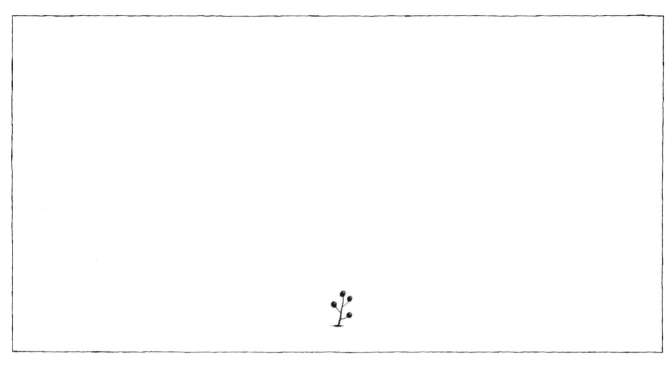

It was the day after Tuesday and the day before Wednesday.

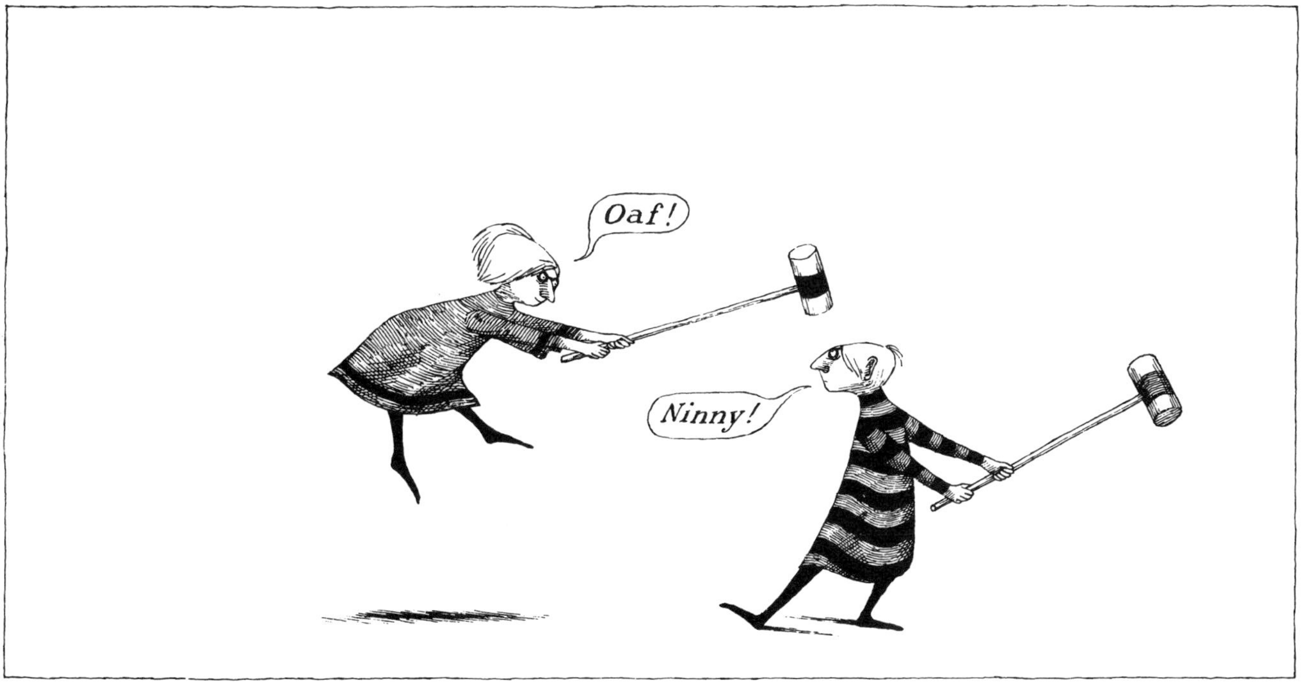
Oaf!
Ninny!

CHAPTER ONE

Embley and Yewbert were hitting one another with croquet mallets

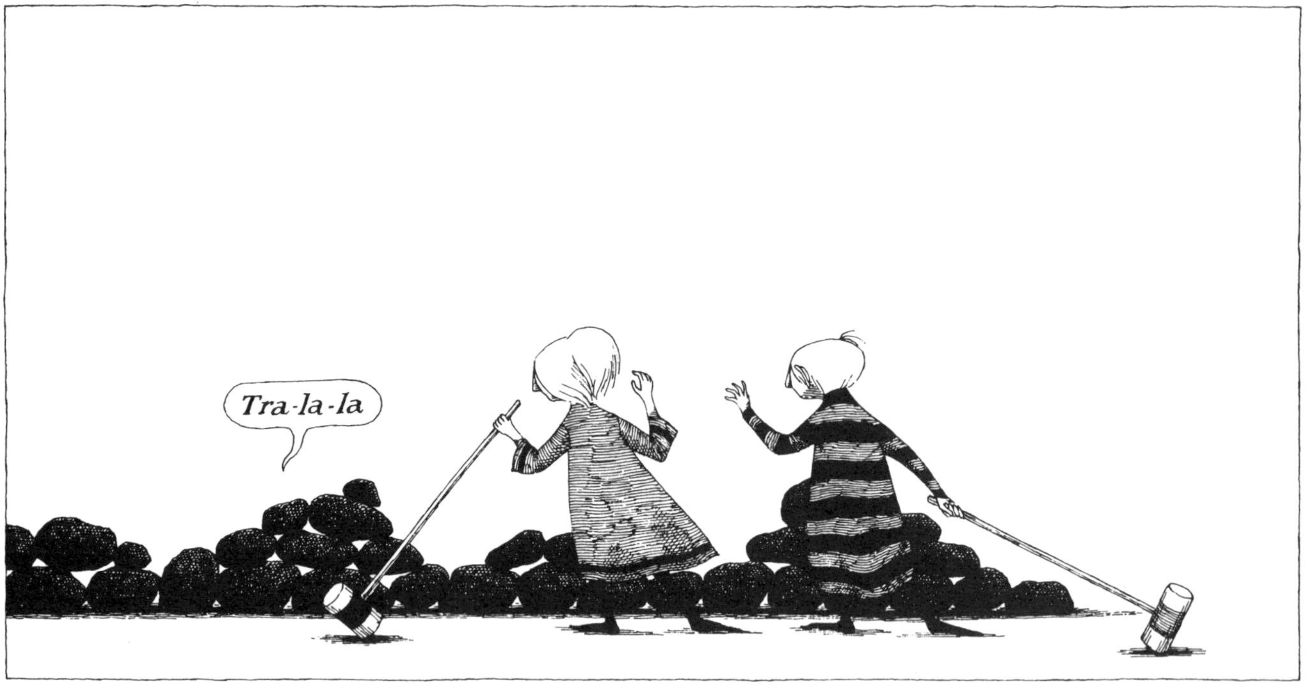
Tra-la-la

when they heard a noise behind the wall

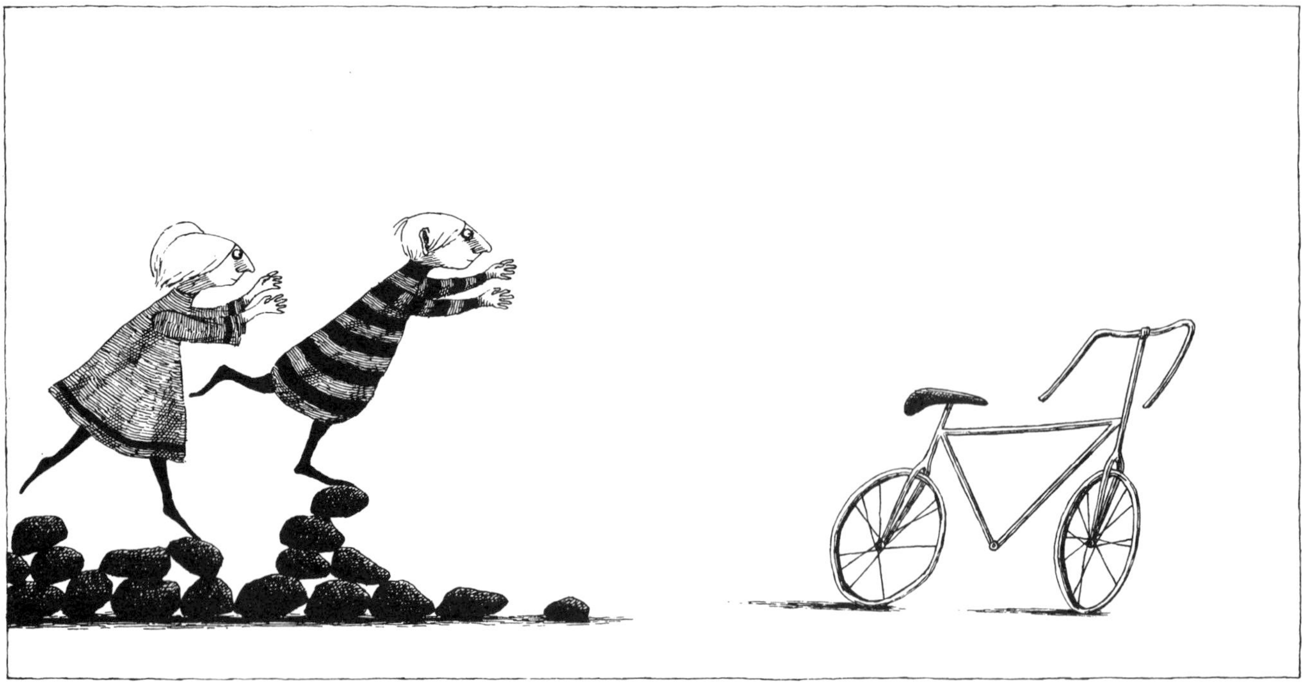

and an untenanted bicycle rolled into view.

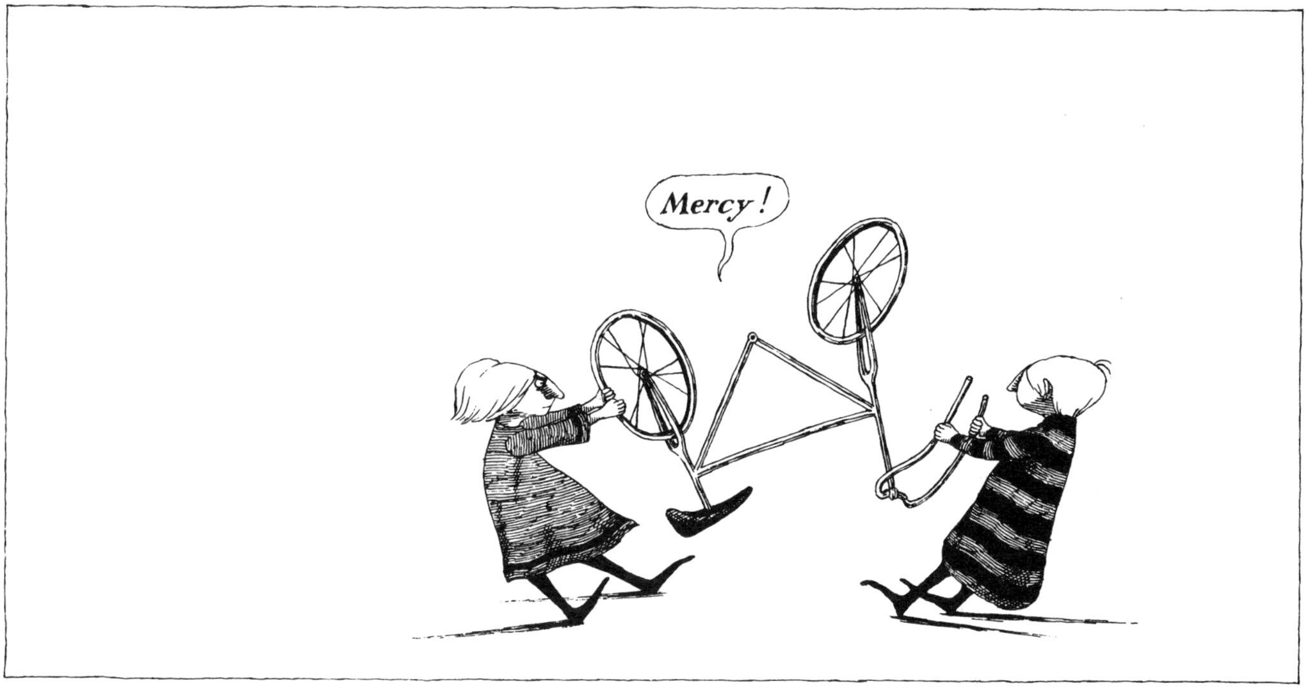
Mercy!

CHAPTER TWO

Brother and sister tried to take sole possession of it

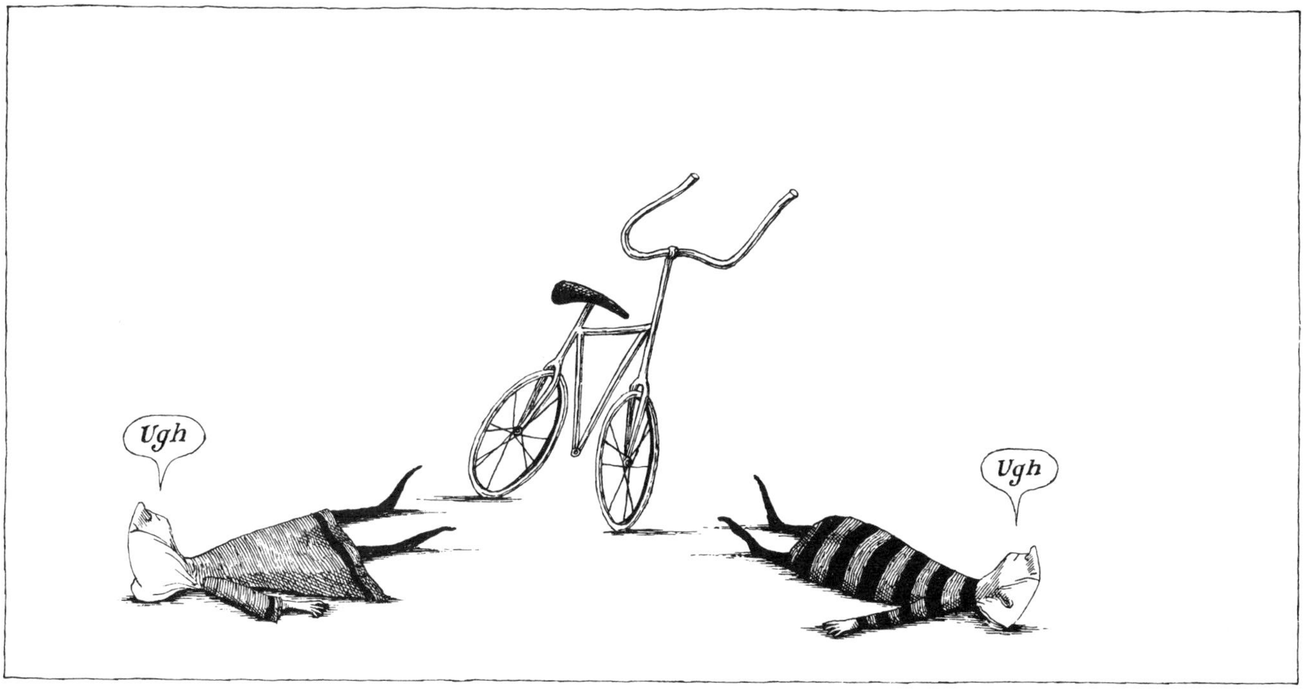
Ugh
Ugh

until they both fell exhausted;

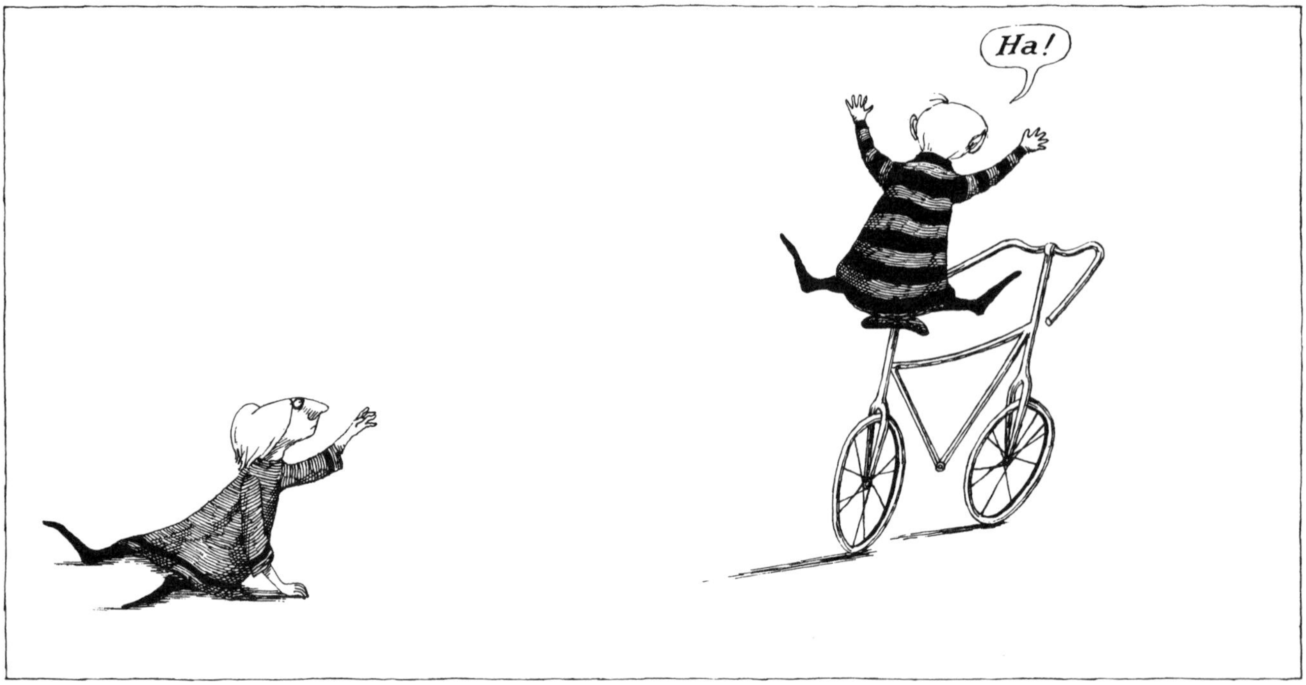
Ha!

Yewbert recovered first and leapt onto the seat

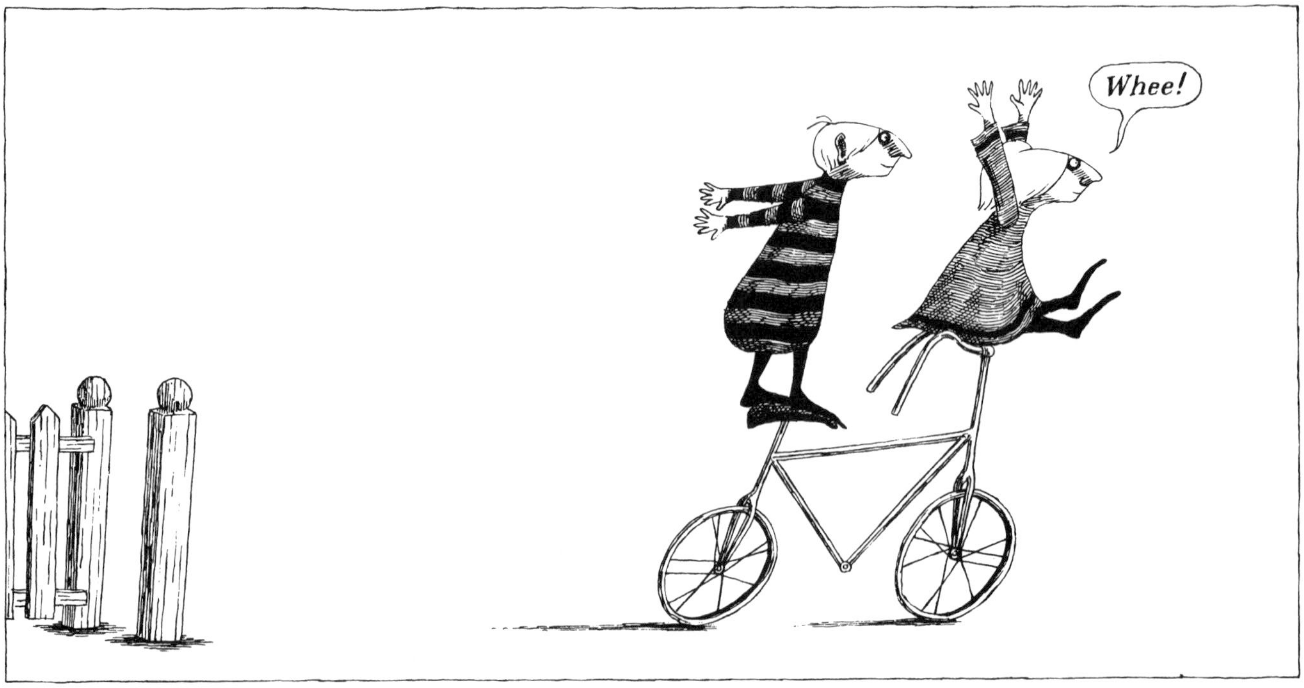
Whee!

so Embley had to sit on the handlebars as they flew out the gate.

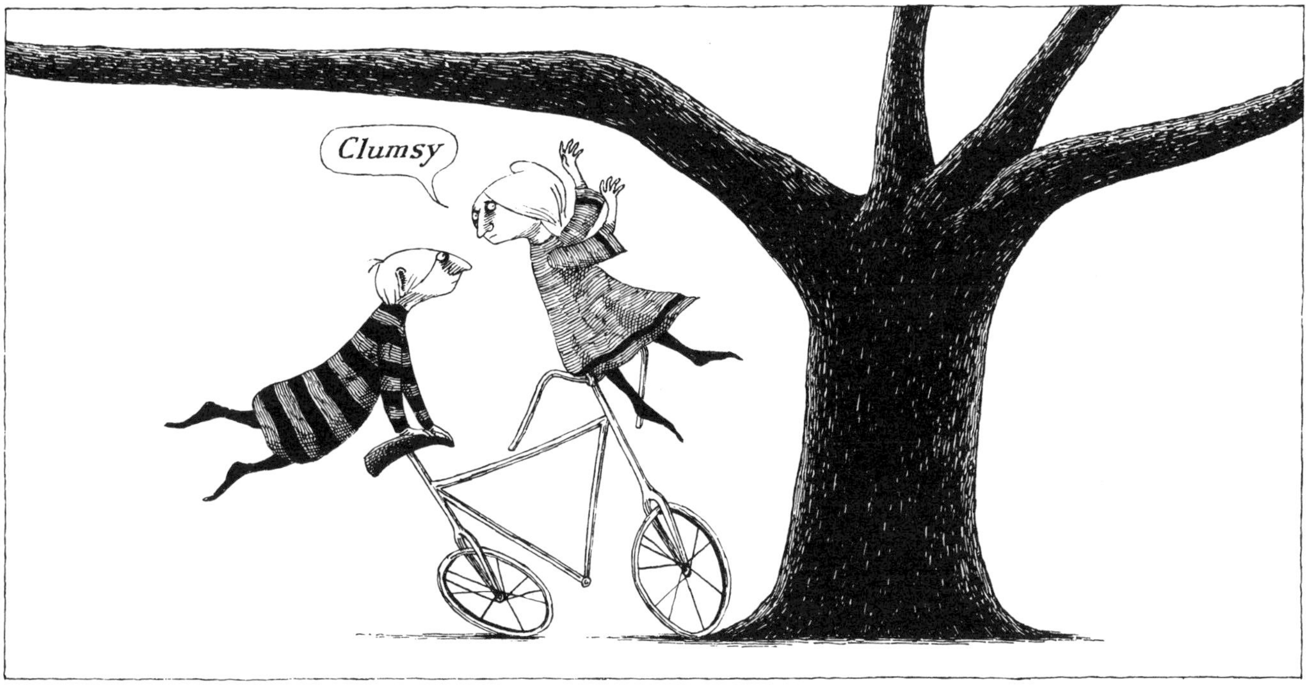
Clumsy

CHAPTER FOUR

After that they almost ran into a tree

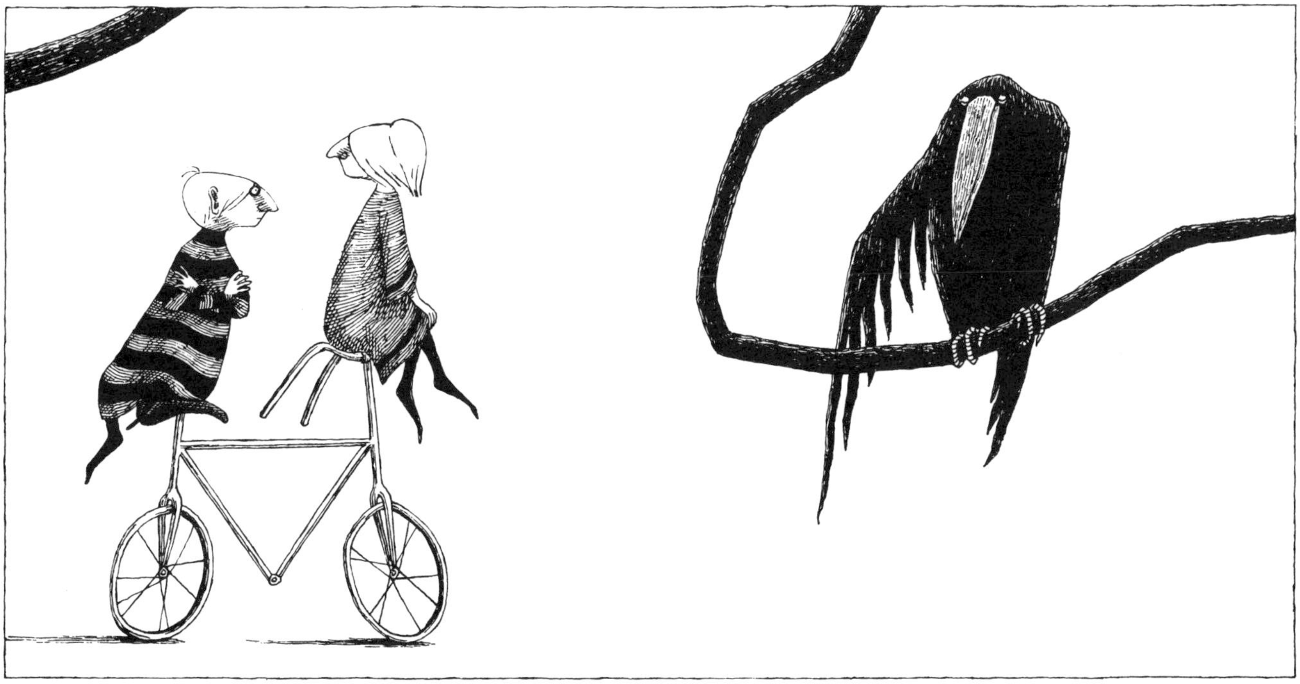

on which was perched a large bird

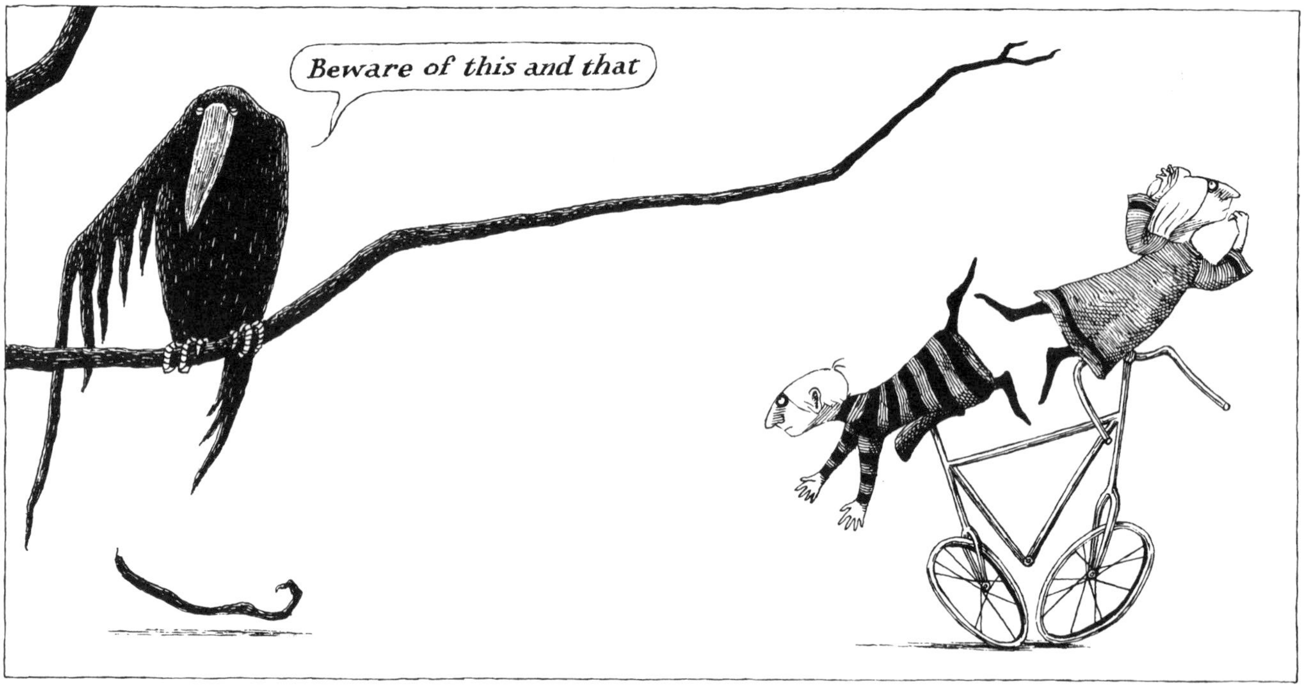
Beware of this and that

who muttered as they went by.

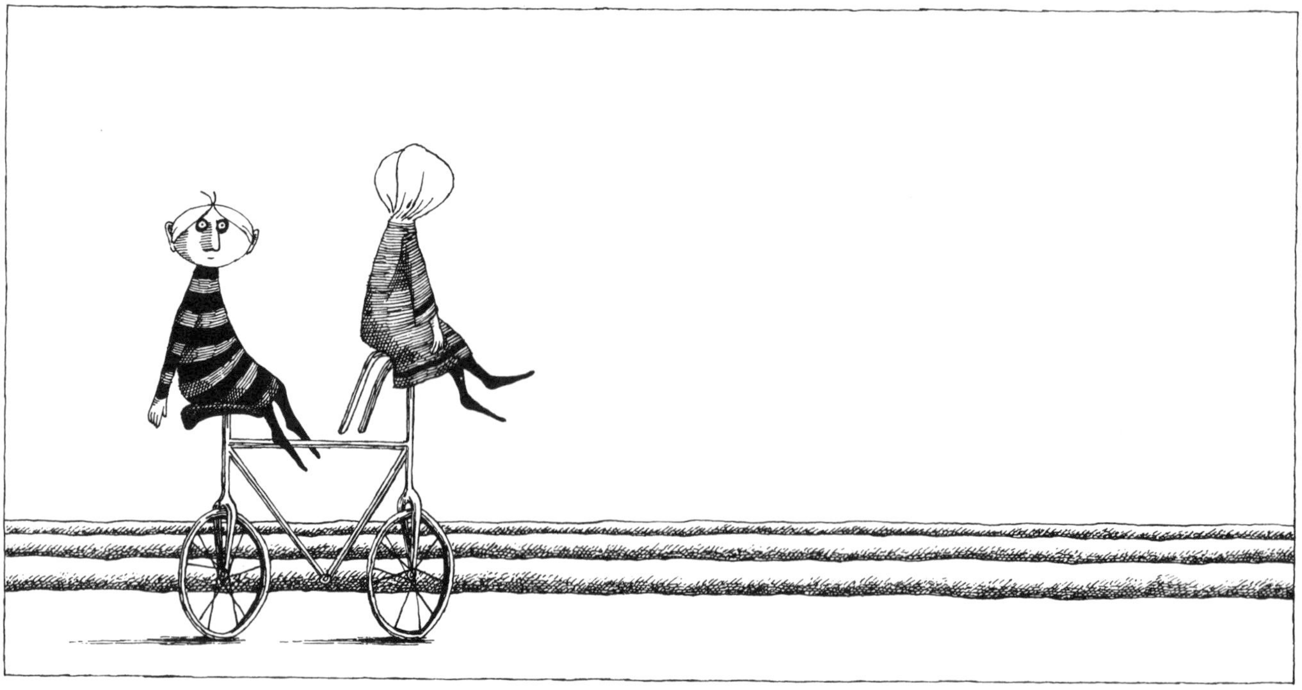

CHAPTER SEVEN

They rode past a great many turnip fields

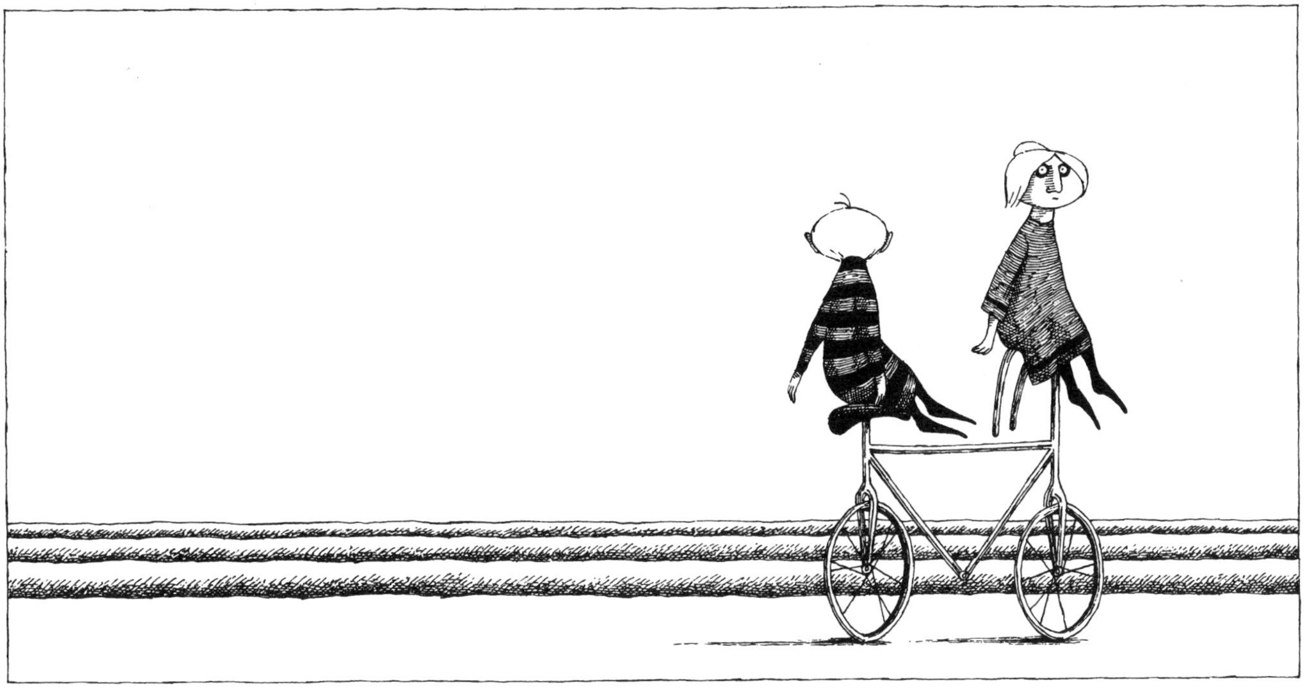

but as *it* was the wrong time of year, they didn't see any turnips.

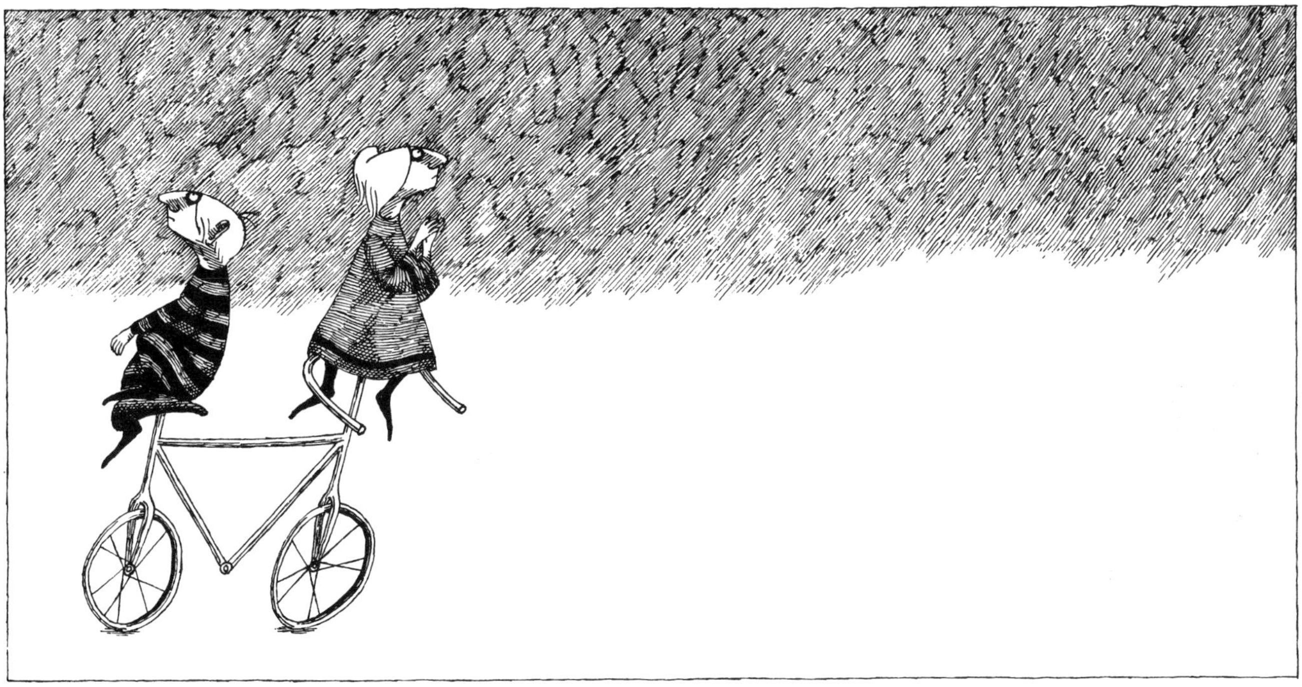

CHAPTER ELEVEN

A horrid storm came up ;

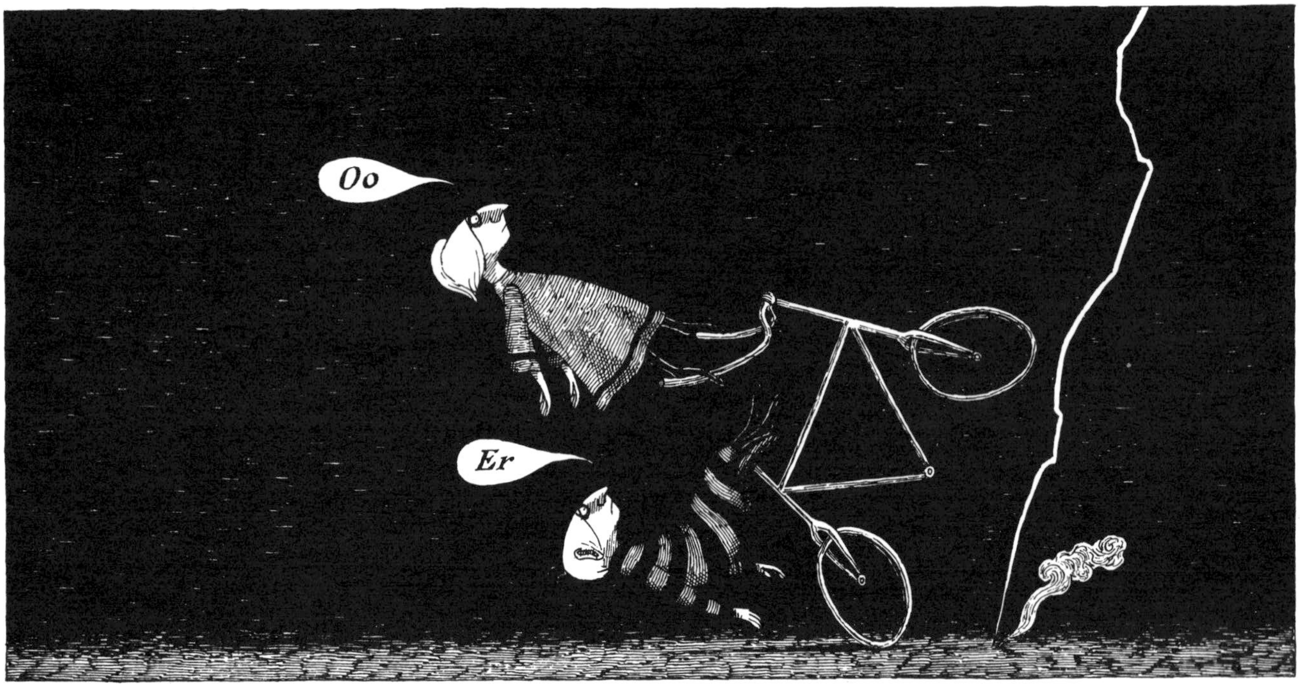
Oo
Er

they were nearly *struck* by lightning

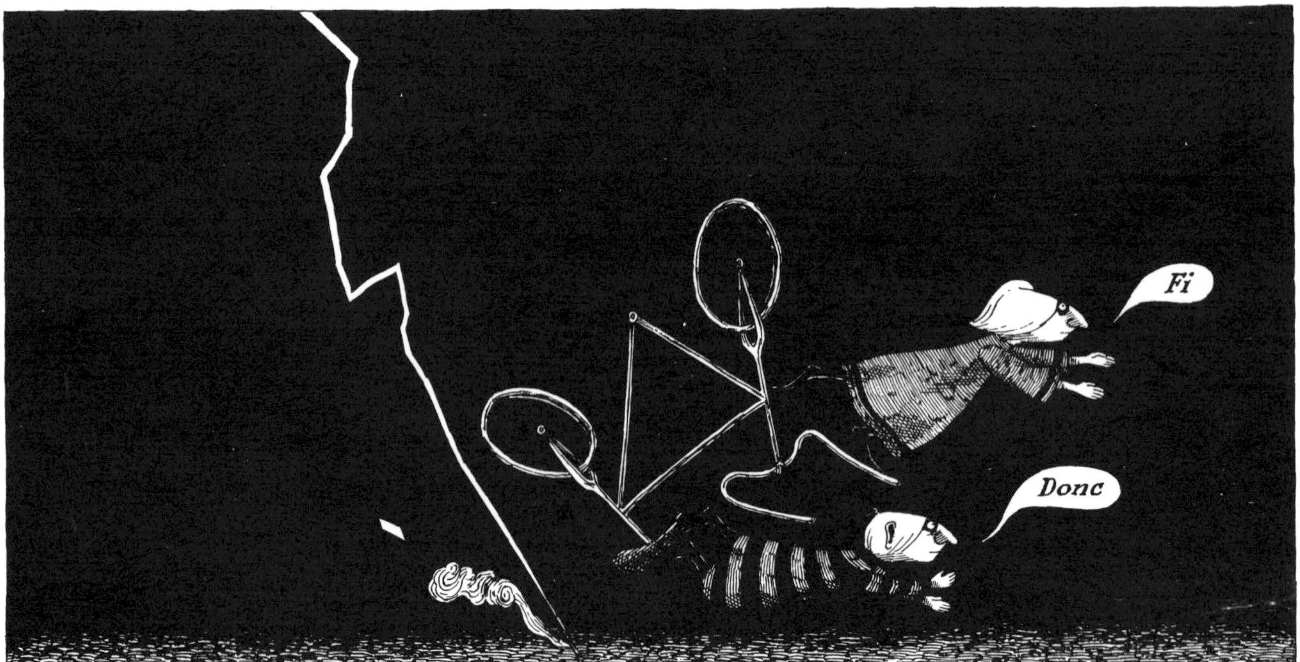
Fi
Donc

several times.

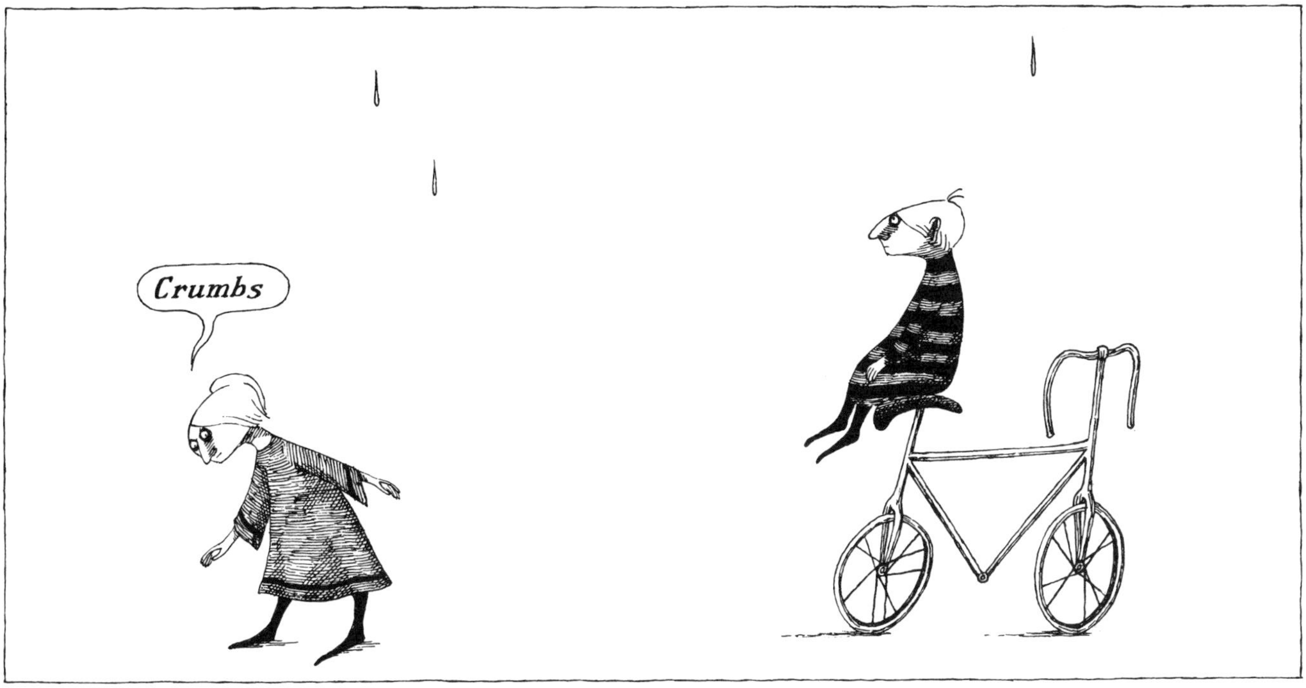
Crumbs

When it was over Embley found she had lost her fourteen pairs of yellow shoes

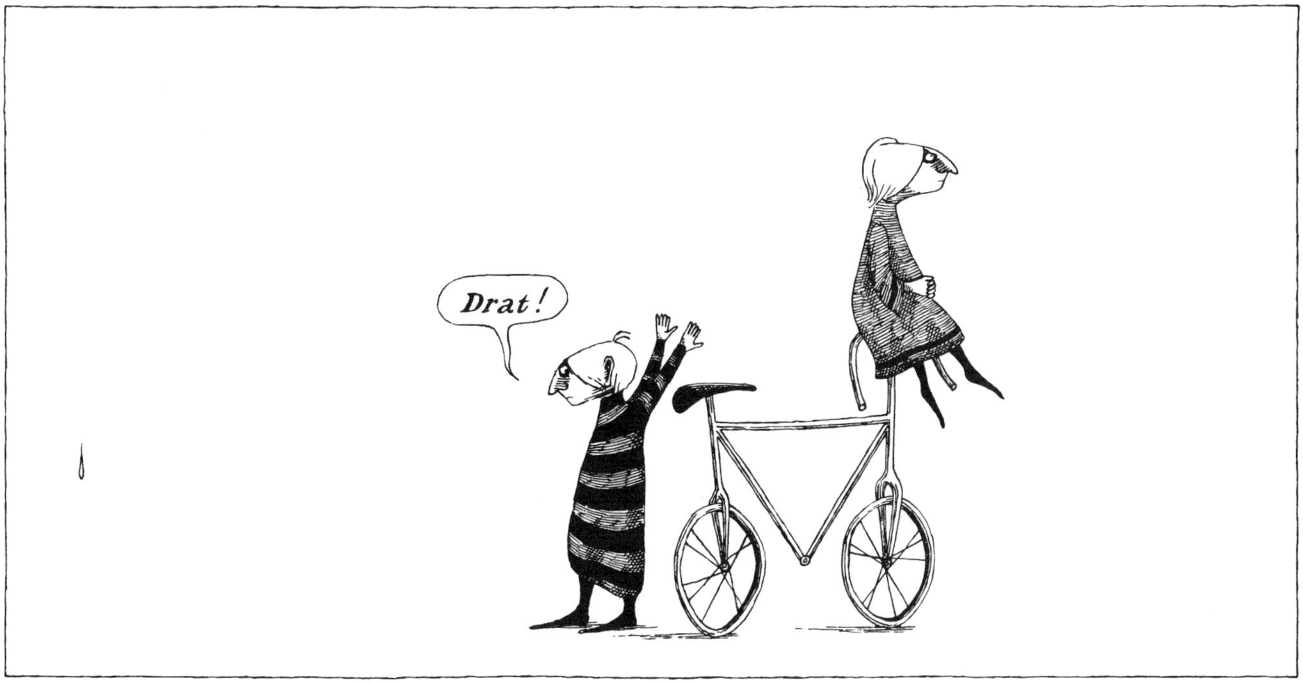
Drat!

and Yewbert his spotted-fur waistcoat.

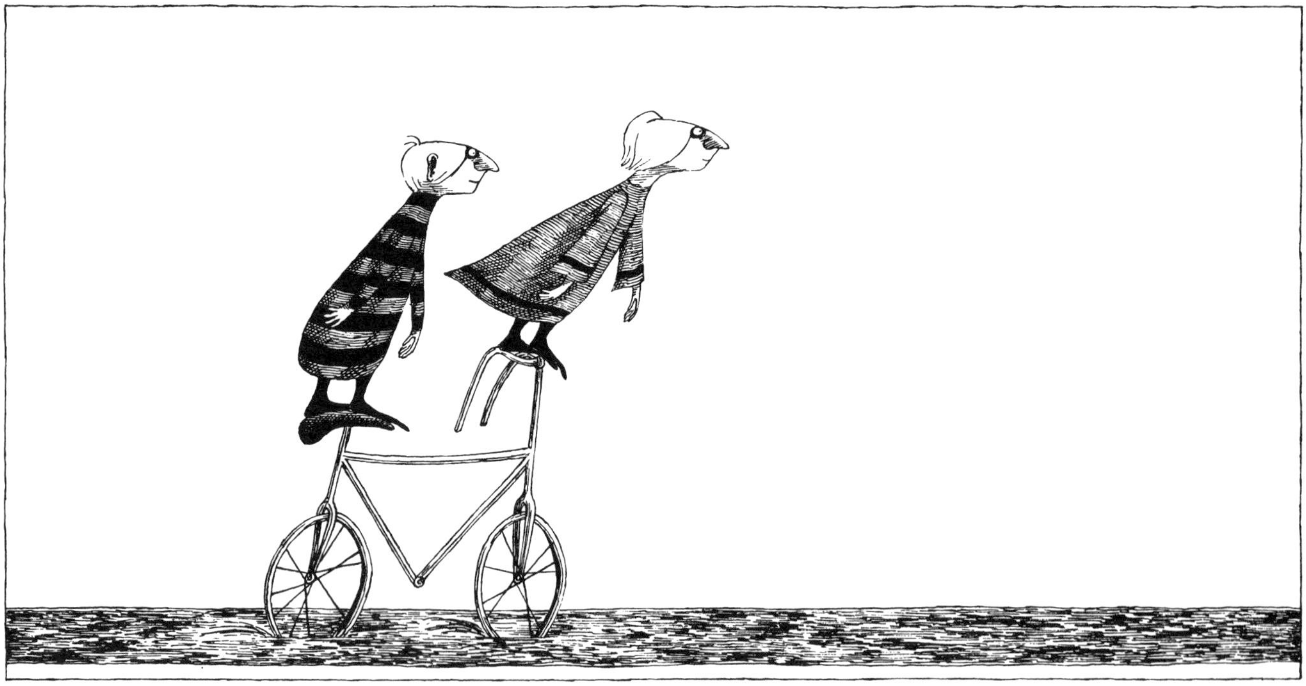

CHAPTER TWELVE

As they were riding through a lengthy puddle

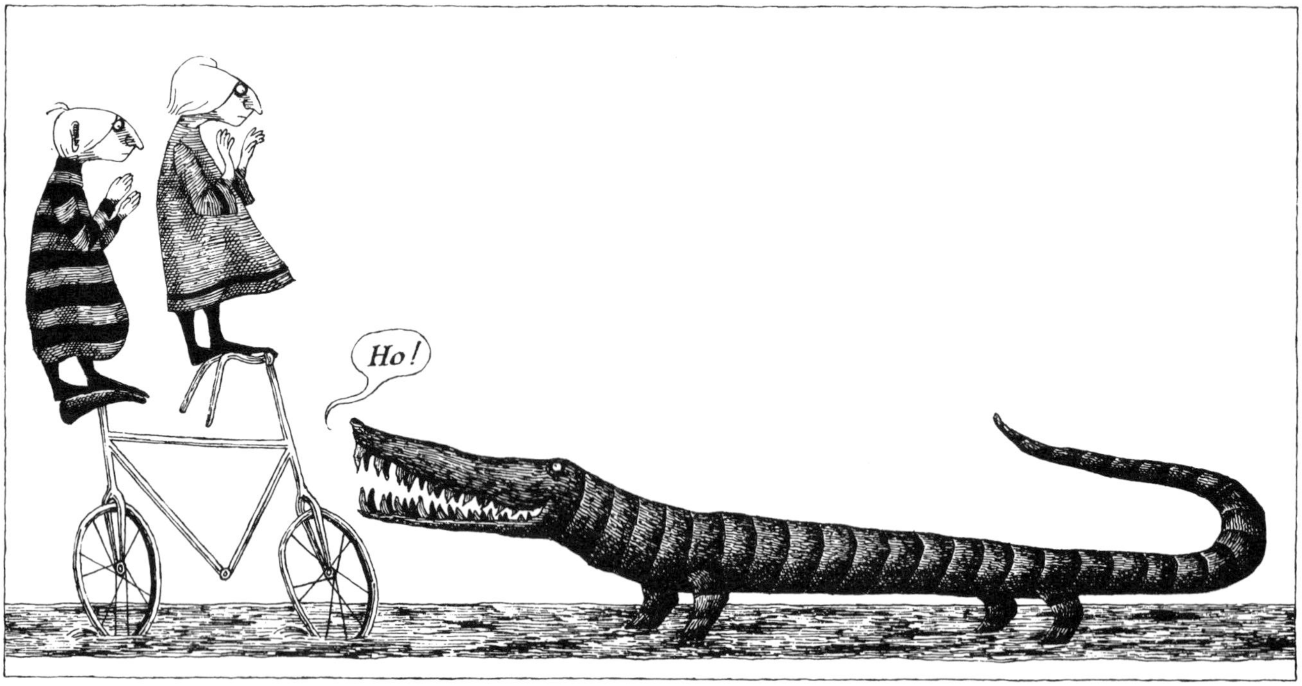
Ho!

an alligator rose up in front of them;

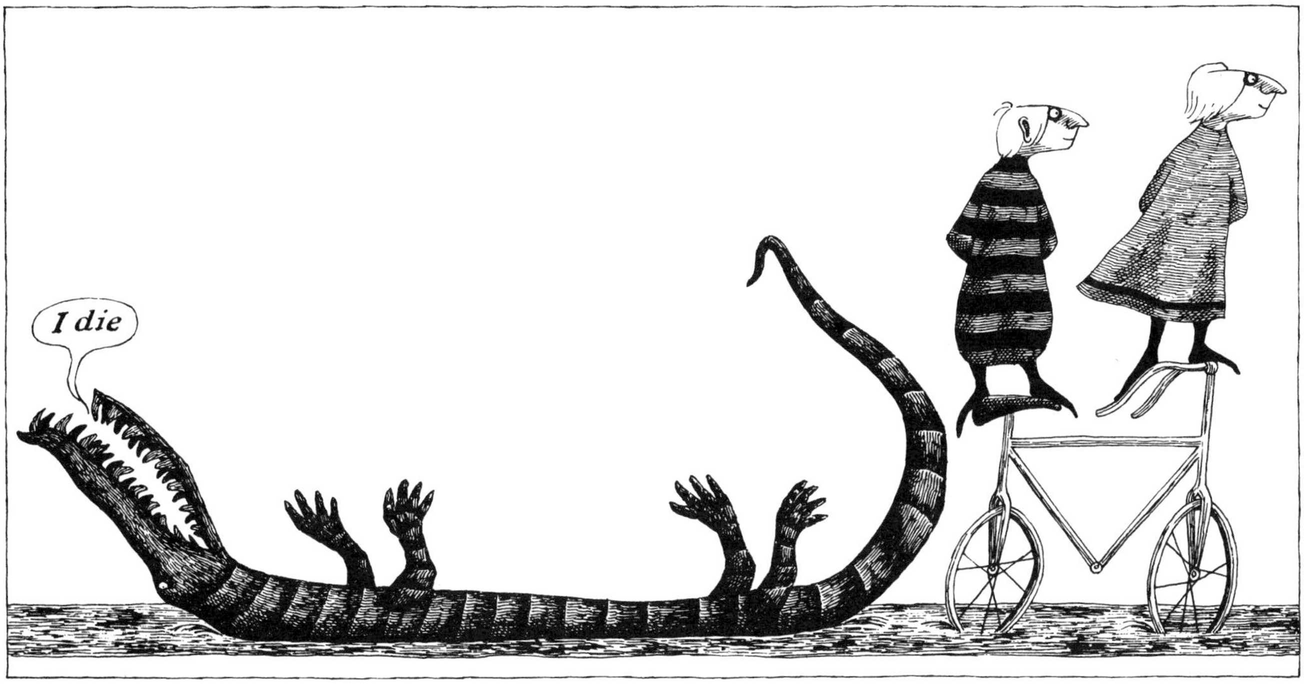
I die

Embley kicked it on the end of its nose, and it expired.

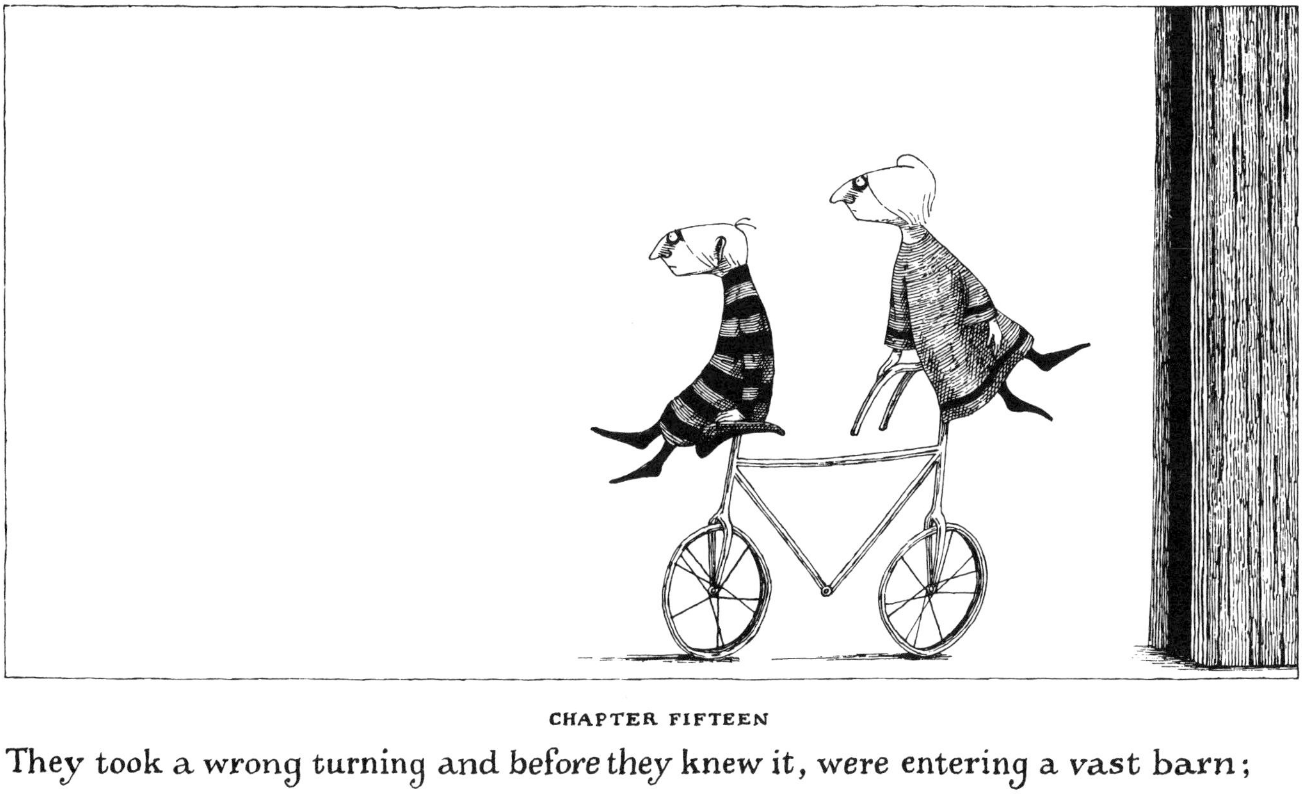

CHAPTER FIFTEEN

They took a wrong turning and before they knew it, were entering a vast barn;

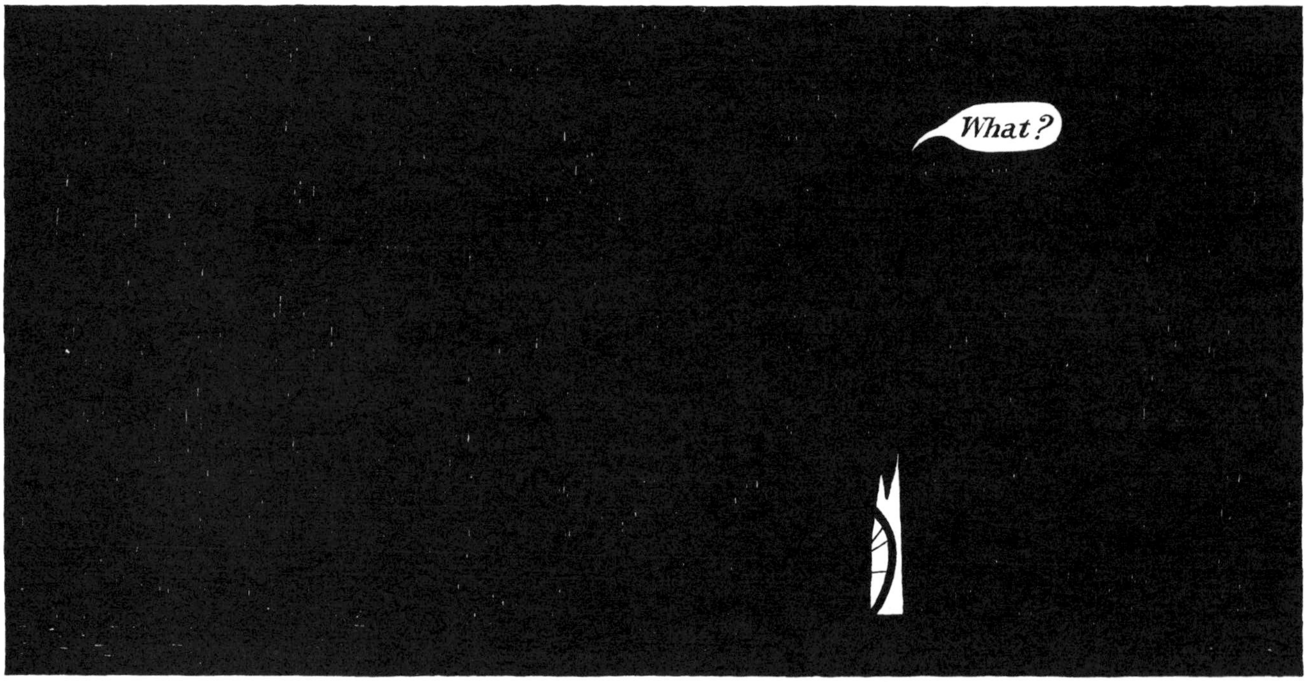
What?

it was too dark to hear anything;

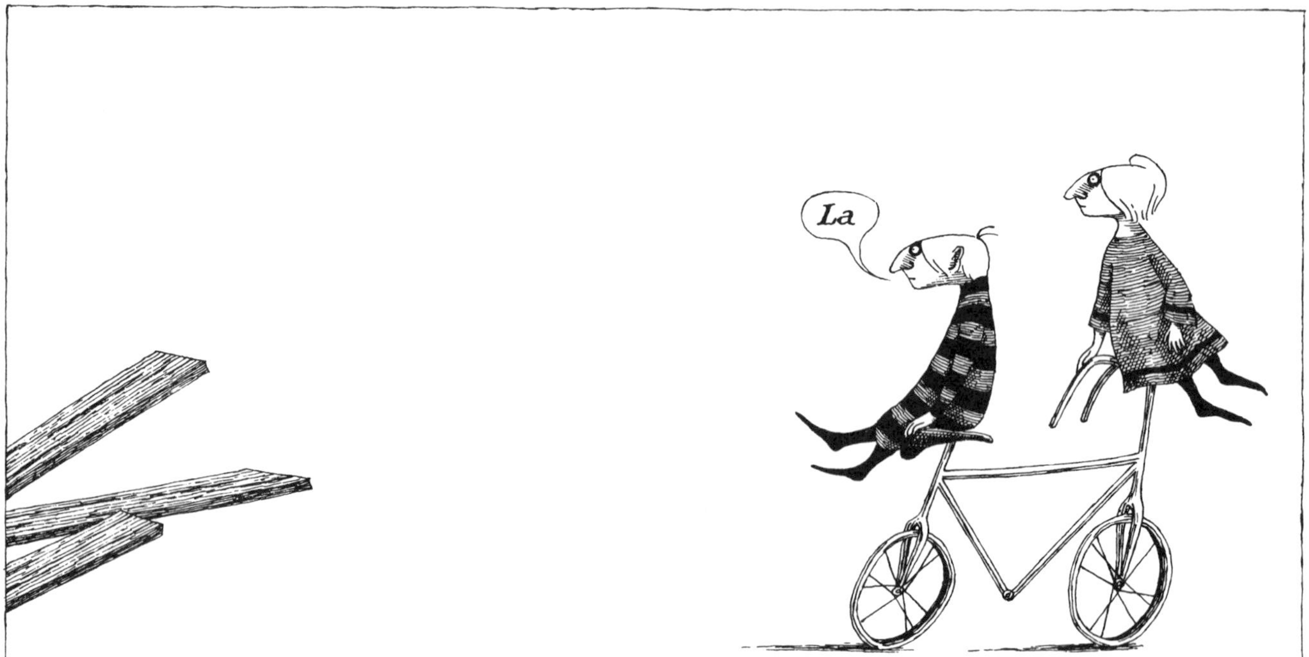
La

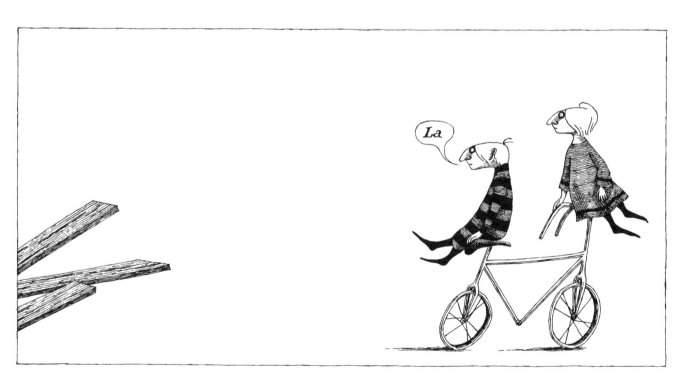

it fell down as they came out the other end.

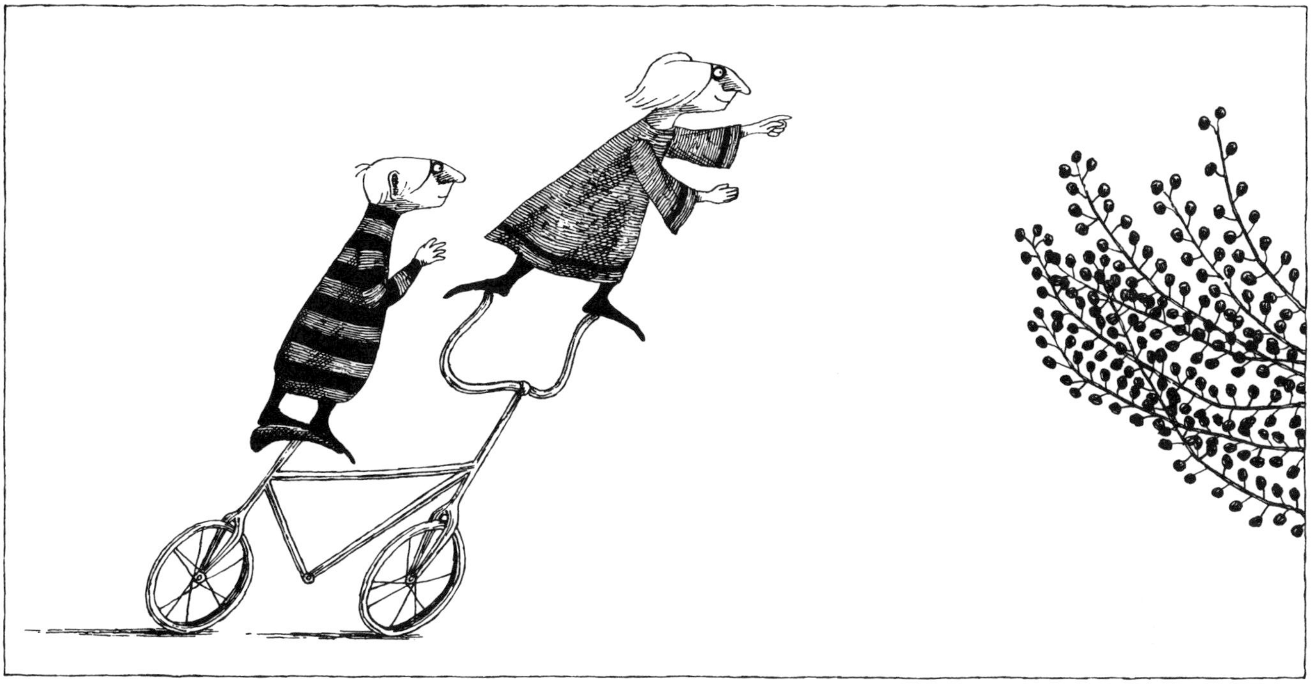

CHAPTER NINETEEN

They made for a huge bush

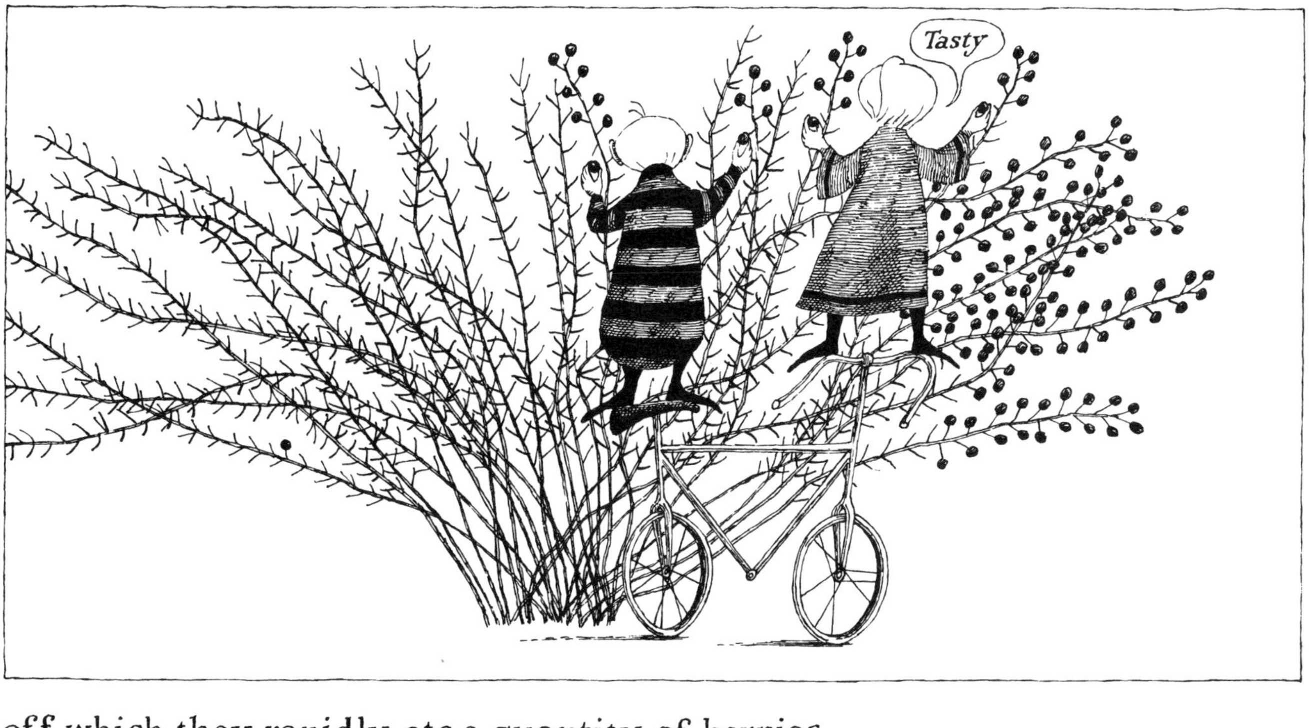
Tasty

off which they rapidly ate a quantity of berries.

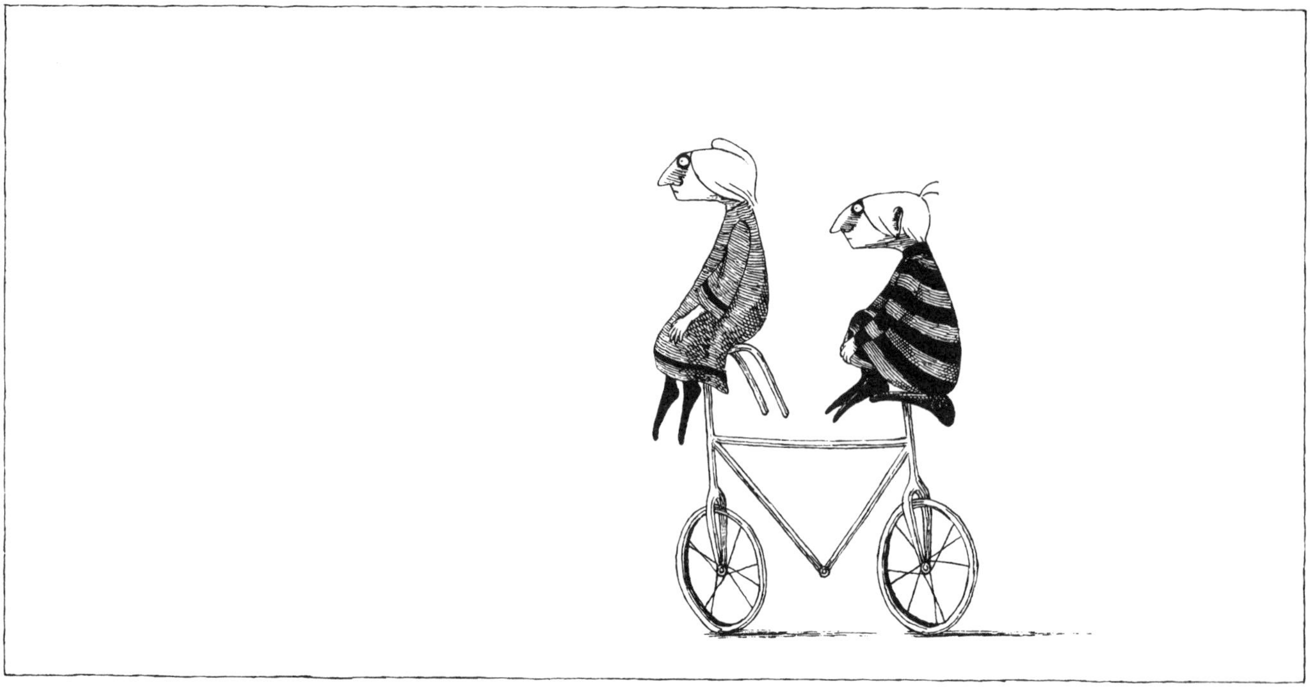

CHAPTER TWENTY-TWO (AND THE LAST)

They returned home

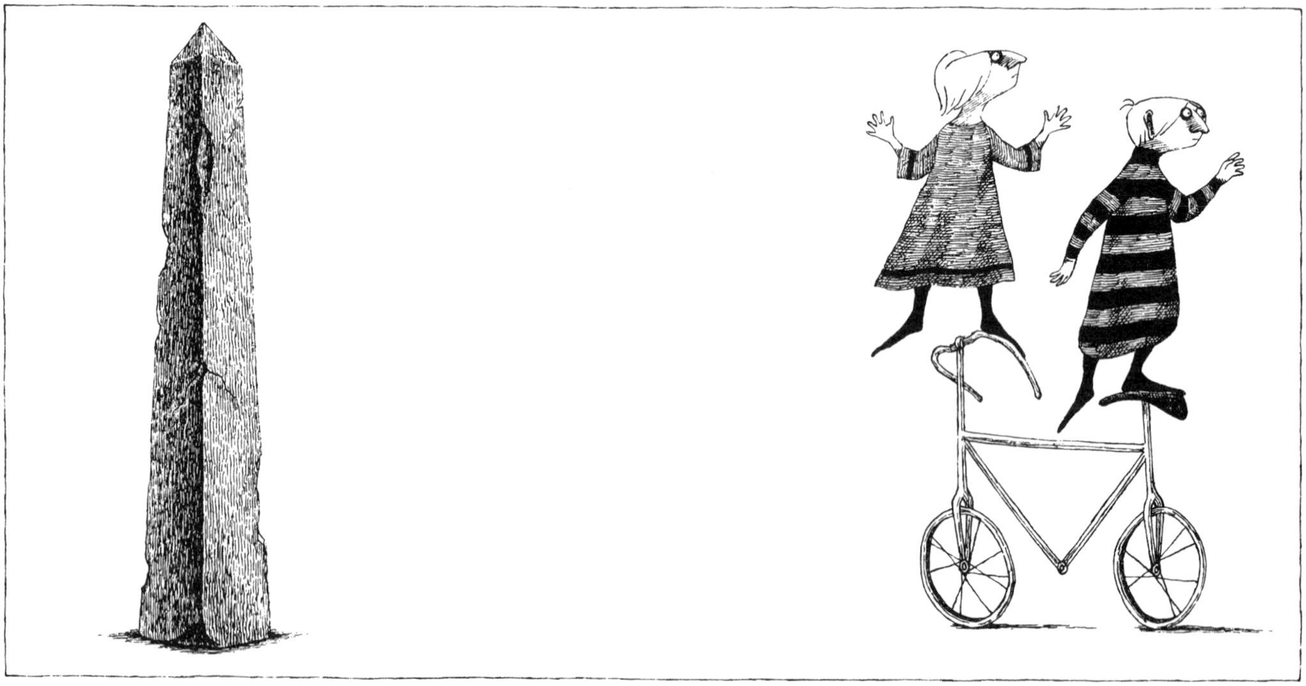

to discover there was nothing to be seen but an obelisk

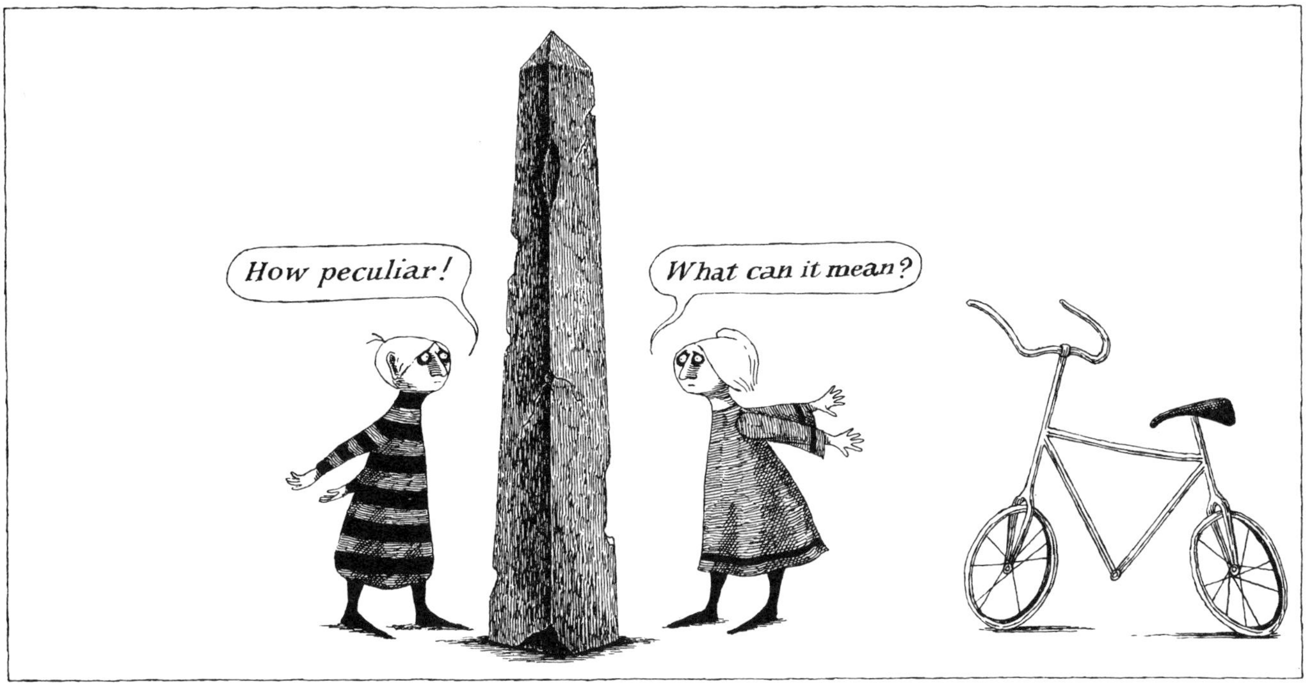
How peculiar!
What can it mean?

which said it had been raised to their memory 173 years ago;

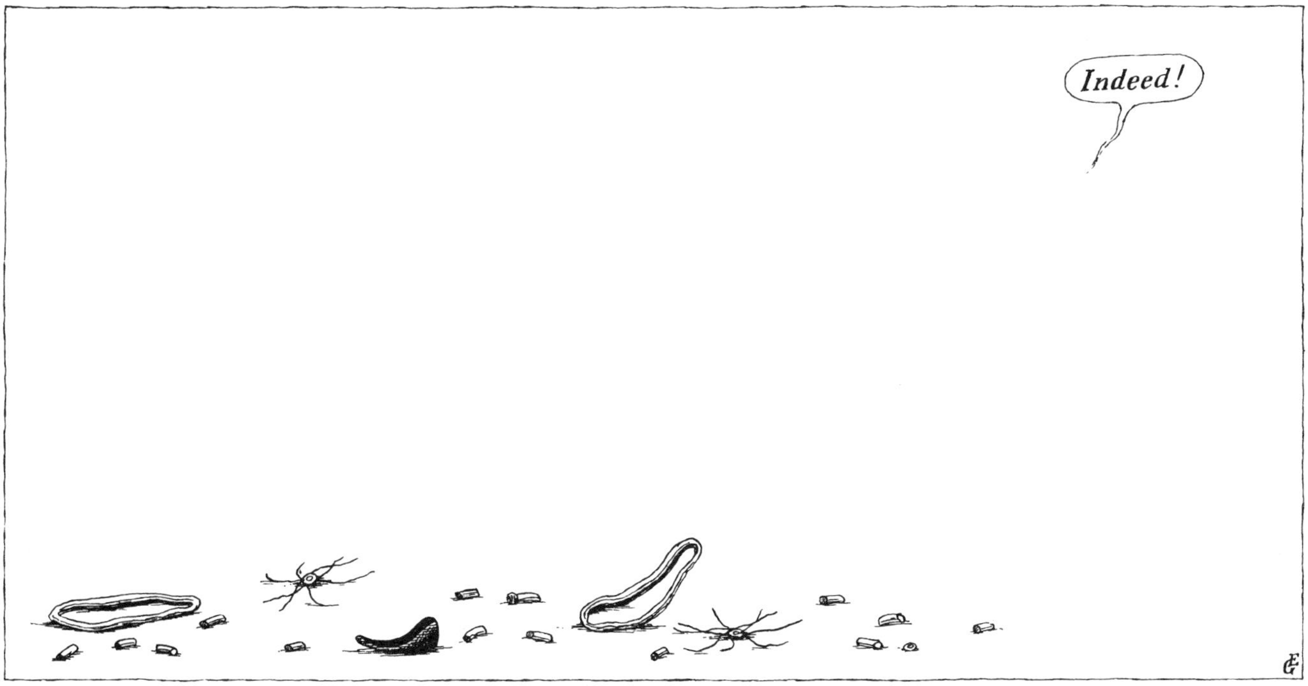
Indeed!

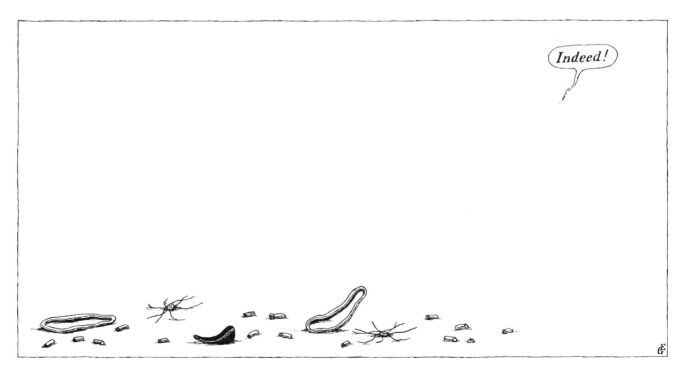

the bicycle uttered for the last time and fell to bits.

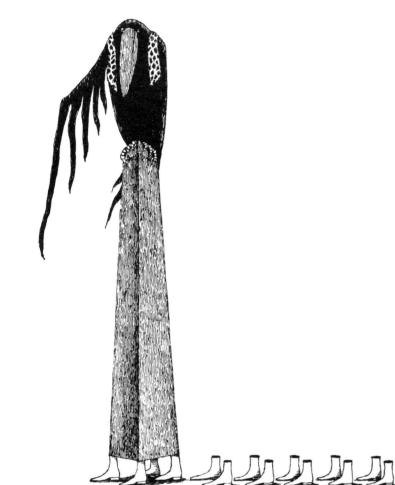

The Sopping Thursday by Edward Gorey

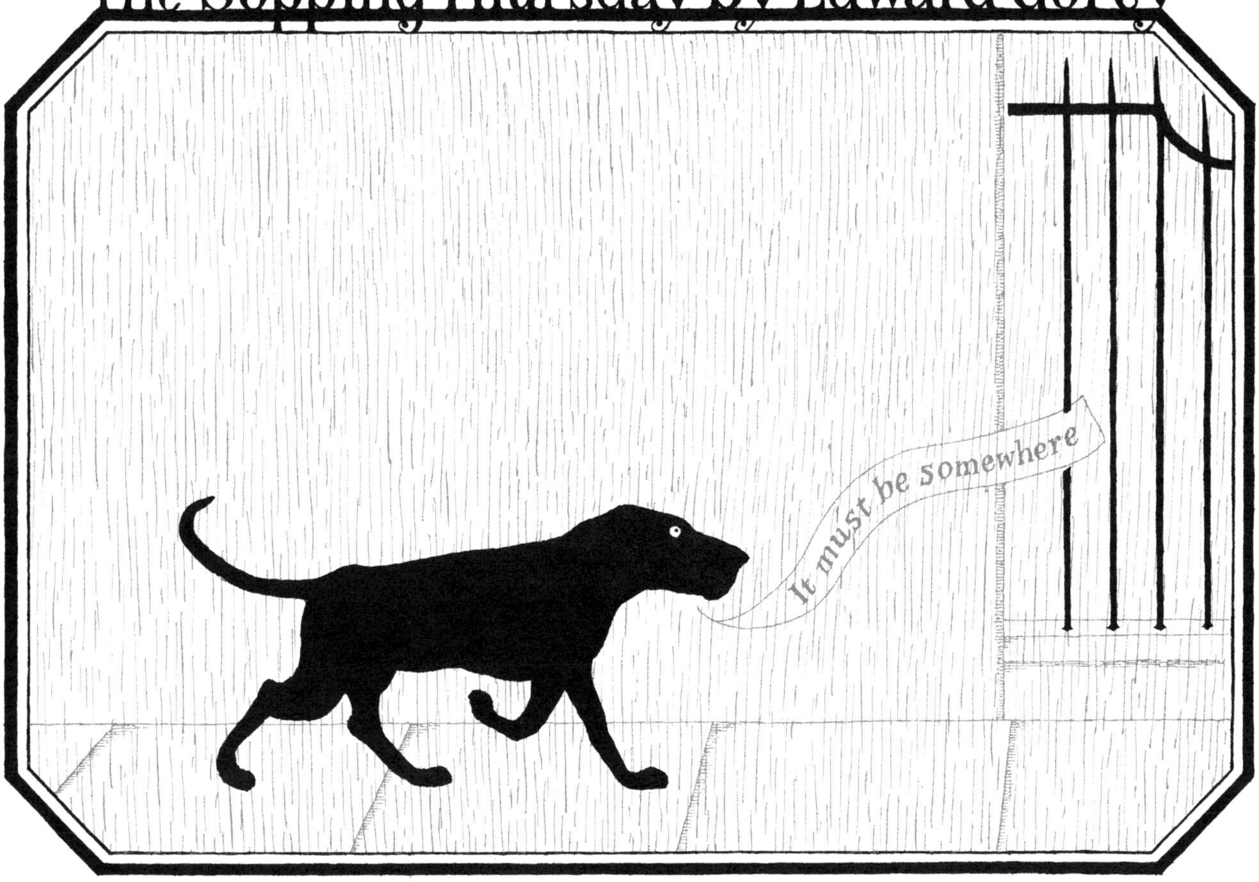
It must be somewhere

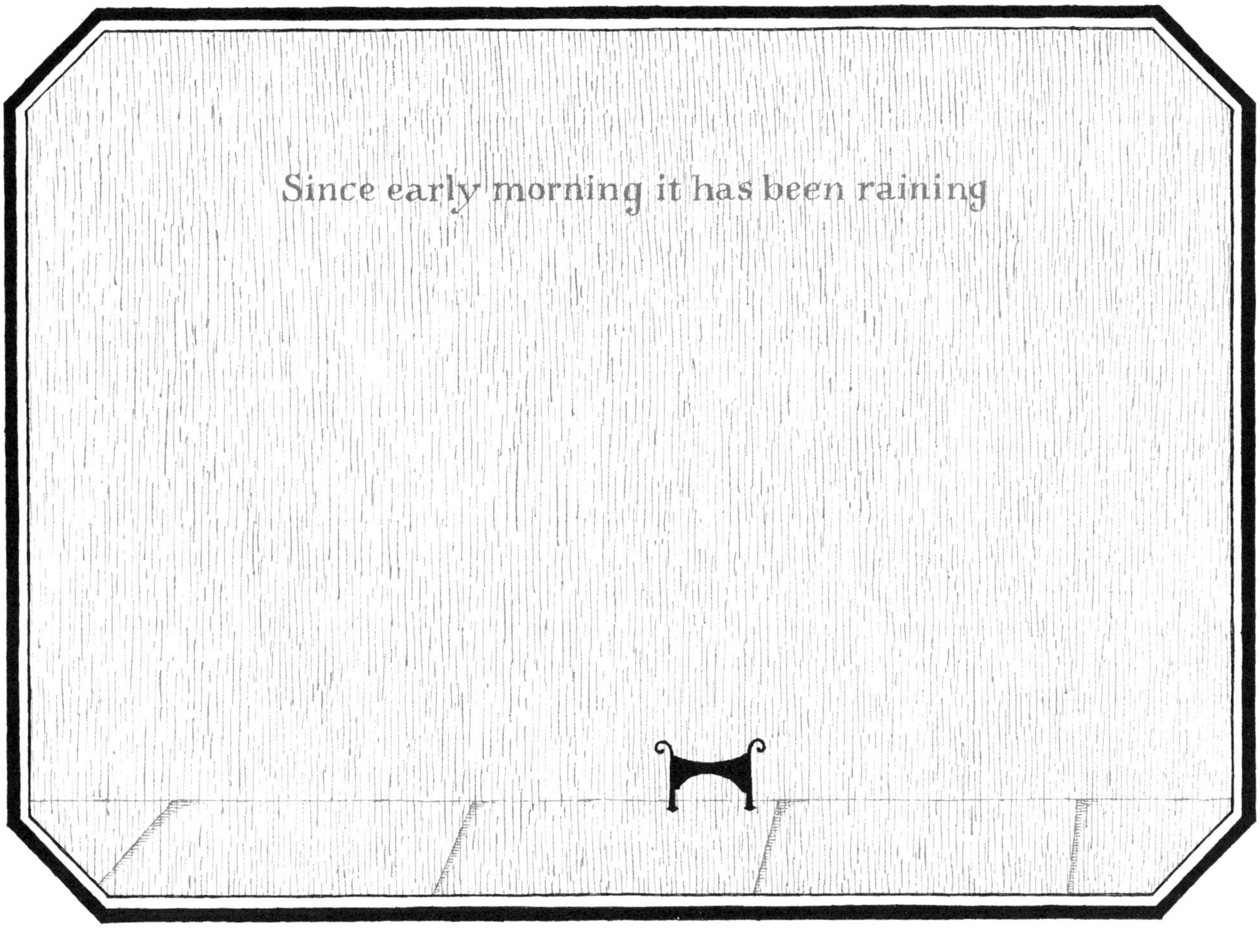
Since early morning it has been raining

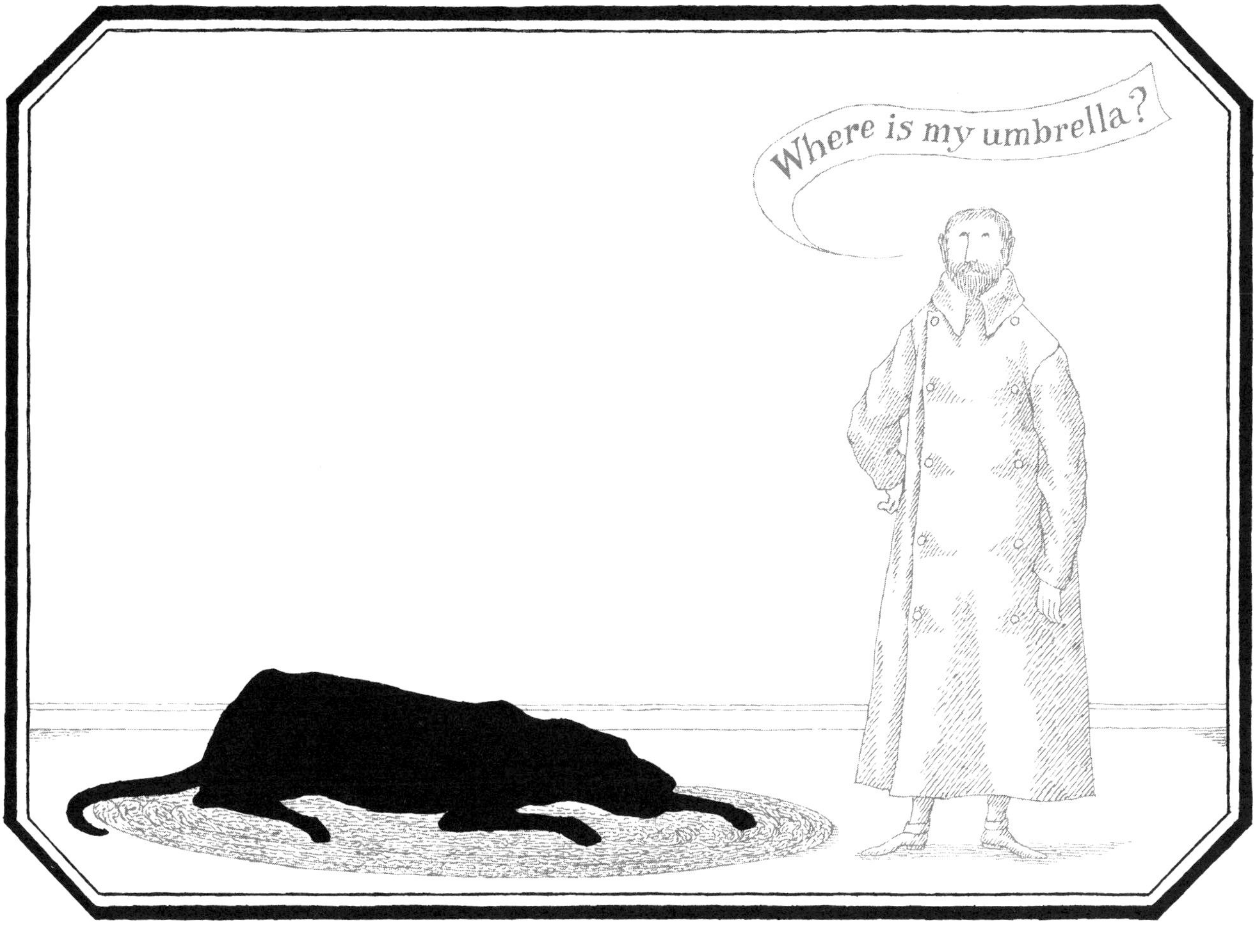
Where is my umbrella?

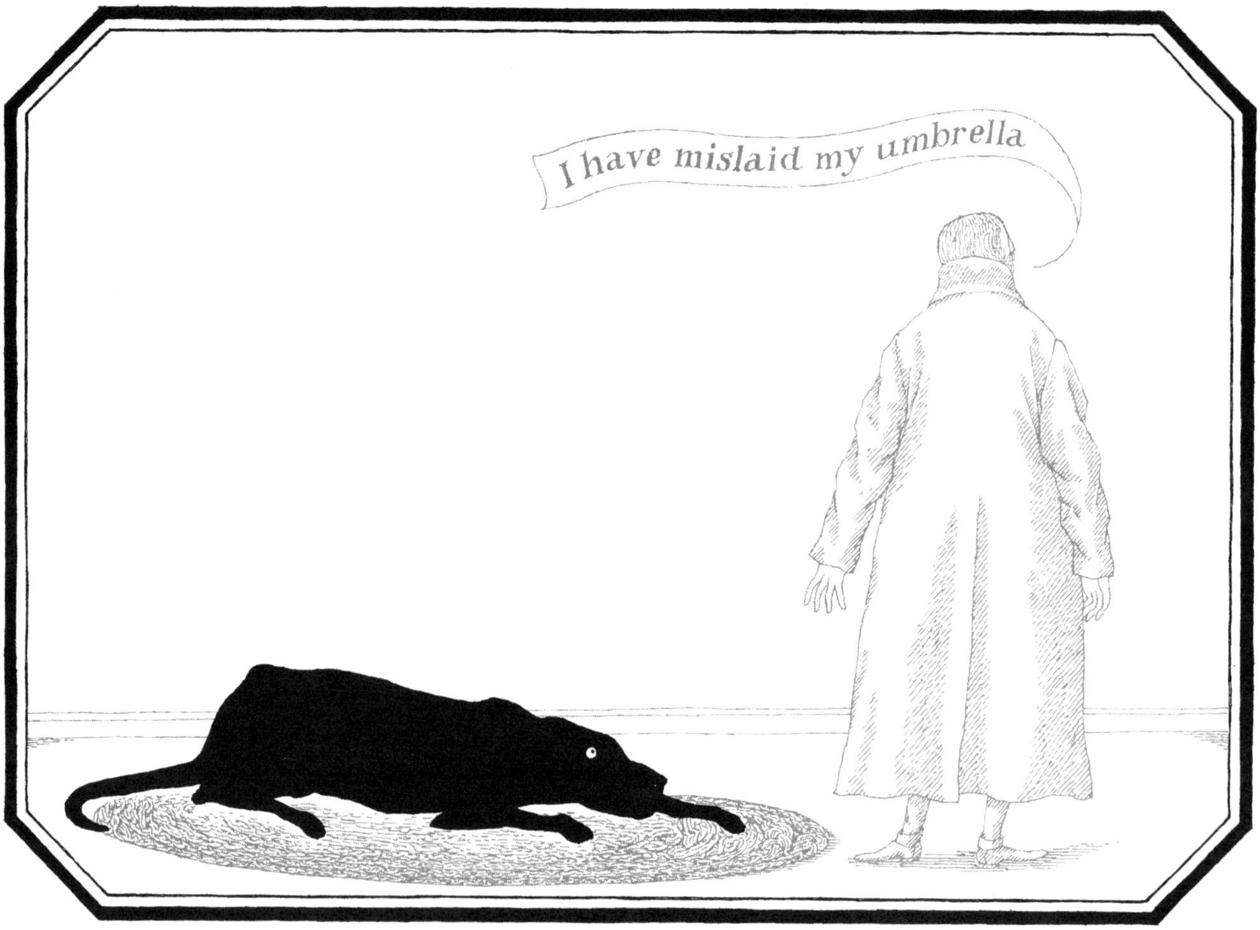
I have mislaid my umbrella

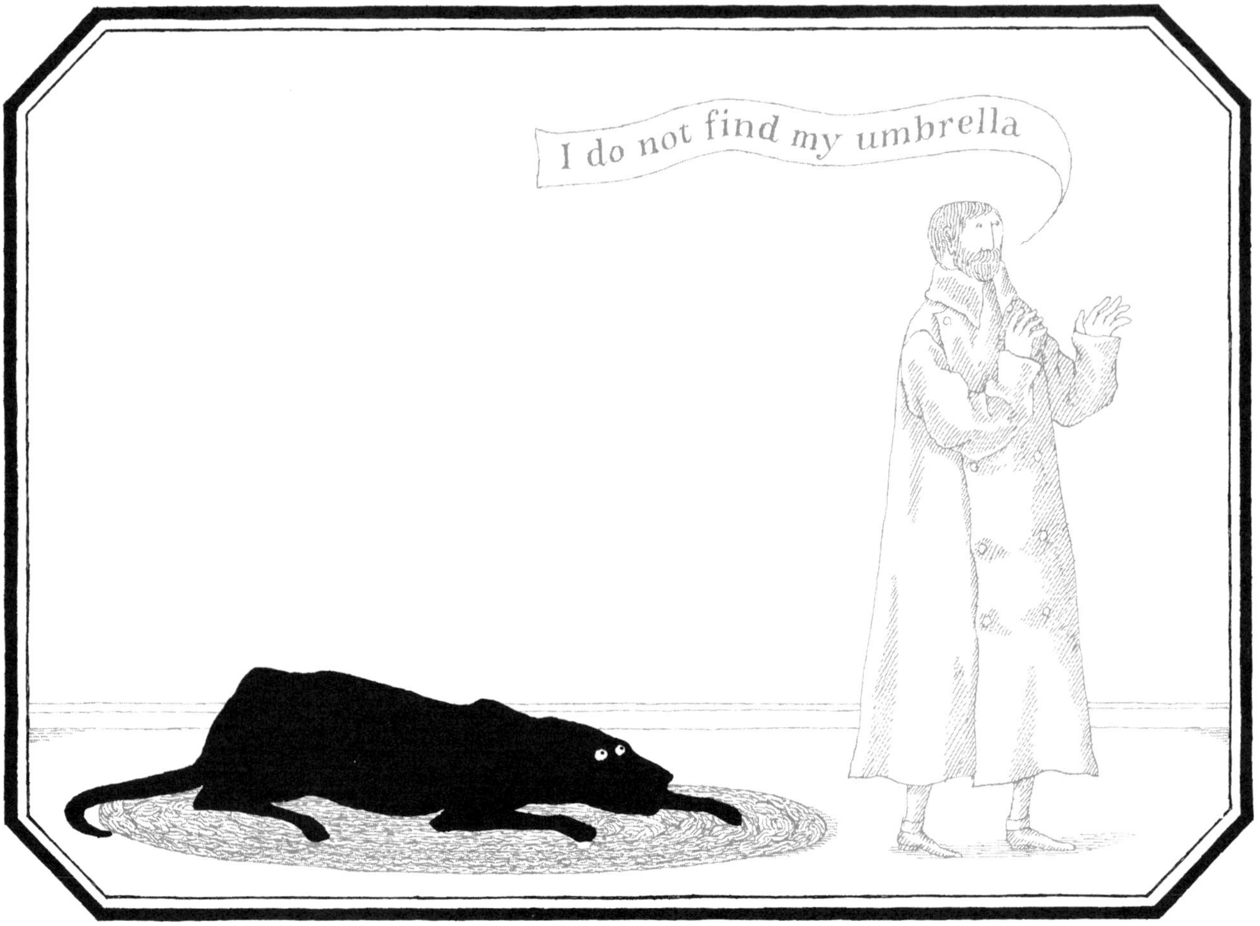
I do not find my umbrella

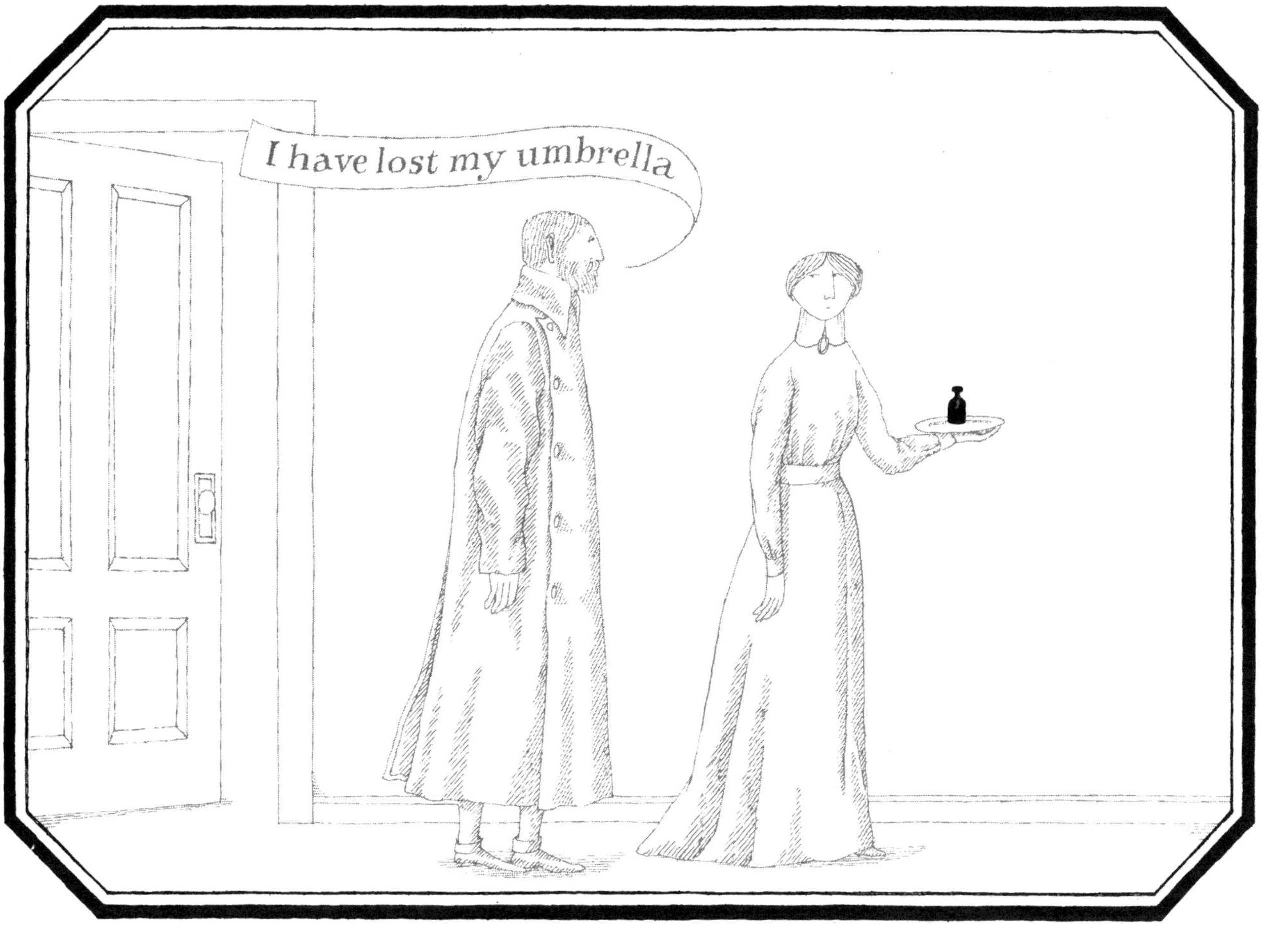
I have lost my umbrella

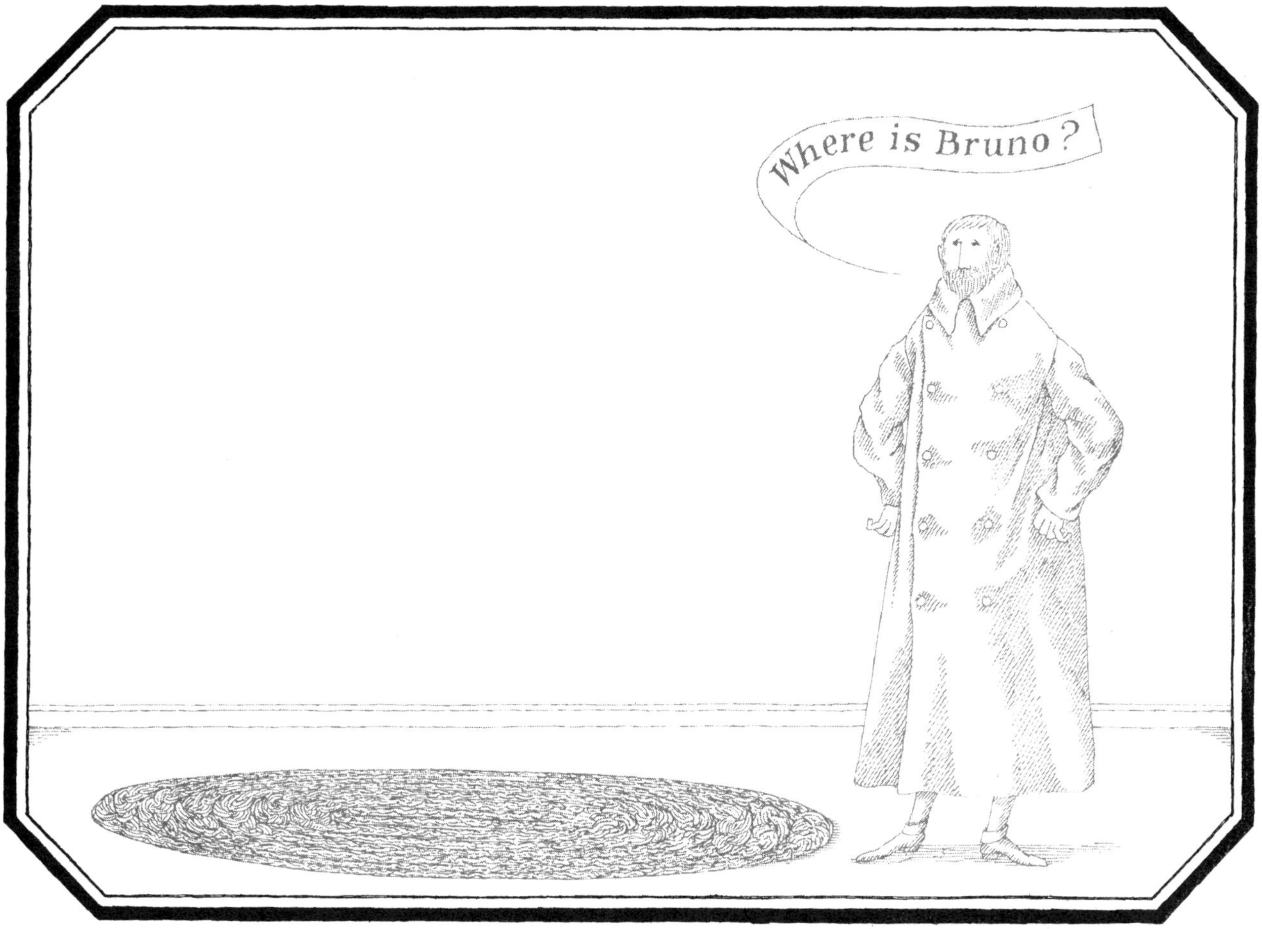
Where is Bruno?

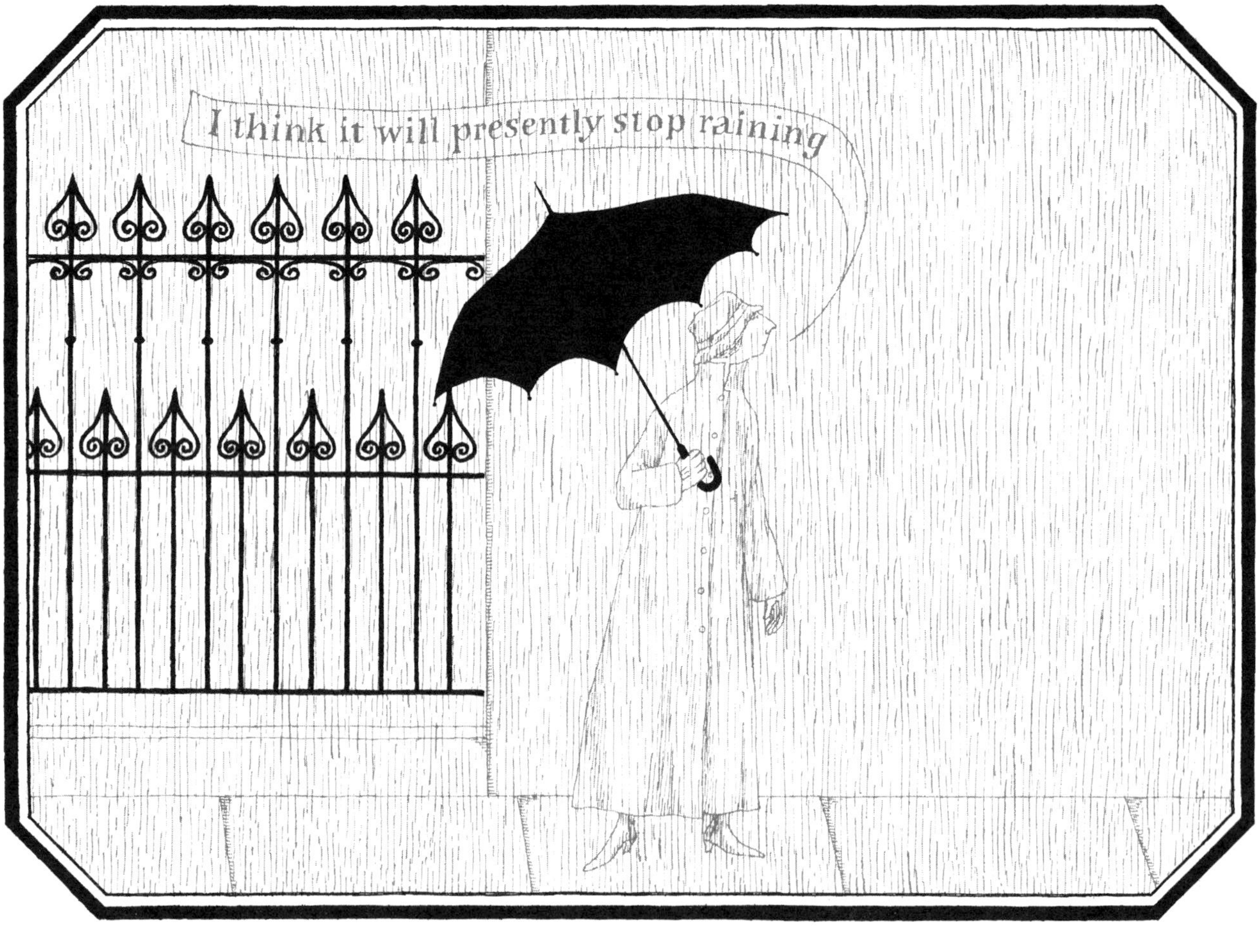
I think it will presently stop raining

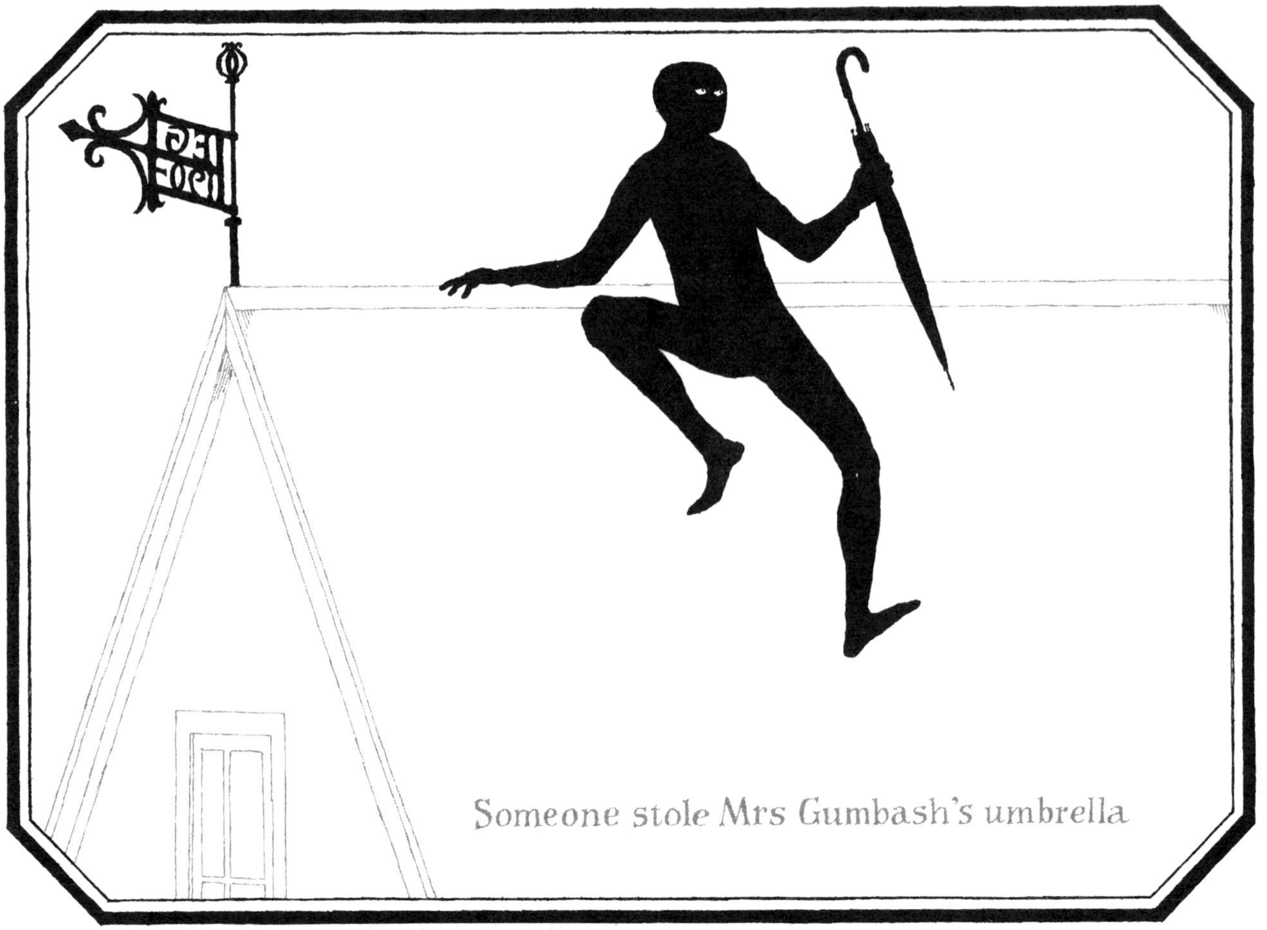
Someone stole Mrs Gumbash's umbrella

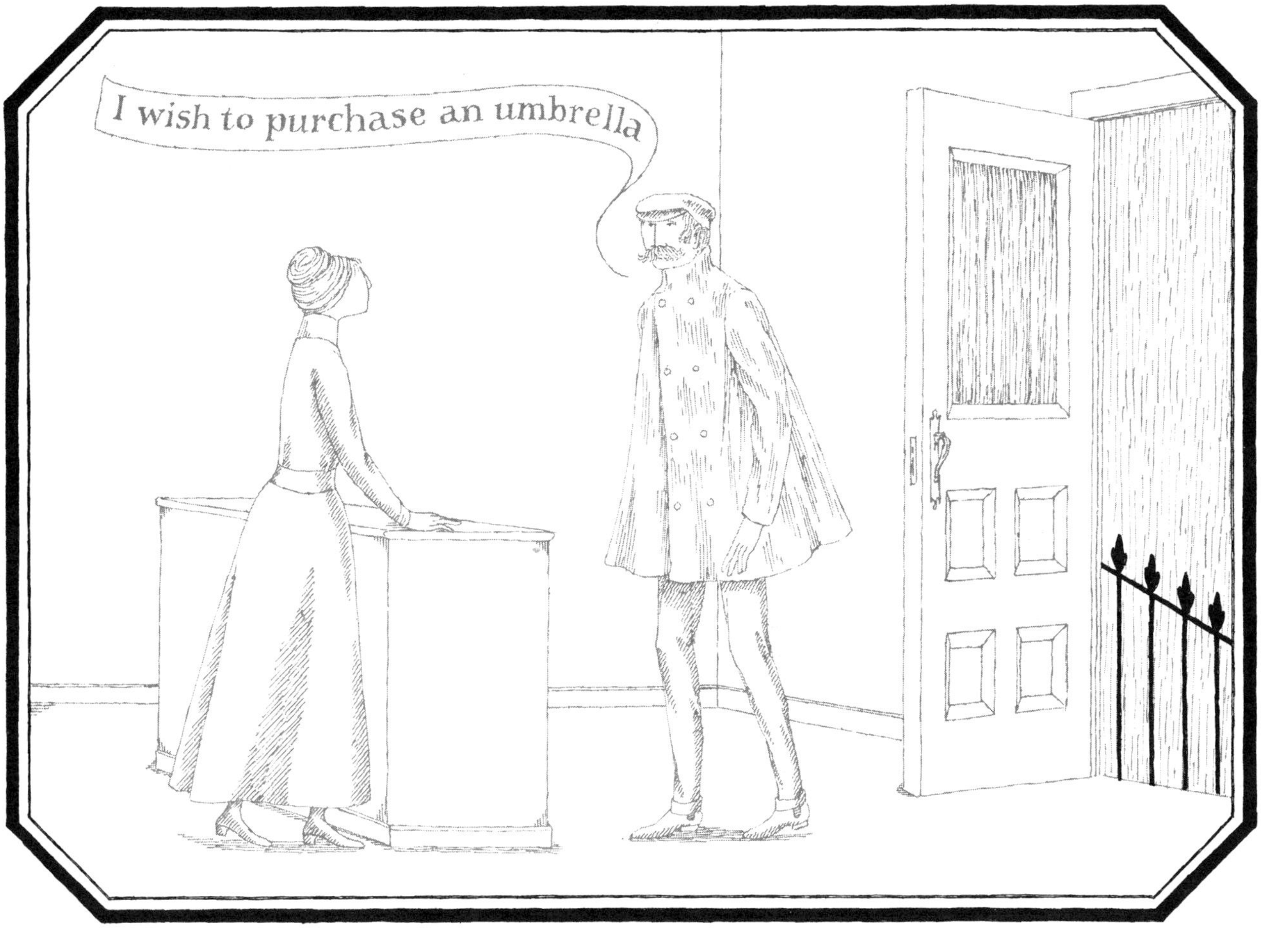
I wish to purchase an umbrella

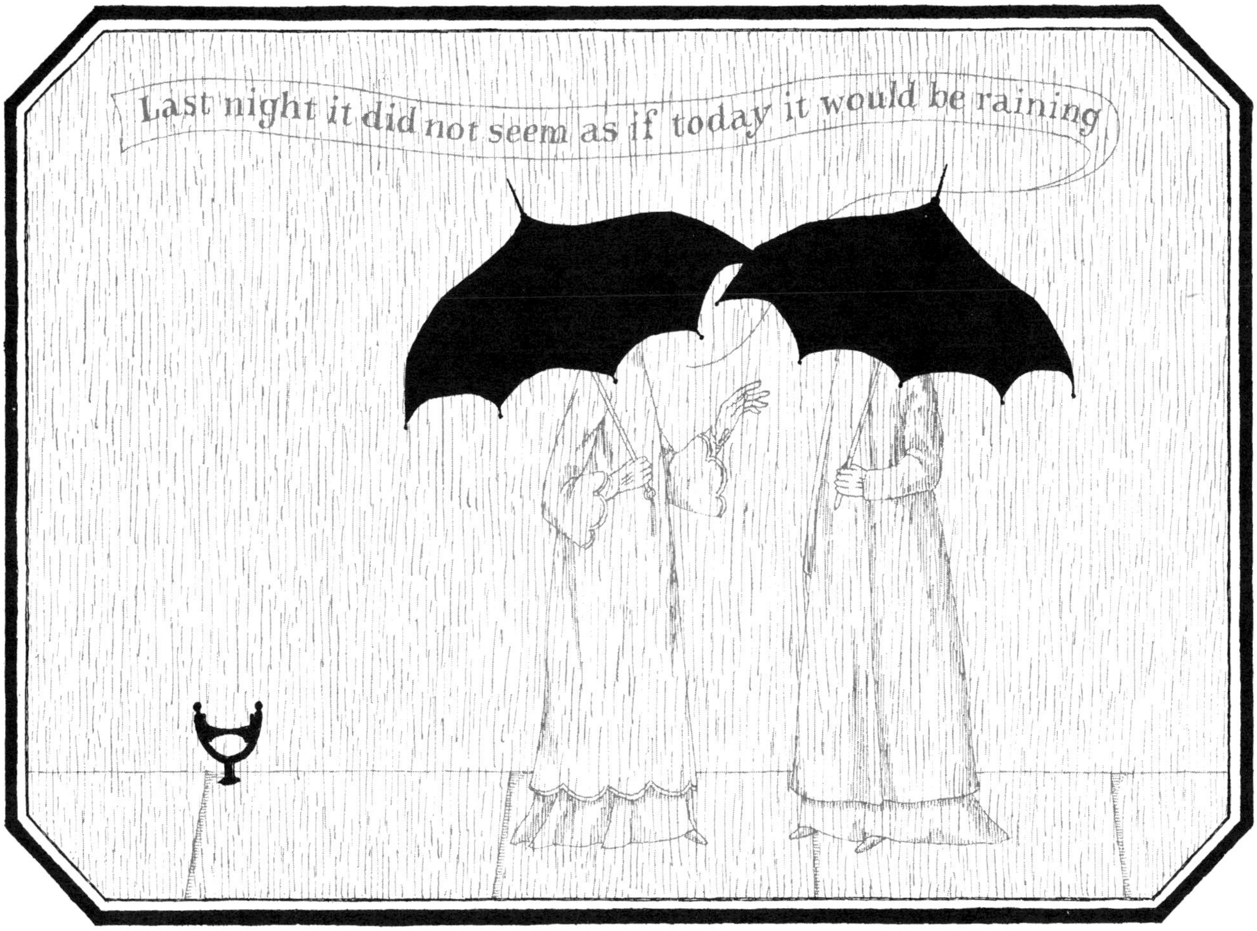
Last night it did not seem as if today it would be raining

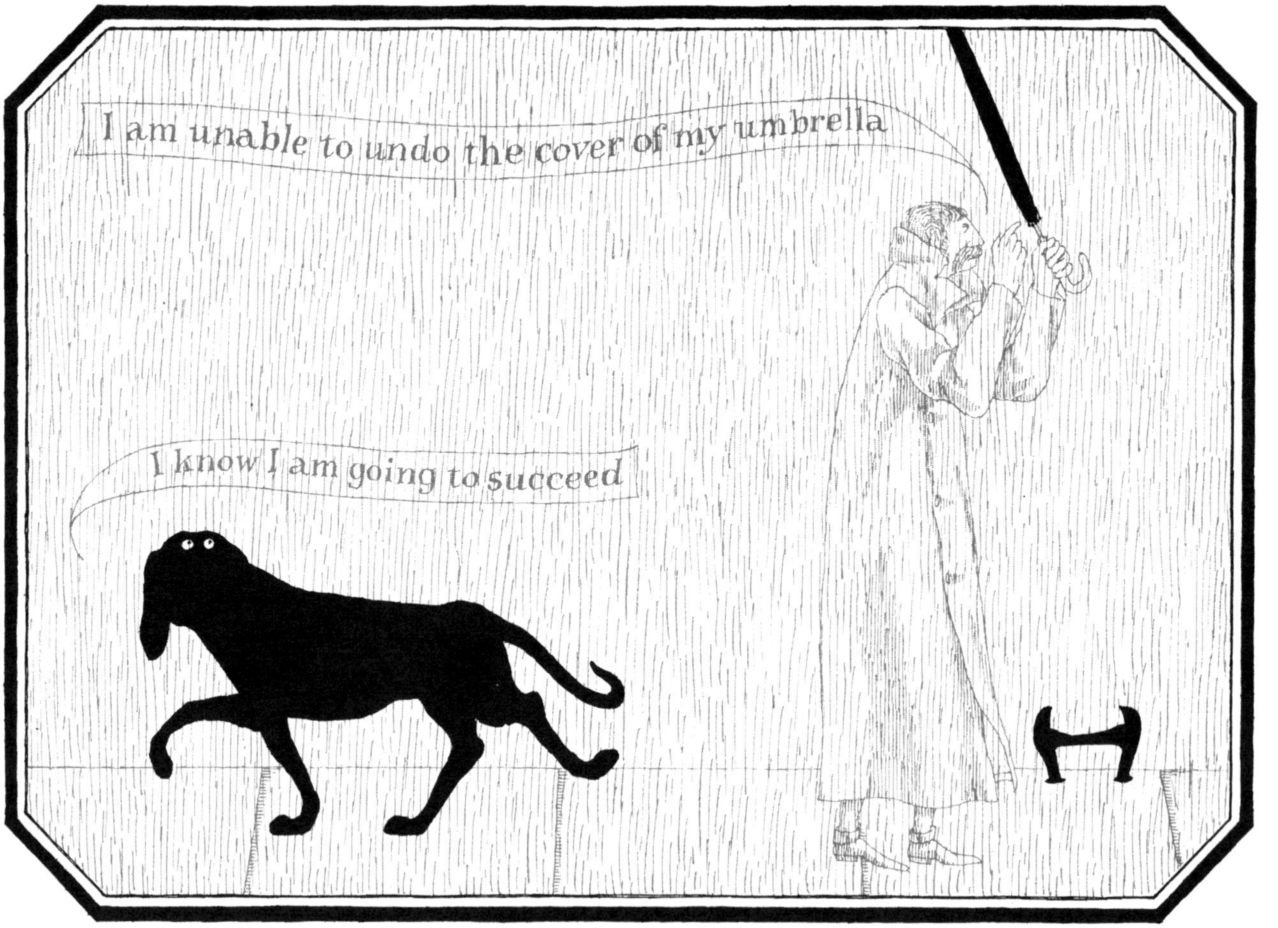
I am unable to undo the cover of my umbrella
I know I am going to succeed

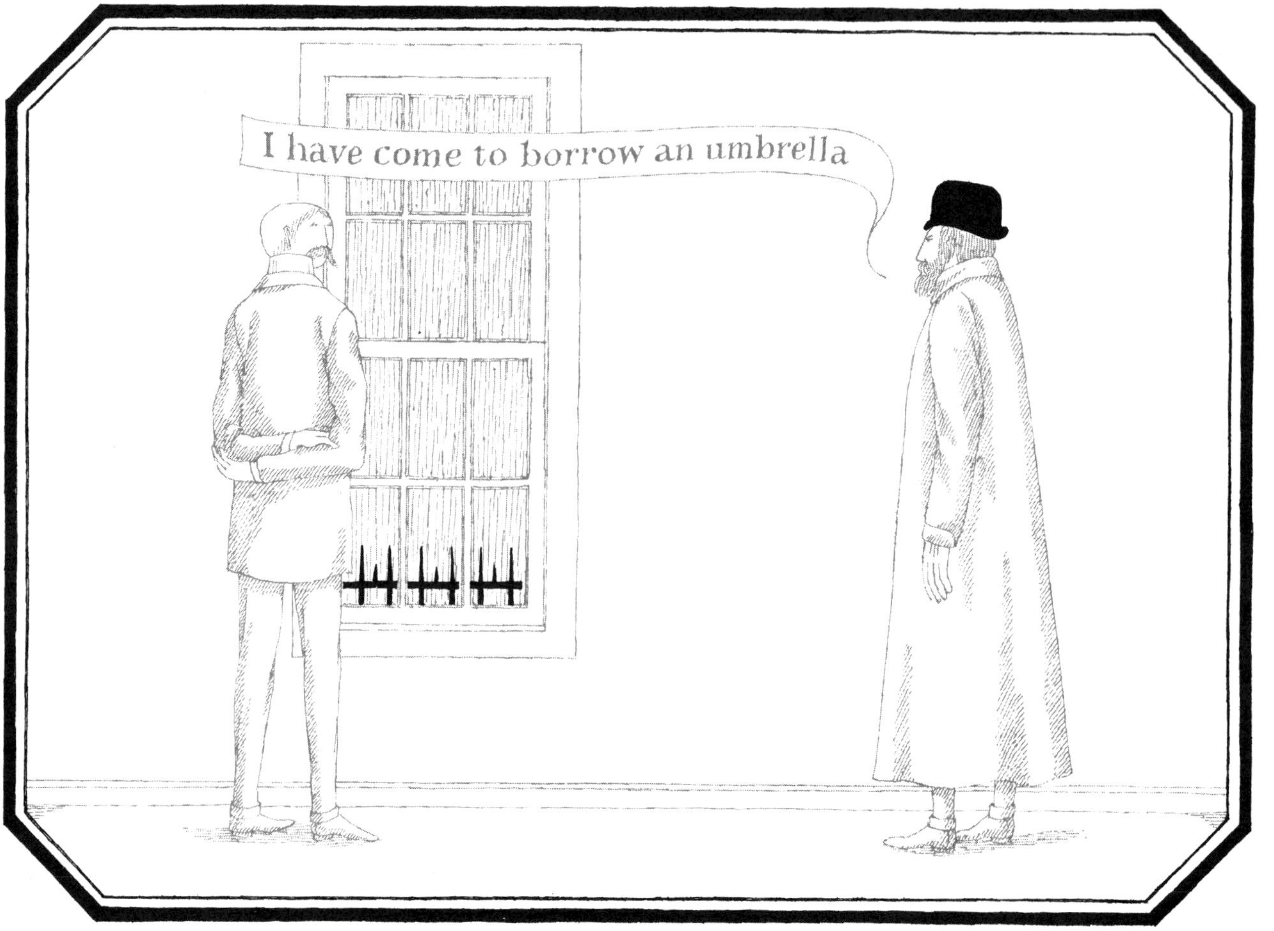
I have come to borrow an umbrella

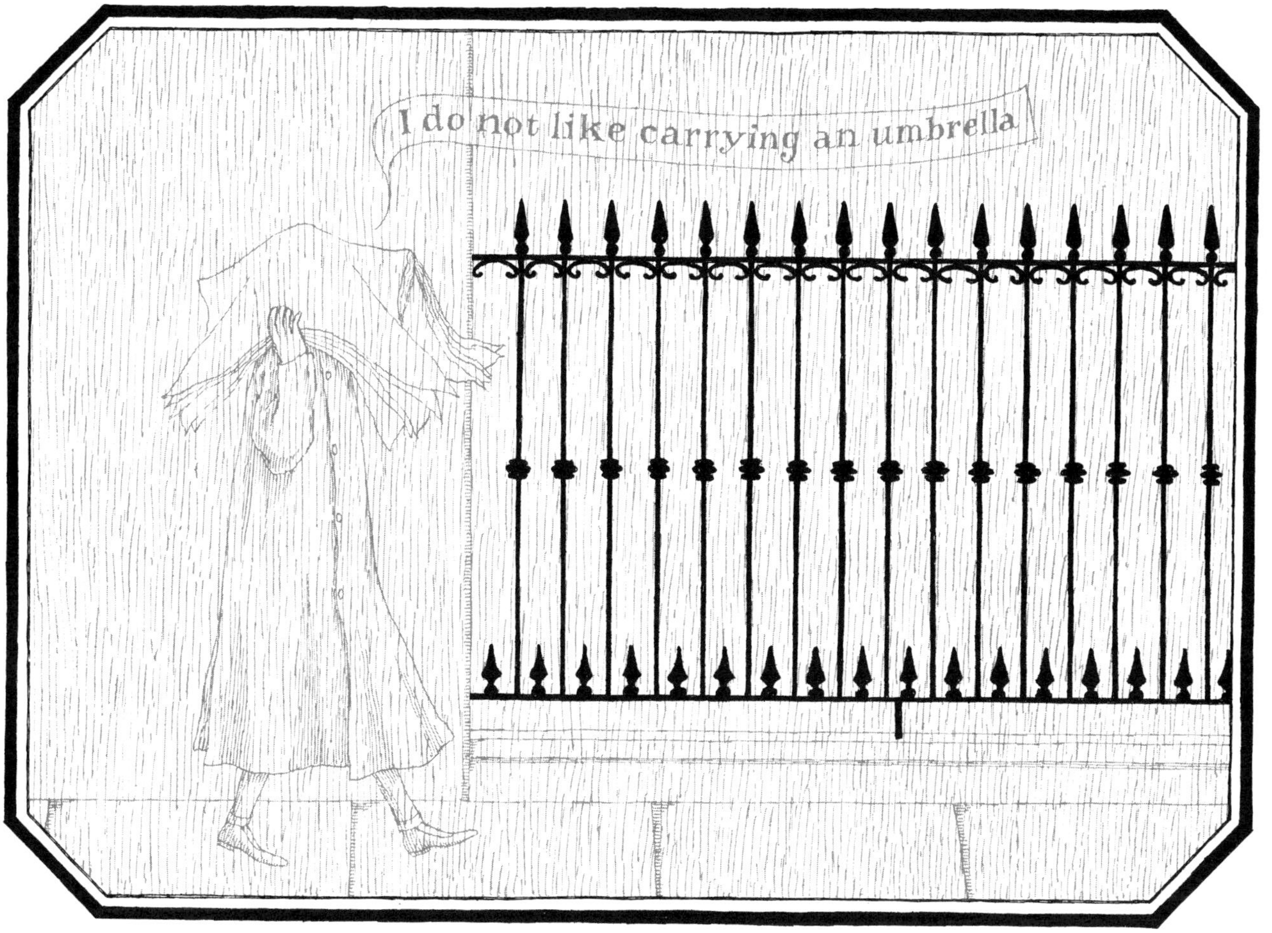
I do not like carrying an umbrella

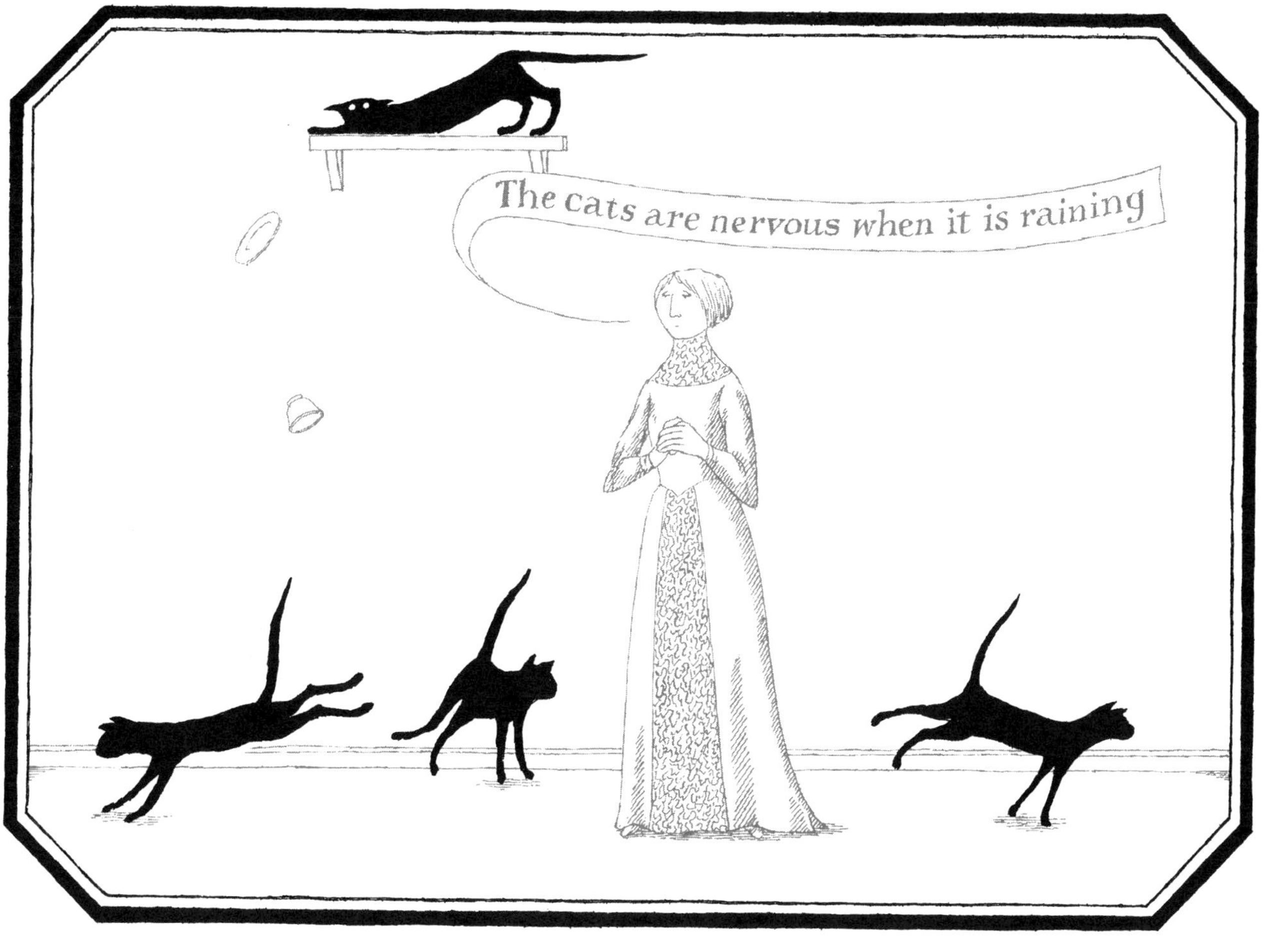
The cats are nervous when it is raining

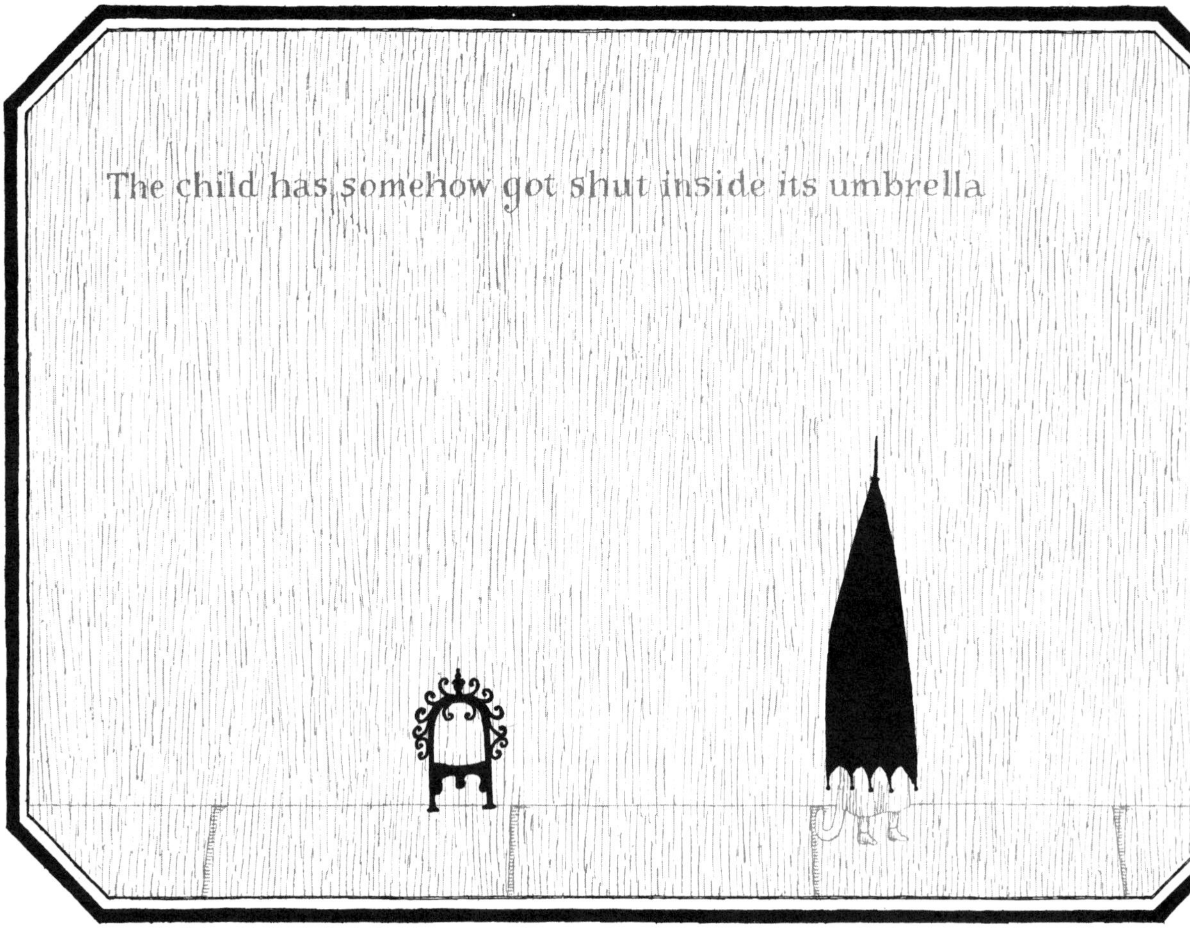
The child has somehow got shut inside its umbrella

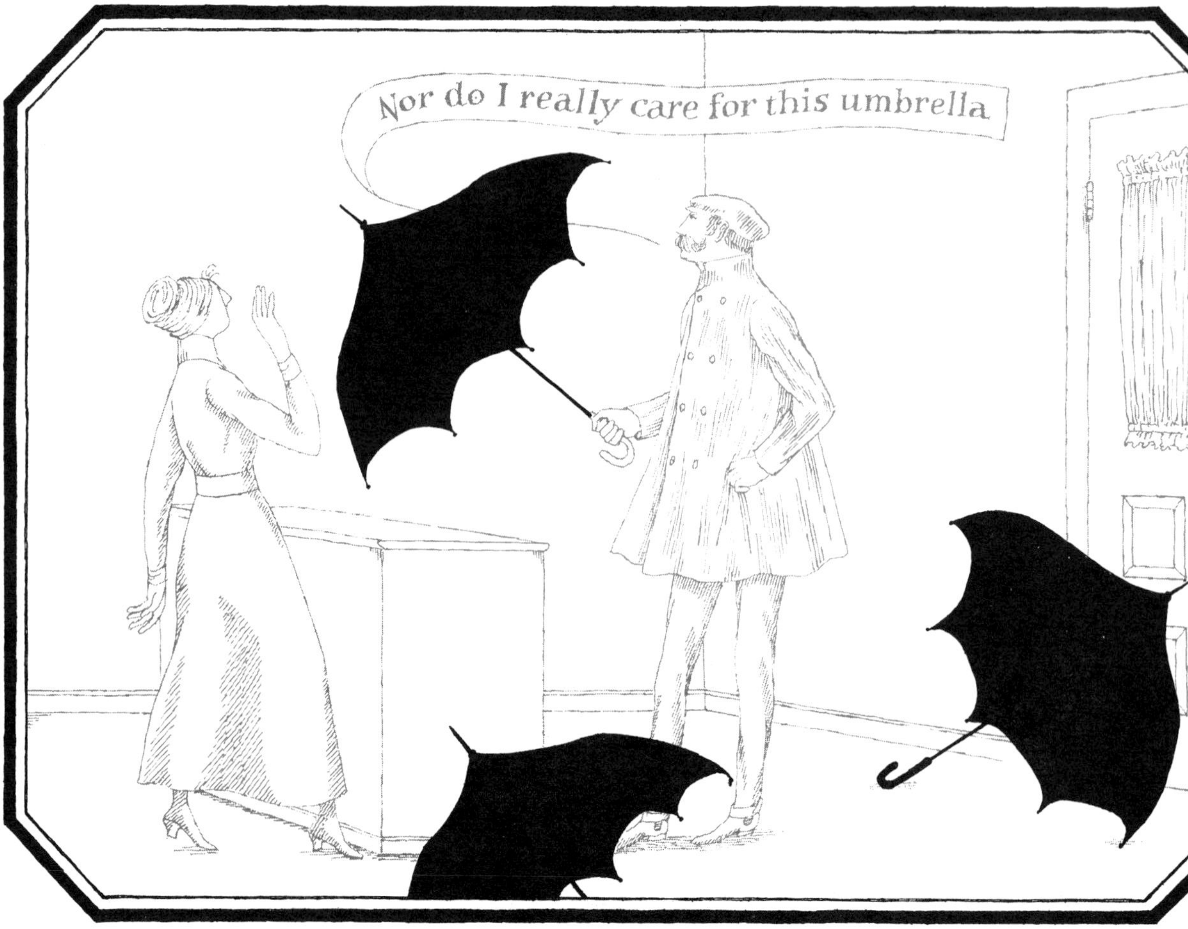
Nor do I really care for this umbrella

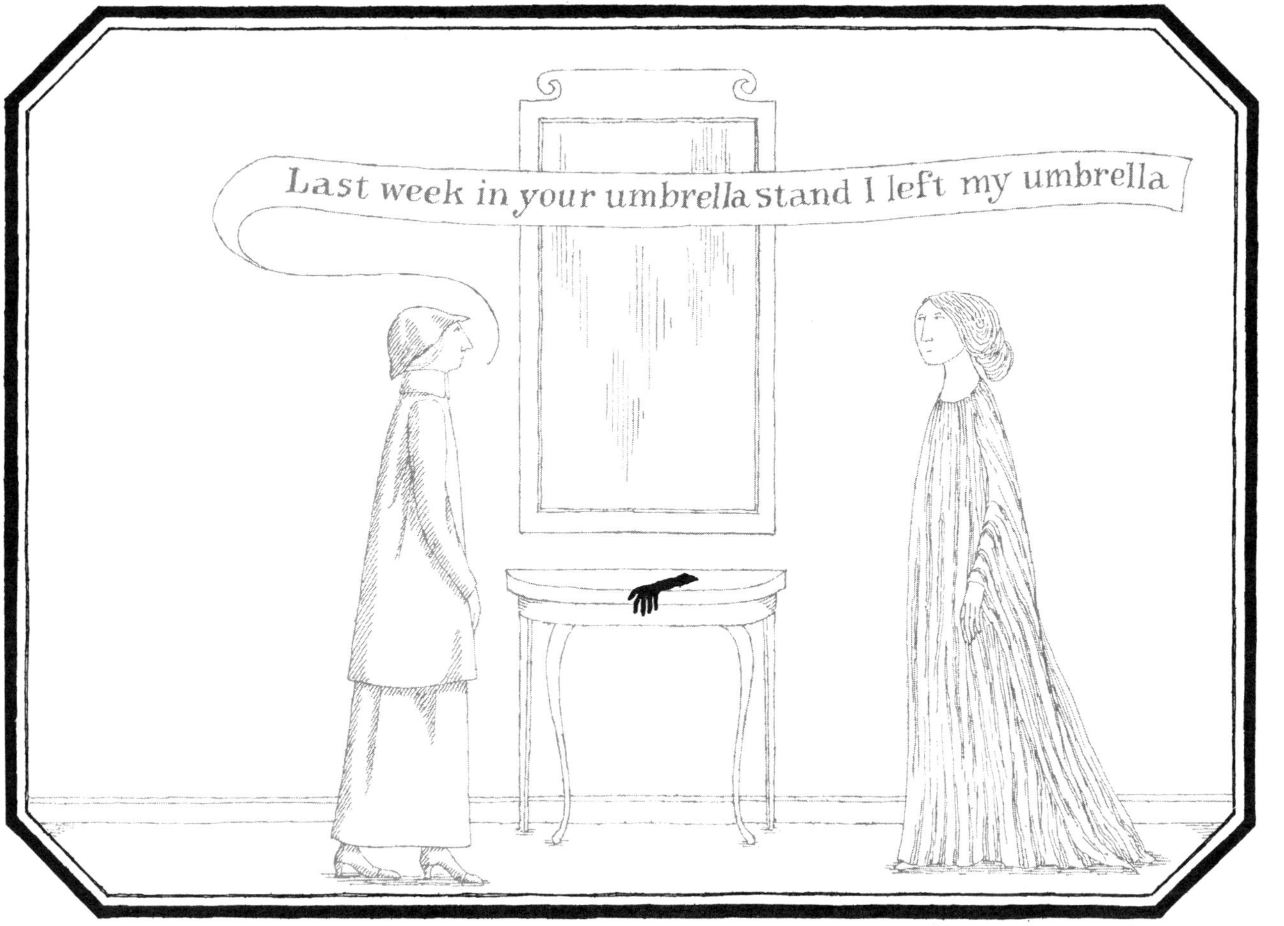
Last week in your umbrella stand I left my umbrella

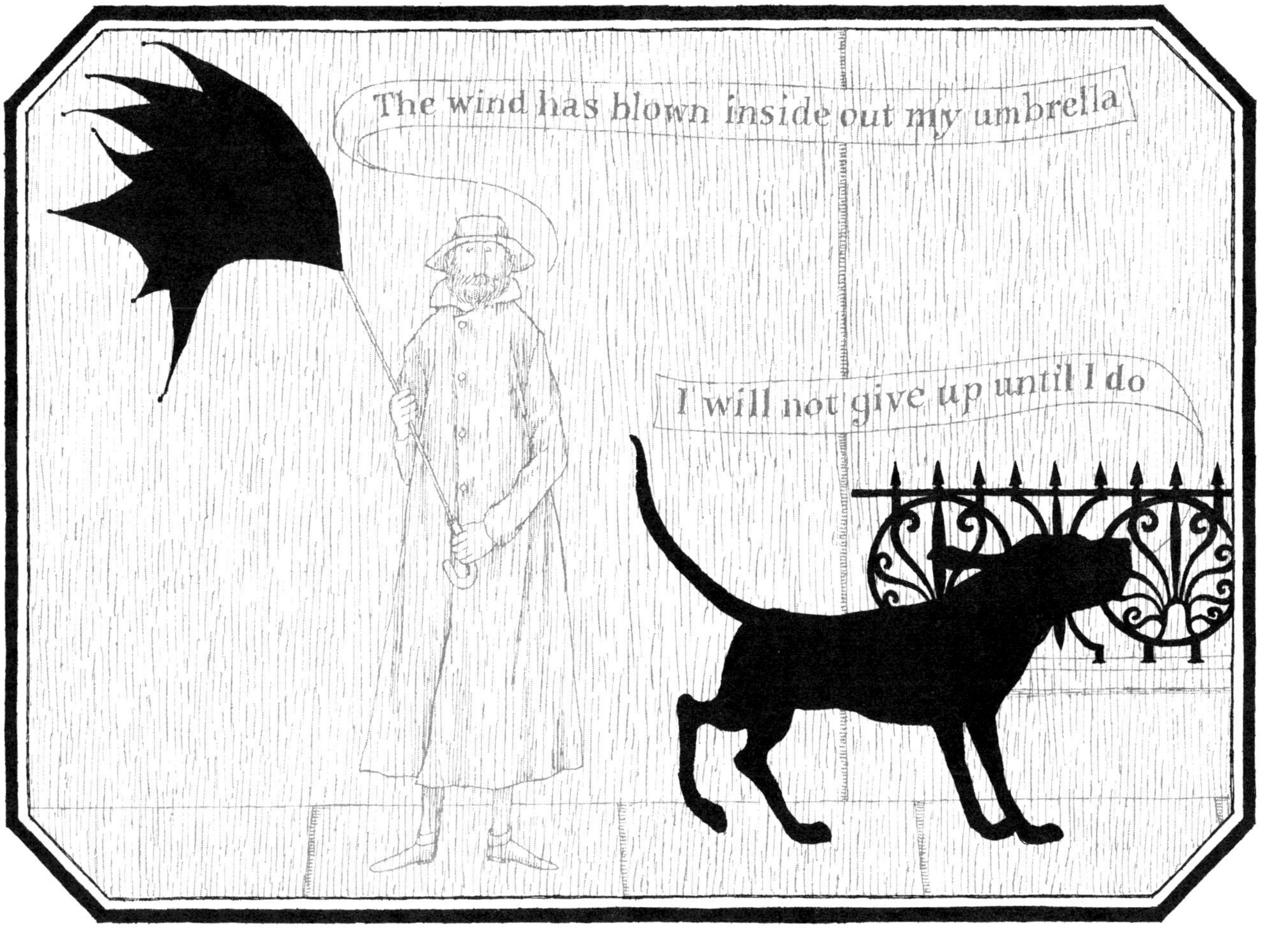
The wind has blown inside out my umbrella
I will not give up until I do

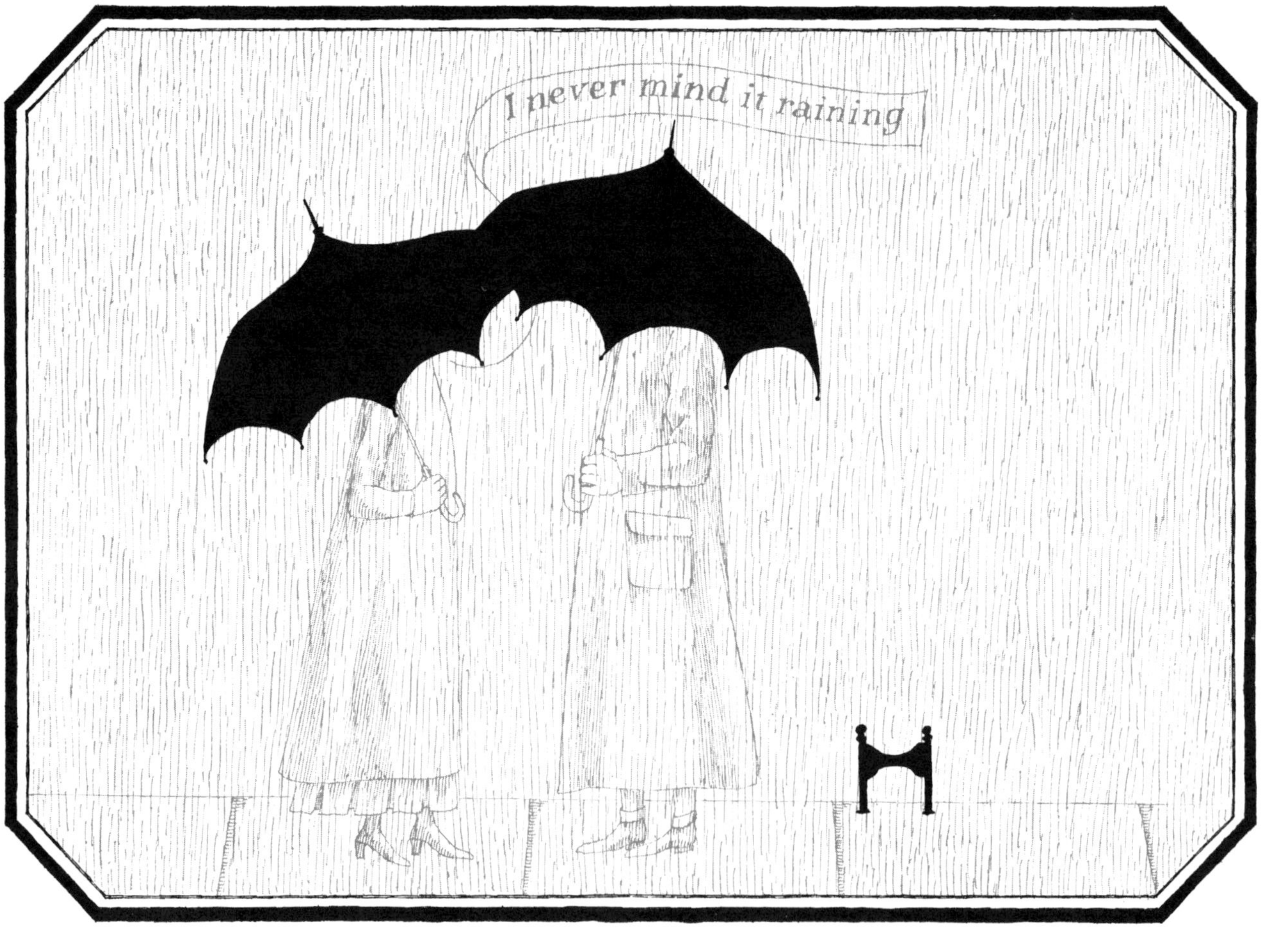
I never mind it raining

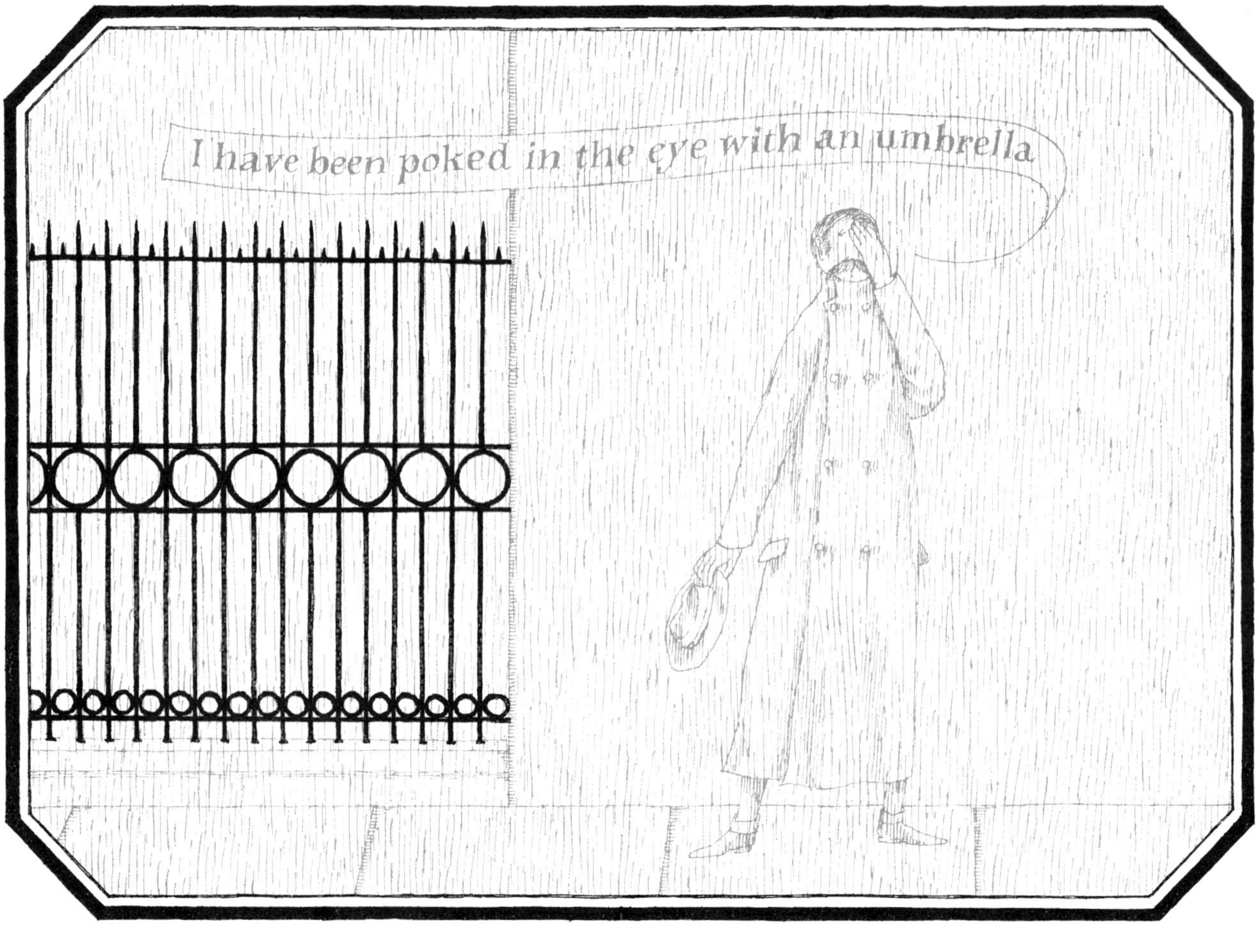
I have been poked in the eye with an umbrella

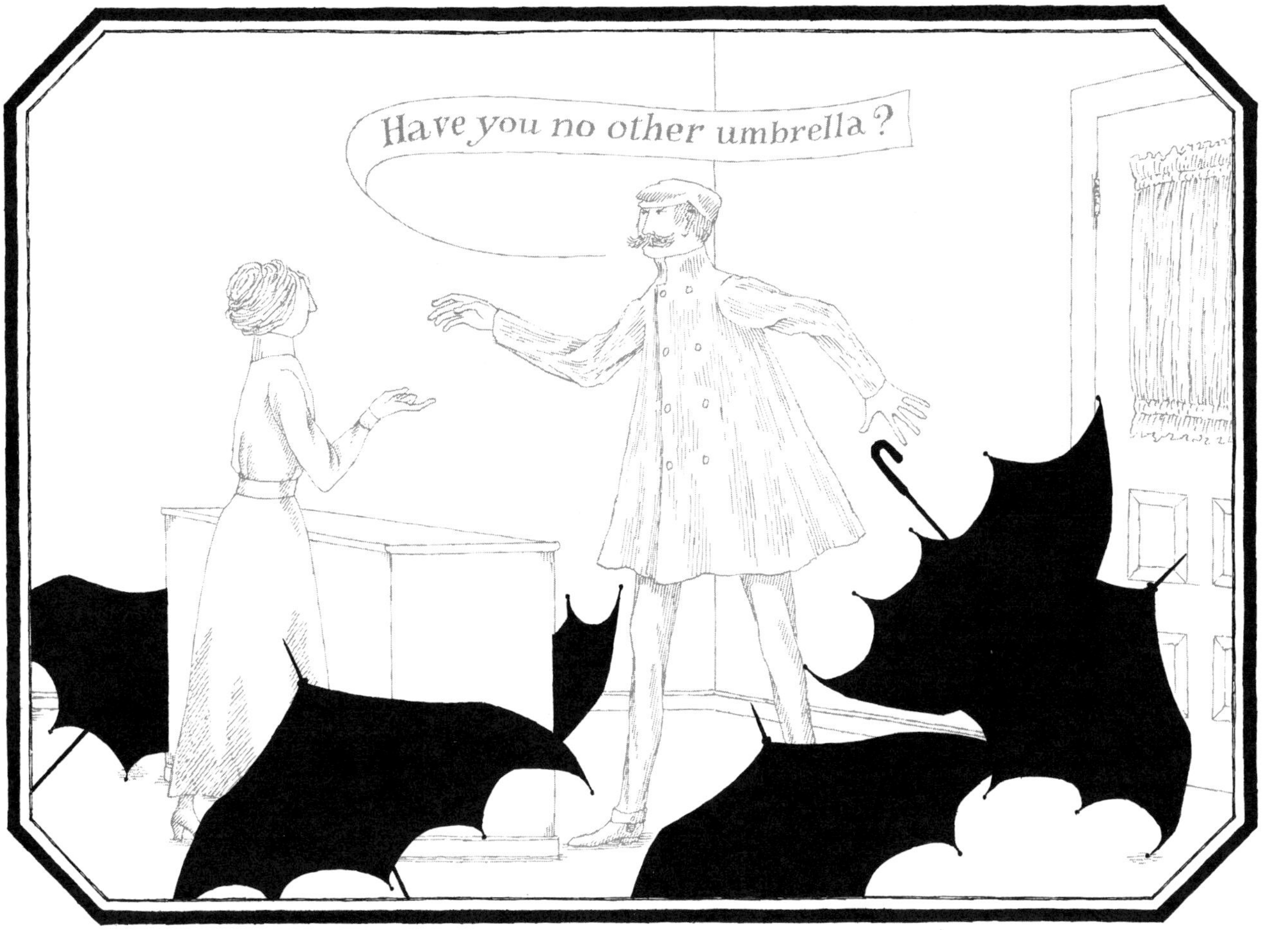
Have you no other umbrella?

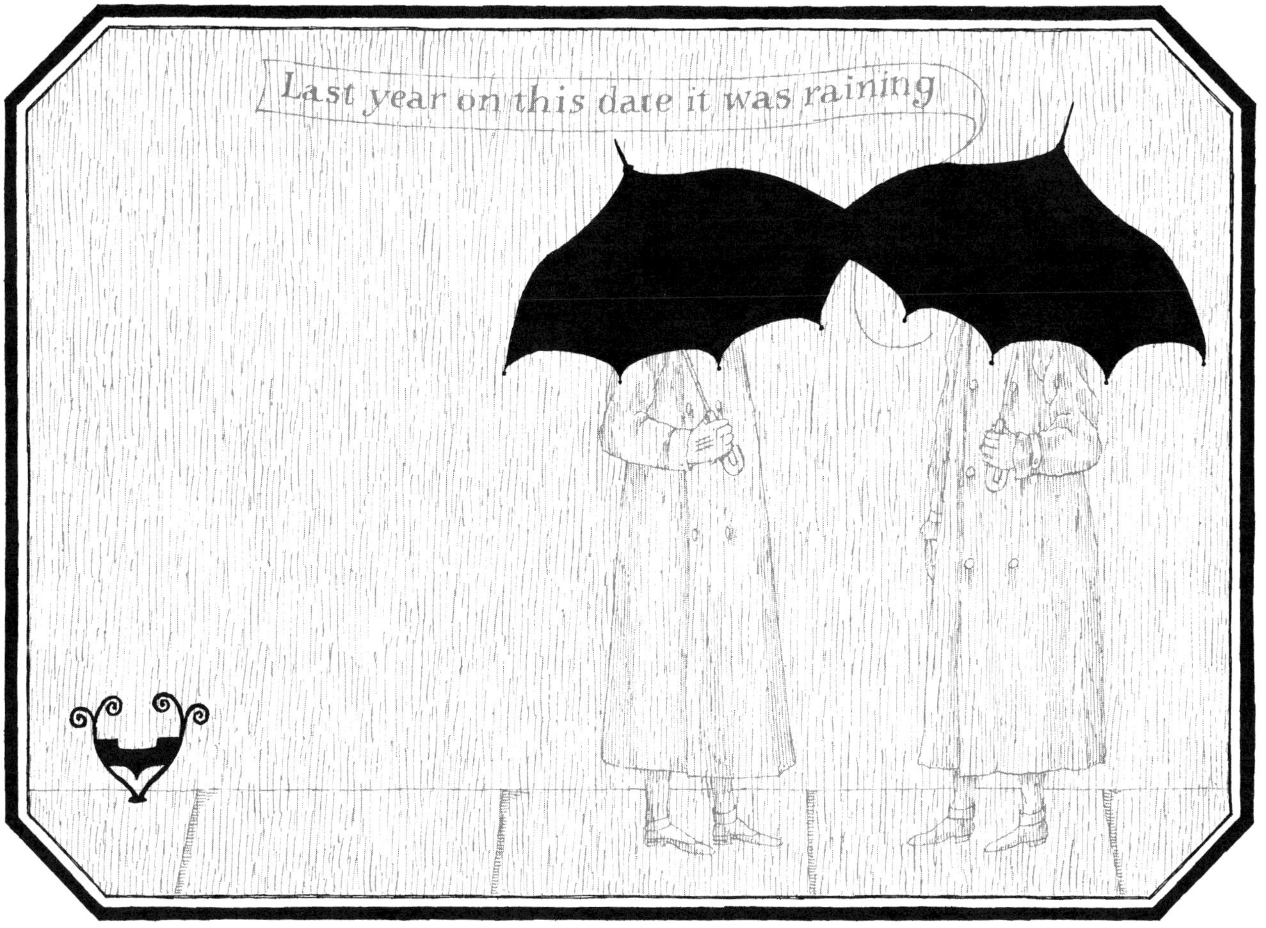
Last year on this date it was raining

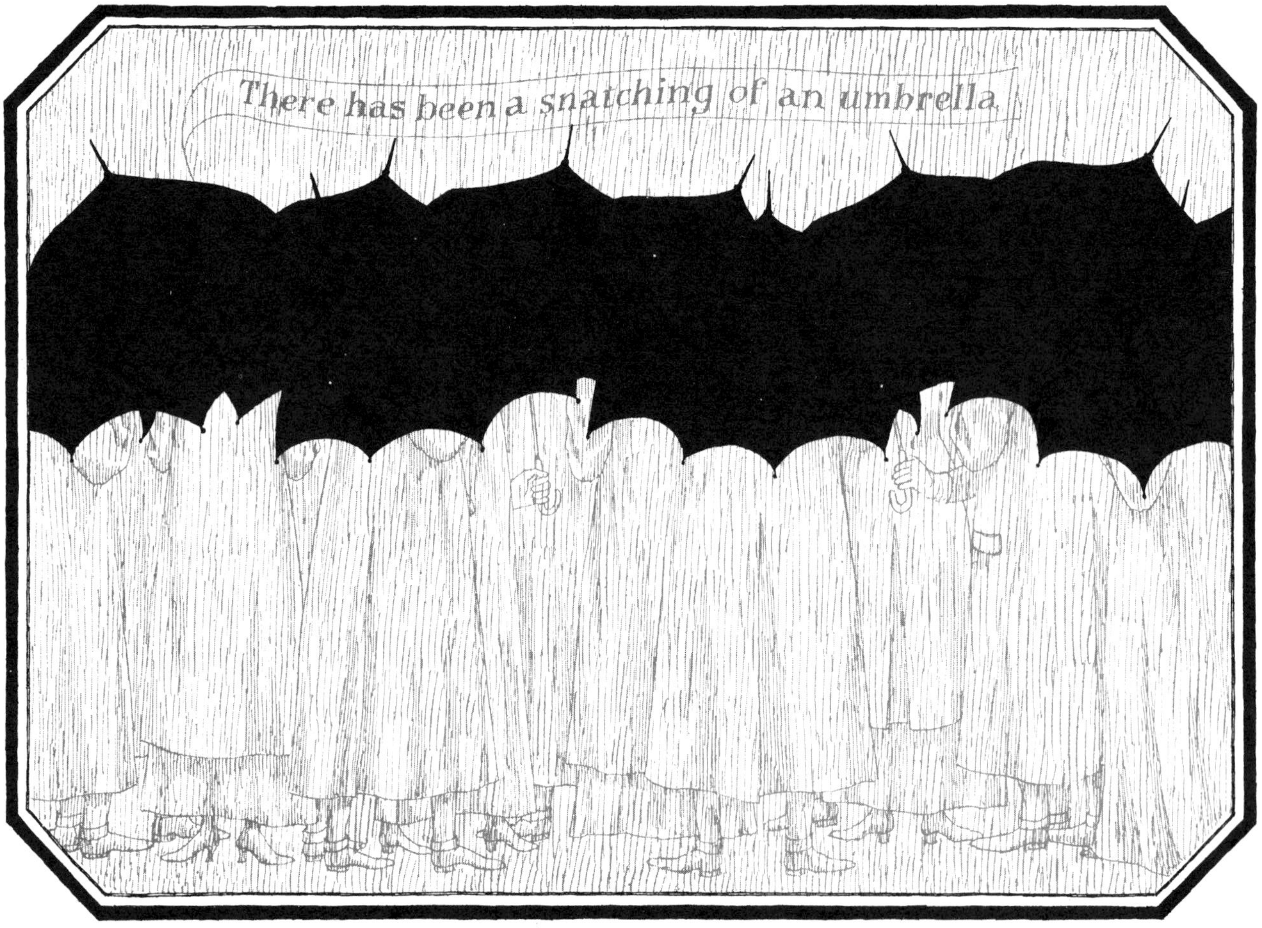
There has been a snatching of an umbrella

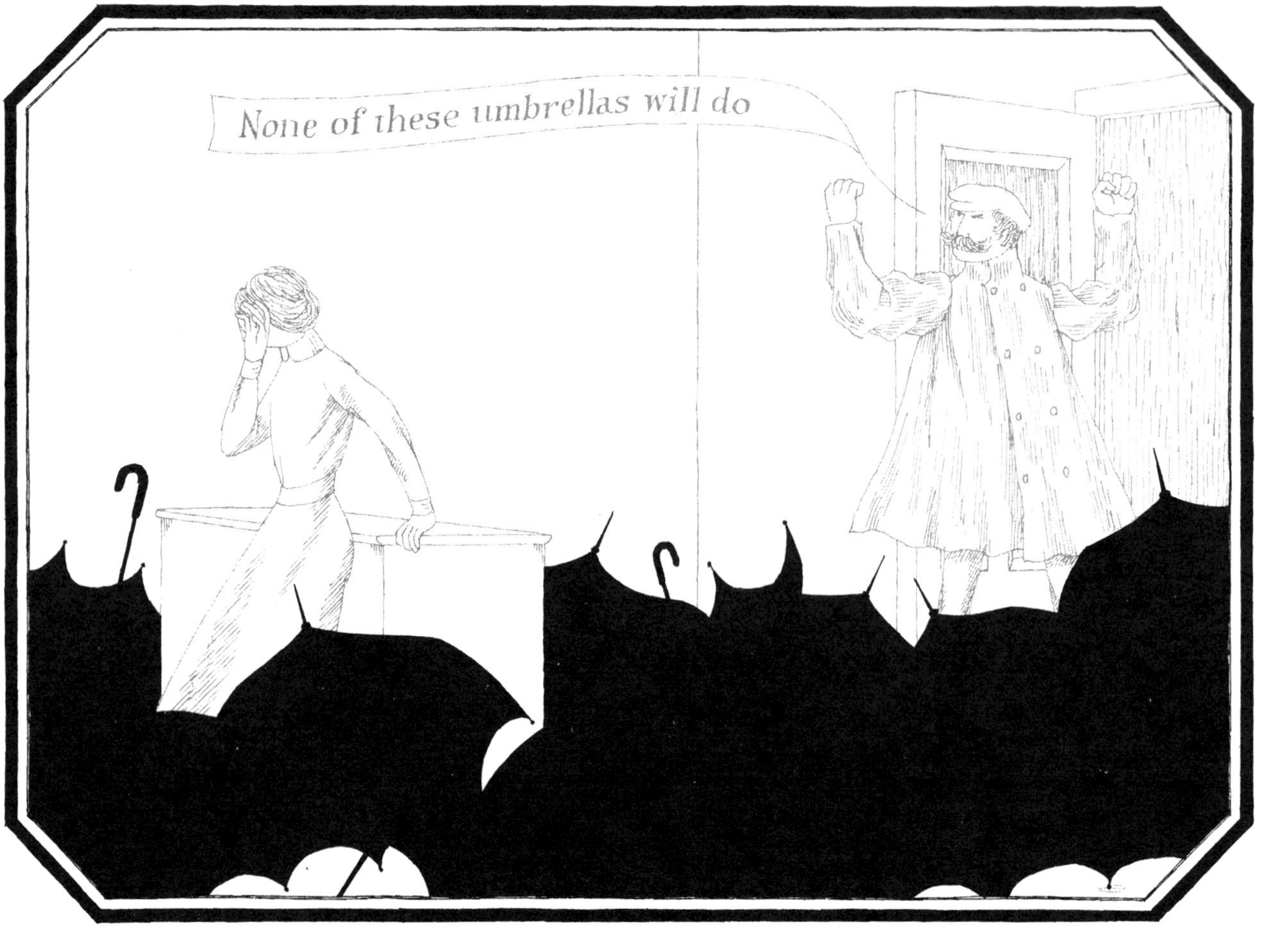
None of these umbrellas will do

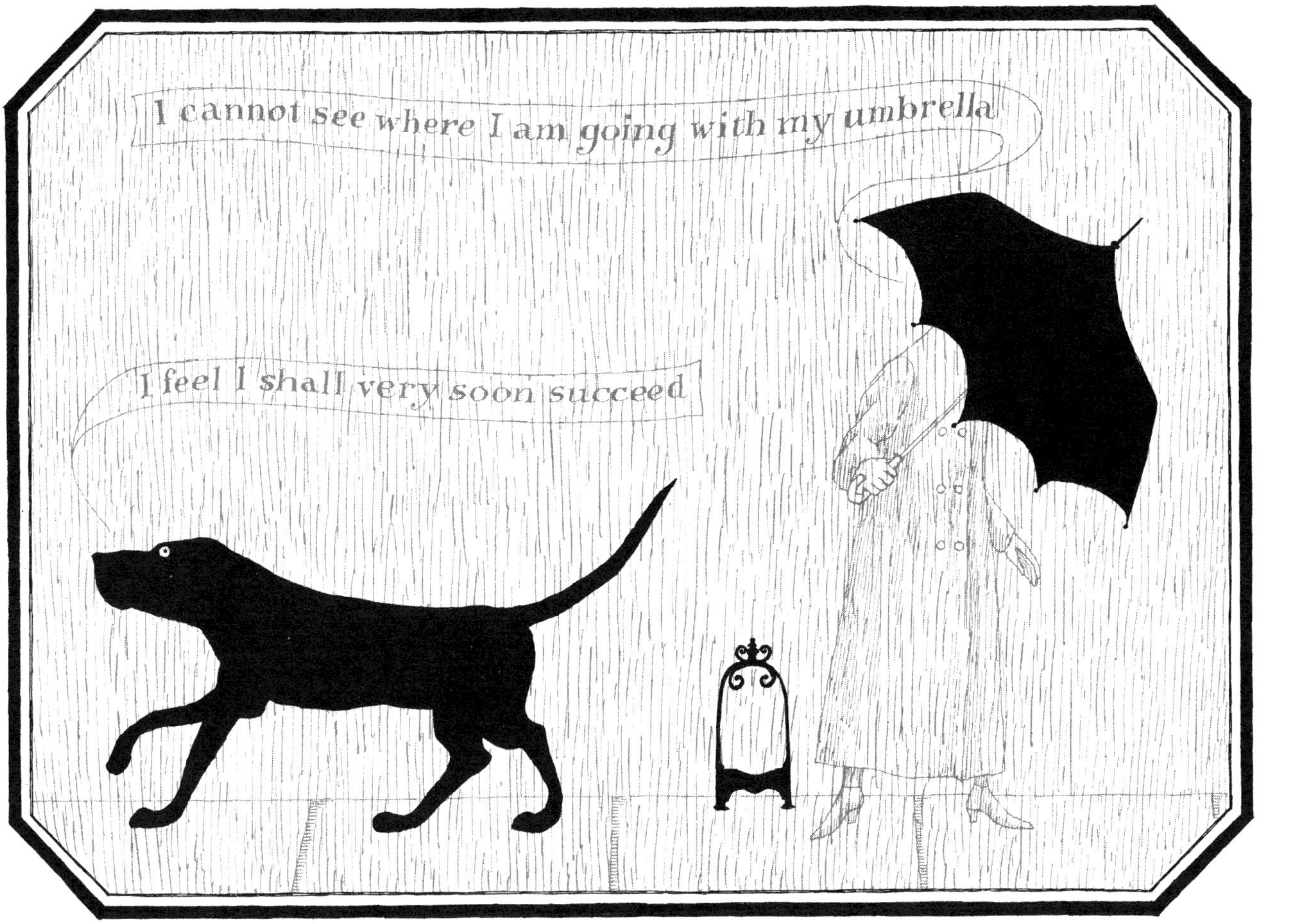
I cannot see where I am going with my umbrella
I feel I shall very soon succeed

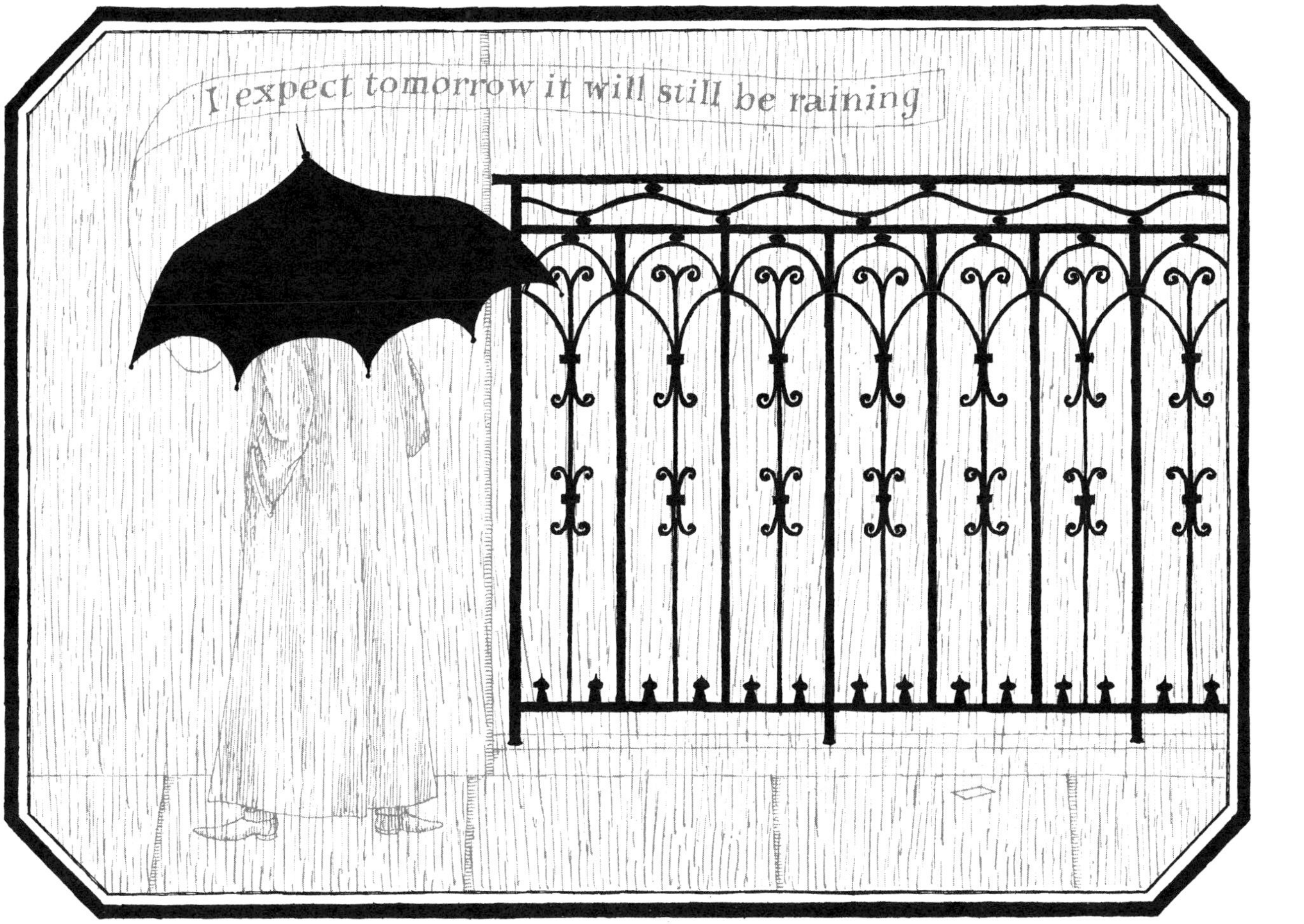
I expect tomorrow it will still be raining

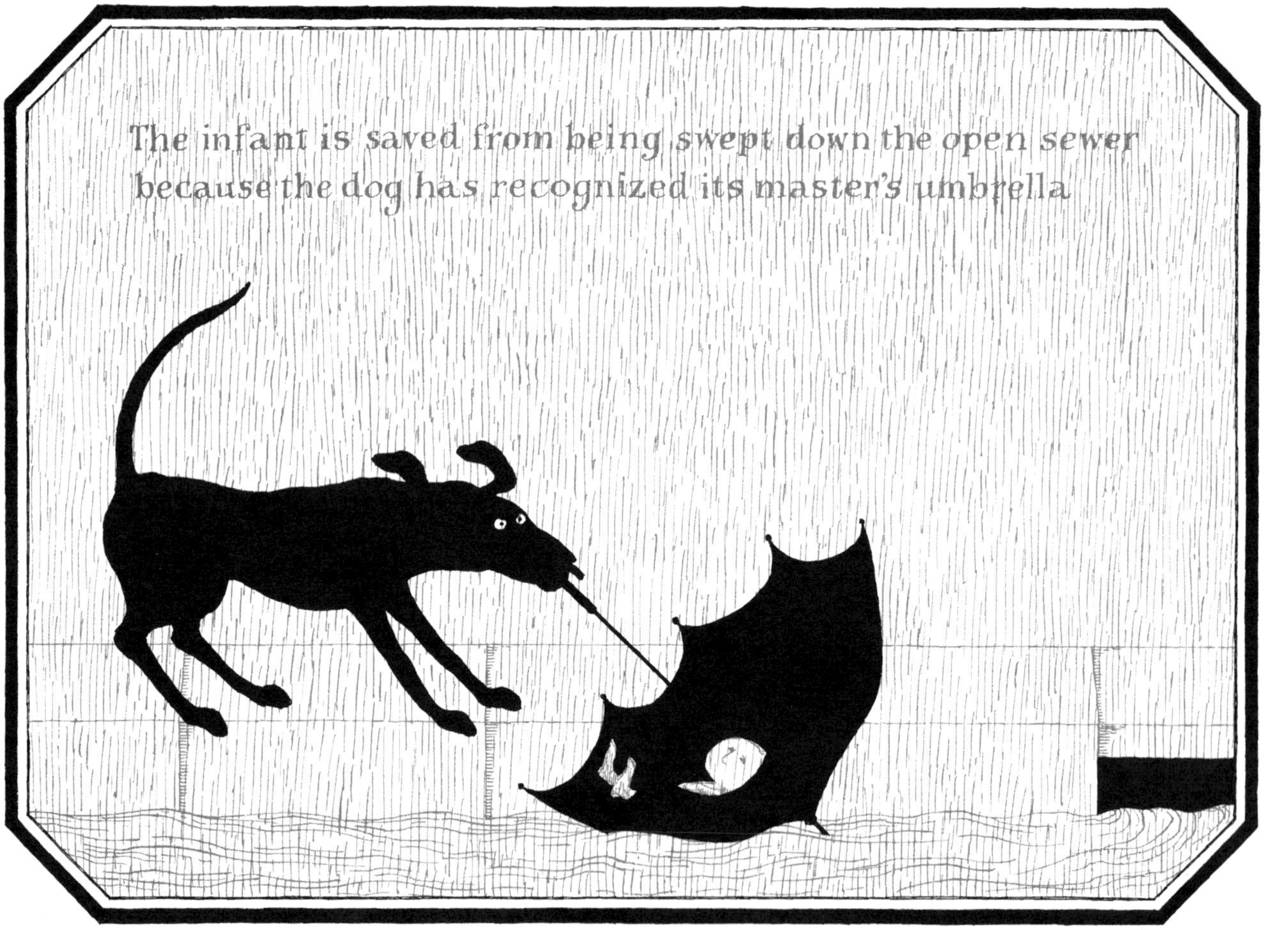
The infant is saved from being swept down the open sewer because the dog has recognized its master's umbrella

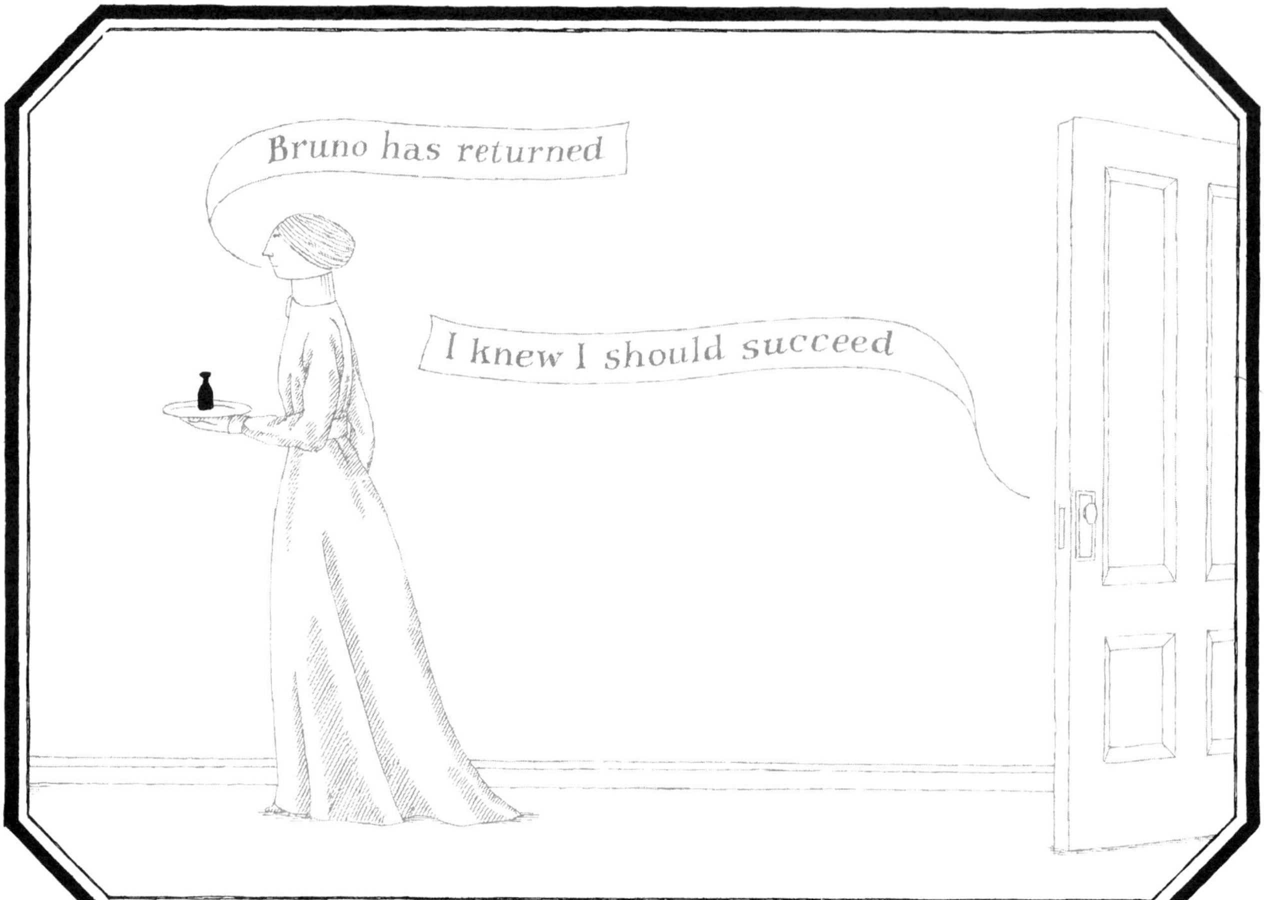
Bruno has returned
I knew I should succeed

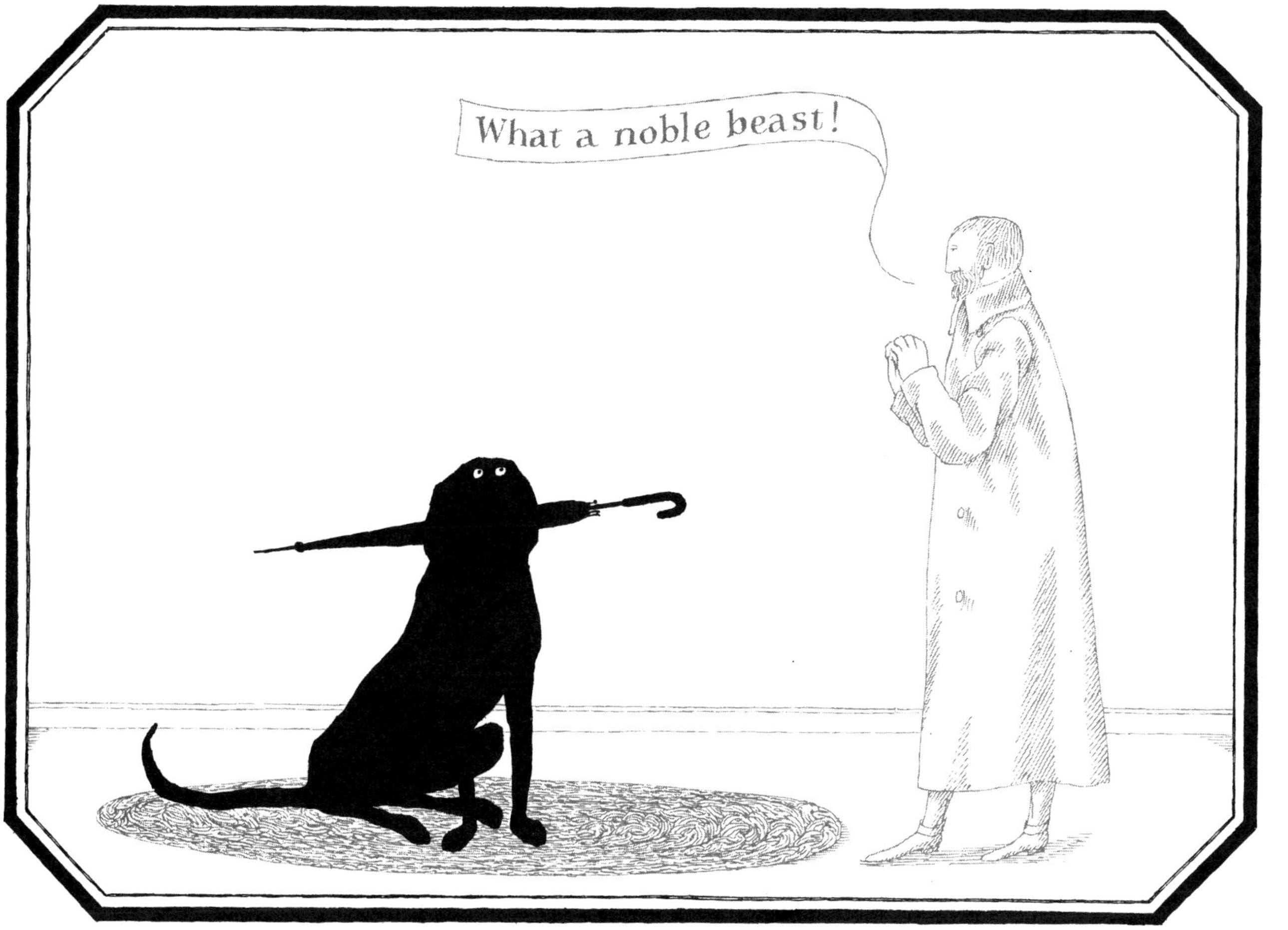
What a noble beast!

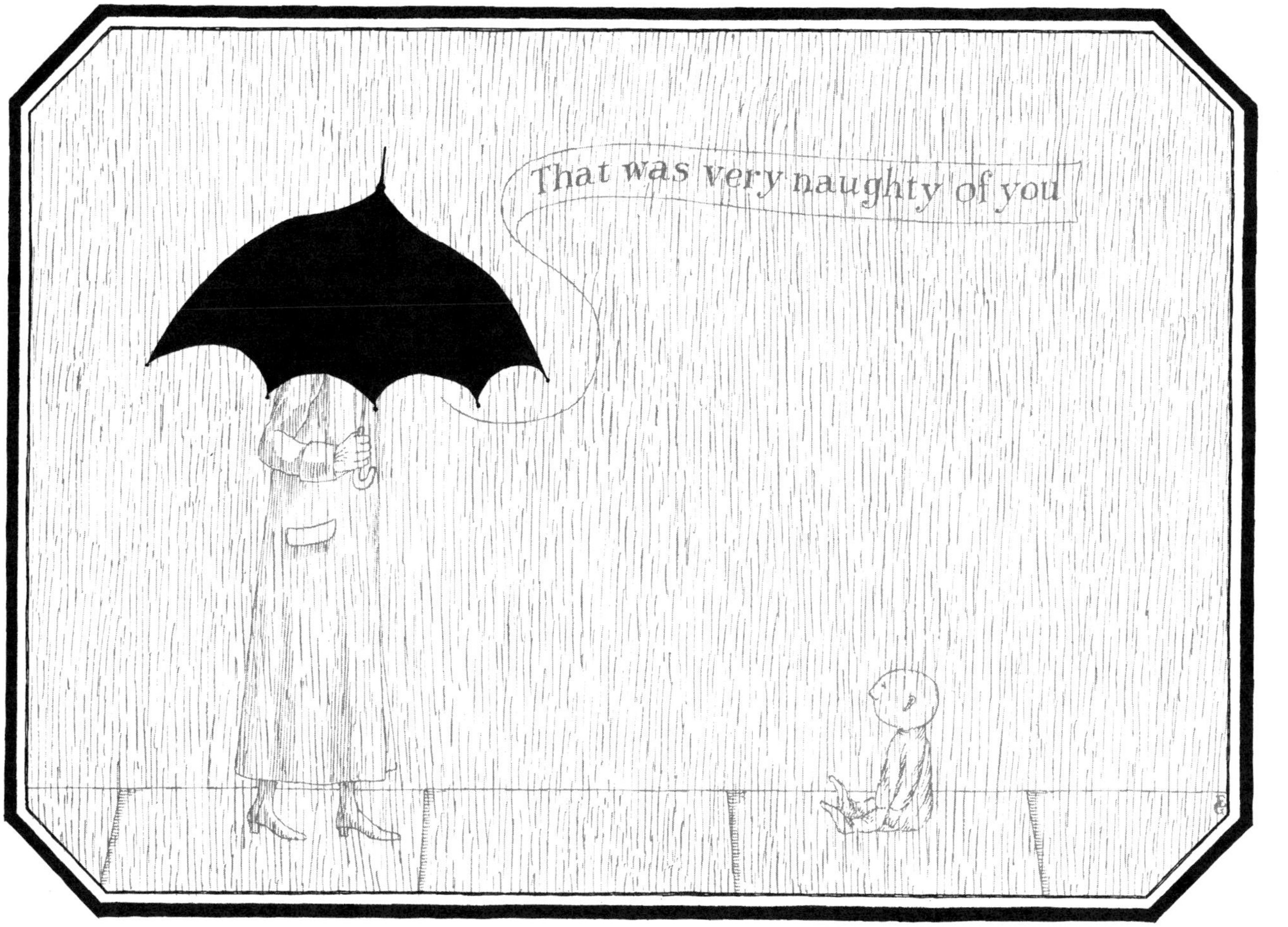
That was very naughty of you

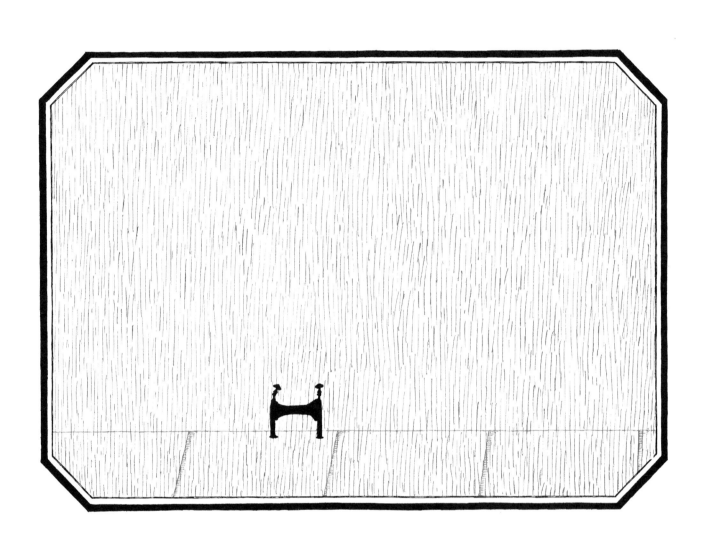

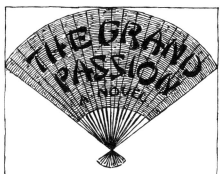

THE GRAND PASSION
A NOVEL

Englished anonymously
from the Conton Dialect (1930)
and illustrated by
EDWARD GOREY

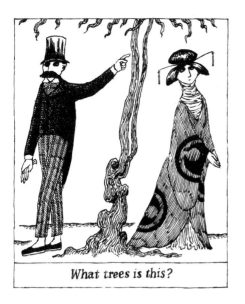

What trees is this?

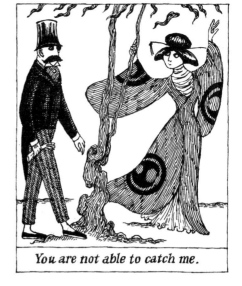

You are not able to catch me.

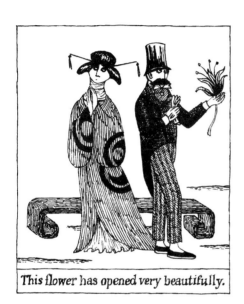

This flower has opened very beautifully.

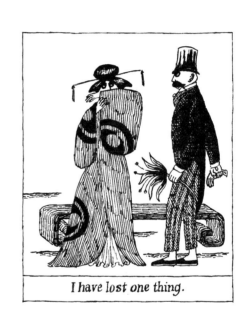

I have lost one thing.

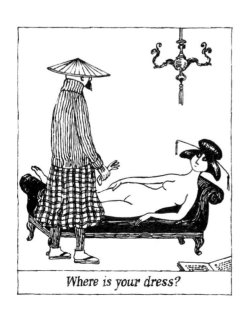

Where is your dress?

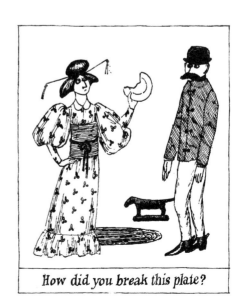

How did you break this plate?

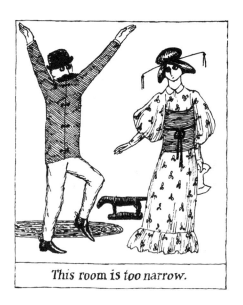

This room is too narrow.

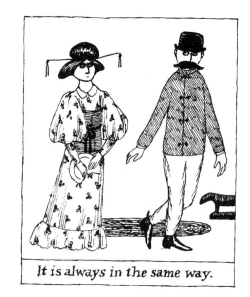

It is always in the same way.

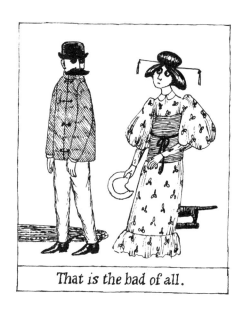

That *is* the bad of all.

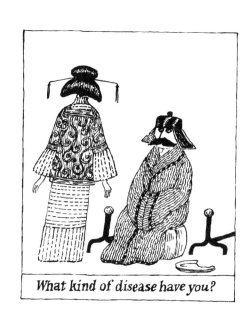

What kind of disease have you?

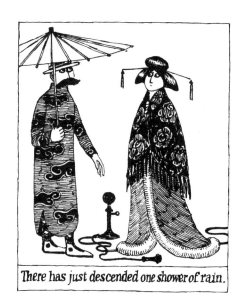

There has just descended one shower of rain.

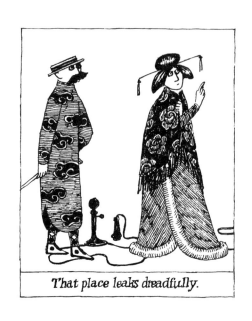

That place leaks dreadfully.

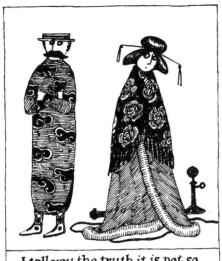

I tell you the truth it is not so.

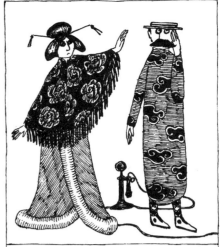

That is altogether different from this.

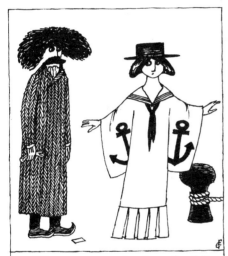

When are you going to embrak?

Les
Passementeries
Horribles
by
Edward
Gorey

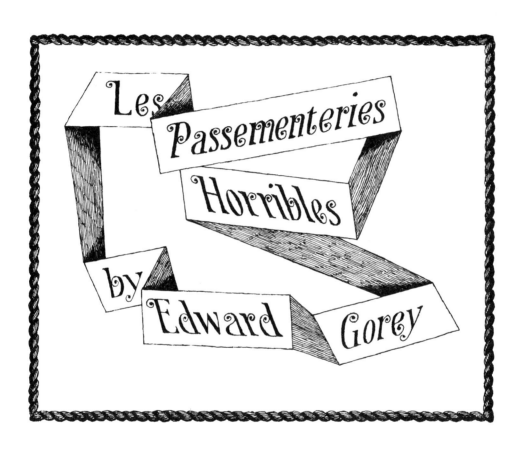

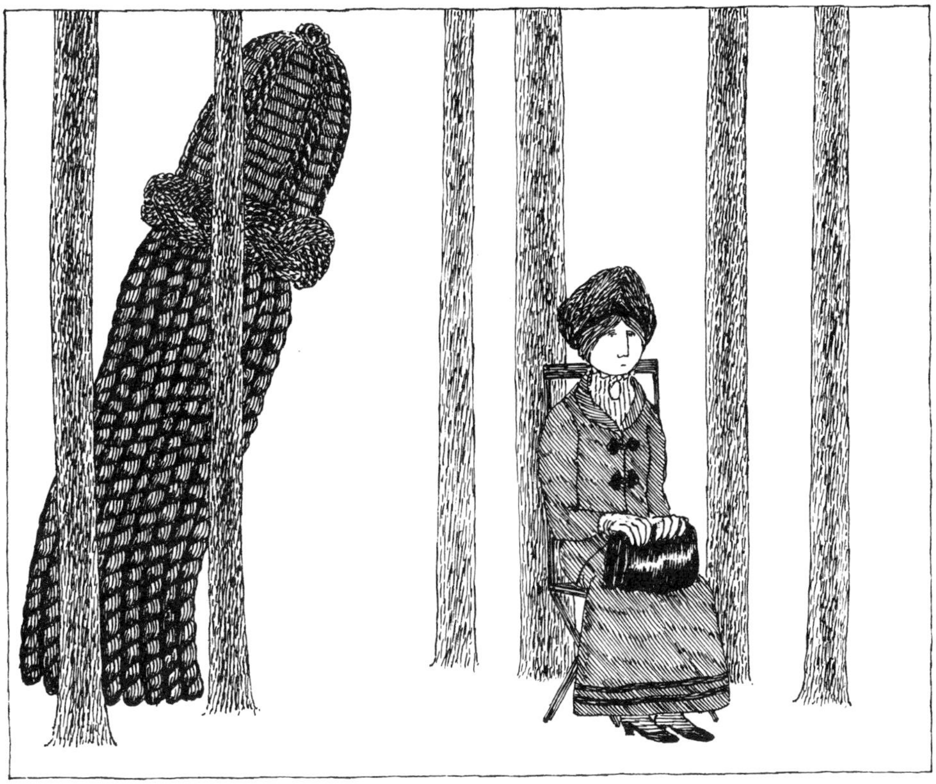

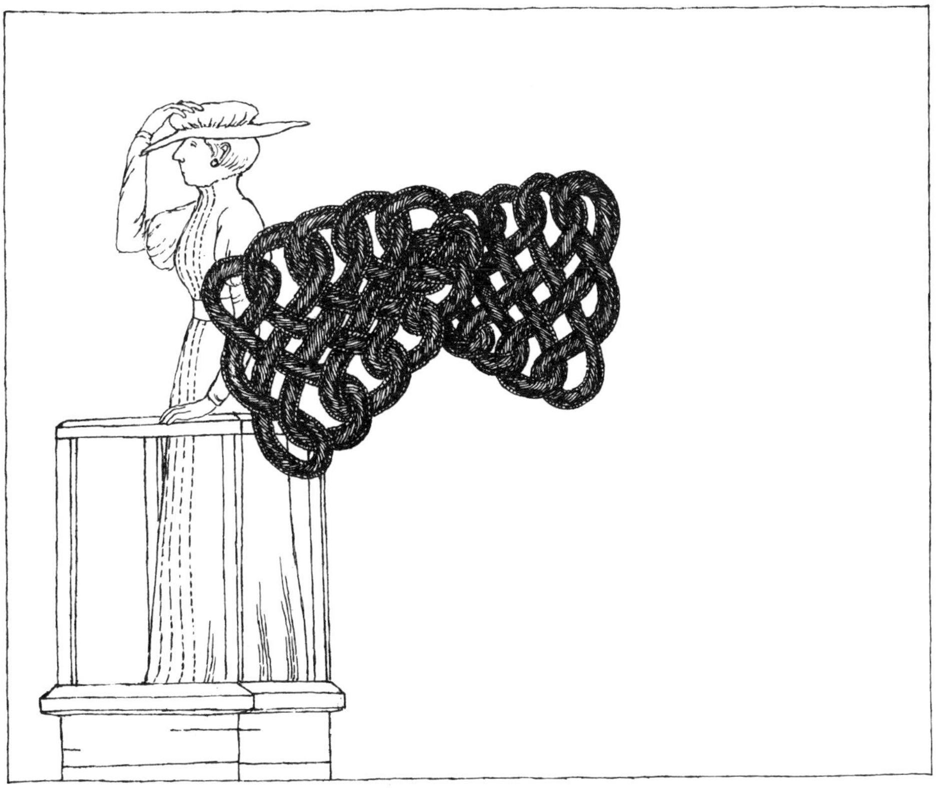

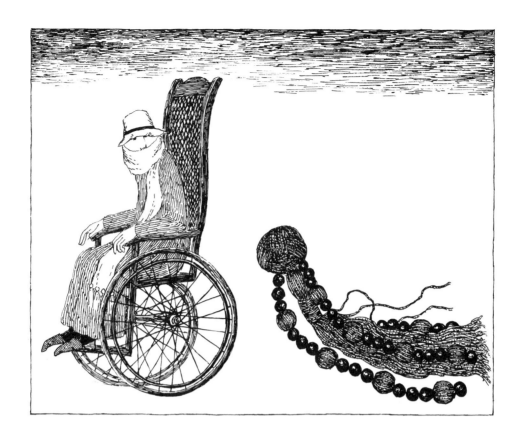

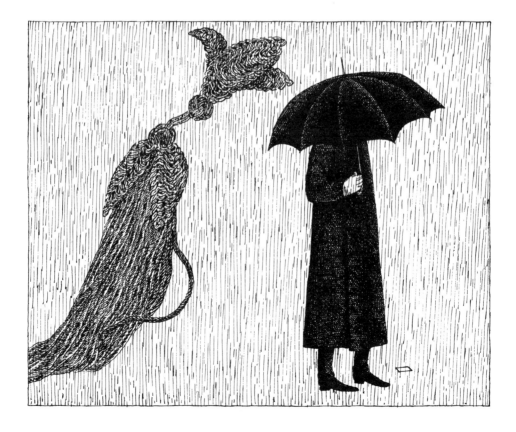

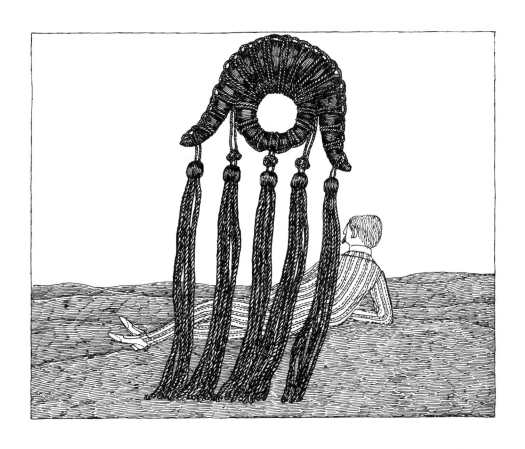

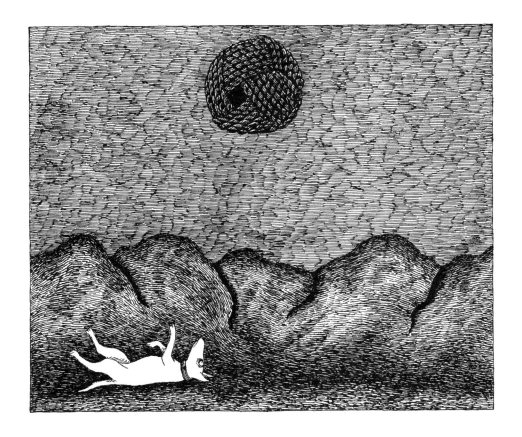

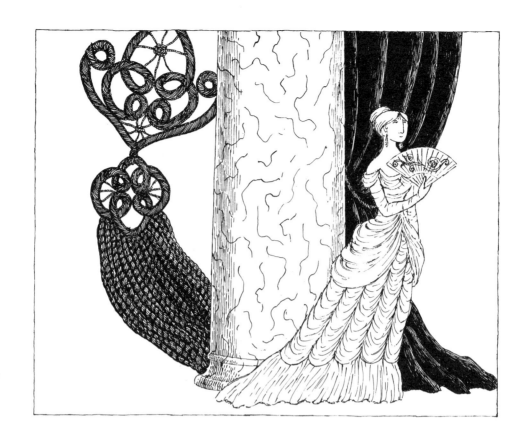

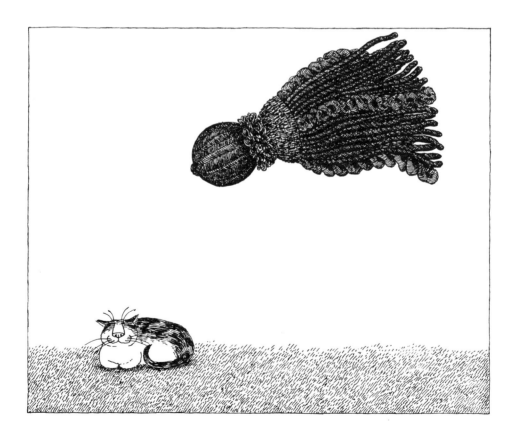

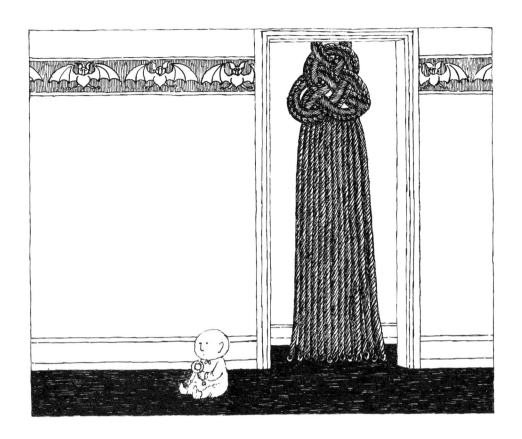

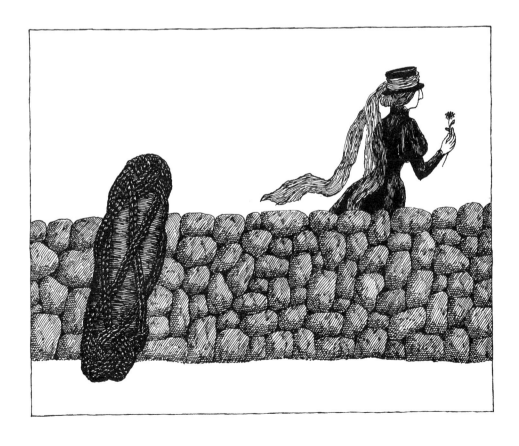

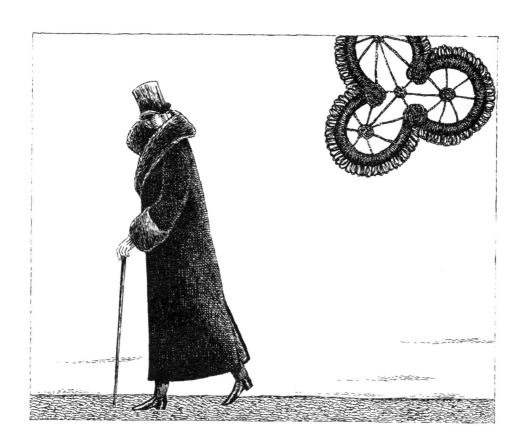

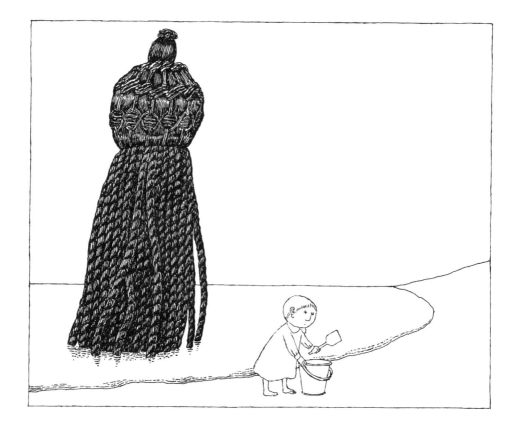

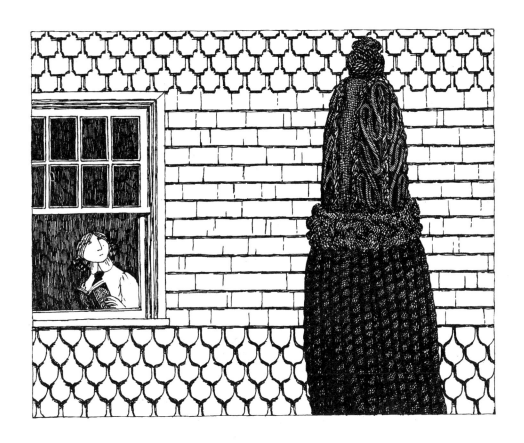

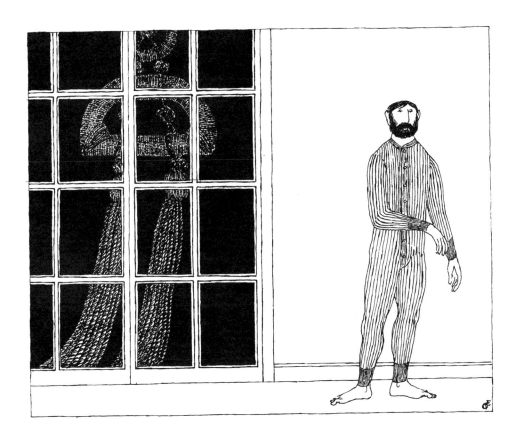

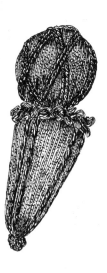

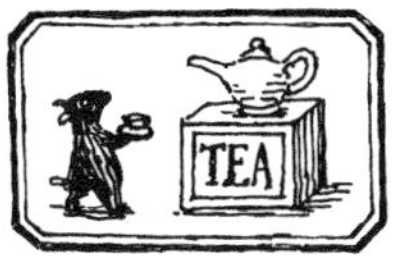
TEA

The Eclectic Abecedarium

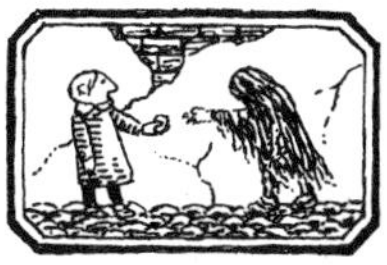

Betray no qualms
When asked for Alms.

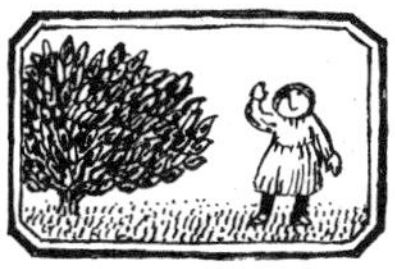

A hidden Bird
Is often heard.

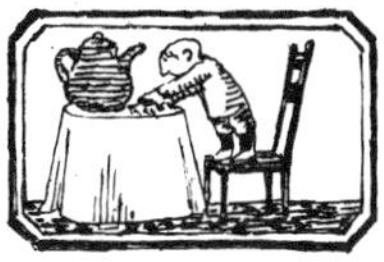

Pick up loose Crumbs
Upon your thumbs.

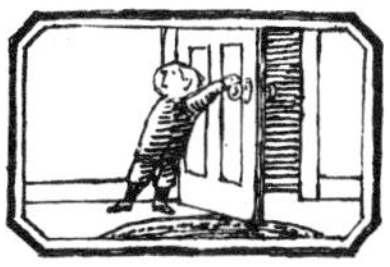

Look back before
You close a Door.

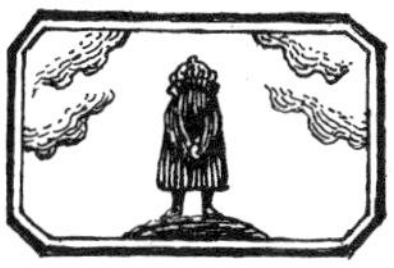

There is an Eye
Up in the sky.

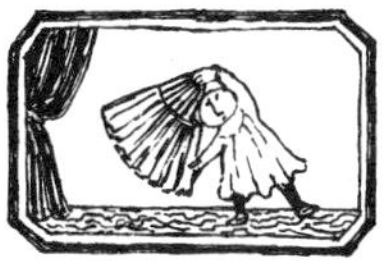

It takes elan
To wield a Fan.

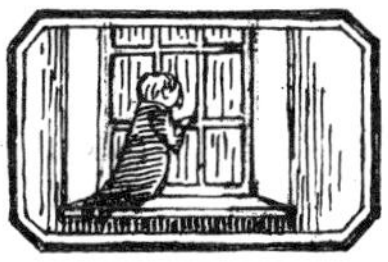

Beyond the Glass
We see life pass.

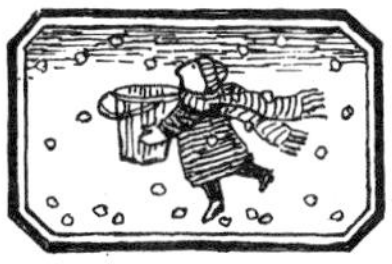

For catching Hail
Keep by a pail.

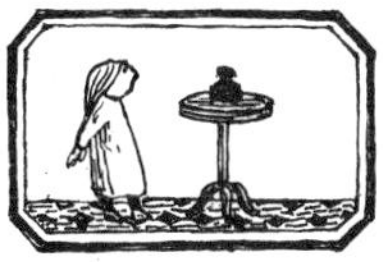

Be loath to drink
Indian Ink.

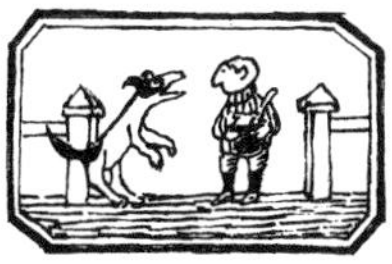

Don't try to cram
The dog with Jam.

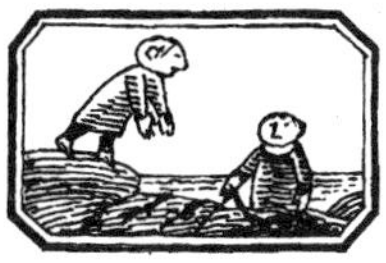

In sorting Kelp
Be quick to help.

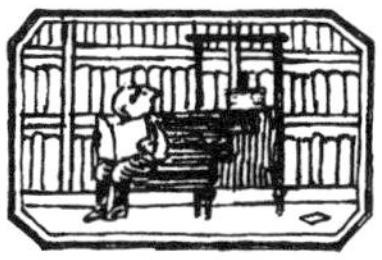

Forbear to taste
Library Paste.

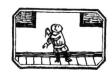

Be sure a Mouse
Lurks in the house.

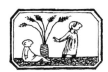

A careless No
Leads on to woe.

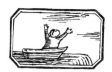

Don't leave the shore
Without an Oar.

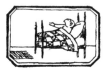

Request a Pill
When you are ill.

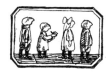

Find tasks to do
While in a Queue.

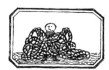

Attempt to cope
With tangled Rope.

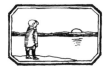

See down the Sun
When day is done.

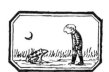

On any road
May sit a Toad.

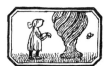

Don't overturn
The garden Urn.

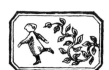

Beware the Vine
Which can entwine.

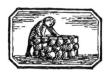

The way to Hell
Is down a Well.

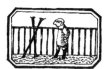

The letter X
Was made to vex.

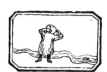

With every Yawn
A moment's gone.

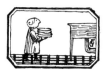

The kitchen sink
Is made of Zinc.

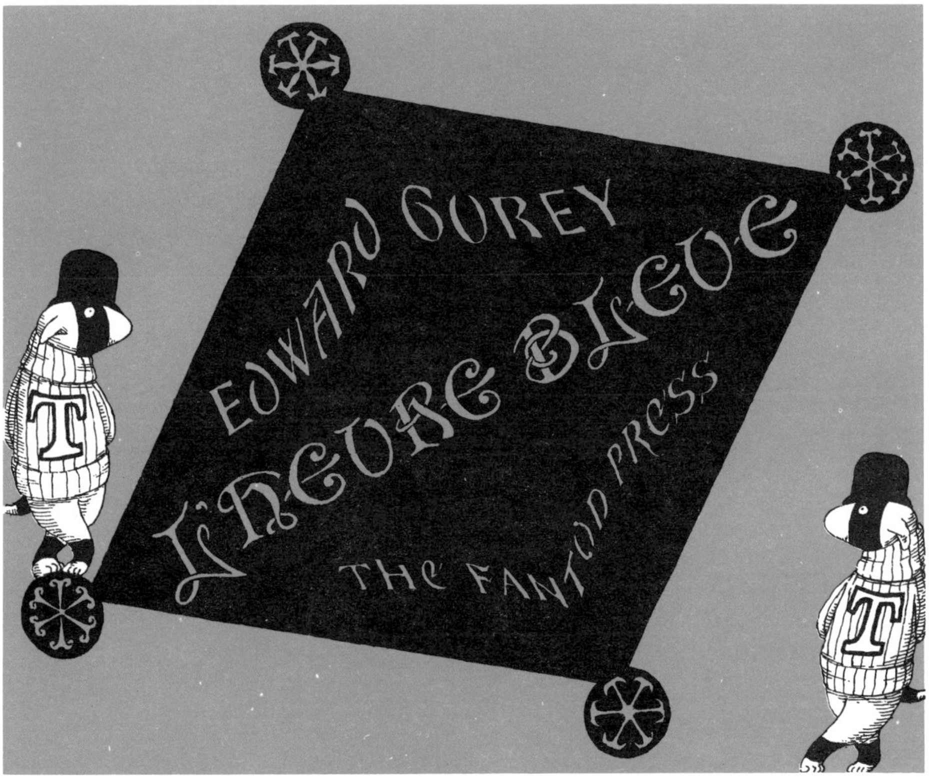

EDWARD GOREY
L'HEURE BLEUE
THE FANTOD PRESS

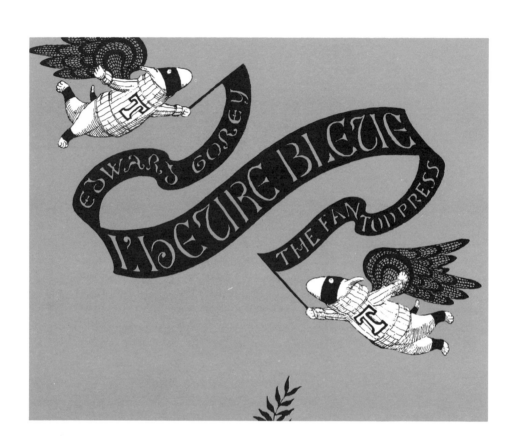

EDWARD GOREY
L'HEURE BLEUE
THE FANTOD PRESS

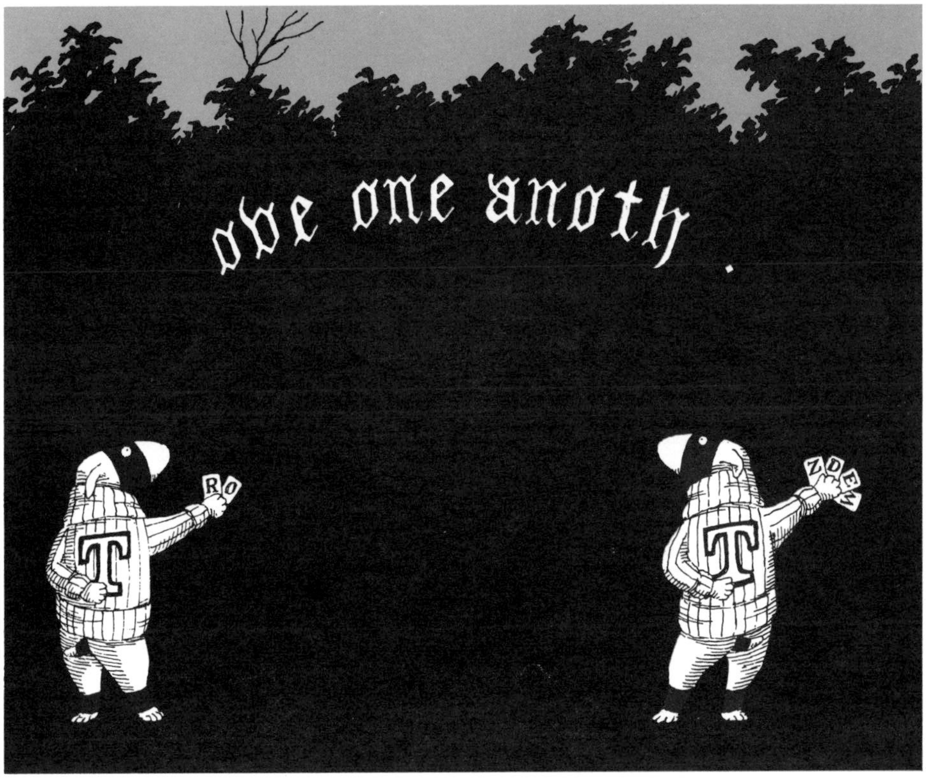
ove one anoth .
T
RO
T
ZDEW

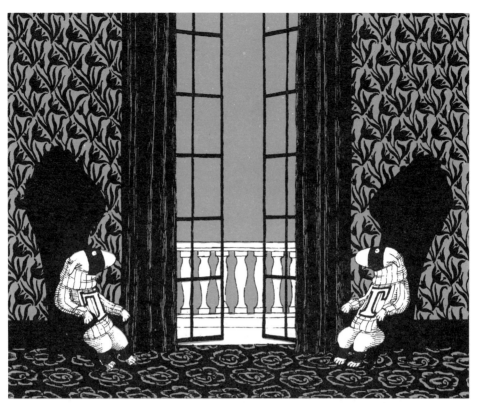

It is not the living, it is the being lived on.

I must remember to write that, along with some other things, down.

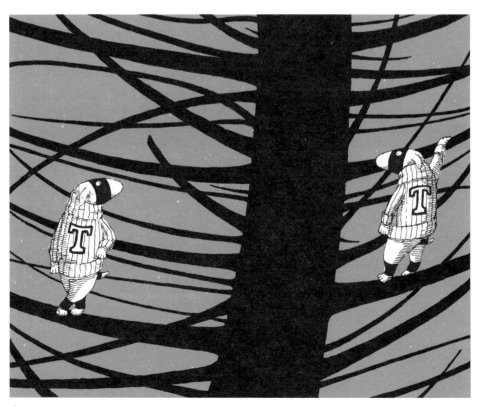

One day a week I don't _____, but I never tell anyone which day it is.

Last week it was Thursday, wasn't it?

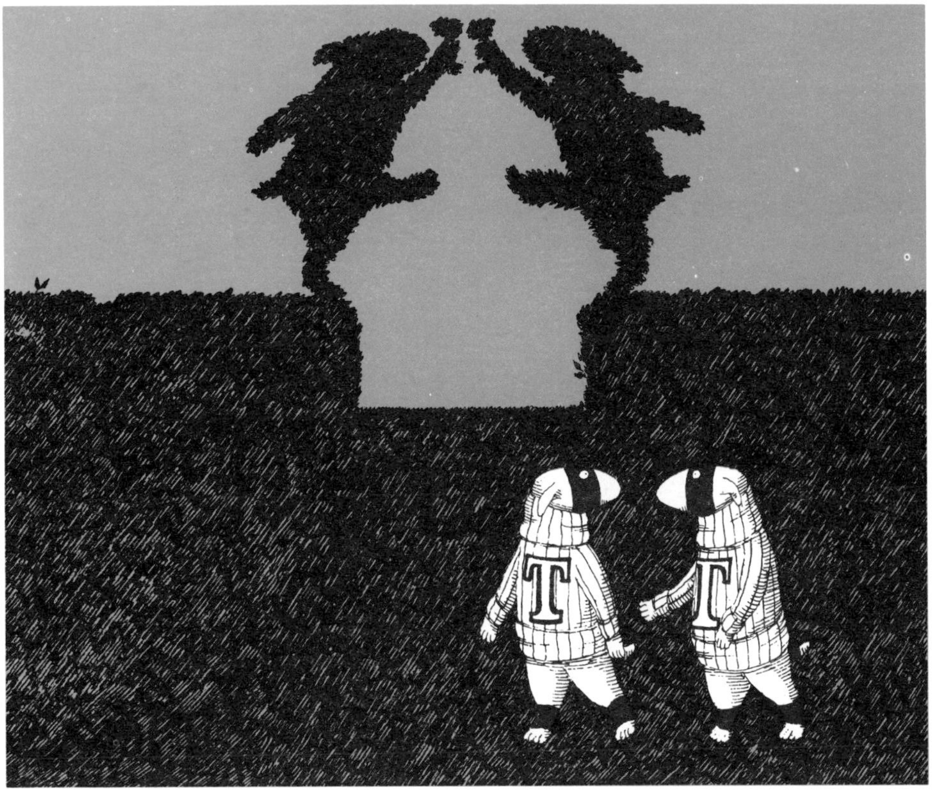

It seems to me wine warms up very quickly.

I never know what you think is important.

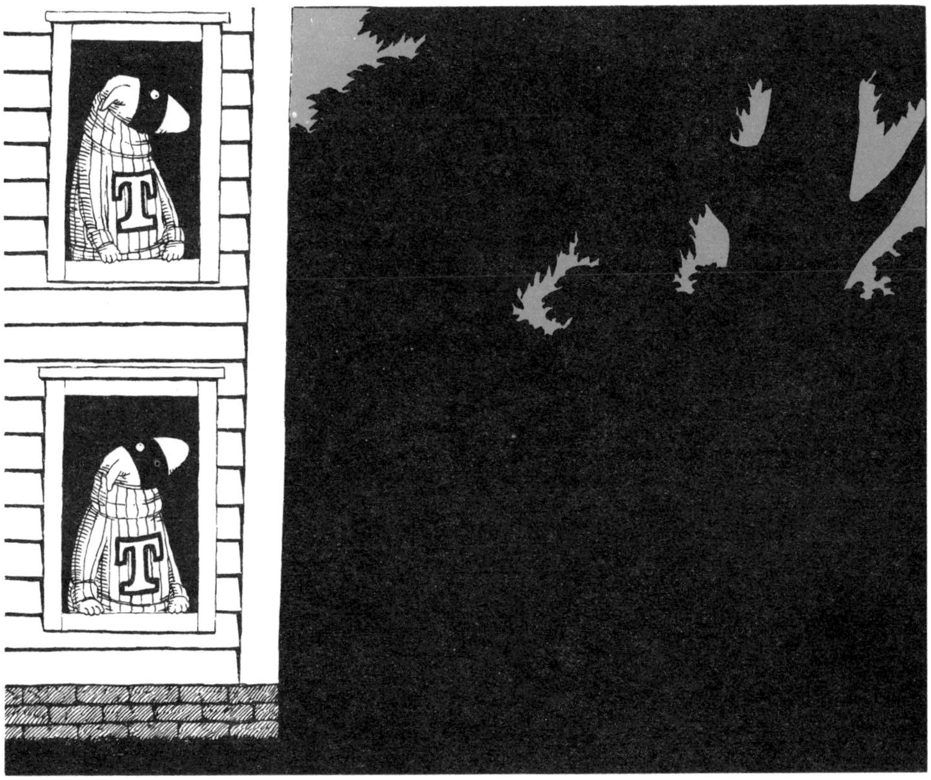

T
T

The ______s have it all over us.

Only if you live there.

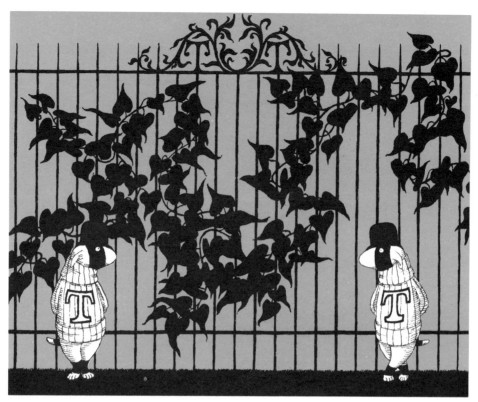

I never insult you in front of others.

I keep forgetting that everything you say is connected.

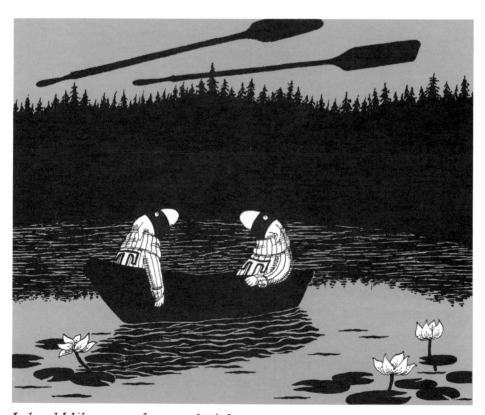

I should like a parsley sandwich.

To the best of my knowledge they are not in season.

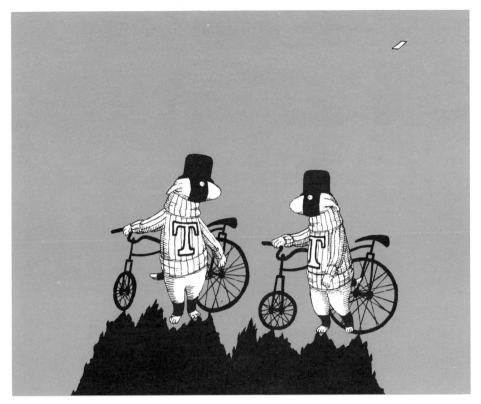

Not everything in life can be interpreted metaphorically.

That's because things fall out on the way.

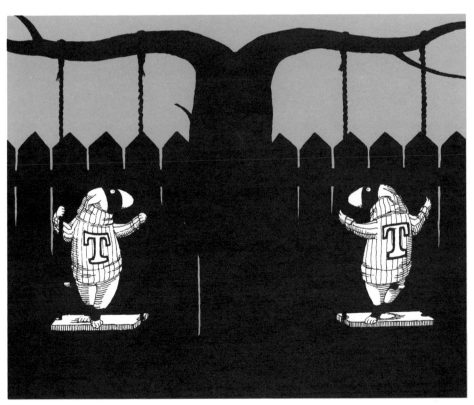

As I always say.

I know you do, although I don't believe I've ever actually heard you.

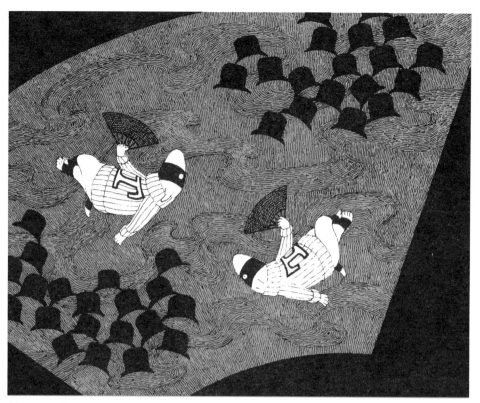

Kampan'yō-isu no ryōkin wa tokubetsu ni ikura desu ka?

Kibun ga warui.

   What is the extra charge for a deck chair?

   I feel sick.

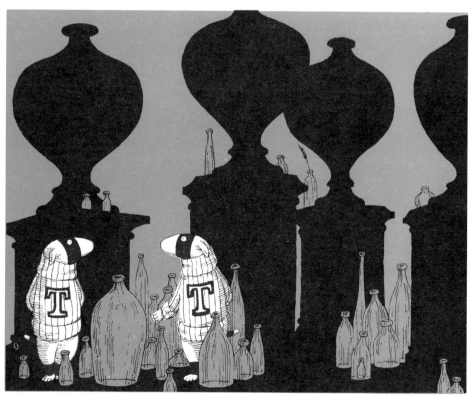

It seems to me a fate worse than sinking.

But there isn't any other kind.

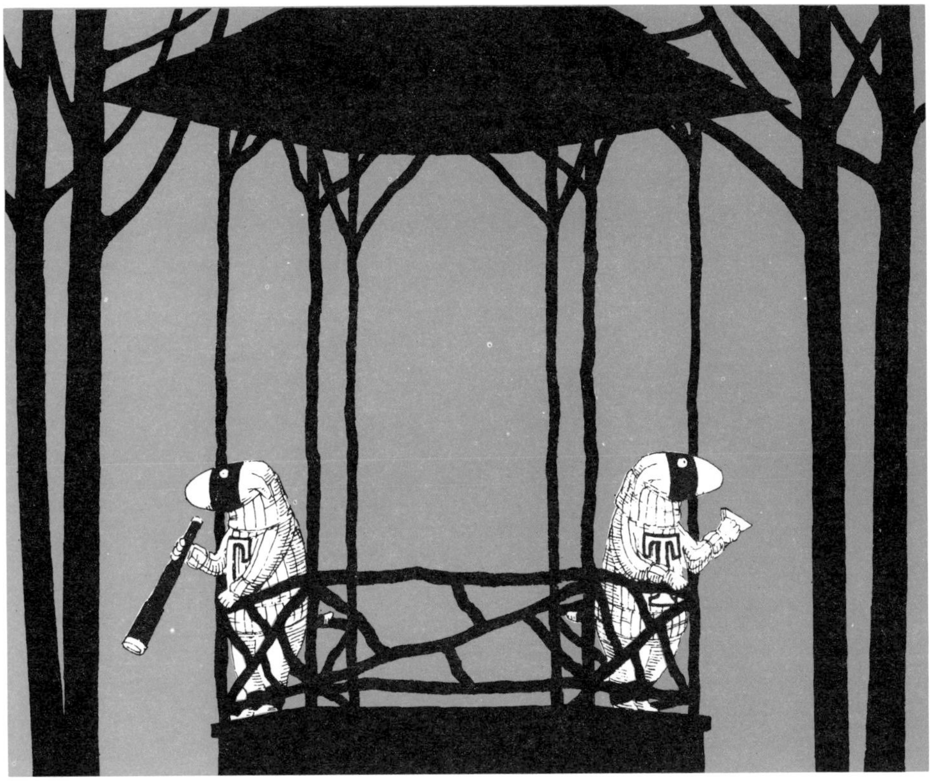

I understand ________ is an author.

I am not certain I can arrange an introduction.

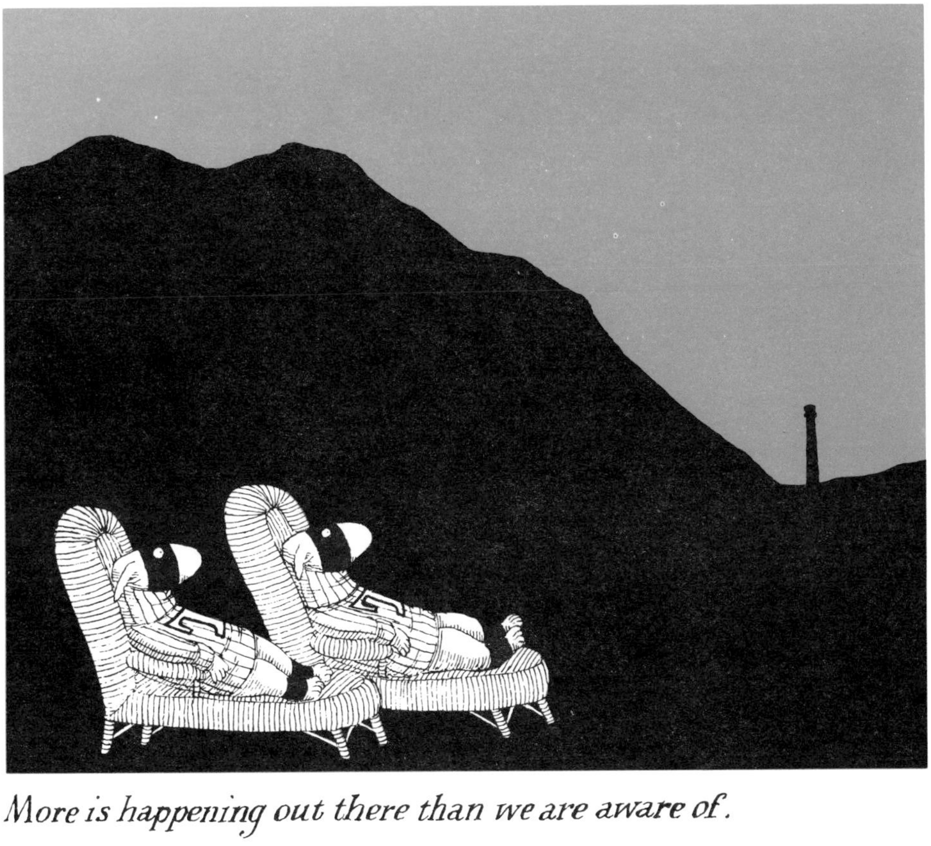

More is happening out there than we are aware of.

It is possibly due to some unknown direful circumstance.

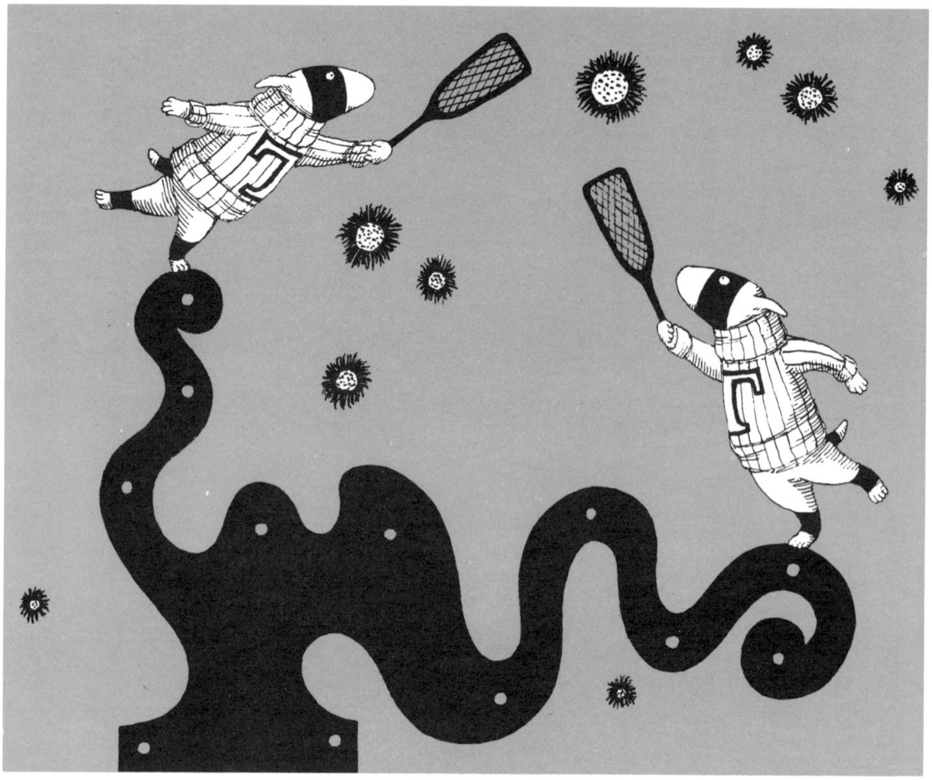

I thought it was going to be different;
It turned out to be(,) just the same.

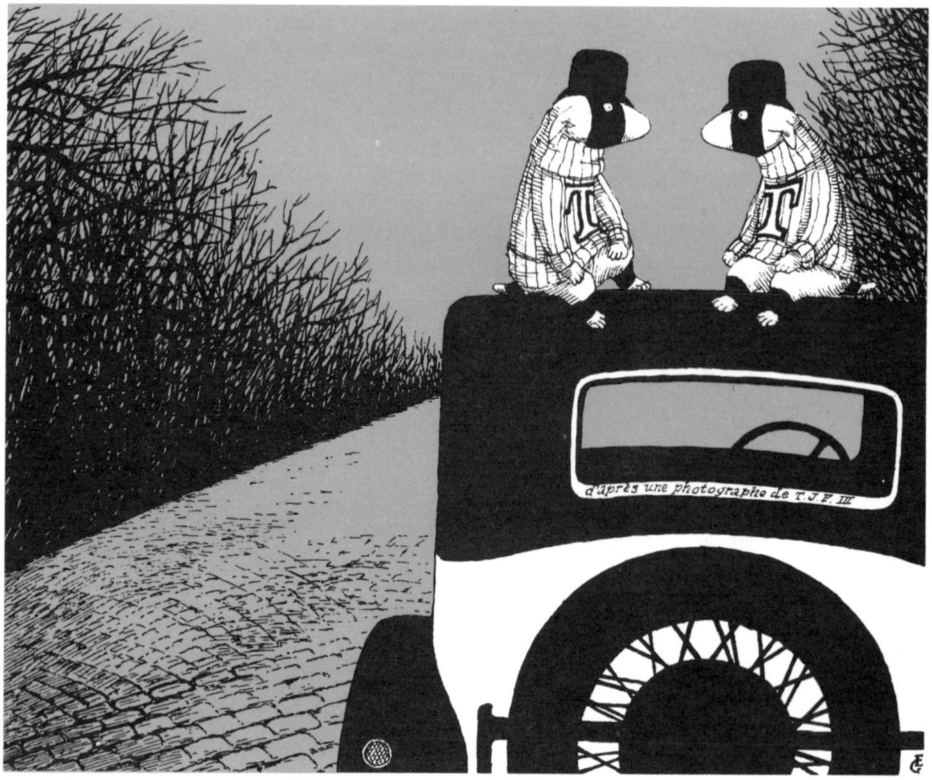
d'après une photographe de T. J. F. III

What is Food?
It's a small town in New Hampshire.

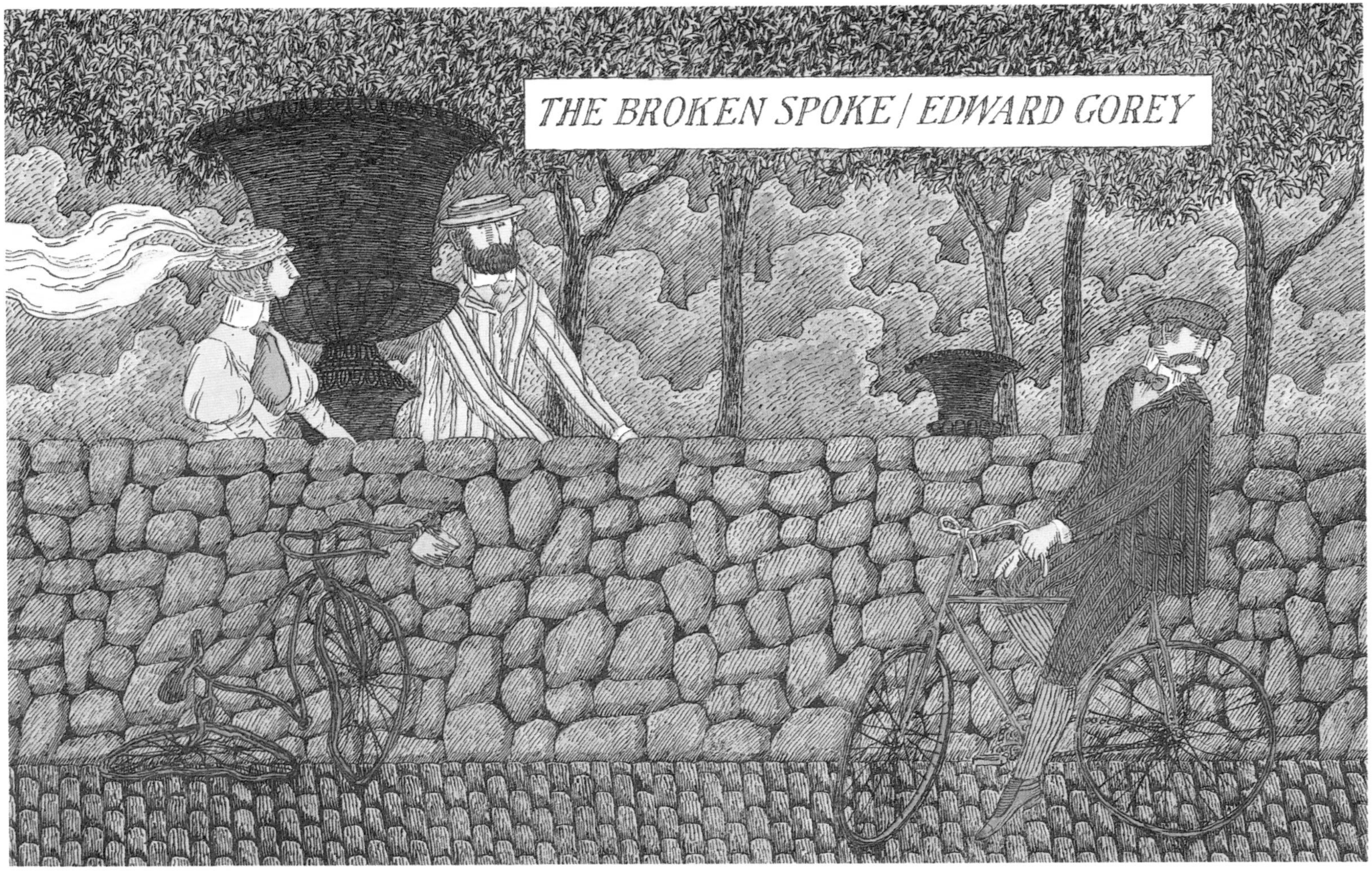
THE BROKEN SPOKE / EDWARD GOREY

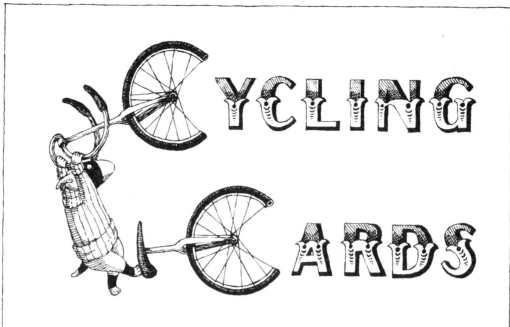

CYCLING CARDS

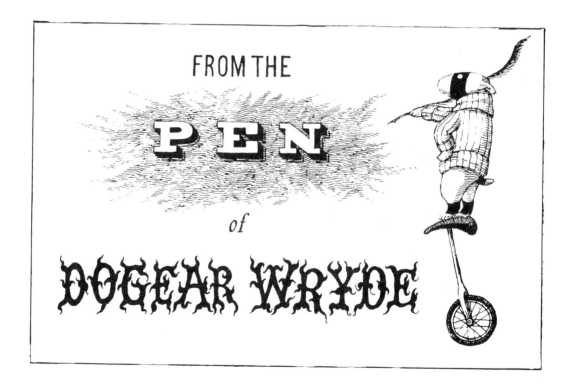

FROM THE

PEN

of

DOGEAR WRYDE

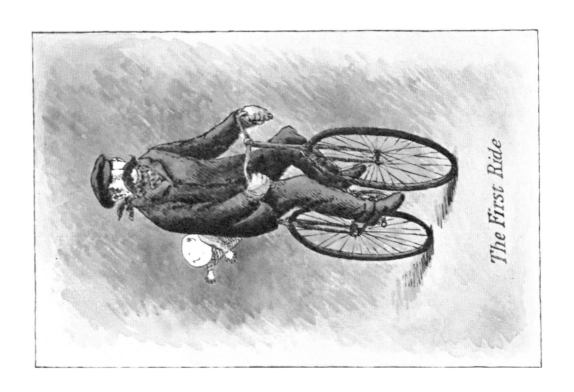

The First Ride

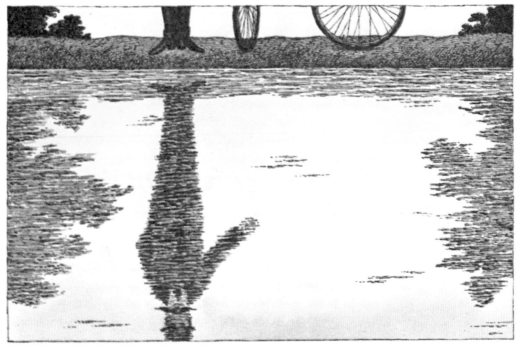

Monsieur Bandage-Herniaire and his famous Unreflecting Bicycle

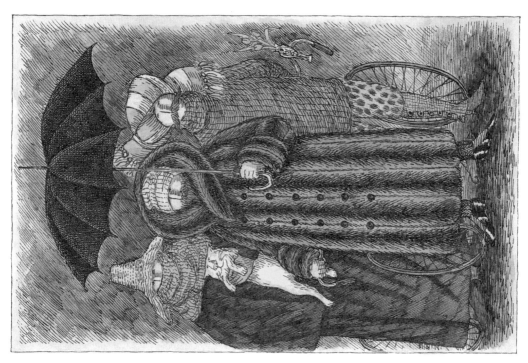

Contestants in the annual Trans-Novaya Zemlya Bicycle Race

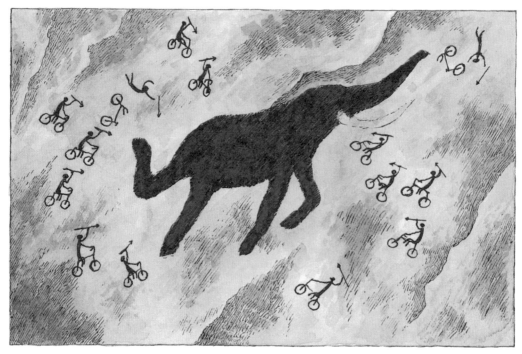

After a photograph of a painting found on the wall of a cave near Afazia, Ohio, the location of the entrance to which is no longer known

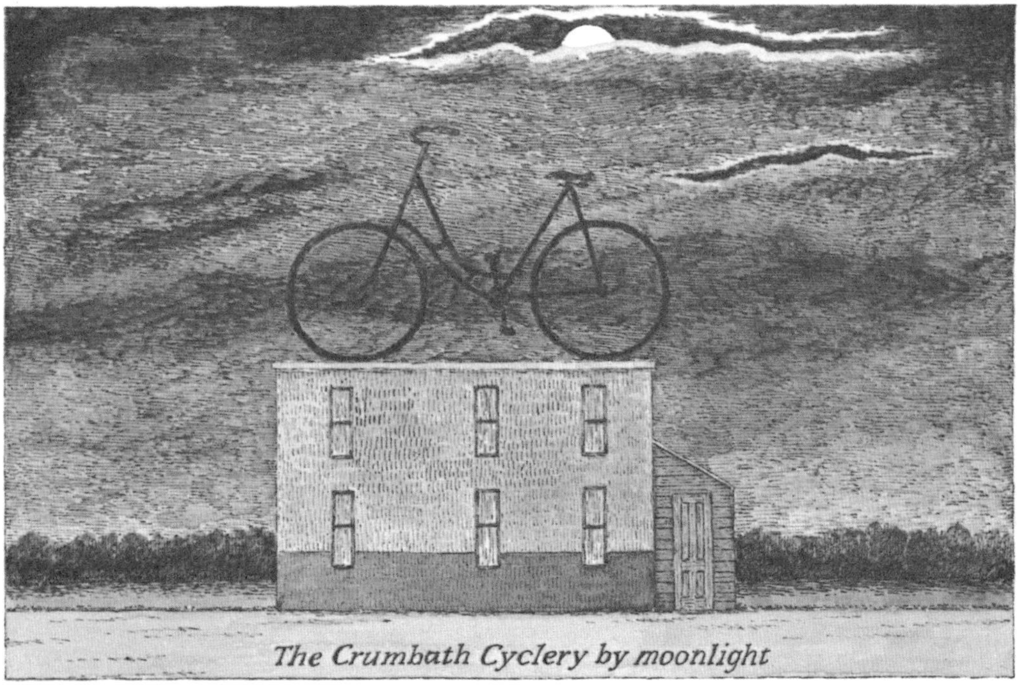

The Crumbath Cyclery by moonlight

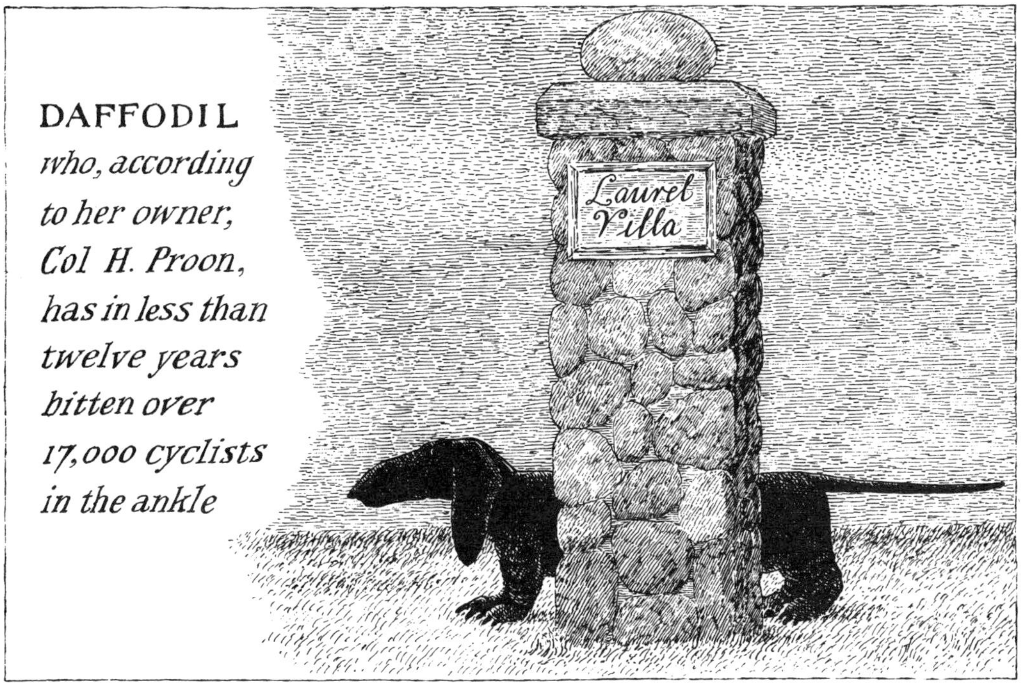
Laurel
Villa

DAFFODIL
who, according to her owner, Col H. Proon, has in less than twelve years bitten over 17,000 cyclists in the ankle

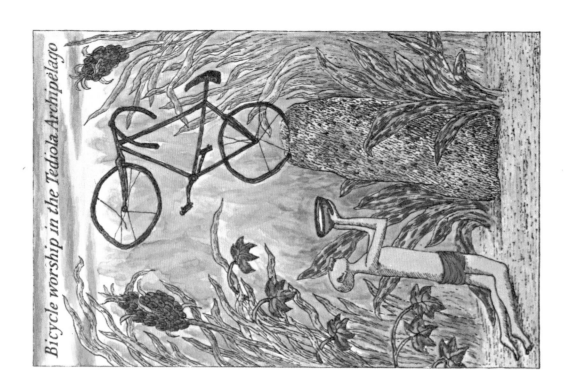

Bicycle worship in the Tediola Archipelago

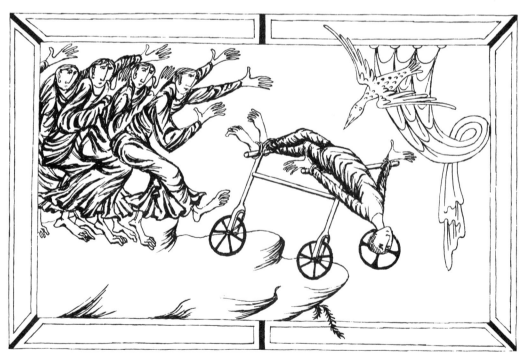

The Martyrdom of St Egfroth. Eleventh century drawing, Hollowtooth Museum, Mortshire

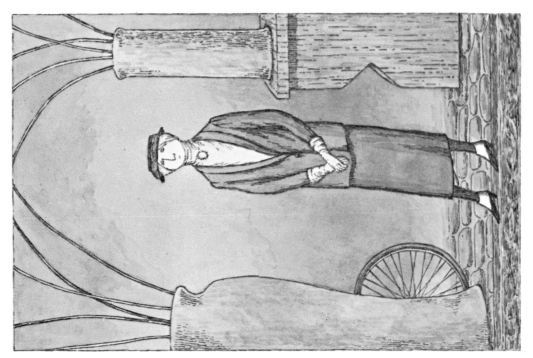

Miss A. Sprigknot, the first lady to cross the suspension bridge over Porphyria Falls on a bicycle

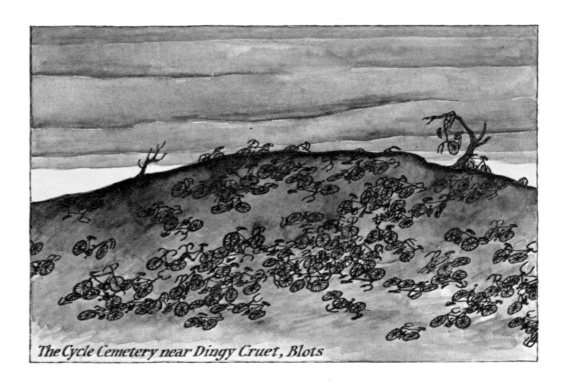

The Cycle Cemetery near Dingy Cruet, Blots

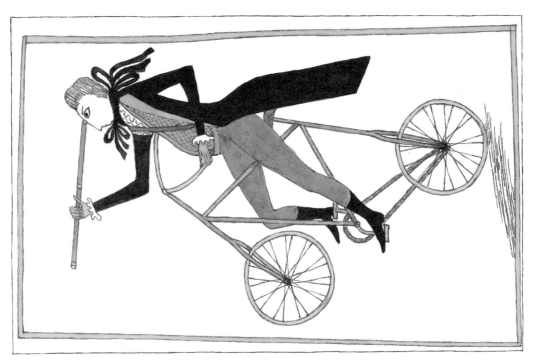

Major O'Twiddy, the hero of Falling Forks. Anonymous water-colour, c.1825

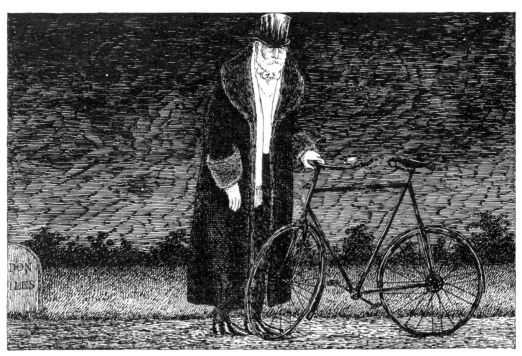

Celebrated Cycling Calamities No. 23. The Duke of Aught suffers a puncture on his way to the first performance of Crudele, Queen of Corinth in 178 years

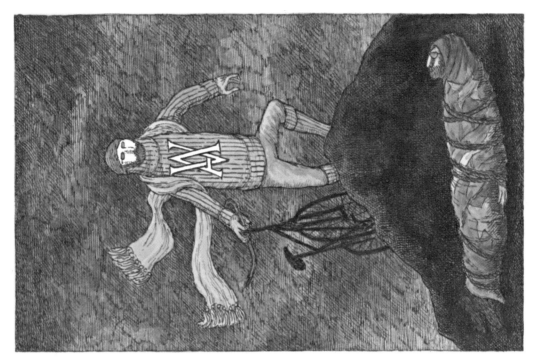

The rescue of Sir Odo Fitzaddle from the top of Mt Radish

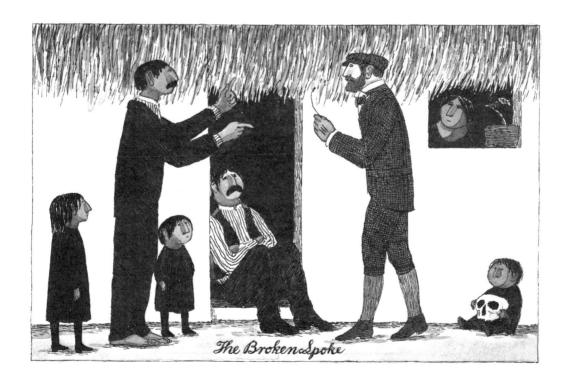

The Broken Spoke

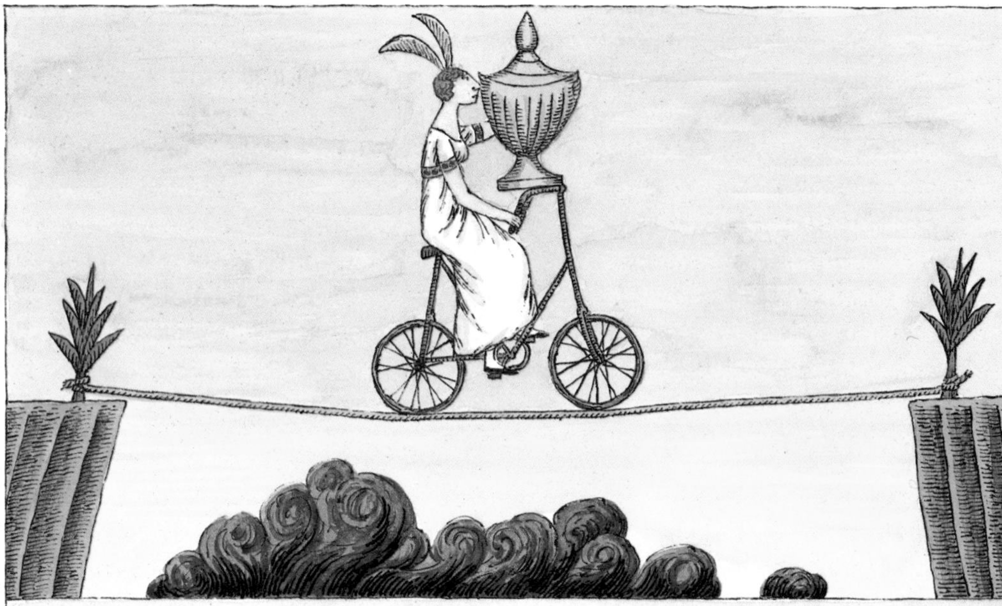

Innocence, on the Bicycle of Propriety, carrying the Urn of Reputation safely over the Abyss of Indiscretion

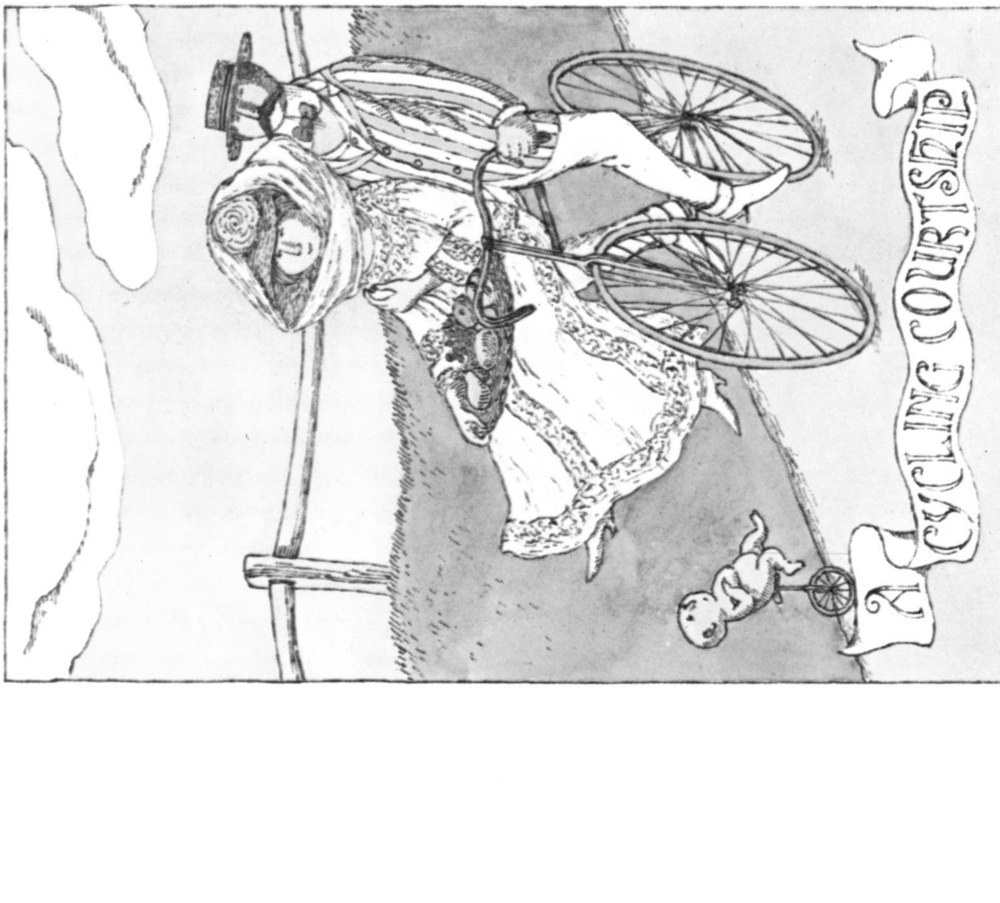
A CYCLING COURTSHIP

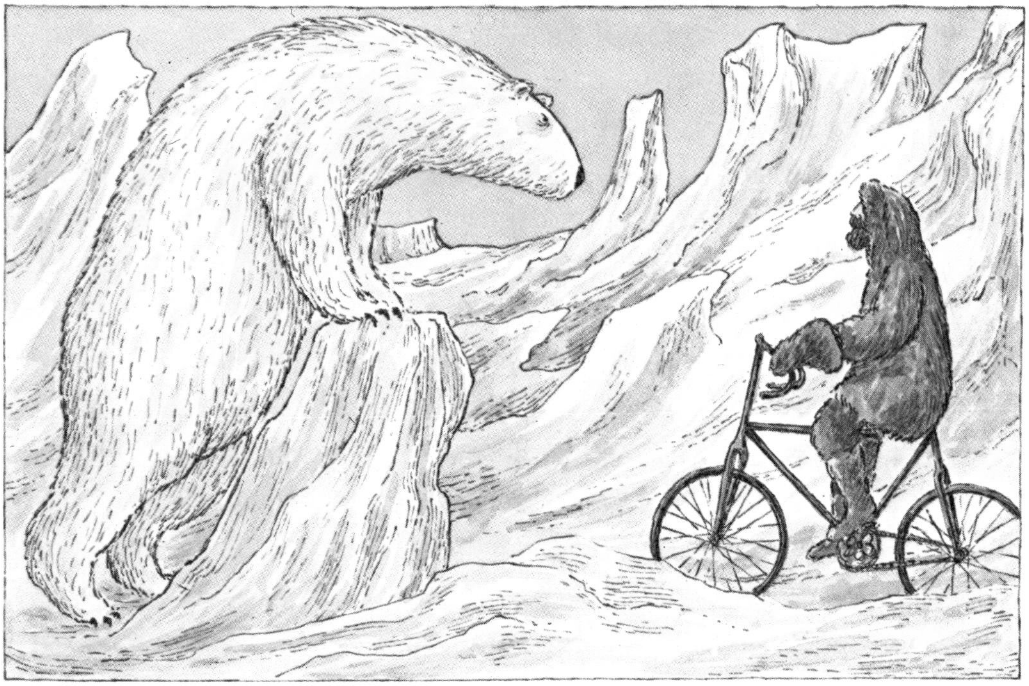

The Crumpet-Fanlight Expedition: Capt. Mousegrave's fatal reconnaissance at Ulna Bay

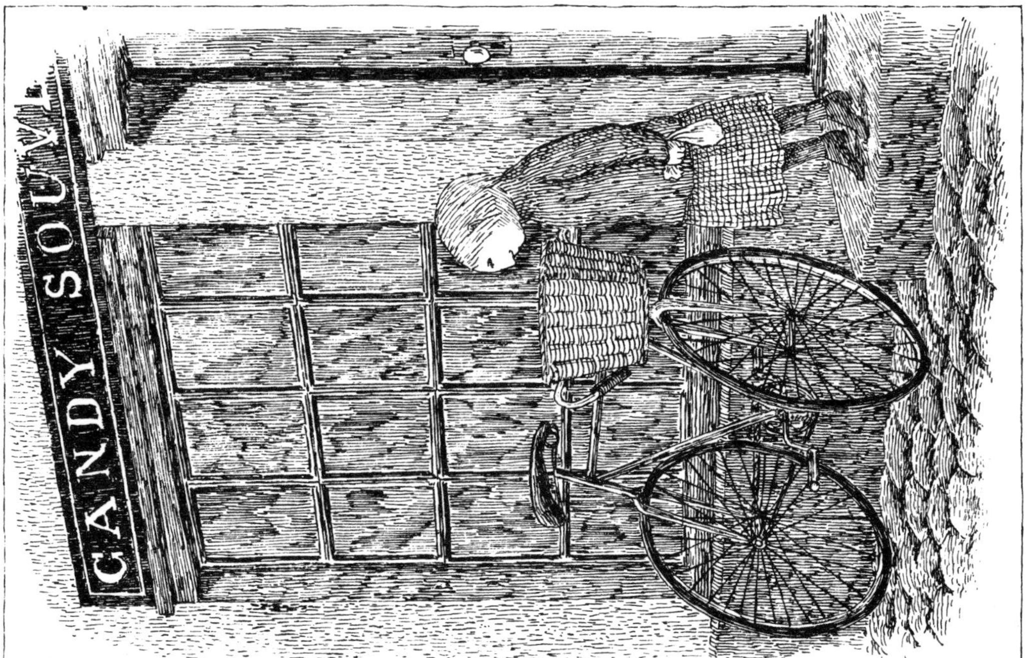
CANDY SOU

The Orange Bicycle Case: the discovery of Nesba Macsplosh's head

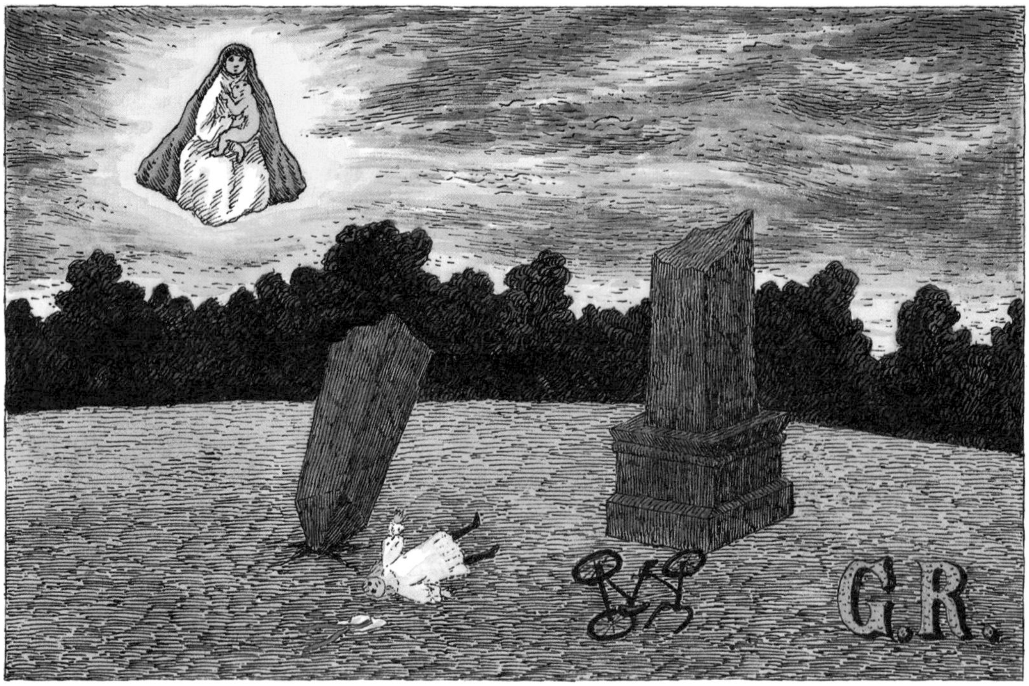
G.R.

Ex-voto, formerly in the possession of G.E. Deadworry

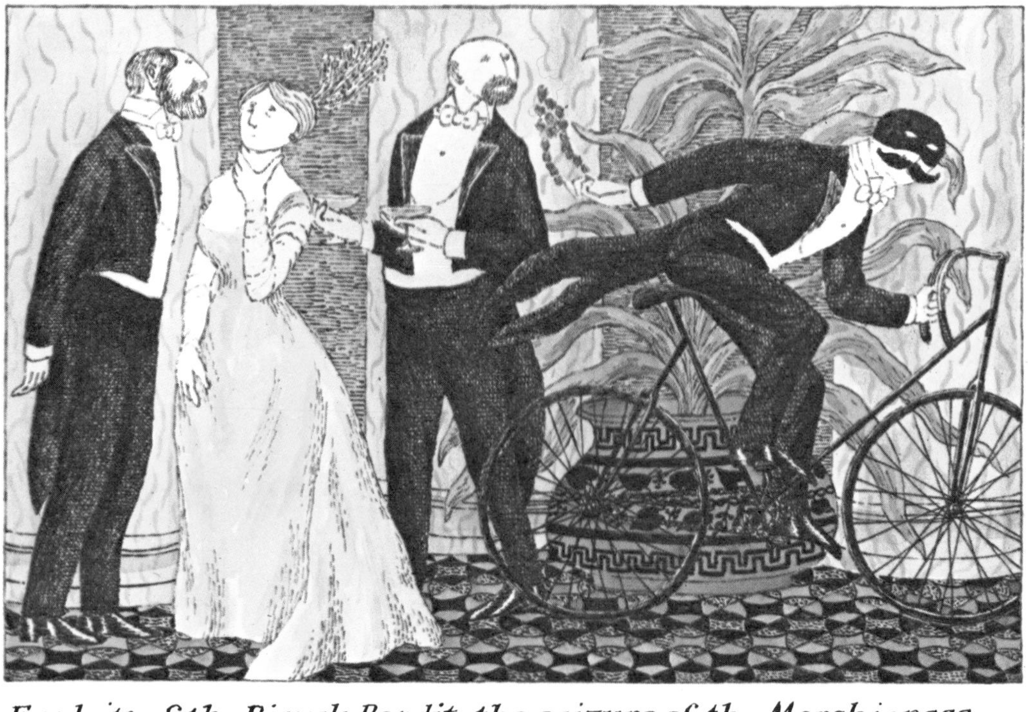

Exploits of the Bicycle Bandit: the seizure of the Marchioness of Bunworry's emeralds during a ball at Condiment House

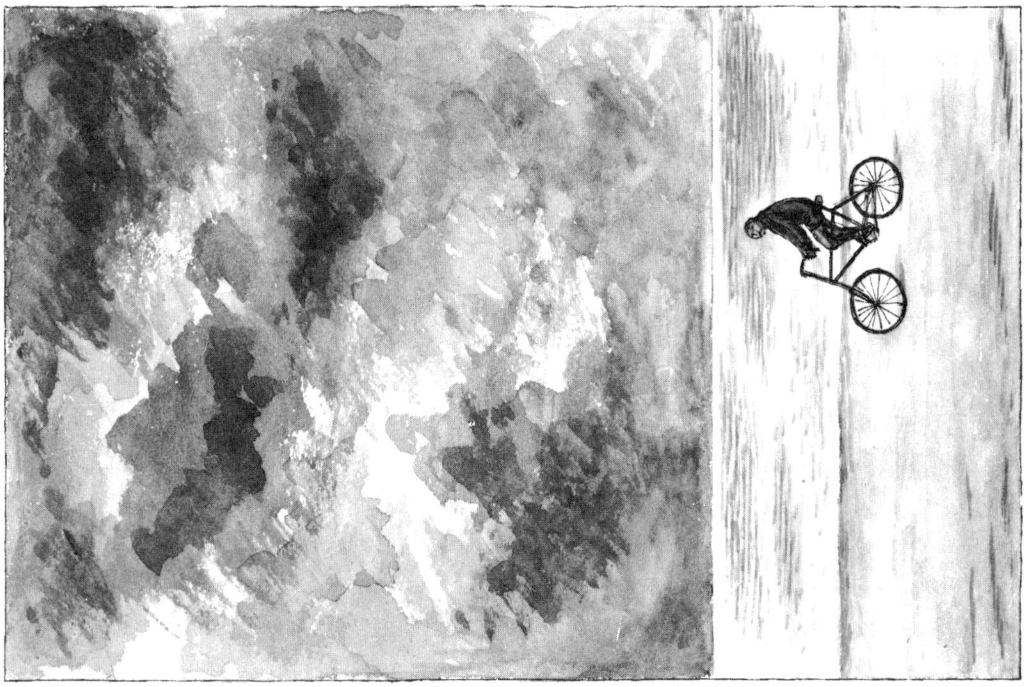

Arthur Igleby, the long-distance champion, working out on Nattering Sands

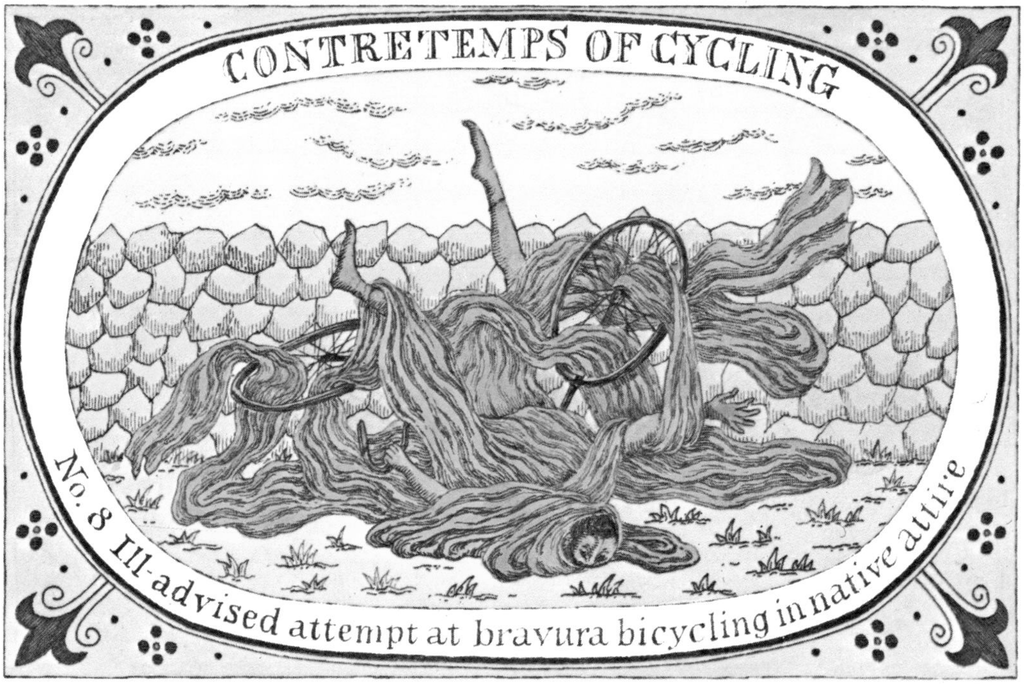
CONTRETEMPS OF CYCLING
No. 8 Ill-advised attempt at bravura bicycling in native attire

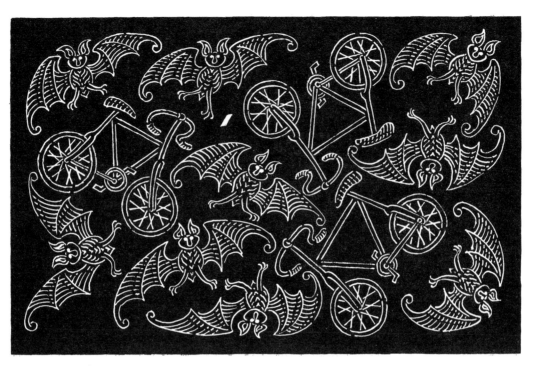

Nineteenth century Japanese stencil: bats and bicycles

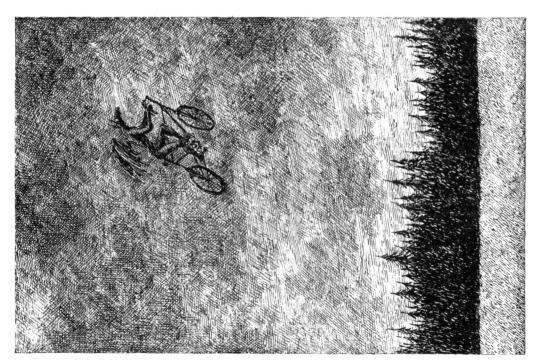

Apparition of demon cyclist that appeared in the sky over Gasket, Maine several times during the second week in November, 1911

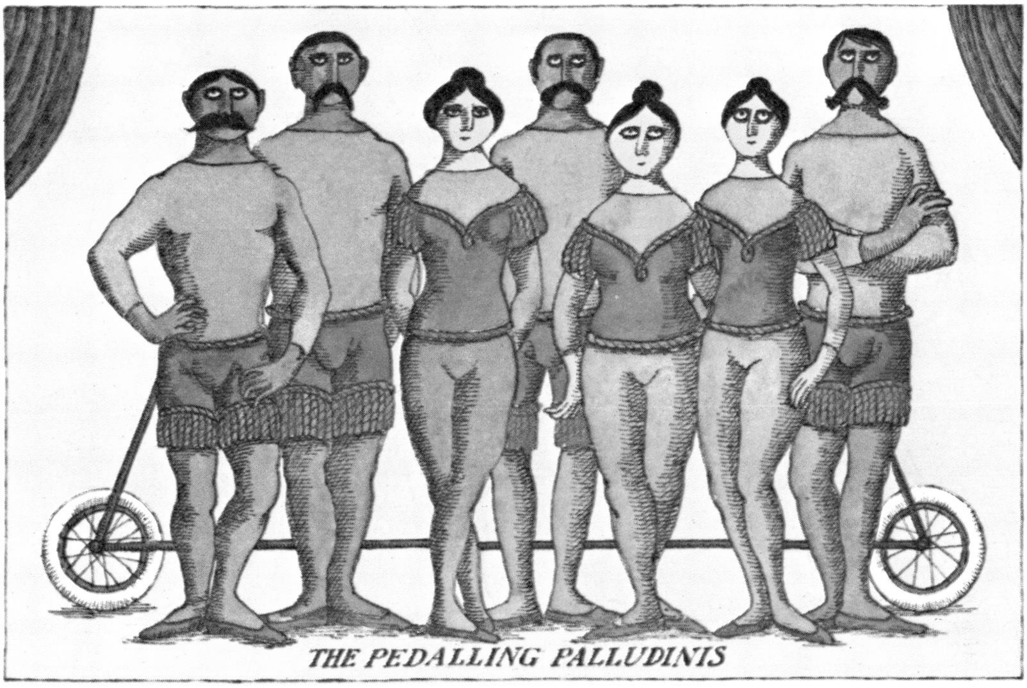

THE PEDALLING PALLUDINIS

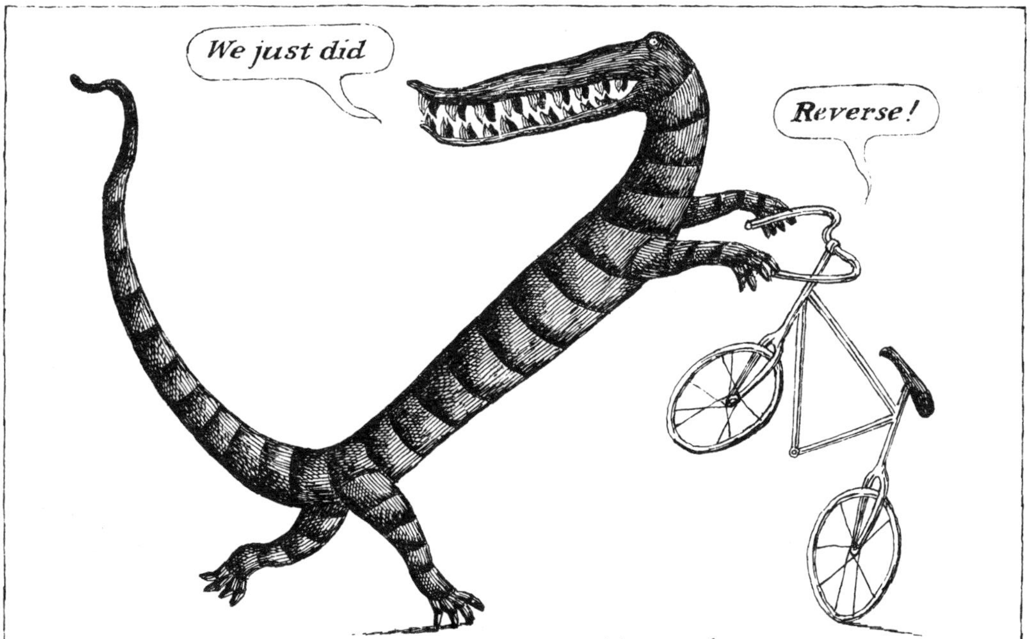
We just did
Reverse!

Valse dégueulasse

(Advertisement)

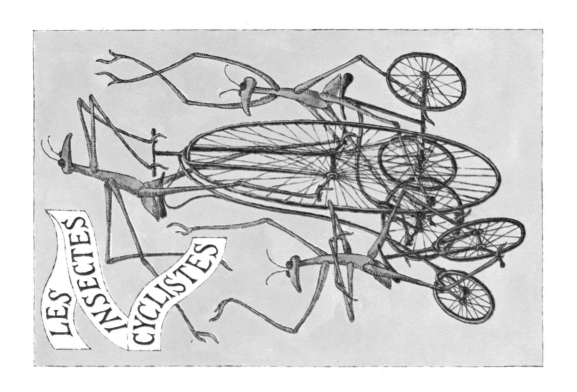

LES INSECTES CYCLISTES

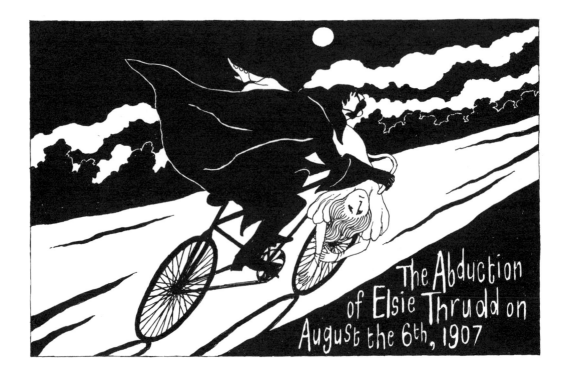

The Abduction of Elsie Thrudd on August the 6th, 1907

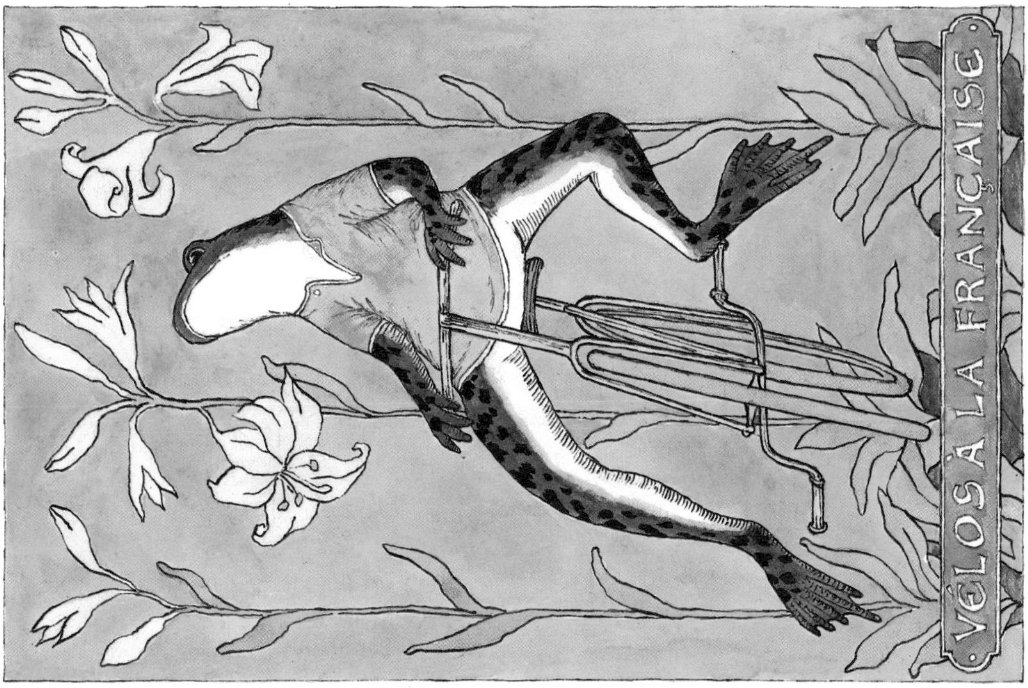
VÉLOS À LA FRANÇAISE

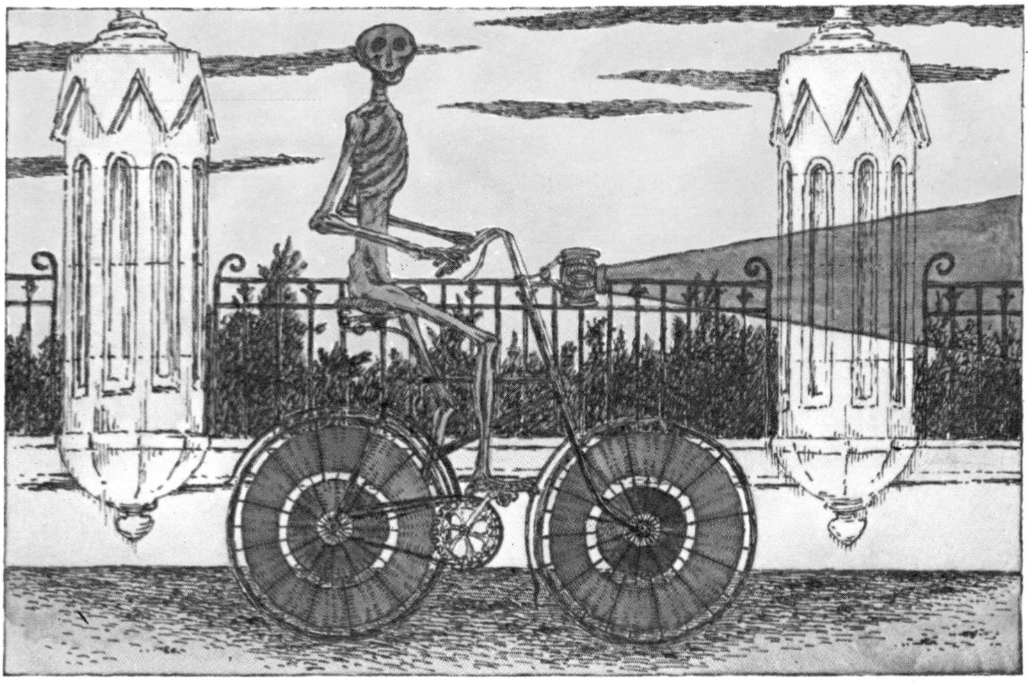

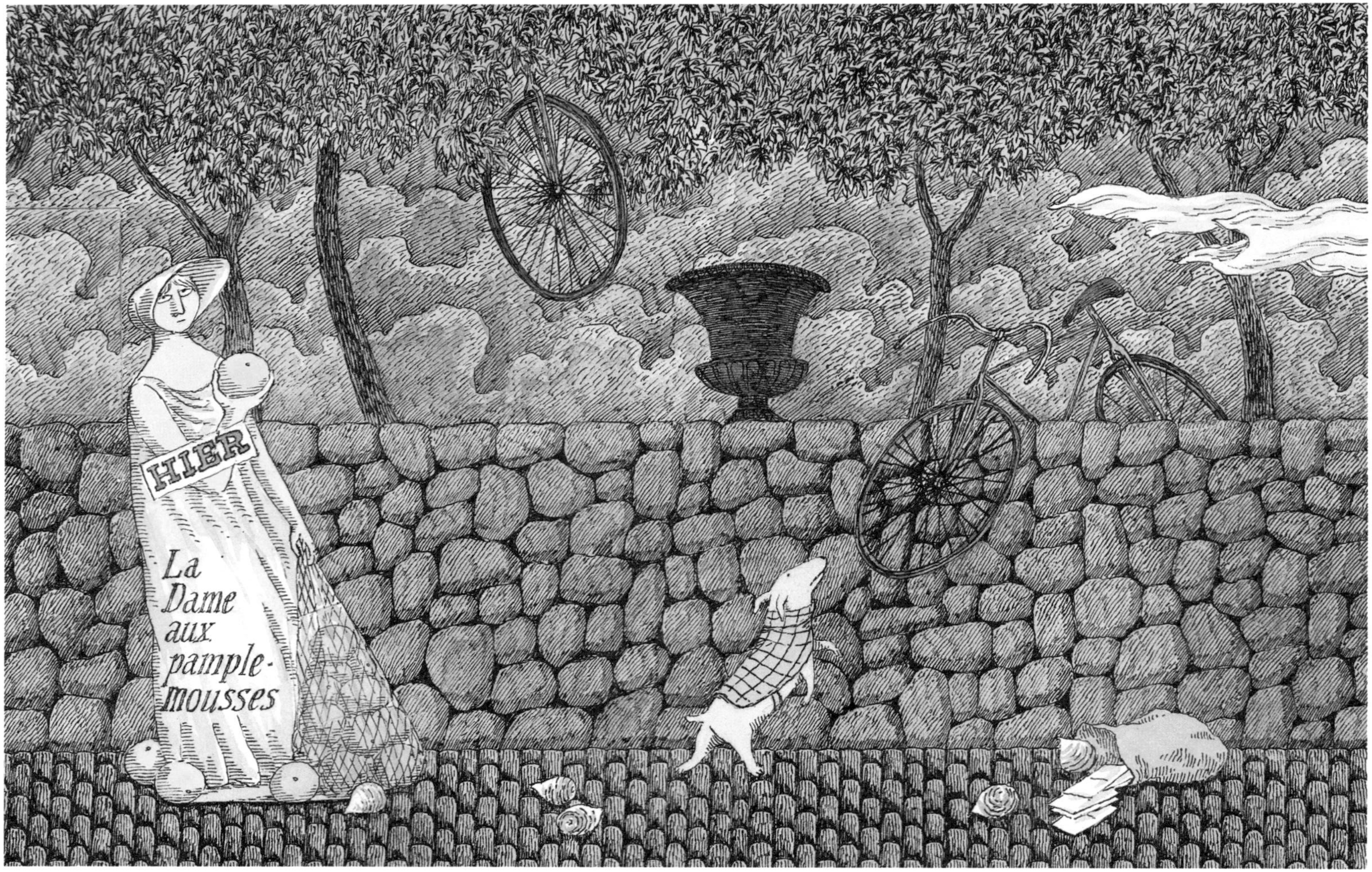
HIER
La Dame aux pample-mousses

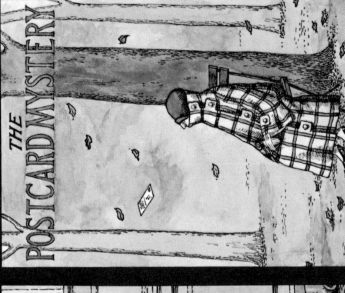

THE
POSTCARD MYSTERY
BY D. AWDREY-GORE

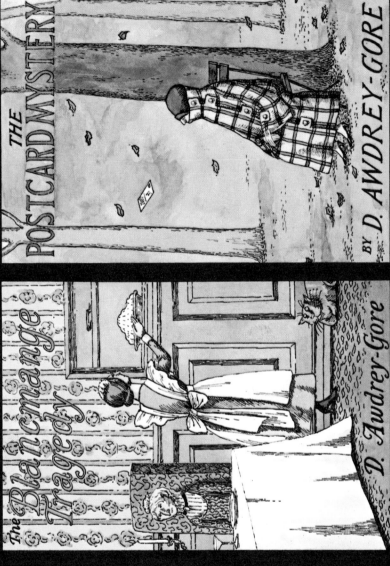

The Blancmange Tragedy

D. Audrey-Gore

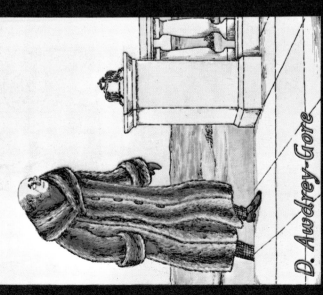

The
Toastrack Enigma

D. Awdrey-Gore

THE AWDREY-GORE LEGACY
EDWARD GOREY

THE PINCUSHION AFFAIR
D. AWDREY-GORE
THE Toothpaste Murder
D. AWDREY-GORE
THE DUSTWRAPPER SECRET
D. AWDREY-GORE

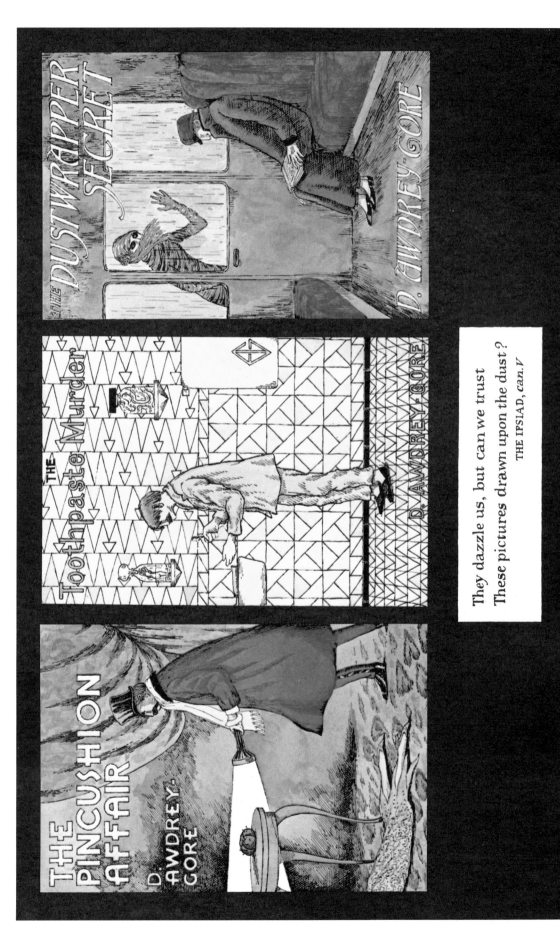

They dazzle us, but can we trust
These pictures drawn upon the dust?
THE IPSIAD, *can.V*

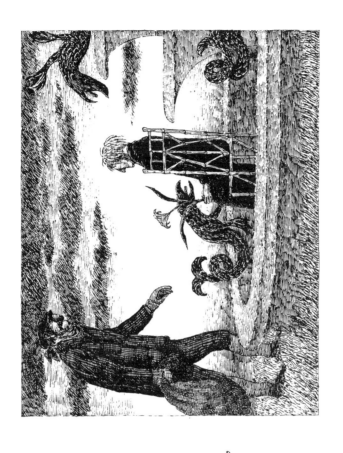

INTRODUCTORY NOTE BY E. G. DEADWORRY

On last St Spasmus's day Miss D. Awdrey-Gore was found dead at the age of 97. Just before dawn a nameless poacher came upon her body in a disused fountain on the estate of Lord Ravelflap; she was seated bolt upright on a gilt ballroom chair, one of a set of seventeen then on display at Suthick & Upter's Auction Rooms in Market Footling; her left hand clutched a painted tin lily of cottage manufacture, inside which was rolled up a Cad's Relish label of a design superseded in 1947; something illegible was pencilled on the back. That she had been murdered was obvious, though as yet the cause of death has not been determined.

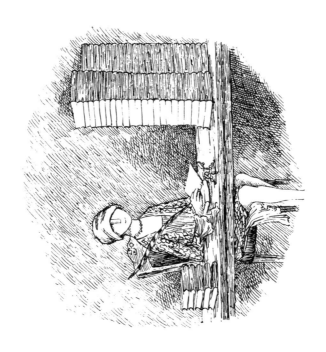

One moment she was sitting there;
The next, she'd vanished into air.
THE IPSIAD, *can.VI*

It will be remembered that Miss Awdrey-Gore was one of the most prolific (*vide our* Two-Shilling Reprint Library) and celebrated writers of detective stories at the time of her unexpected disappearance on St Spasmus's eve in 1927. On various occasions since then, she has been reported (among a number of other possibilities) in a private lunatic asylum, living in Taormina dressed as a man, married to a Salubrian nobleman in Slobgut, or alternately, a garage mechanic in Idle-on-Sea, in religious retreat on the slopes of Kanchenjunga. But always falsely: her whereabouts for the past forty-four years remain unknown.

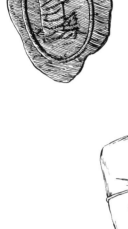

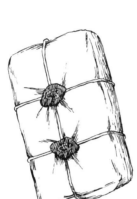

Several days after her reappearance, in a nearby suburban villa an oiled-silk packet came to light beneath the false bottom of an elephant's foot umbrella stand. Done up with mauve string and indigo blue sealing wax, it was addressed to my late grandfather, G. E. Deadworry, then (in 1927) head of Deadworry and Silt, her publishers. The packet's contents in their entirety— though certain things are patently missing— are reproduced on the following pages.

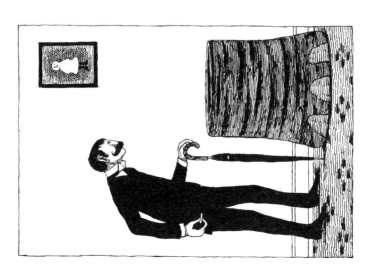

Waredo Dyrge
Half Irish, half Japanese
Has been soldier of fortune and progressive
victim of explosions all over the world
Now England's most sought-after private
detective
Has possibly world's most valuable collection
of artificial hands, many of them given to
him by grateful clients
Will never take up a case on a Tuesday

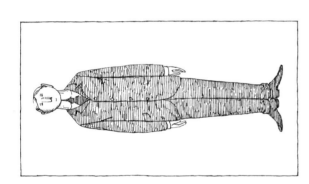

To catch and keep the public's gaze
One must have lots of little ways.
THE IPSIAD, can.IV

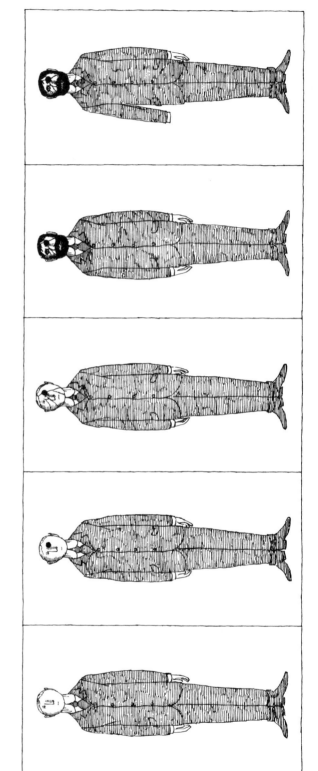

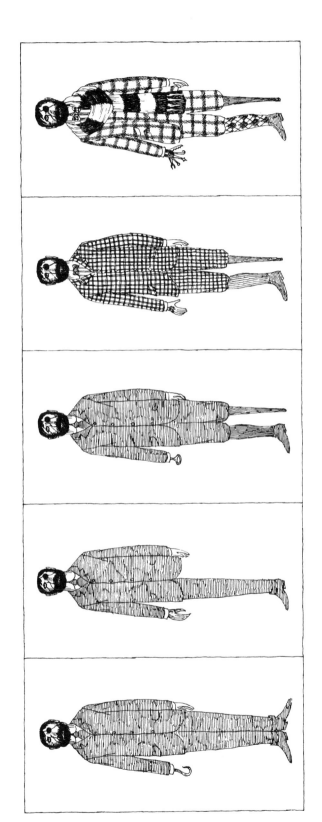

His deductions concerning each case are given in the form of a linked series of haiku in Gaelic of his own composition; each is presented to the reader as it is made in a literal English translation that, while strange and vague in the extreme, turns out to have been perfectly fair and even obvious.

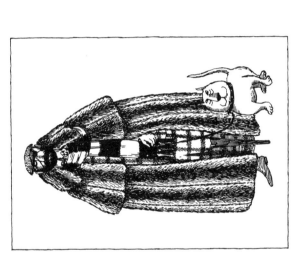

Deary, his inseparable and ferocious companion, is named for his master's favourite reading – the Deary Rewdgo Series for Intrepid Young Ladies (*D.R. on the Great Divide, D.R. in the Yukon, D.R. at Baffin Bay*, etc.) by Dewda Yorger. He is familiar with thirty-seven different hand signals, and has a passionate fondness for Cad's Relish on water biscuits.

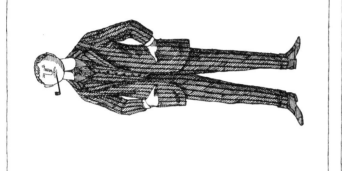

Amateur cricketer/sailor/explorer   Architect   Heir to title and/or estate   Childhood friend

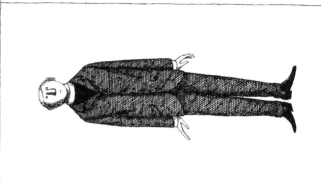

Curate/Vicar/Dean/Bishop   Escaped lunatic   Cousin from Tasmania

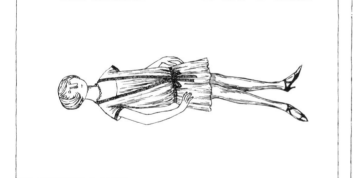

Heroine (if she turns out to be the murderer, have a second with different hair colour)

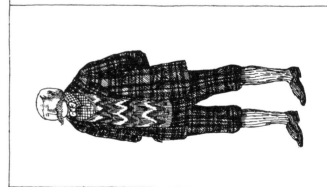

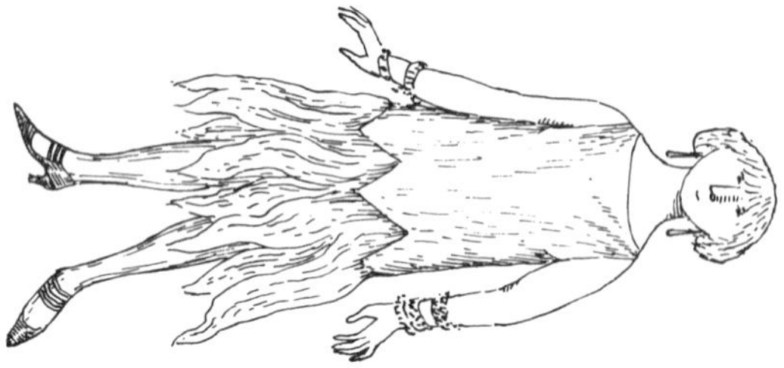

County/not quite county lady   Owner of fabulous jewels   Hostess of weekend house party

Owner of great estate   Local magistrate   Baronet   M.F.H.   Member of Parliament

Of all the people on the scene
Some are betwixt and some
between.

THE IPSIAD, *can. II*

Member of the upper class gone to the bad   Lower class person with a grudge

Duke/Dowager duchess   Village ancient   Superannuated governess/gardener

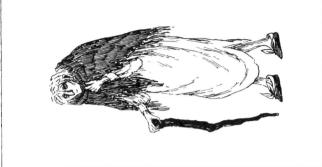

Author of standard work on string figures   Indigent cousin   Axe murderess in forgotten cause *célèbre*

Lady novelist   Lady with passion for Flowers/dogs/other ladies   Scottish cousin

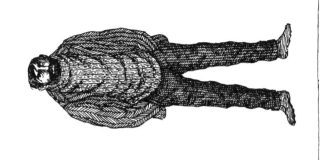

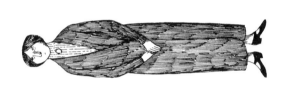

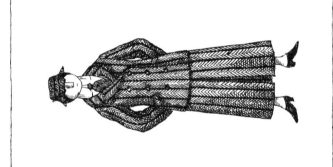

Real/bogus Middle European nobleman   Gigolo   Secret agent for us/them

Unsuccessful poet   Successful interior decorator   Unsuitable friend of heroine/hero

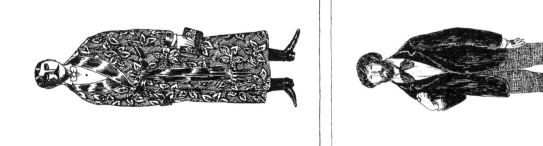

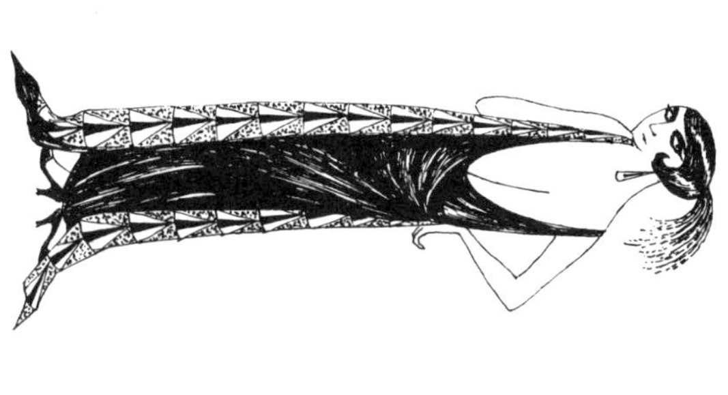

Famous/notorious actress   Unsuitable friend of
hero/heroine   Cousin living at Antibes

The authorities : local / Scotland Yard

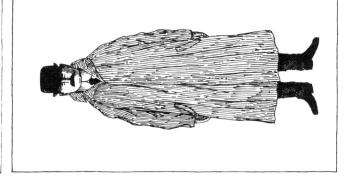

American millionaire   Newspaper proprietor
Prime minister   Condiment tycoon

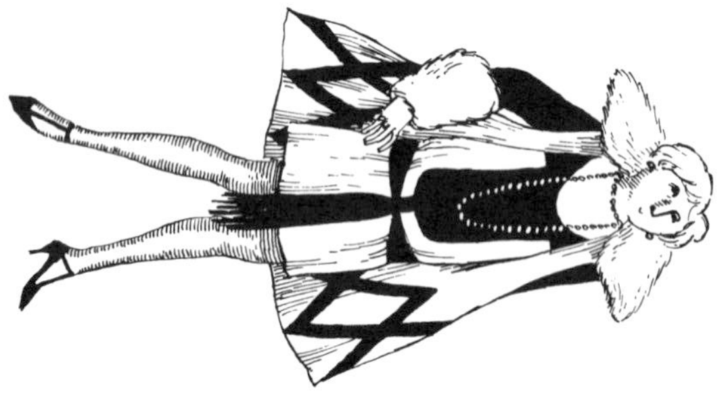

Provincial music-hall star   Owner of fashionable
supper club   Nurse   Cousin by marriage

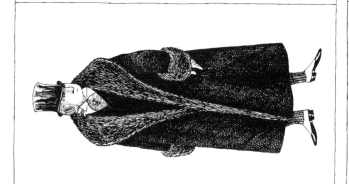

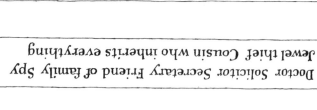

Postmistress   Housekeeper   Seamstress
Companion   Cousin who is retired missionary

Doctor   Solicitor   Secretary   Friend of family   Spy
Jewel thief   Cousin who inherits everything

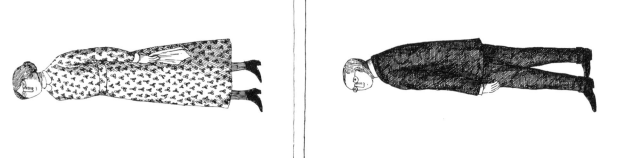

Shell grotto

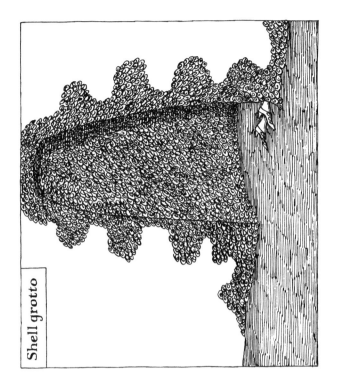

It's most unlikely that his bed
Is where the victim's lying dead.
THE IPSIAD, *Can.III*

Ha-ha

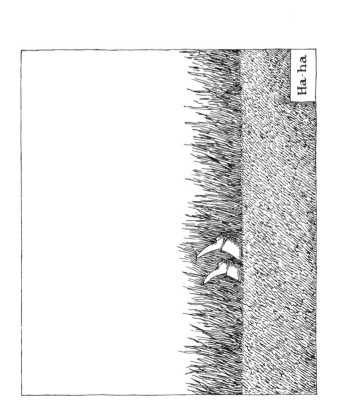

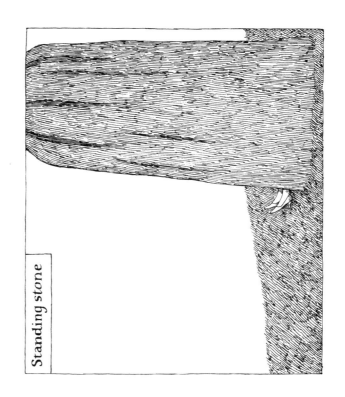

Standing stone

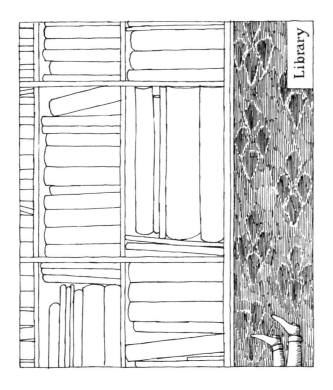

Library

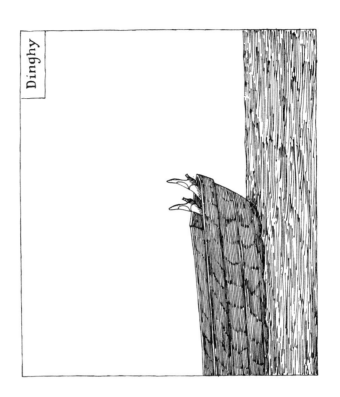

Dinghy

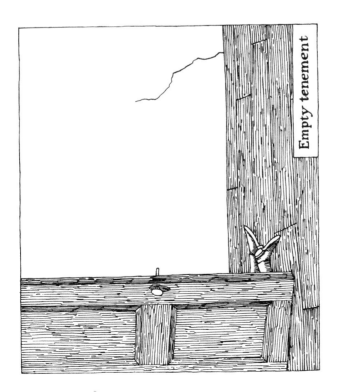

Empty tenement

He was, it's said, somehow done in
With nothing but a safety pin.
THE IPSIAD, can. VI

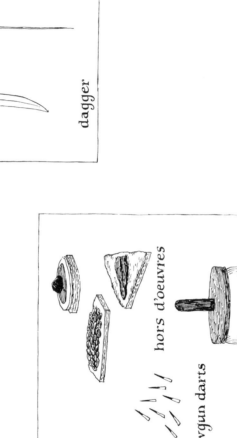

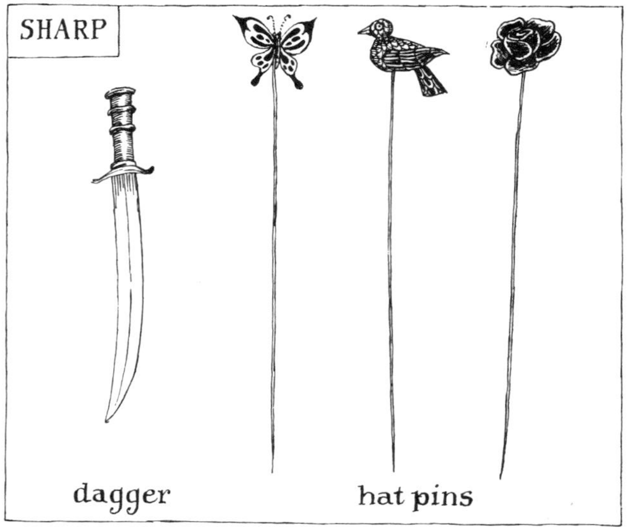

SHARP

hat pins

dagger

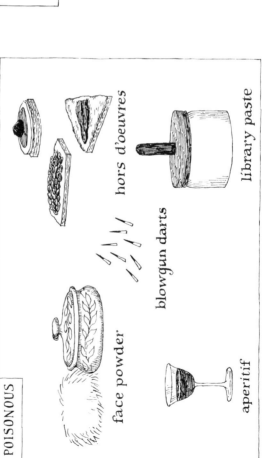

POISONOUS

face powder

blowgun darts

hors d'oeuvres

aperitif

library paste

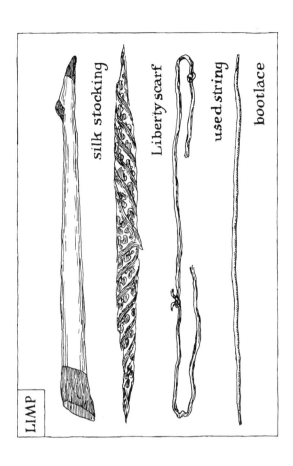

LIMP

silk stocking

Liberty scarf

used string

bootlace

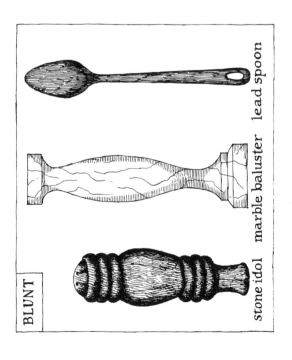

BLUNT

stone idol   marble baluster   lead spoon

GRADUAL

arsenical buns

INSTANTANEOUS

boulder

INEXPLICABLE

confetti

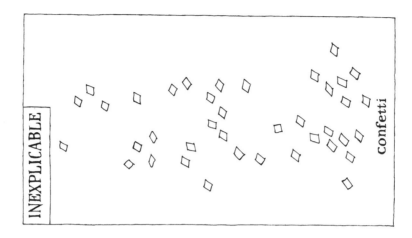

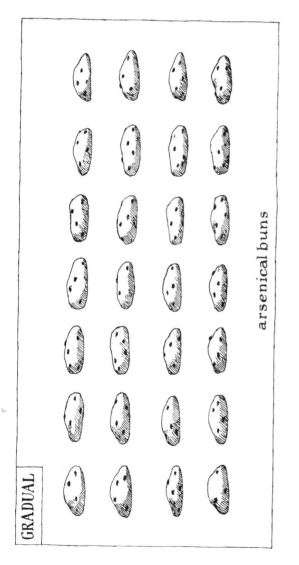

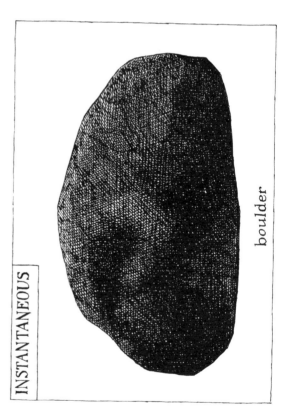

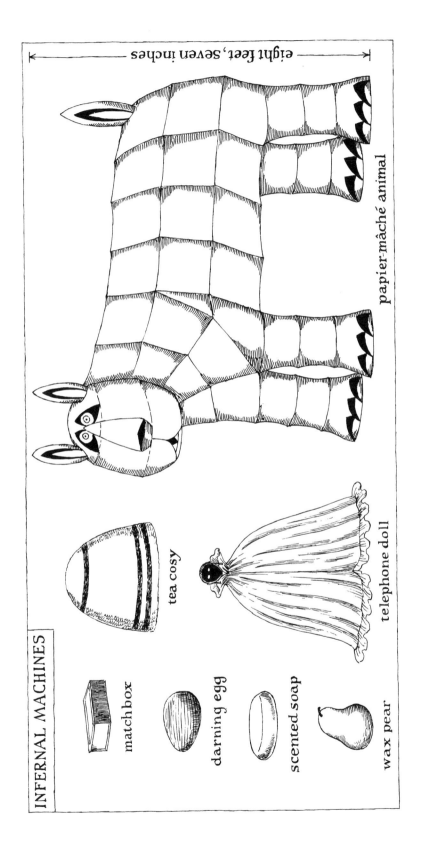

INFERNAL MACHINES

eight feet, seven inches

papier-mâché animal

tea cosy

telephone doll

matchbox

darning egg

scented soap

wax pear

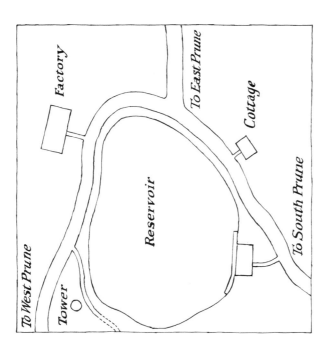

The crucial information can
Be hidden in a simple plan.
THE IPSIAD, *can.* VIII

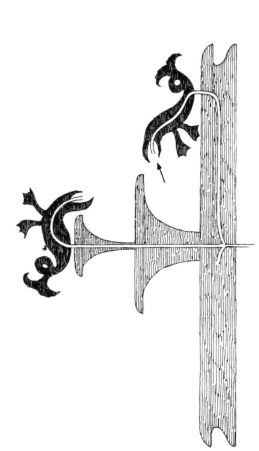

Cross section of fountain from west showing faulty pipe

To West Prune
Tower
Factory
Reservoir
To East Prune
Cottage
To South Prune

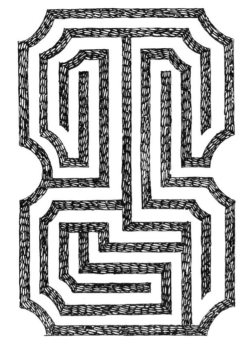

The labyrinth at 4:09 when Harold Tyne-Forque gave up trying to reach its heart

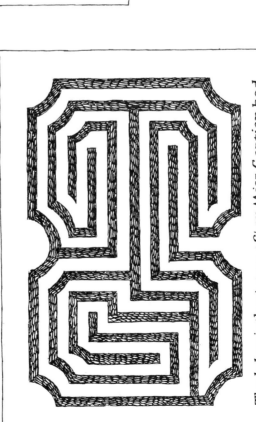

The labyrinth at 3:27 after Miss Gentian had successfully found her way in and back

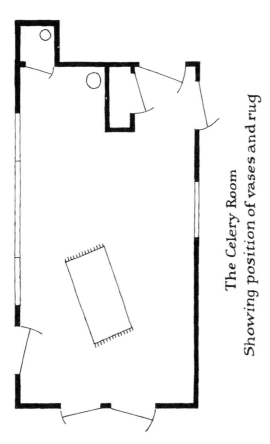

The Celery Room
Showing position of vases and rug

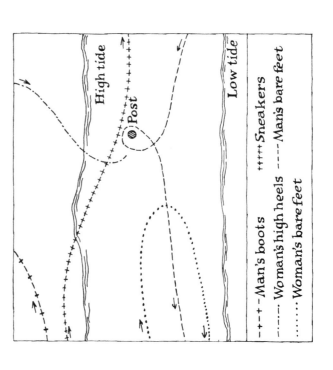

High tide

Post

Low tide

+ + + – Man's boots   +++++ Sneakers
—···— Woman's high heels   – – – – Man's bare feet
············ Woman's bare feet

A
24
H
9²
9¹
7
13
8
R
Jan. 11

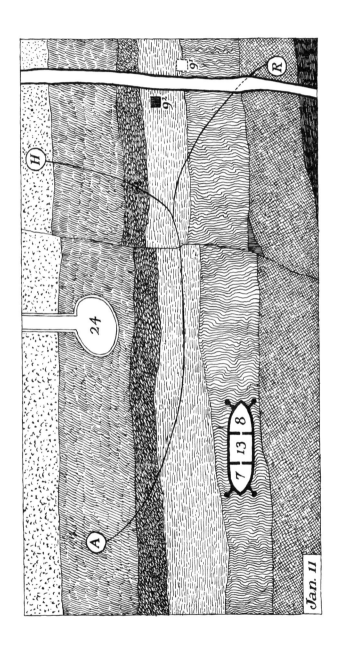

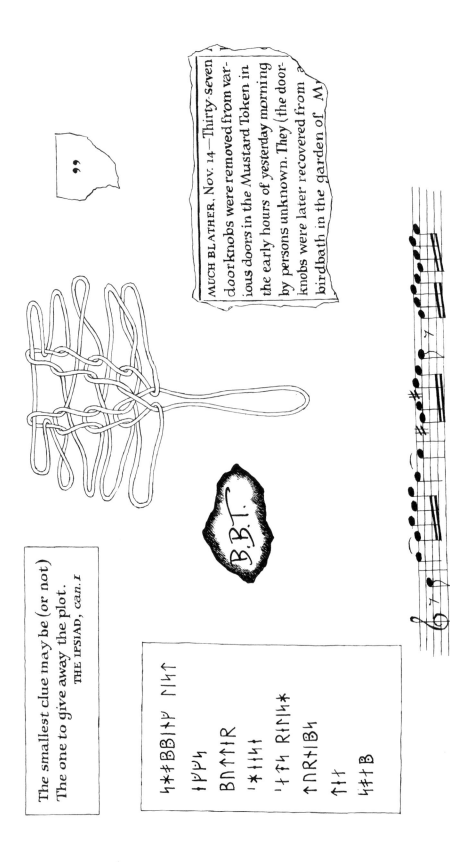

The smallest clue may be (or not)
The one to give away the plot.
THE IPSIAD, *can. 1*

MUCH BLATHER. Nov. 14—Thirty-seven doorknobs were removed from various doors in the Mustard Token in the early hours of yesterday morning by persons unknown. They (the door-knobs were later recovered from a birdbath in the garden of M

P.T.O.
Nº 704G

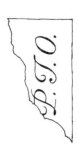

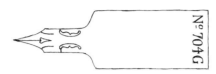

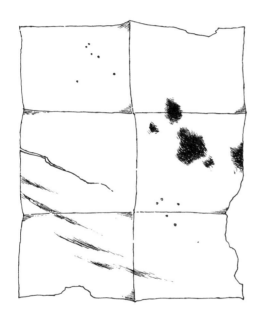

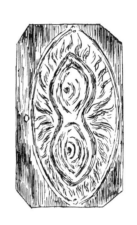

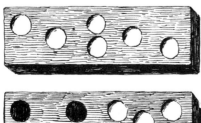

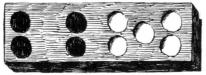

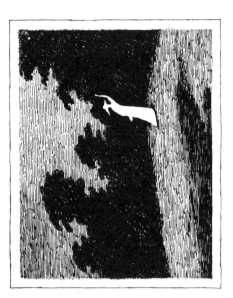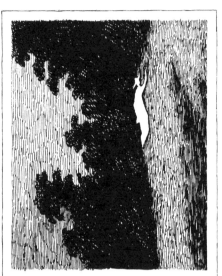

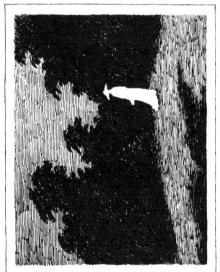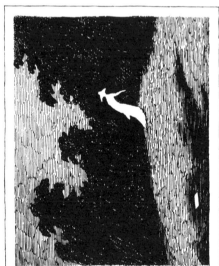

On the 14th of January, was
the 'Larks Sandorga', was
still off the coast of Iceland

What the murderer failed
to realize is that
Grumbletch's salts
are not soluble in
lemonade

Lady Trudi _____ is
_____ really two entirely different
people

What the murderer failed
to realize is that
at high tide the outermost
of Saint Loolai Rocks
is completely submerged

At 11.17 the door to the
winter garden _____ was
already locked and bolted

James Grumesdoul _____ and
Charles Trost
really the same person

What the murderer failed
to realize is that
the Great Northwest
Road does not go
beyond Little Remorse

George Utmost is really
not Daphne Soot _____'s
cousin from Wyoming

Perhaps it might be even subtler
If after all it was the butler.
THE IPSIAD, can. IX

What the murderer failed
to realize is that
there is no Number
Fourteen, Bandage
Terrace

Lola Trope _____ is really
Lord Onion _____'s
great grand-daughter

What the murderer failed
to realize is that
yellow stitchbane
is not yellow at all,
but a pale mauve

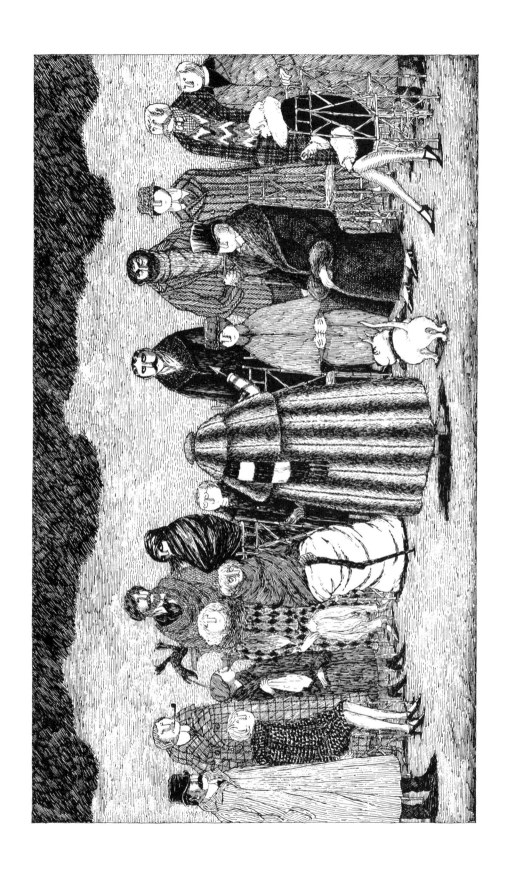

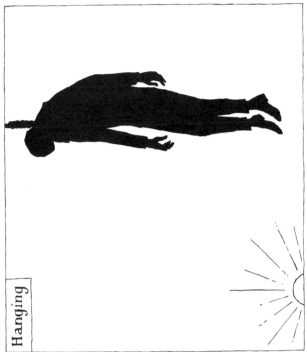

Hanging

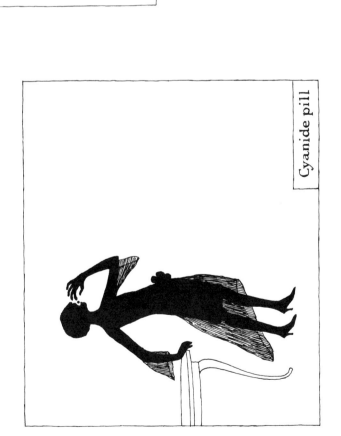

Cyanide pill

The guilty found, there's little wait
Before they're overcome by fate.
THE IPSIAD, *can.xiii*

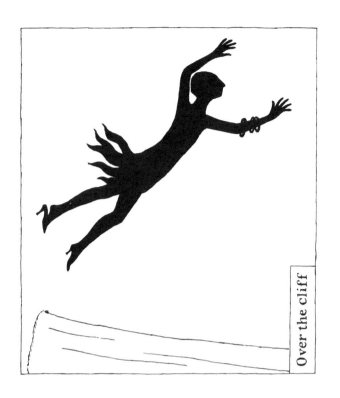

Over the cliff

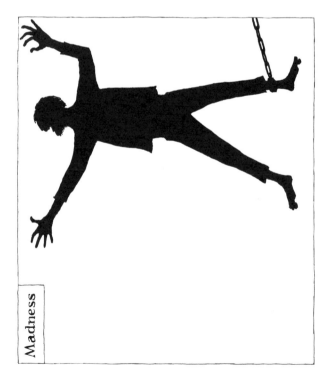

Madness

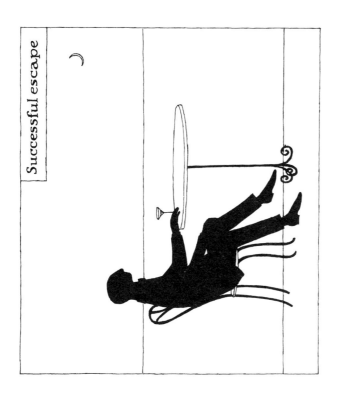

Successful escape

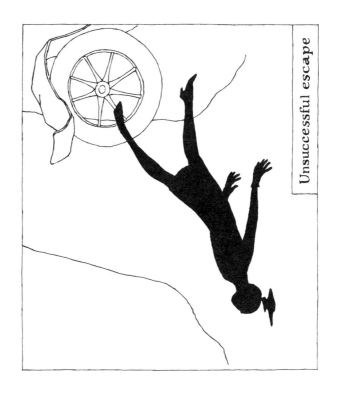

Unsuccessful escape

And what if then we don't find out
What all of it has been about?

THE IPSIAD, *can.XI*

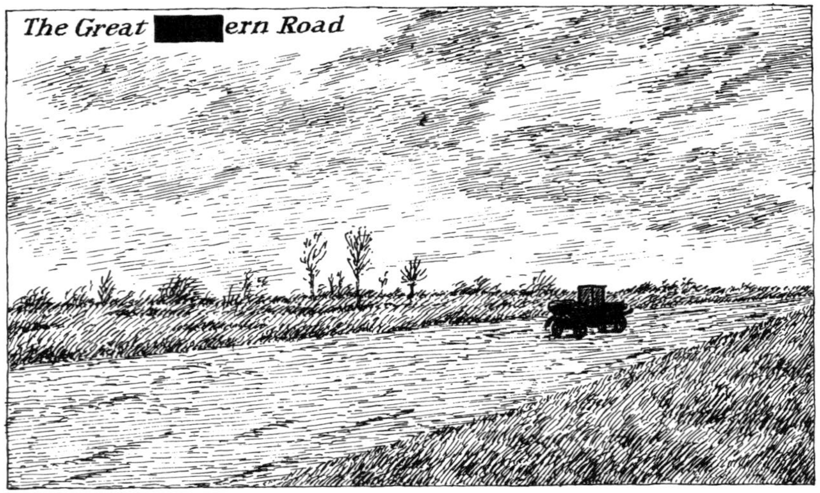
The Great [redacted]ern Road

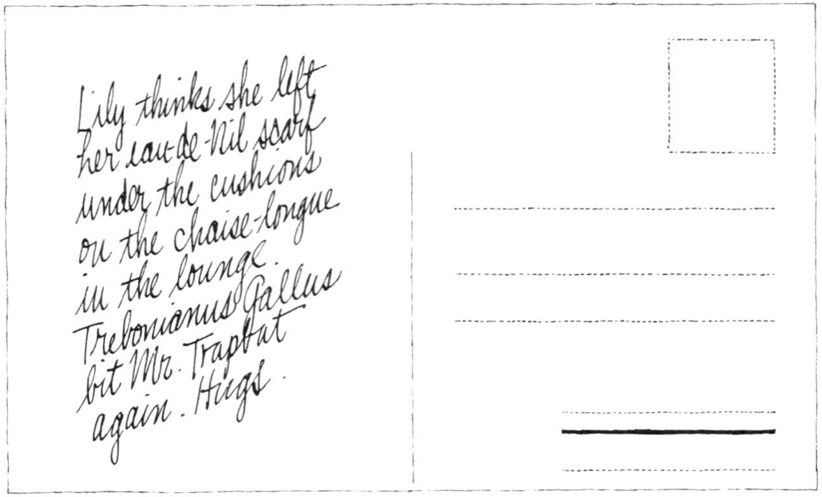
Lily thinks she left
her eau-de-Nil scarf
under the cushions
on the chaise-longue
in the lounge.
Trebonianus Gallus
bit Mr. Trapbat
again. Hugs.

These postcards recently fell out of a discarded lending-library copy of *The Teacosy Crime*, perhaps Miss Awdrey-Gore's most popular work. It will be noticed they were never sent, or, for that matter, even addressed.

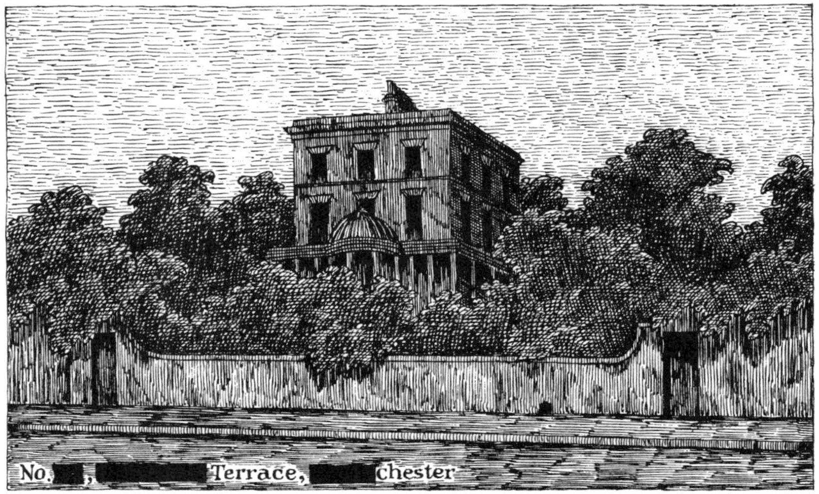
No.[redacted], [redacted] Terrace, [redacted]chester

Post card Carte postale Postkarte Cartolina postale
Dopisnice Открытое письмо Levelező-Lap Briefkaart.

Send at once recipe for plaice with thyme.

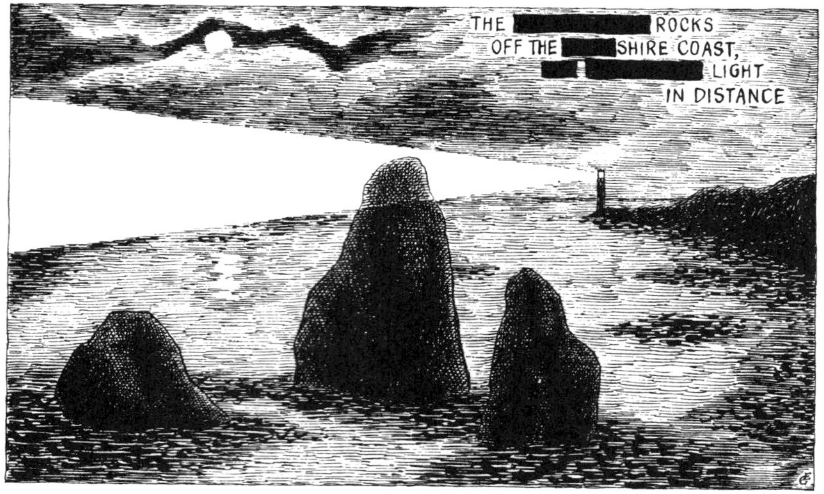
THE [redacted] ROCKS
OFF THE [redacted] SHIRE COAST,
[redacted] LIGHT
IN DISTANCE

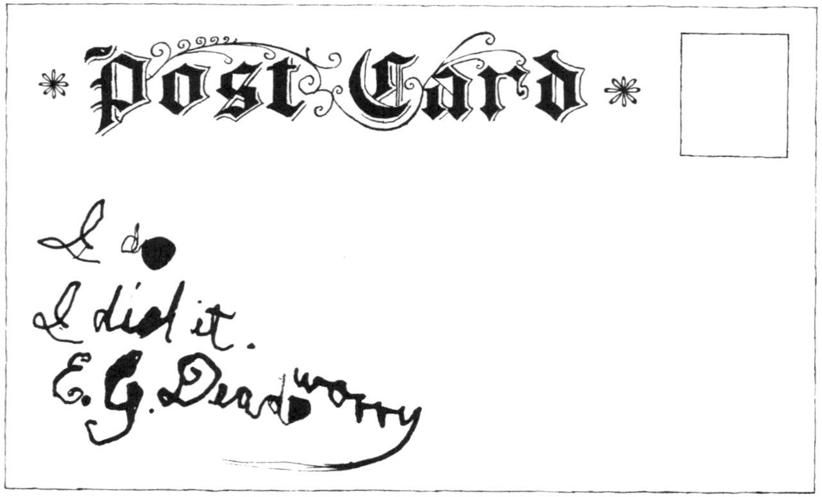
Post Card
I do
I did it.
E. G. Deadworry

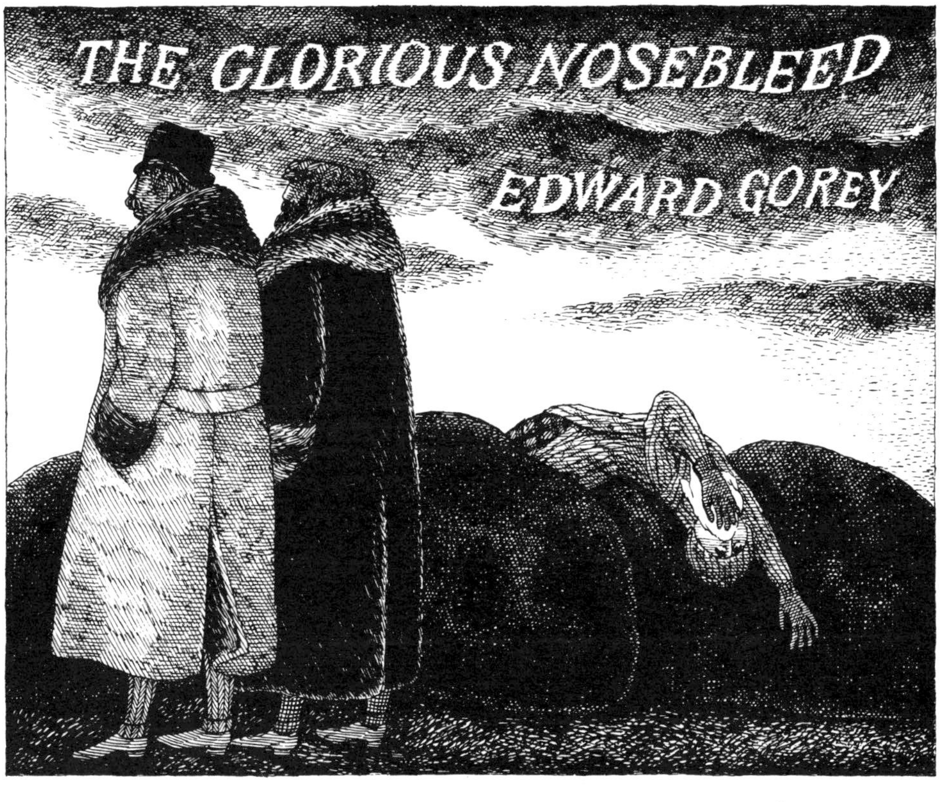
THE GLORIOUS NOSEBLEED
EDWARD GOREY

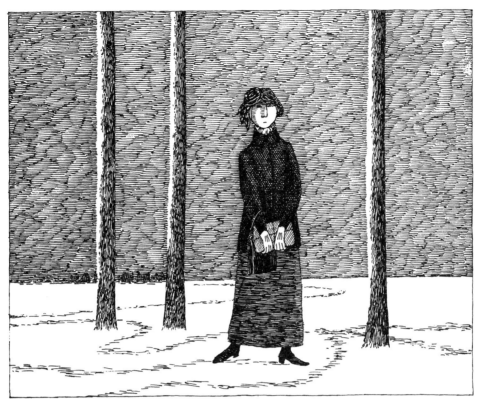

She wandered among the trees Aimlessly.

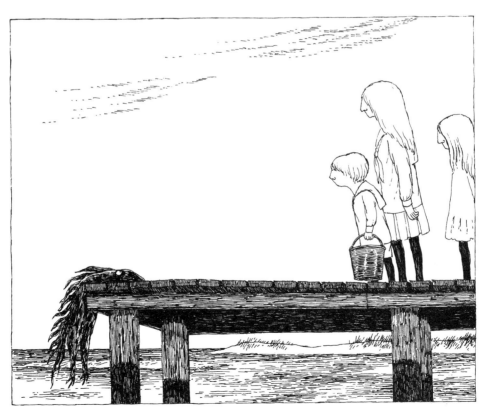

The creature regarded them Balefully.

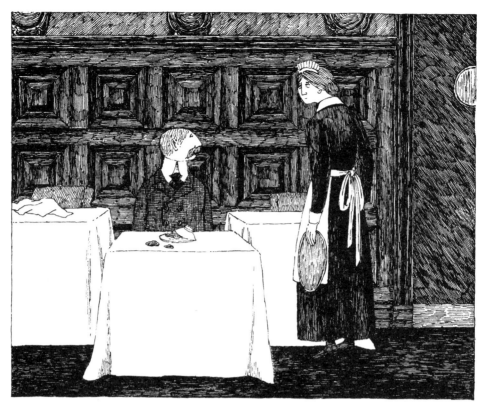

The pudding was served Clumsily.

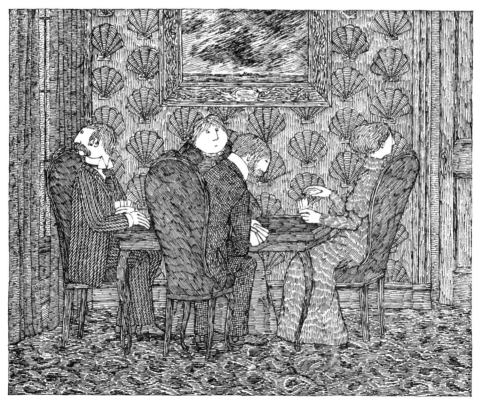

They played whist Distractedly.

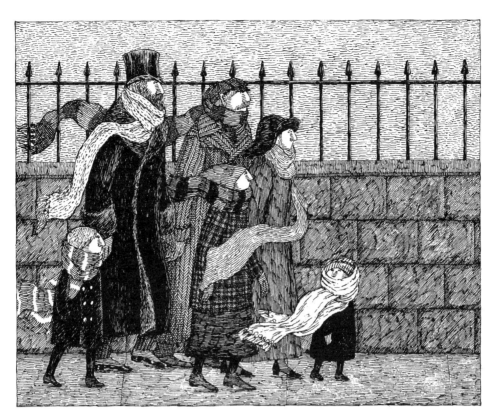

She knitted mufflers Endlessly.

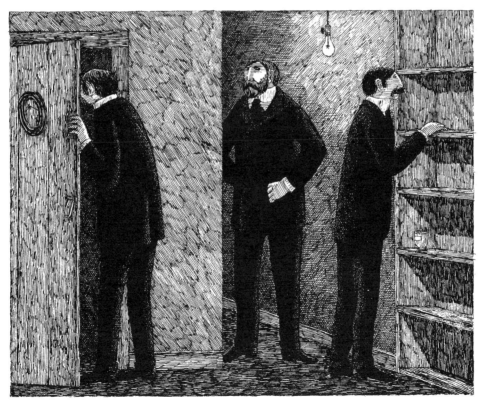

They searched the cellars Fruitlessly.

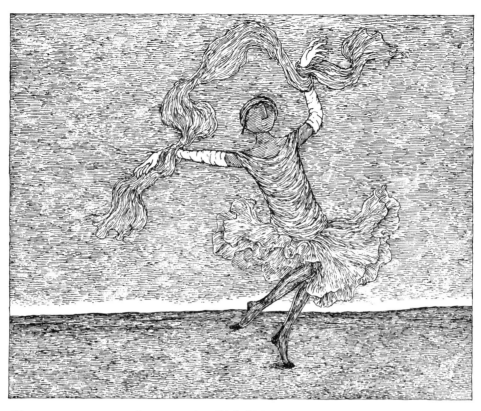

She danced on the sands Giddily.

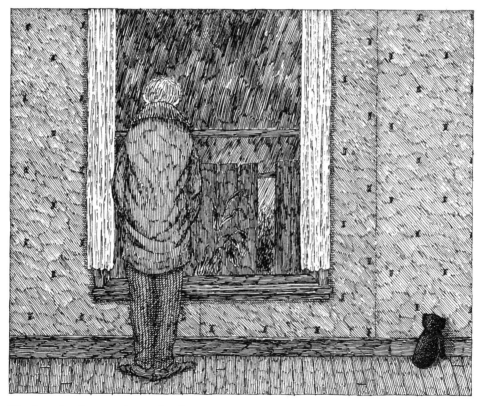

He looked out the window Hopelessly.

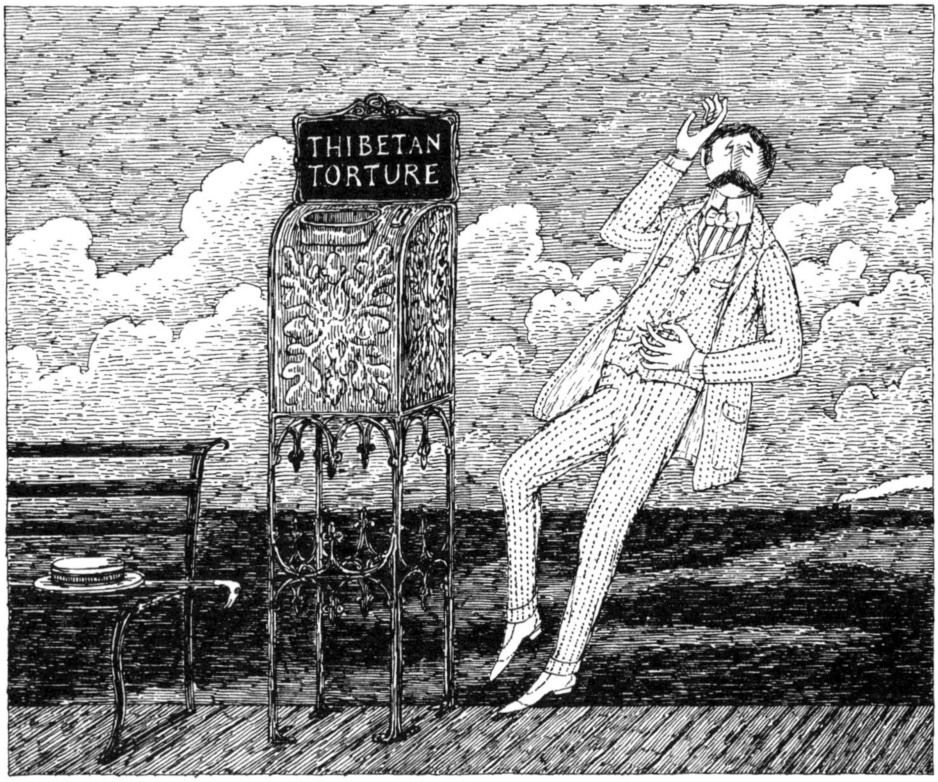
THIBETAN
TORTURE

He fell off the pier Inadvertently.

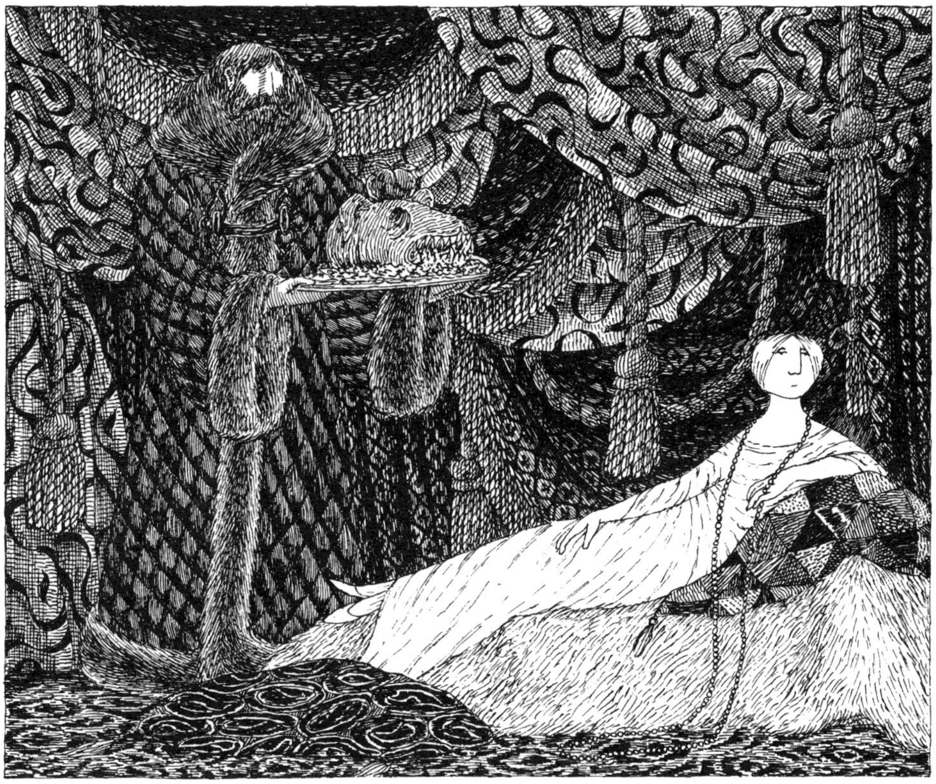

She toyed with her beads Jadedly.

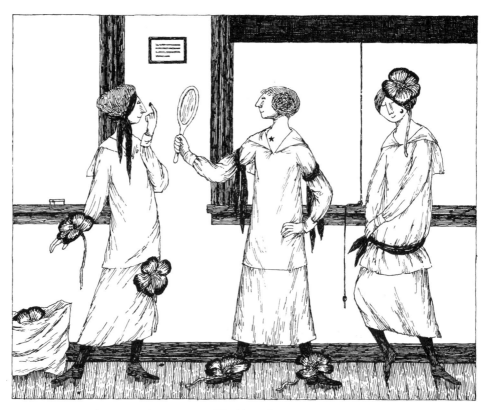

They got themselves up Killingly.

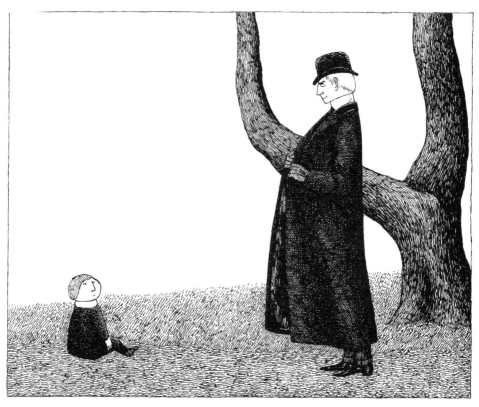

He exposed himself Lewdly.

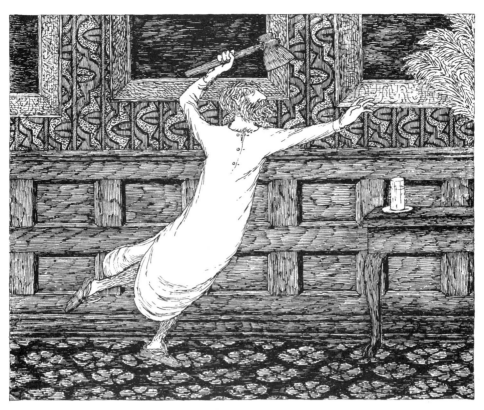

He ran through the hall Maniacally.

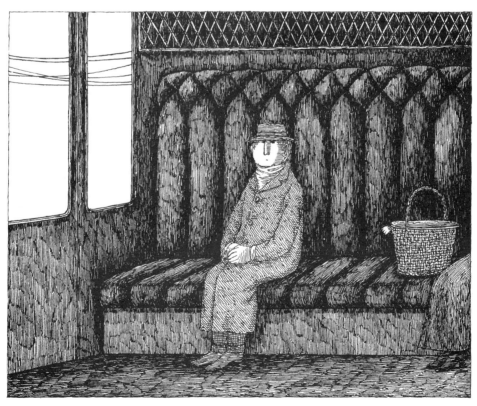

He sat in the train Numbly.

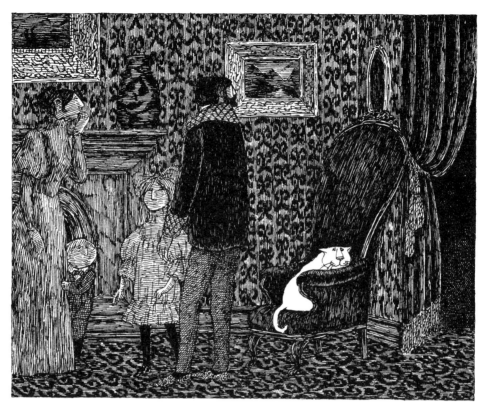

The doorbell rang Ominously.

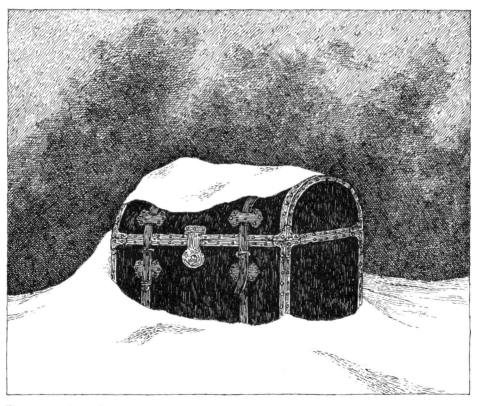

It was in the trunk Presumably.

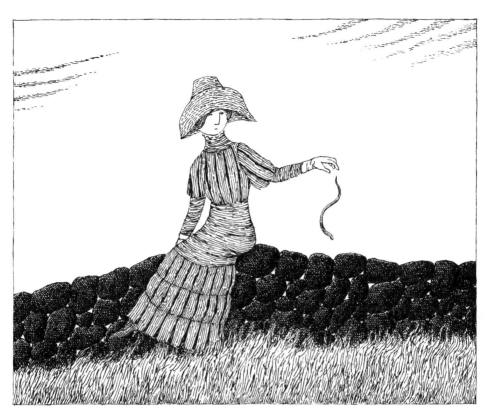

She let go of it Quickly.

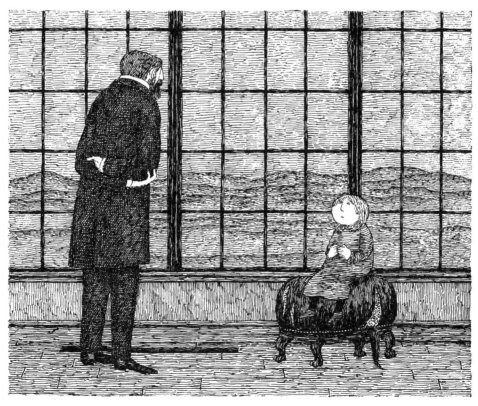

He spoke to the child Repressively.

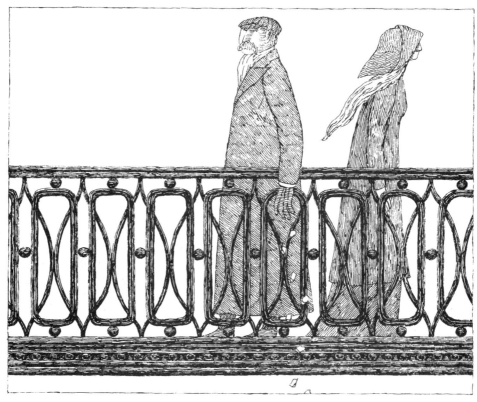

He disposed of the fragments Slyly.

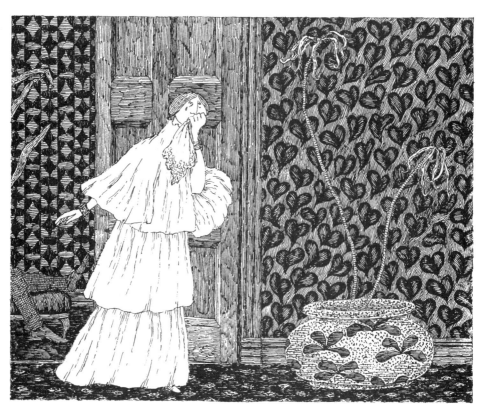

She ran out of the room Tearfully.

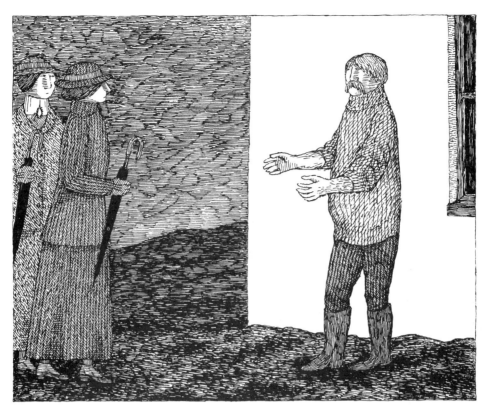

He explained himself Unconvincingly.

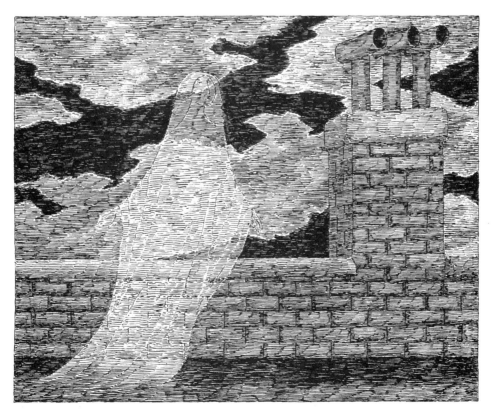

She appeared on the roof Vapourously.

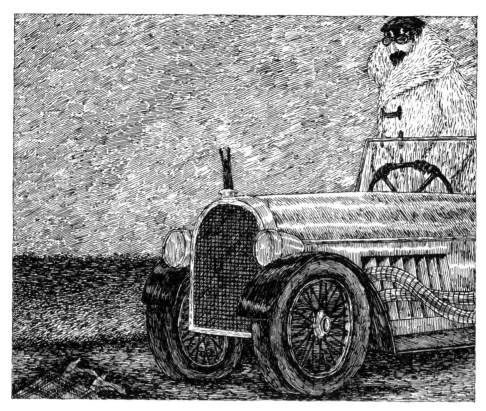

He struck her down Wilfully.

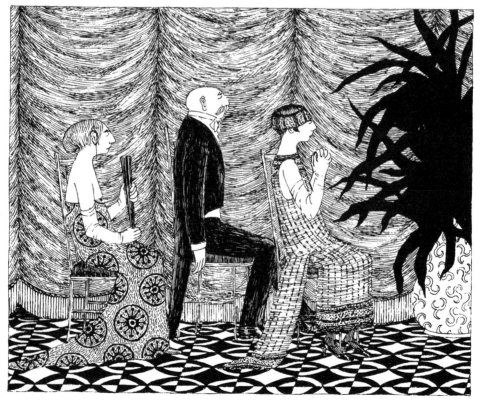

The piece was sung eXcruciatingly.

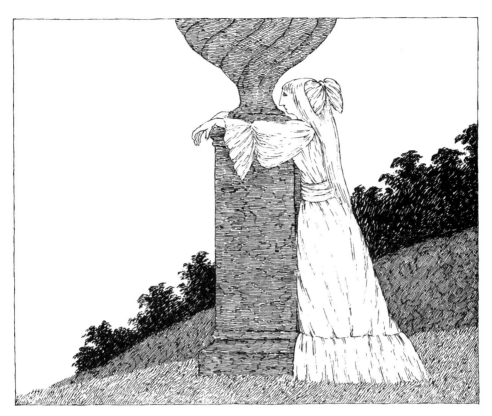

She watched him go Yearningly.

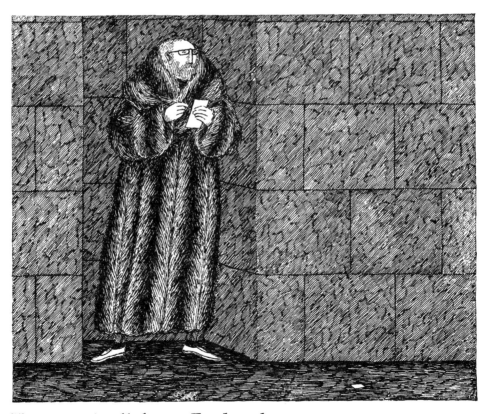

He wrote it all down Zealously.

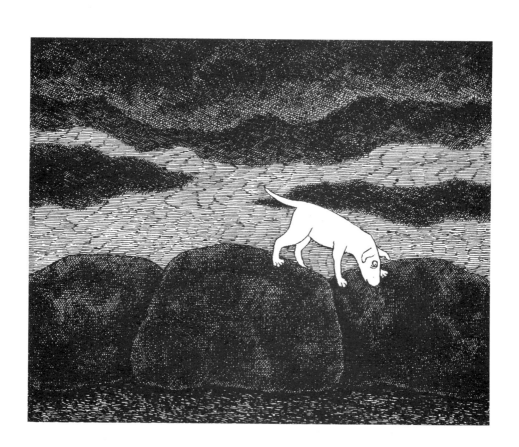

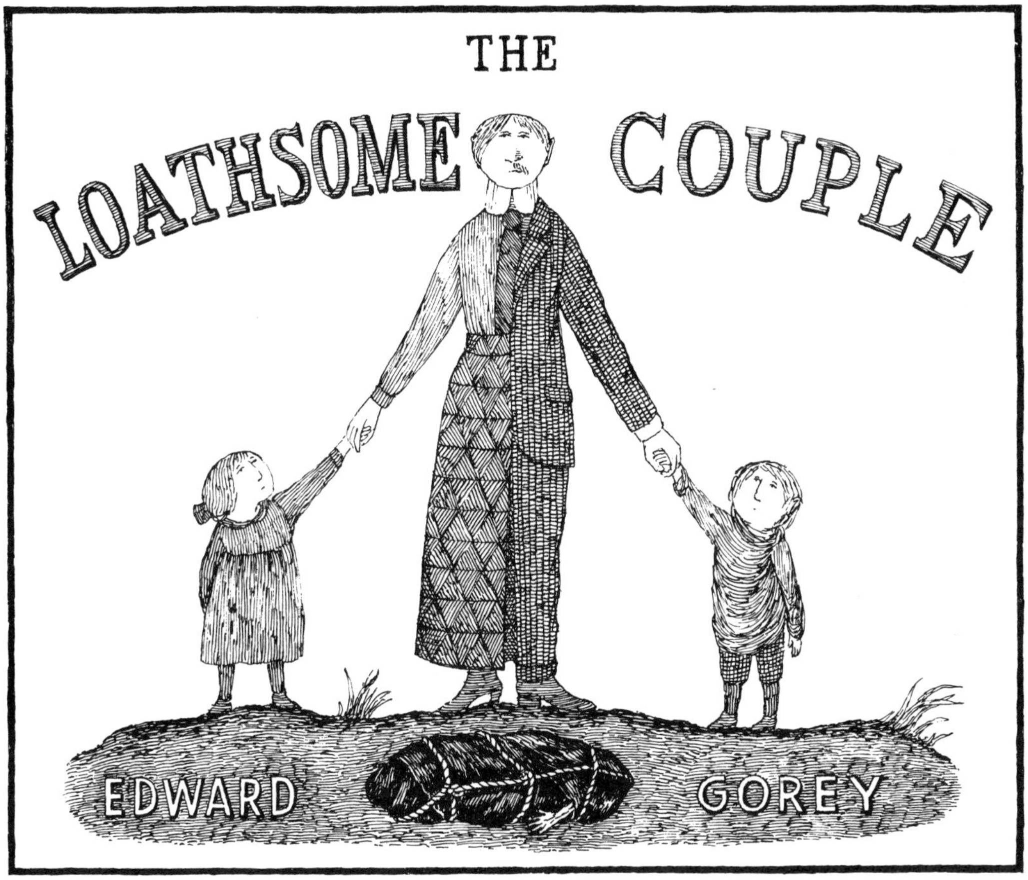
THE
LOATHSOME COUPLE
EDWARD GOREY

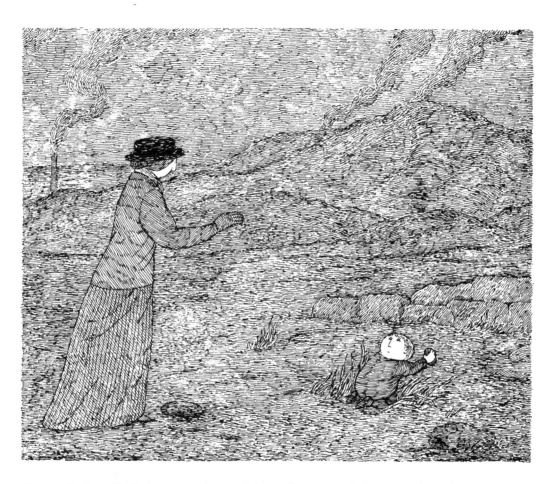

Harold Snedleigh was found beating a sick small animal
to death with a rock when he was five years old.

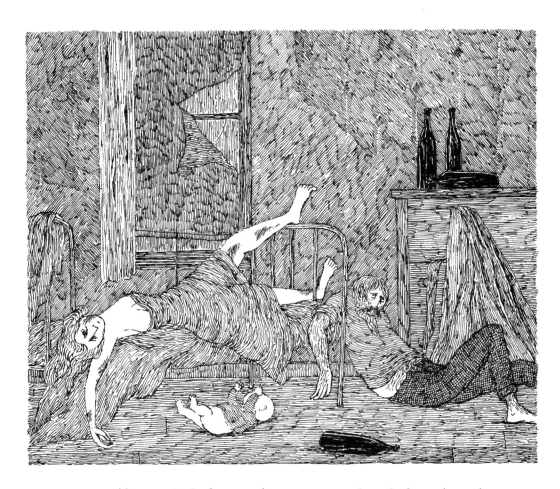

That year Mona Gritch was born to a pair of drunkards.

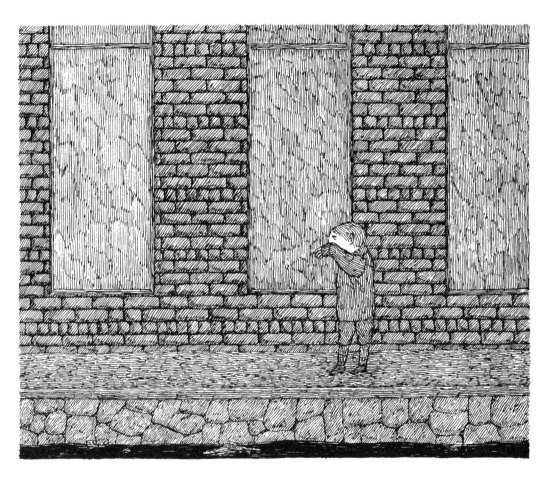

By the time he was twelve Harold had caught the cold that afterwards never left him.

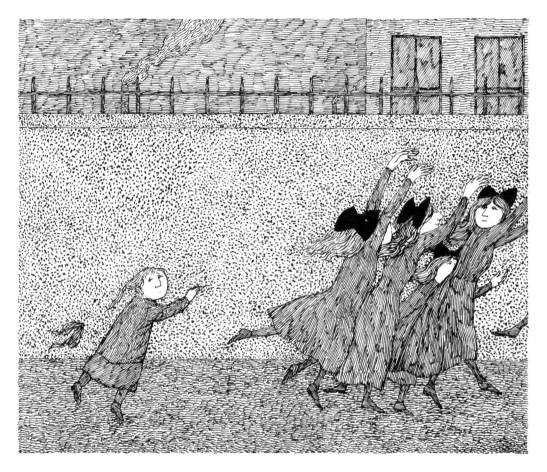

As a child Mona already had thick ankles and thin hair.

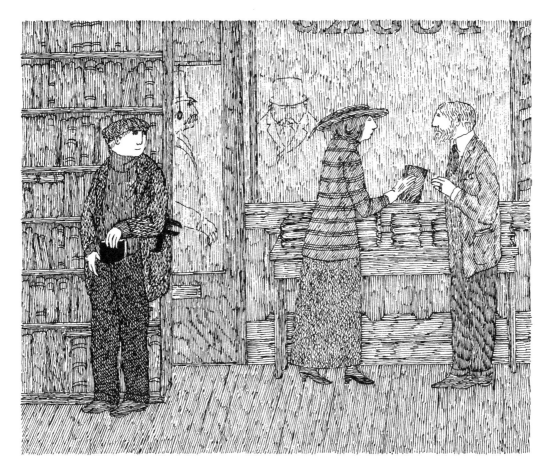

After leaving school Harold went to work in a plumber's office,
and stole curiosa from booksellers whenever he got the chance.

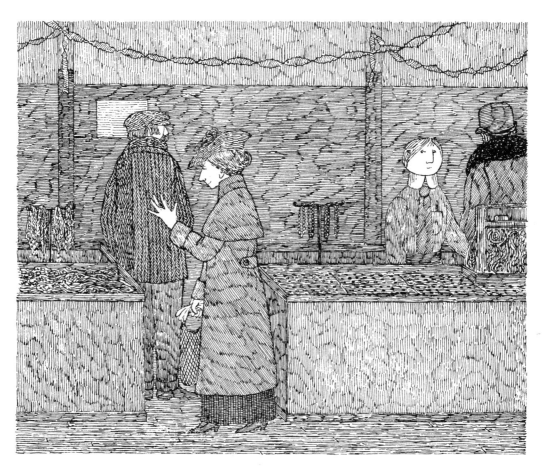

Mona was employed behind the jewelry counter in a five-and-ten, amusing herself by loosening settings with a nailfile so the stones would fall out soon after purchase.

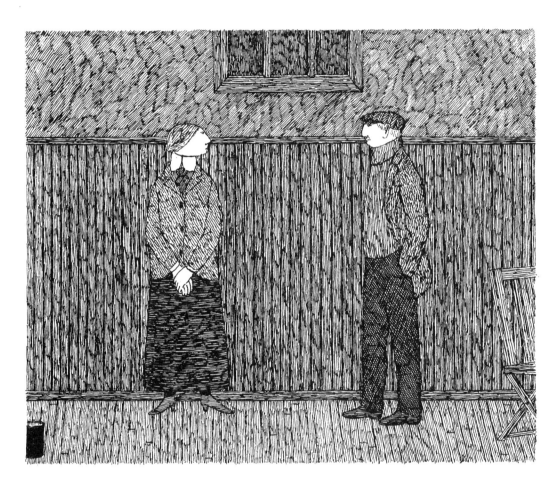

The two met at a Self-Help Institute lecture on the Evils of the Decimal System, and immediately recognized their affinity.

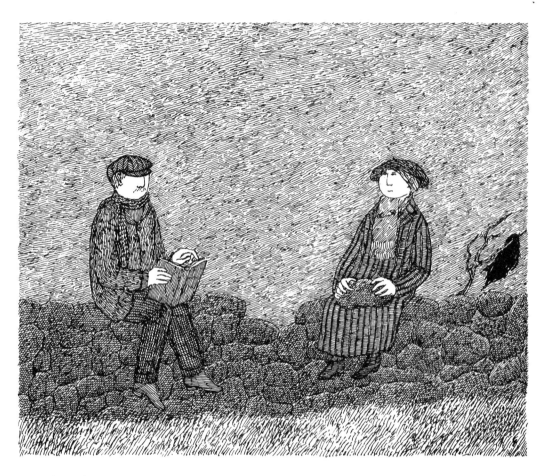

On Sundays they took long walks together, and Harold would bring one of his books.

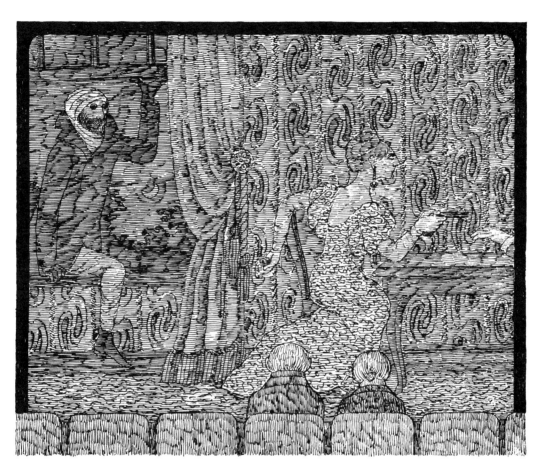

They went to the local cinema whenever there was a crime
film playing.

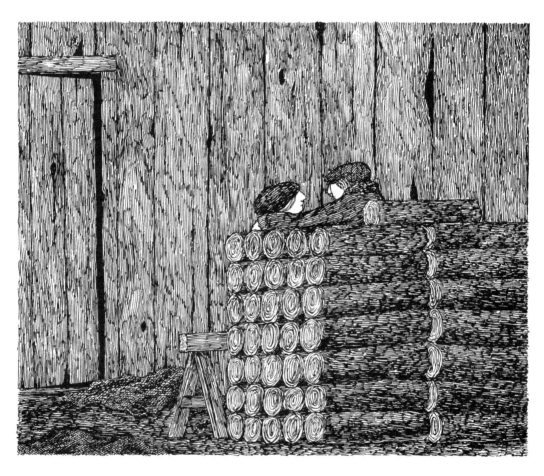

Following one particularly exciting one, they fumbled with
each other in a cold woodshed.

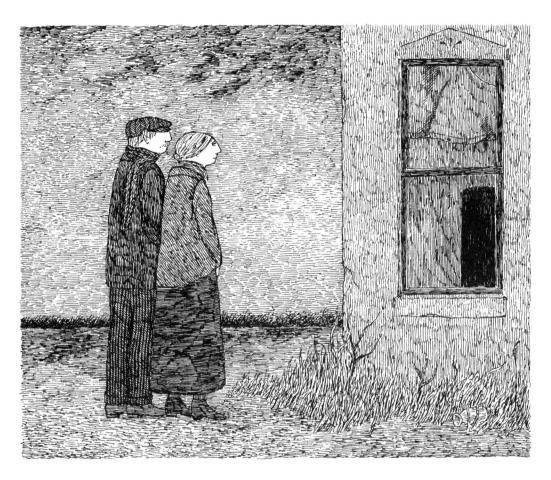

After several years they secretly rented a remote and
undesirable villa.

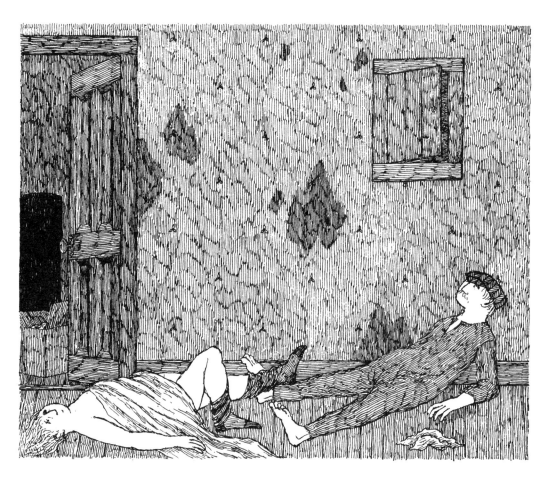

When they tried to make love, their strenuous and
prolonged efforts came to nothing.

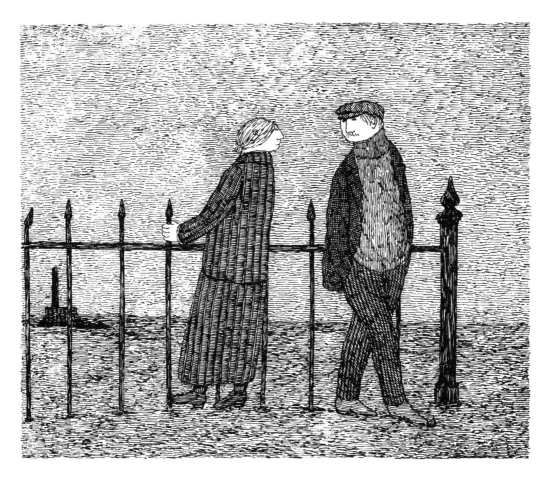

In the autumn of that year they decided to embark upon their life's work.

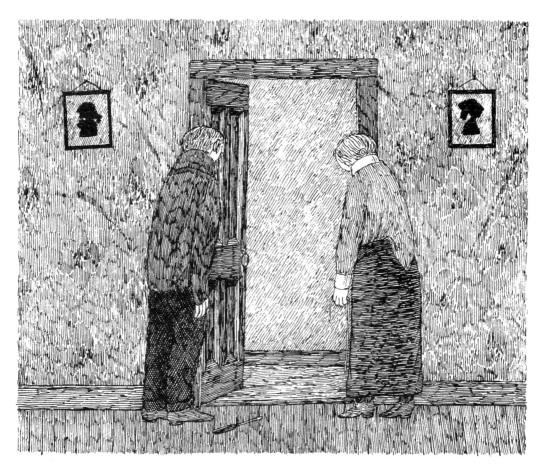

Months later, after many complicated preparations, they felt at last they were ready.

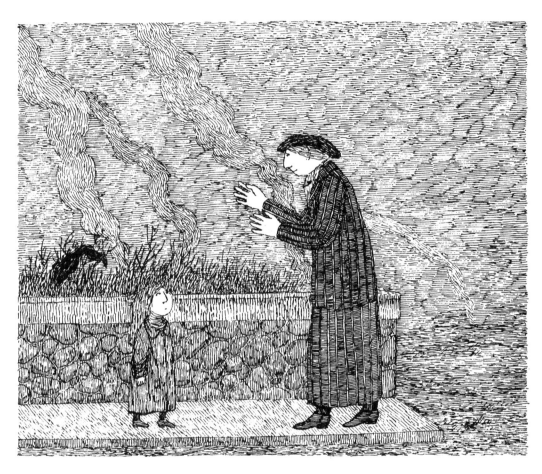

Mona lured a little girl named Eepie Carpetrod to the villa
with promises of a doll wearing a green satin frock.

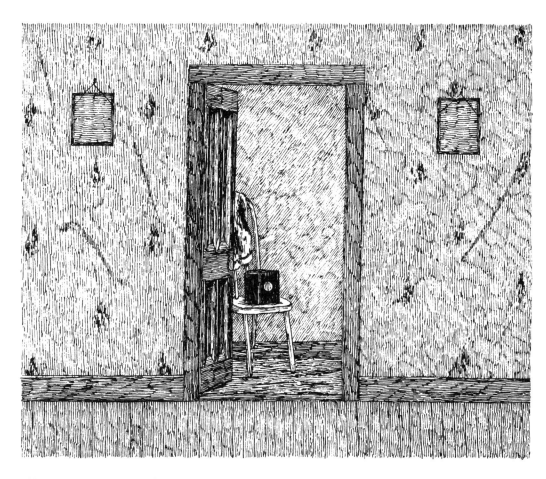

They spent the better part of the night murdering the
child in various ways.

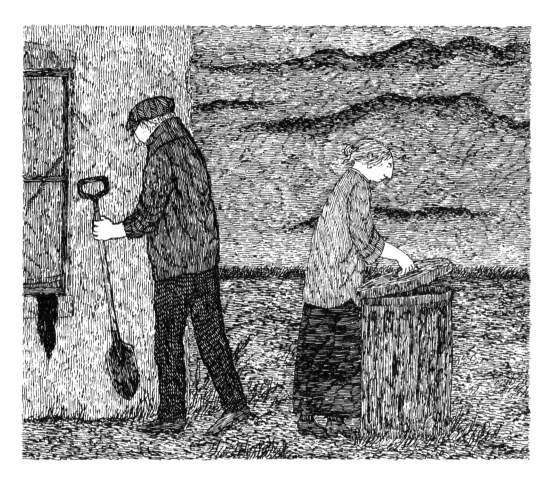

By twilight of the next day the body was buried and
the mess cleaned up.

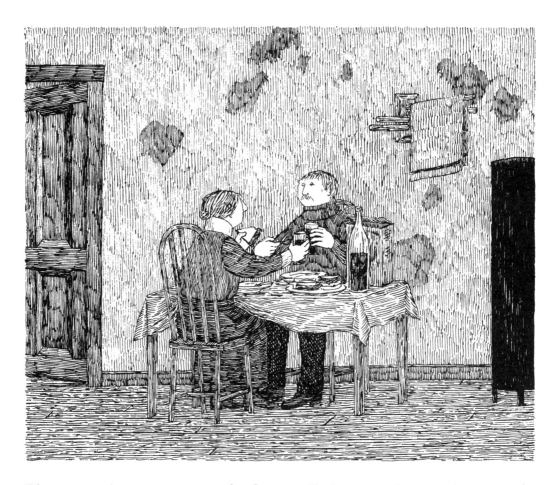

They sat down to a meal of cornflakes and treacle, turnip sandwiches, and artificial grape soda.

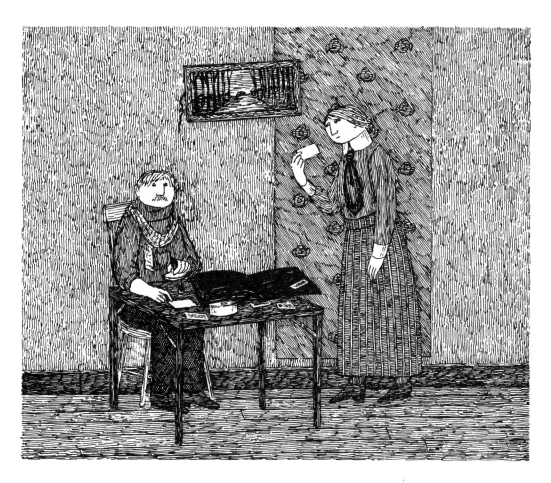

The pictures Mona had taken did not come out very well, being underexposed, but they put them in the new album they had bought anyway.

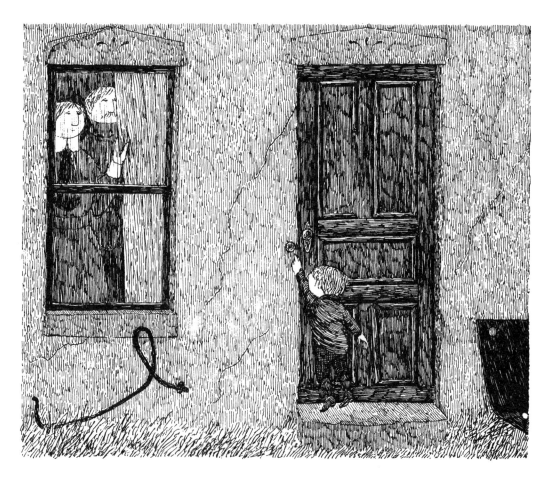

Over the next two years they killed three more children,
but it was never as exhilarating as the first one had been.

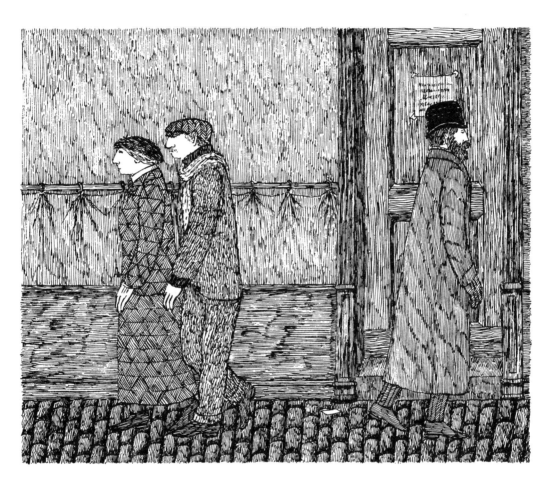

For no very good reason their activities remained unsuspected.

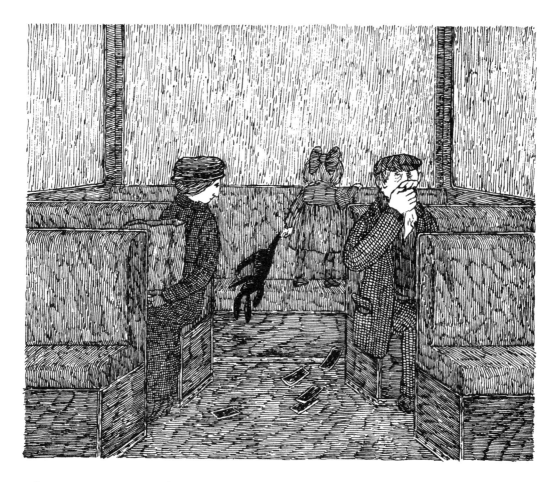

Then one day in April some snapshots fell out of Harold's pocket on a tram.

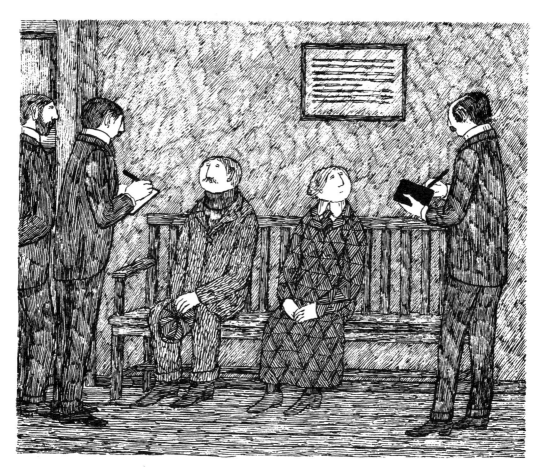

At times they said they had done it all, but other times
they denied everything.

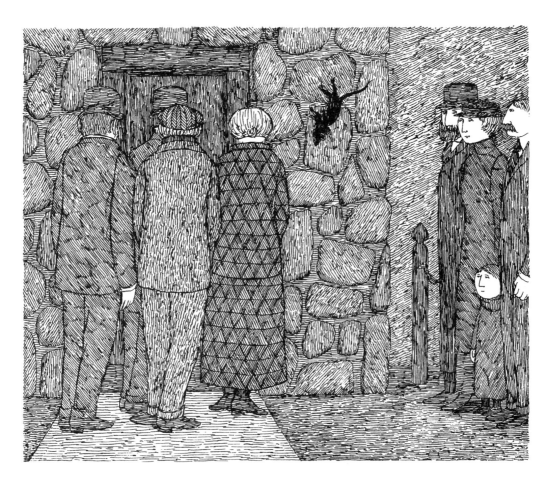

Someone threw a putrescent rat in Mona's face as she
was being taken into the building where the court was.

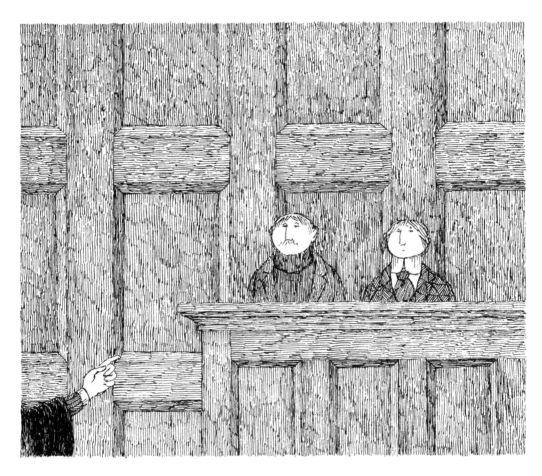

The trial went on and on with both of them sunk in apathy.

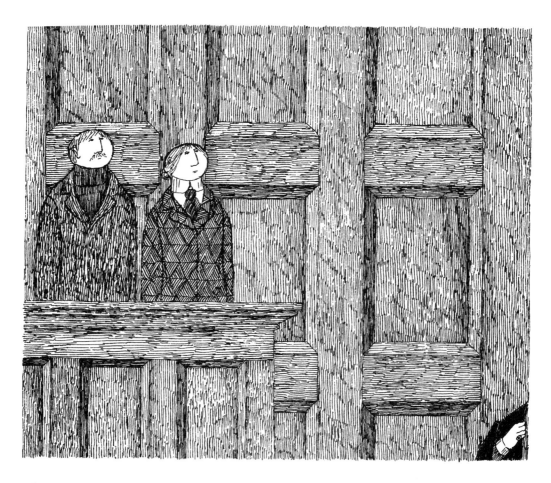

They were found guilty but insane.

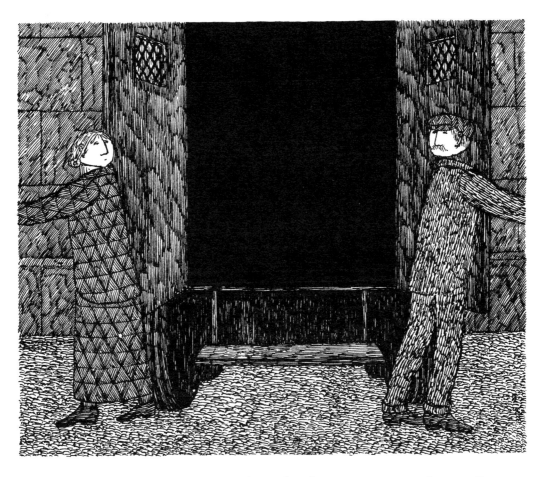

They were taken to the asylum in the same van but after
that they never saw each other again.

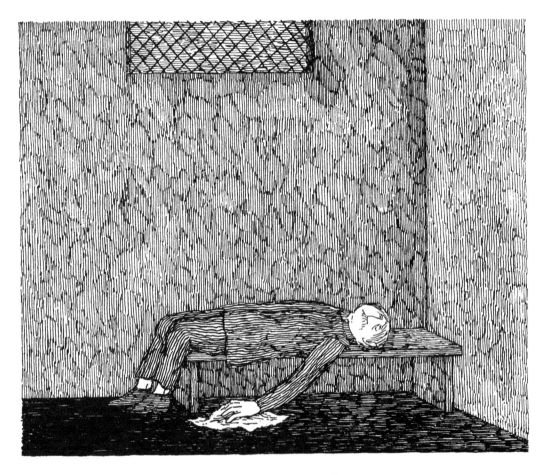

When he was forty-three Harold's cold turned into pneumonia and he died within a few days.

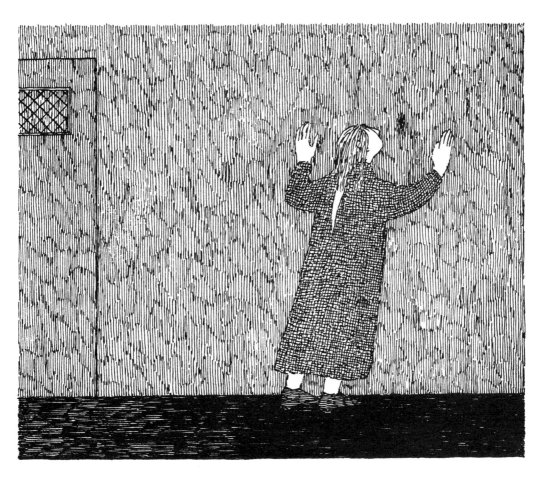

Mona failed to such an extent that for most of her life
she did nothing but lick spots on the walls.

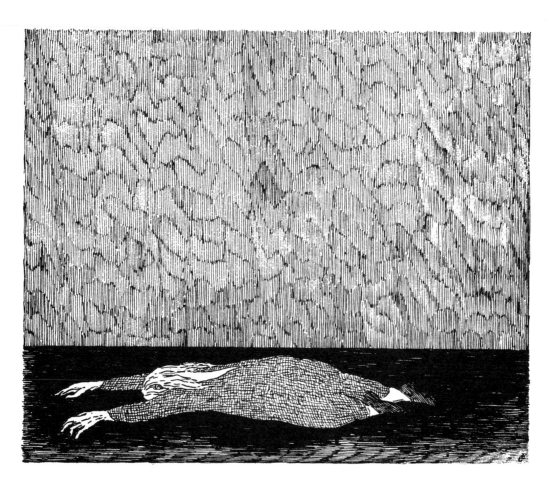

She died at the age of eighty-two or eighty-four.

THE GREEN BEADS
EDWARD GOREY

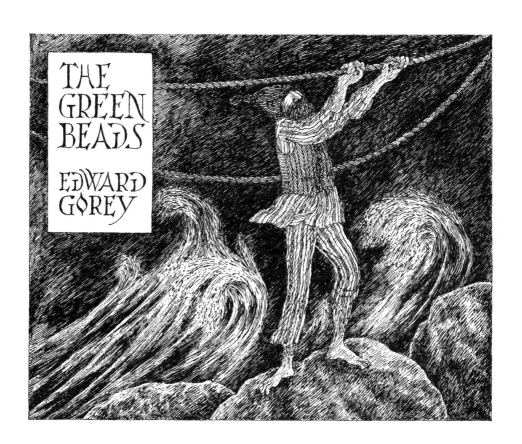

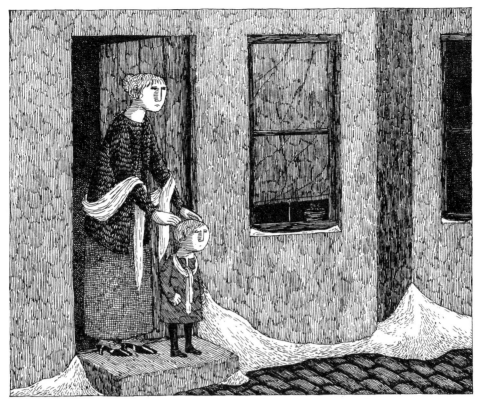

The mother of Little Tancred sent him into the twilight to buy three pennies' worth of tapioca with which to make their evening meal.

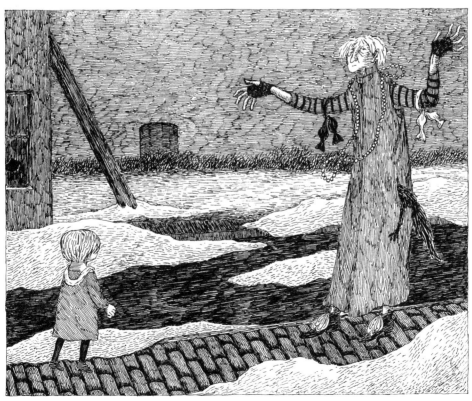

Before he had as yet not got even half-way he saw a disturbed person whose sex was unclear coming towards him while it waved its hands about.

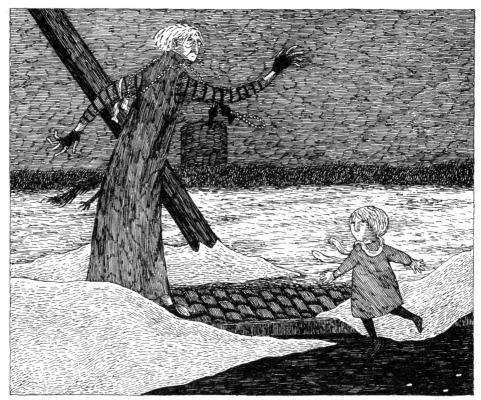

Little Tancred started for the other side of the street, the three pennies falling from his grasp in the middle, but the Disturbed Person was there before him.

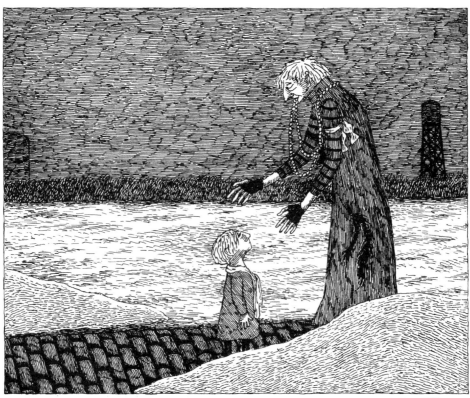

'Is this a visionary child I see, or are you really Tiny Clorinda?' cried the Disturbed Person, chewing on a string of green beads it wore around its neck.

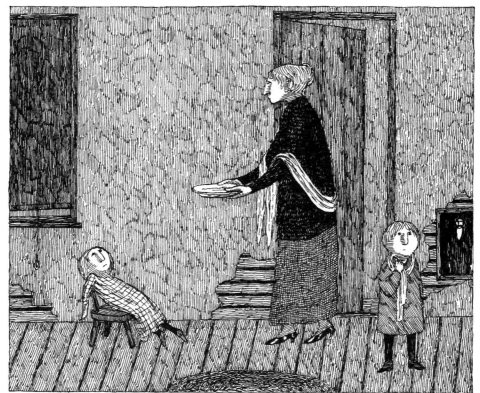

'No—for my name is Little Tancred. If it is of my infant
sister you speak, good sir,' he ventured politely 'she
died last autumn from a disorder of the spine
brought on by a lack of nourishing food'.

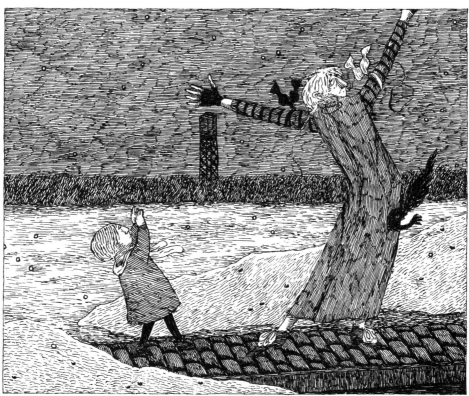

'How it knocks my heart!' moaned the Disturbed Person,
its teeth rending the string asunder, the green beads
flying in all directions and vanishing into the grimy
drifts of snow.

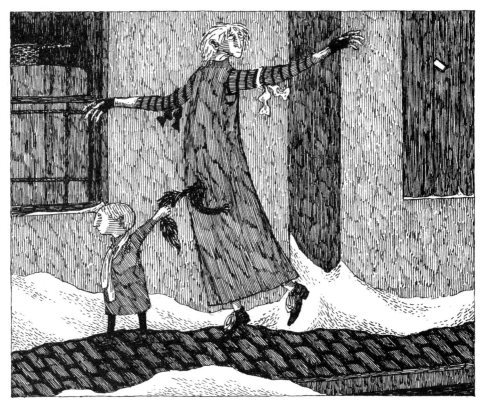

'I am the Baroness von Rettig,' she announced 'your grandmother', and so Little Tancred led her back to where they lived.

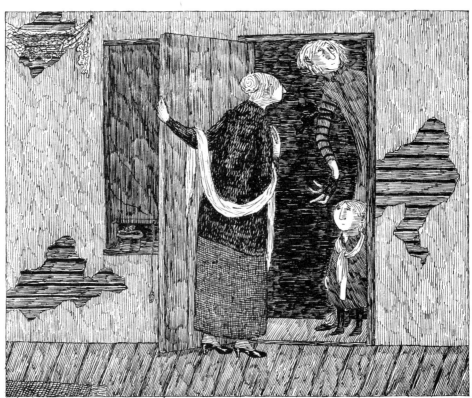

In her astonishment at seeing her son in the company of a disturbed person on the doorstep, Little Tancred's mother forgot to ask the whereabouts of the tapioca.

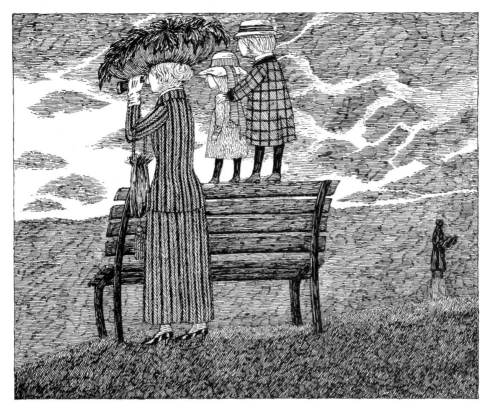

When she was told who the Disturbed Person was, she explained 'We thought you were lost when the *Moon of Valparaiso* went down in the bay three years ago last April.

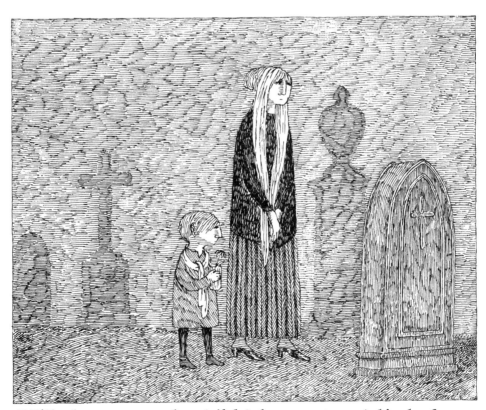

'Wilhelm, your only child,' she went on 'died of pneumonia contracted after helping to man the breeches-buoy all night in vain; those of us who are left visit the cemetery on the seventh of every month.

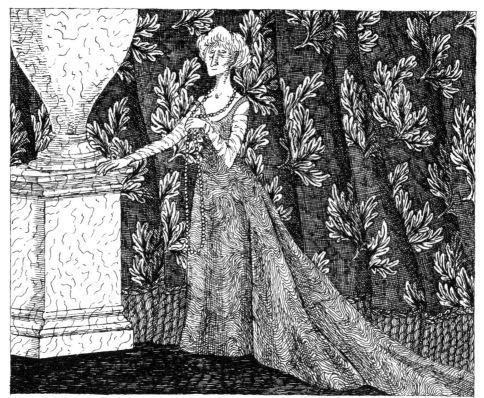

'But if you are not lying on the bottom of the sea,'
she added 'can it be possible that your emerald
necklace is not there after all either?'.

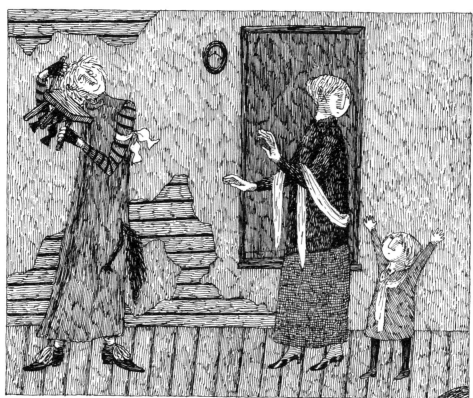

'Grandmother, when I met her,' put in Little
Tancred 'was chewing some green beads, but
they broke and rolled away'.

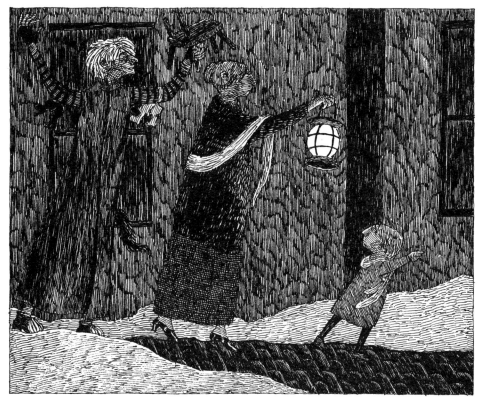

It was now quite dark both indoors and out and so a lantern was lit, and all three rushed into the street.

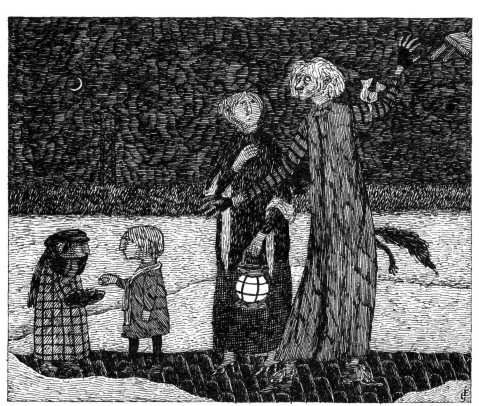

They hunted and hunted, but in the end found only one green bead, and that proved to be a glass marble belonging to a more fortunate little boy named Hugo who lived farther up the block.

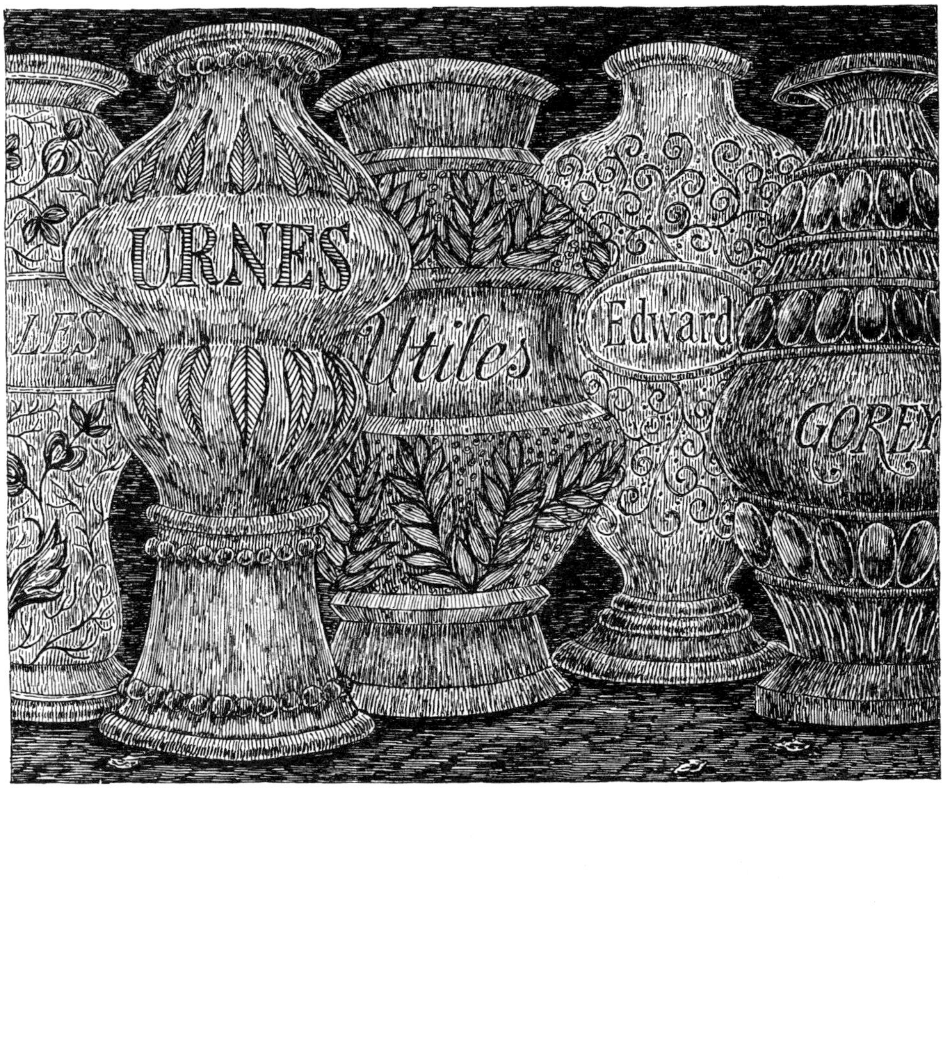
URNES
Utiles
Edward
GOREY

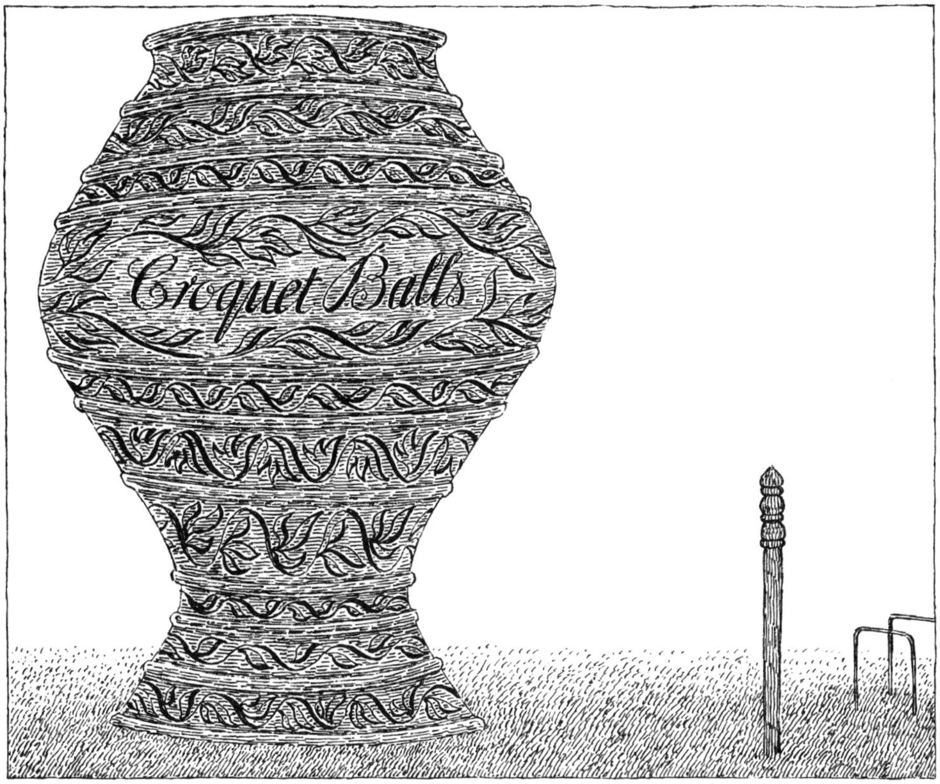
Croquet Balls

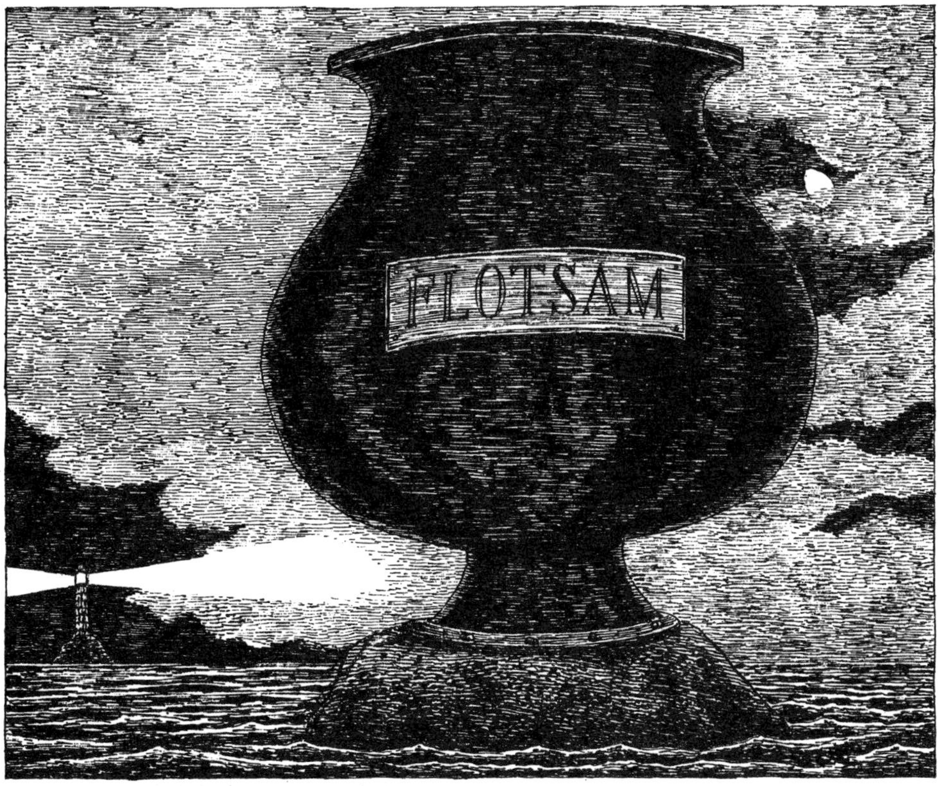
FLOTSAM

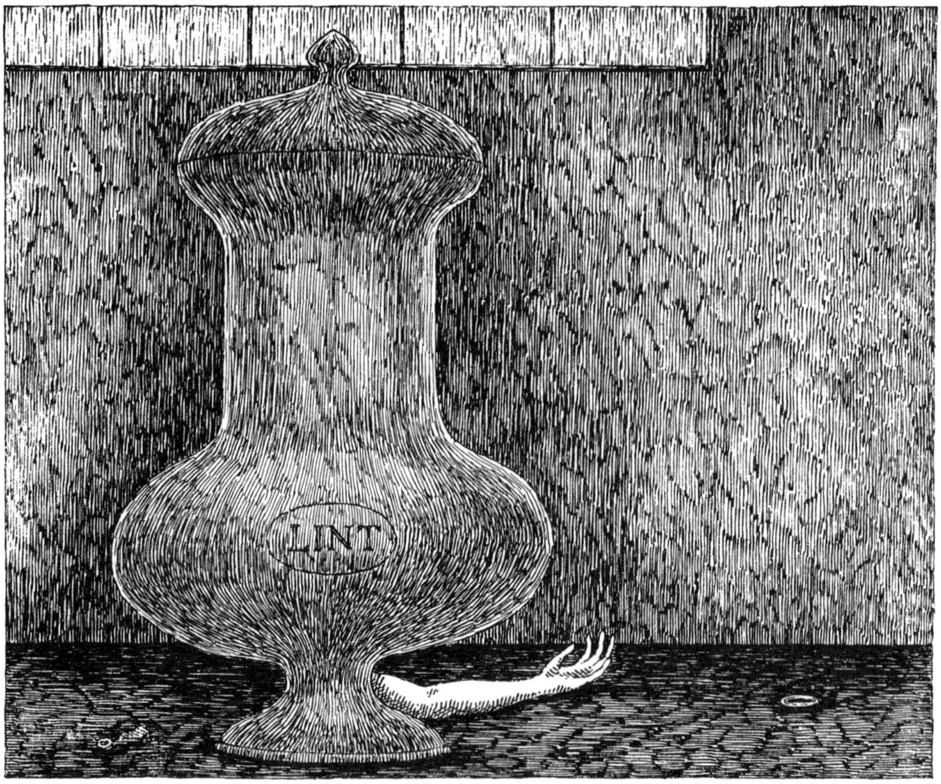
LINT

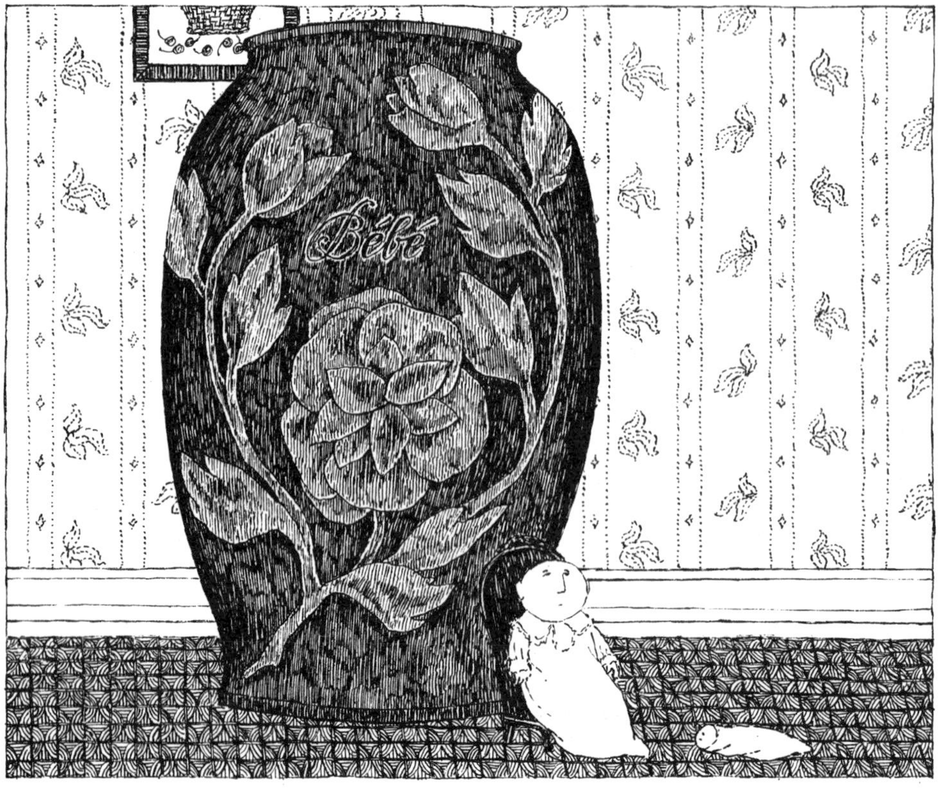
Bébé

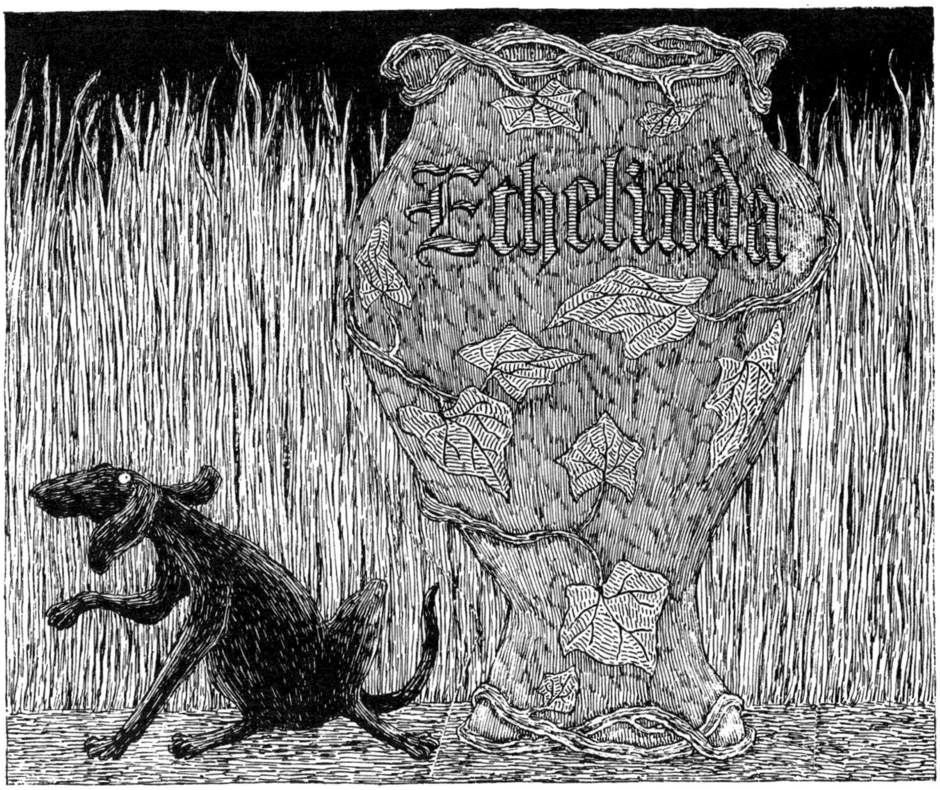
Echelinda

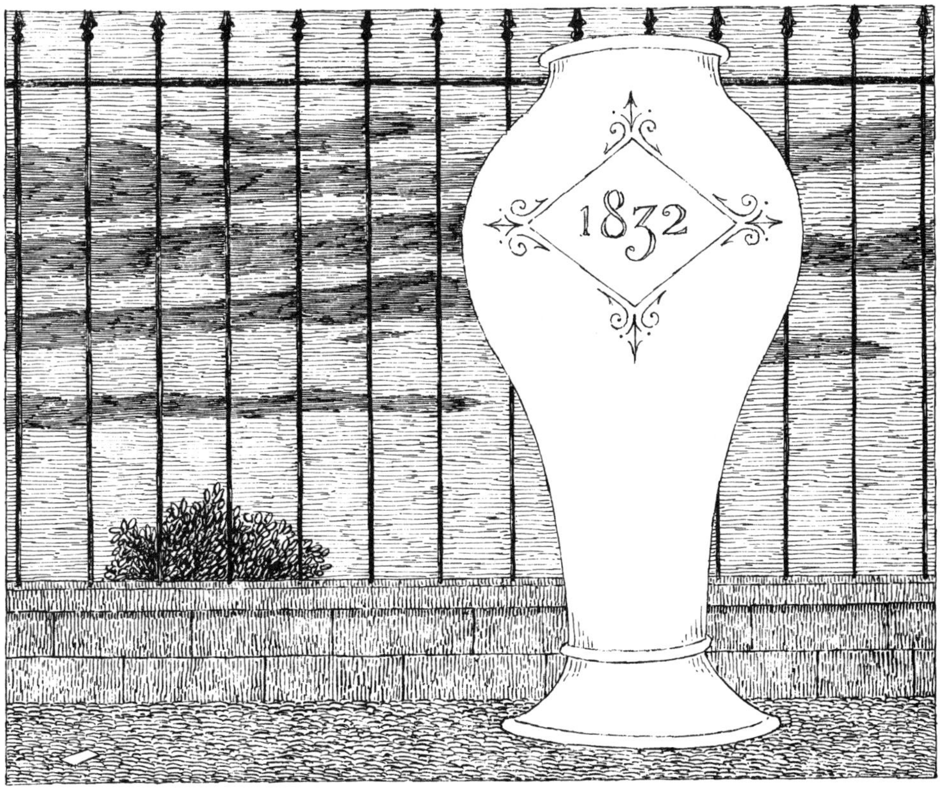
1832

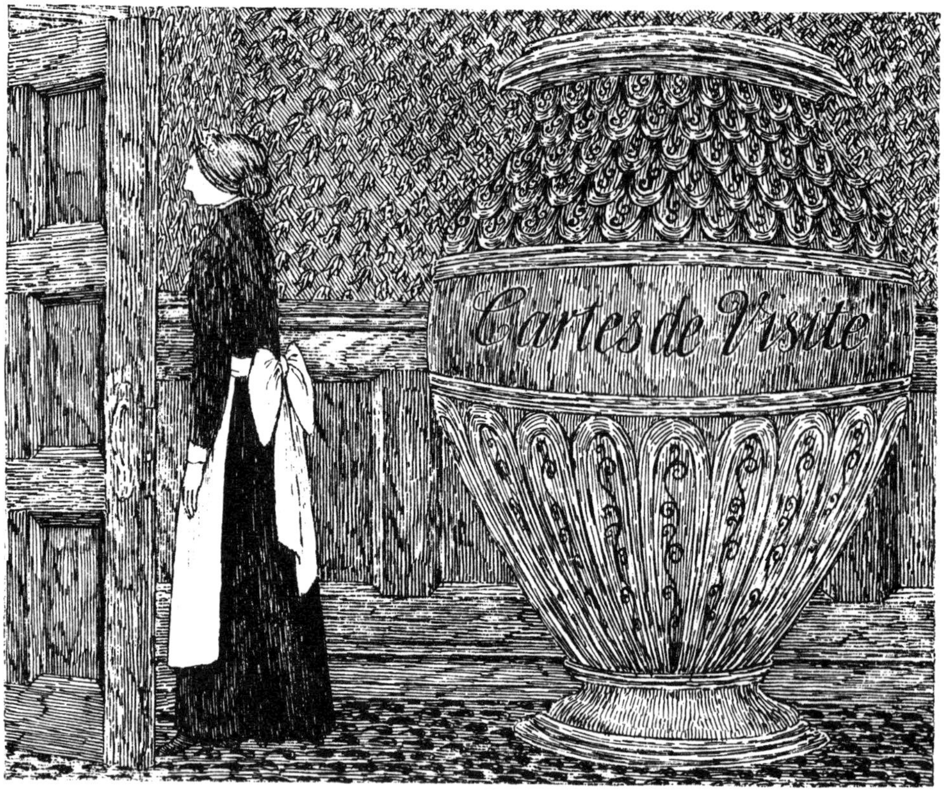
Cartes de Visite

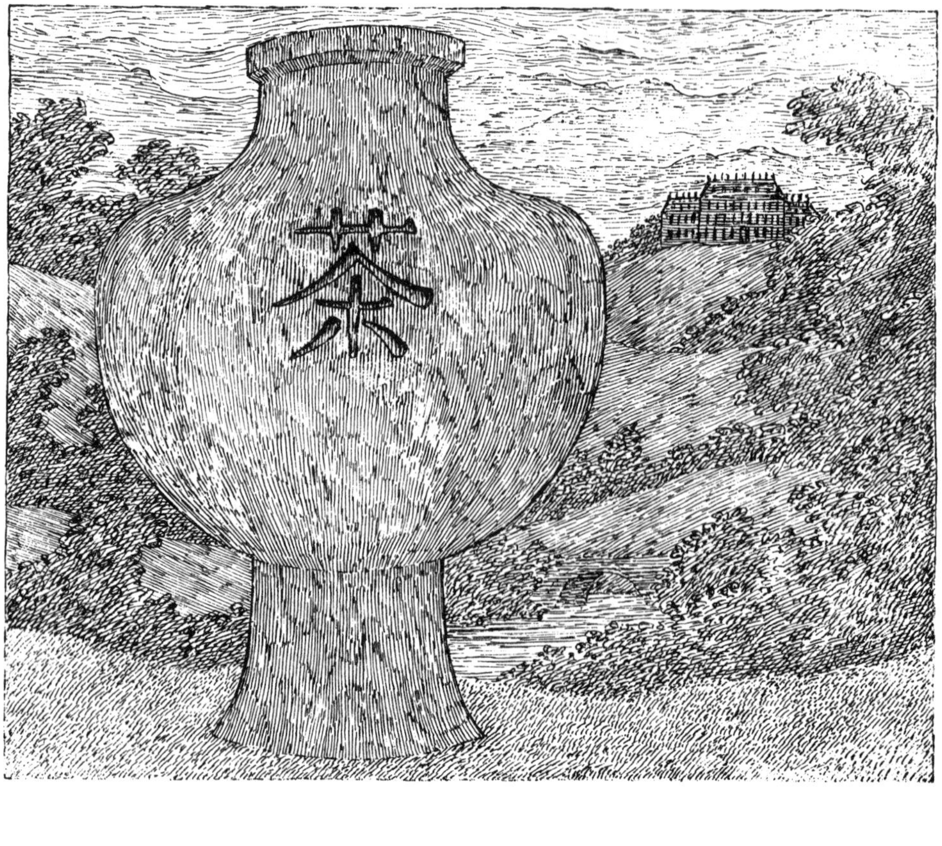
茶

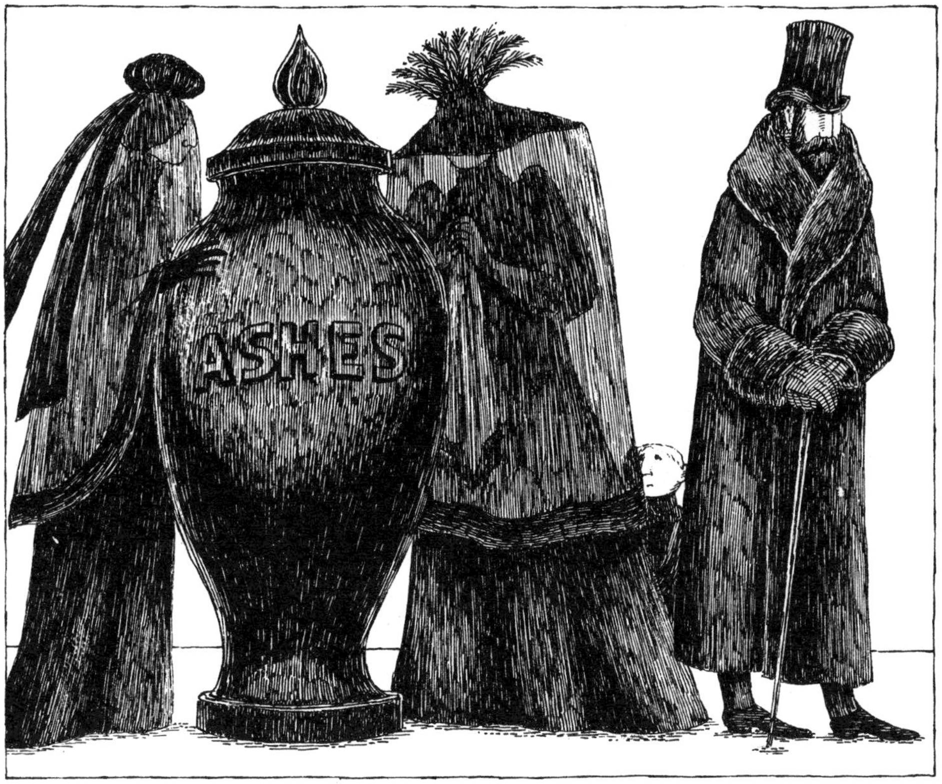
ASHES

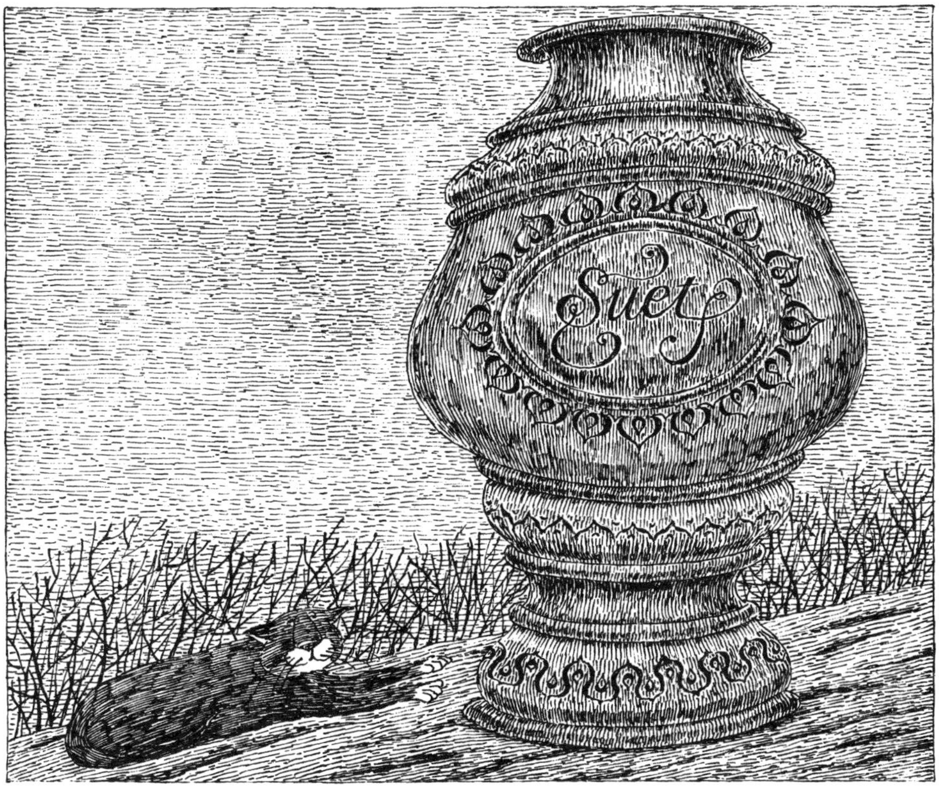
Suet

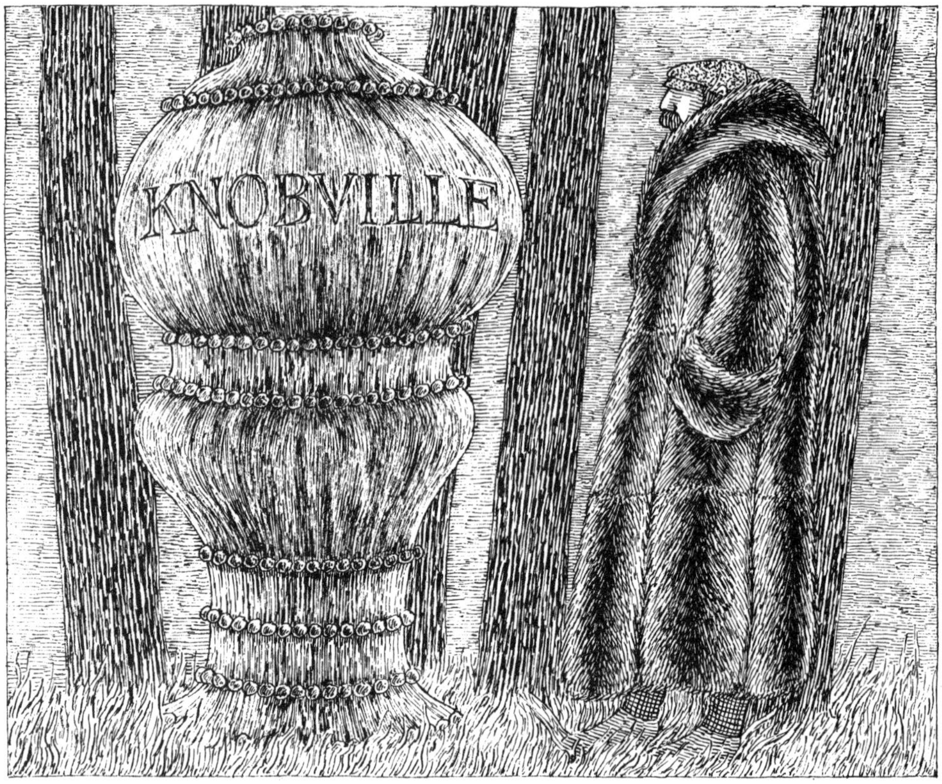
KNOBVILLE

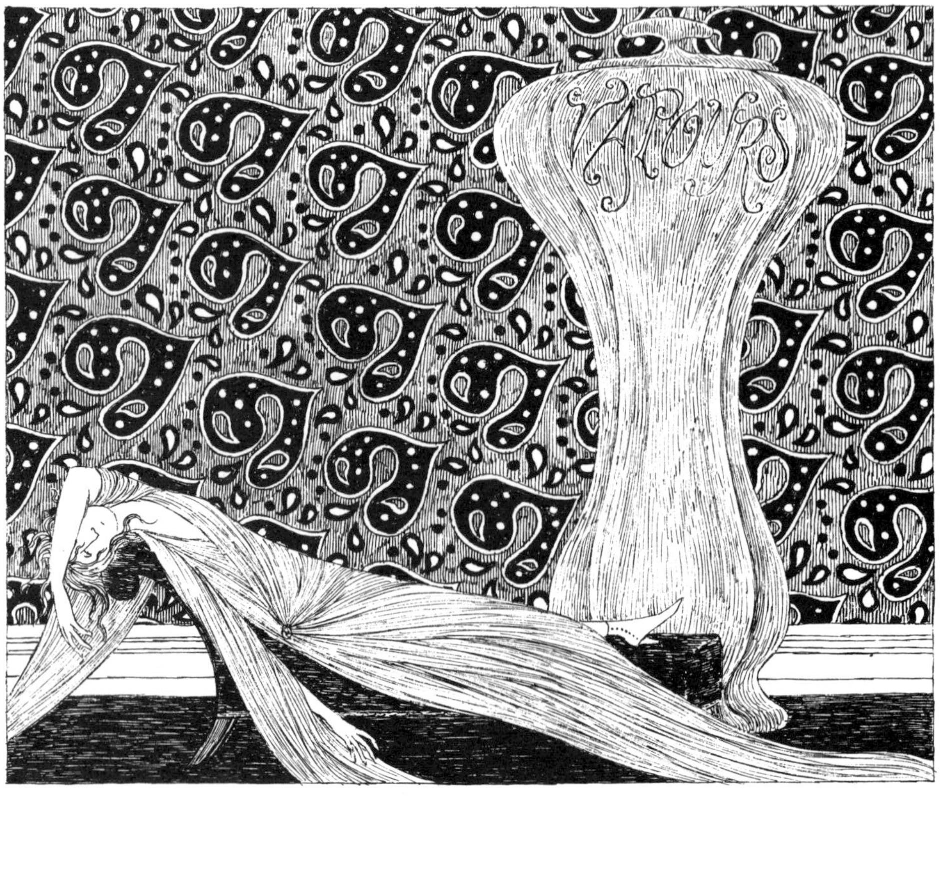
VAPOURS

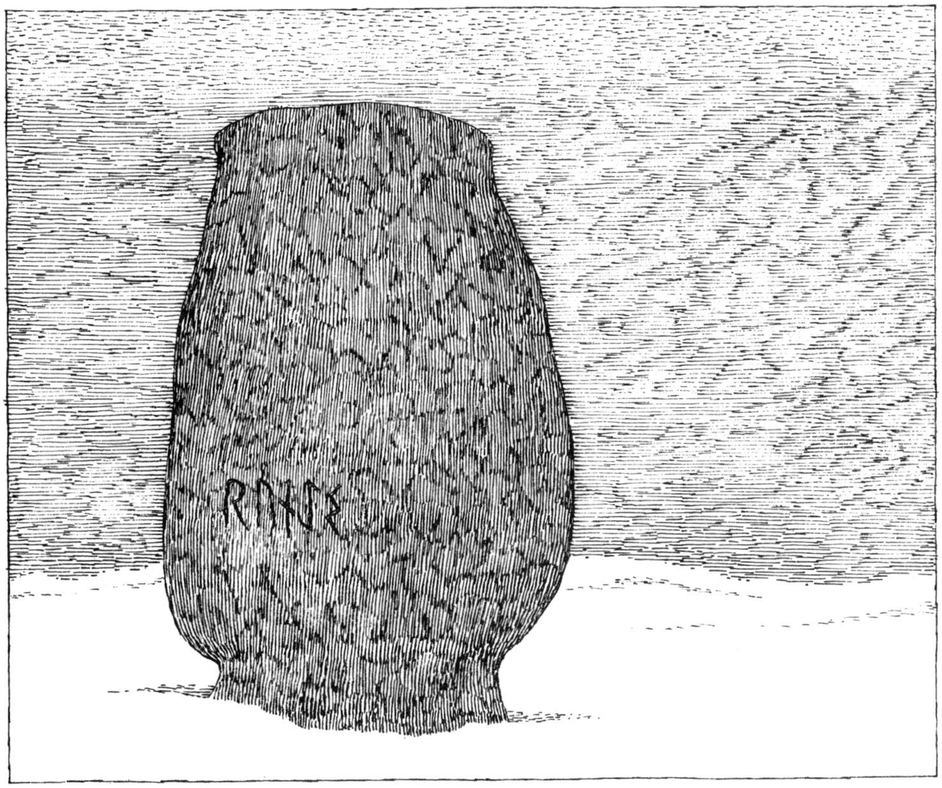

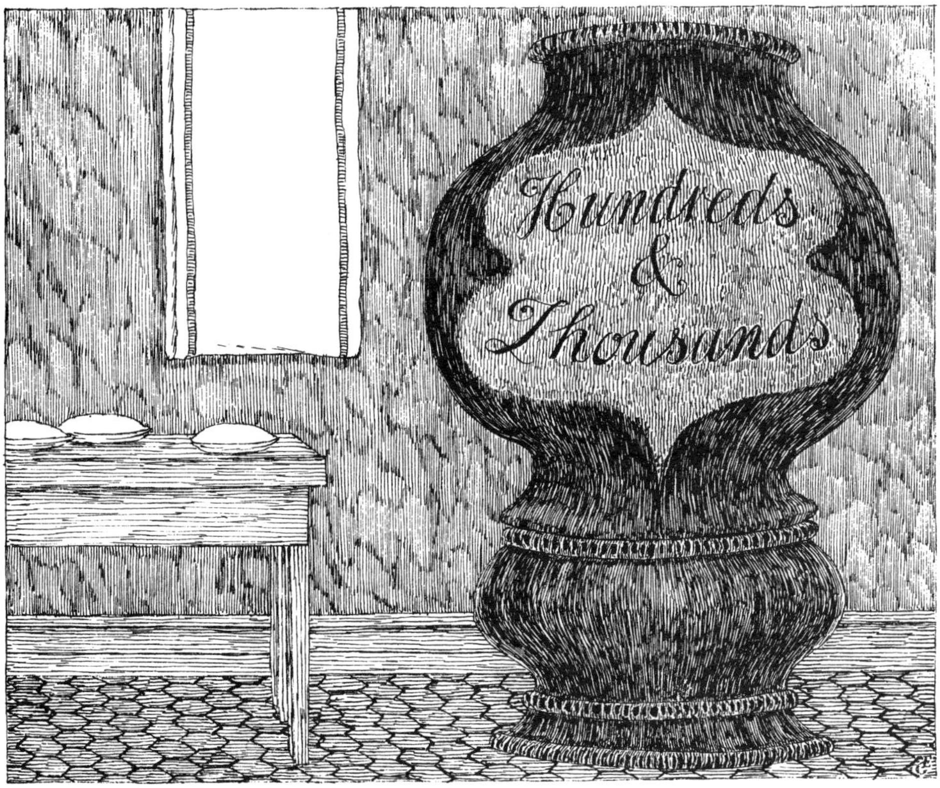
Hundreds
&
Thousands

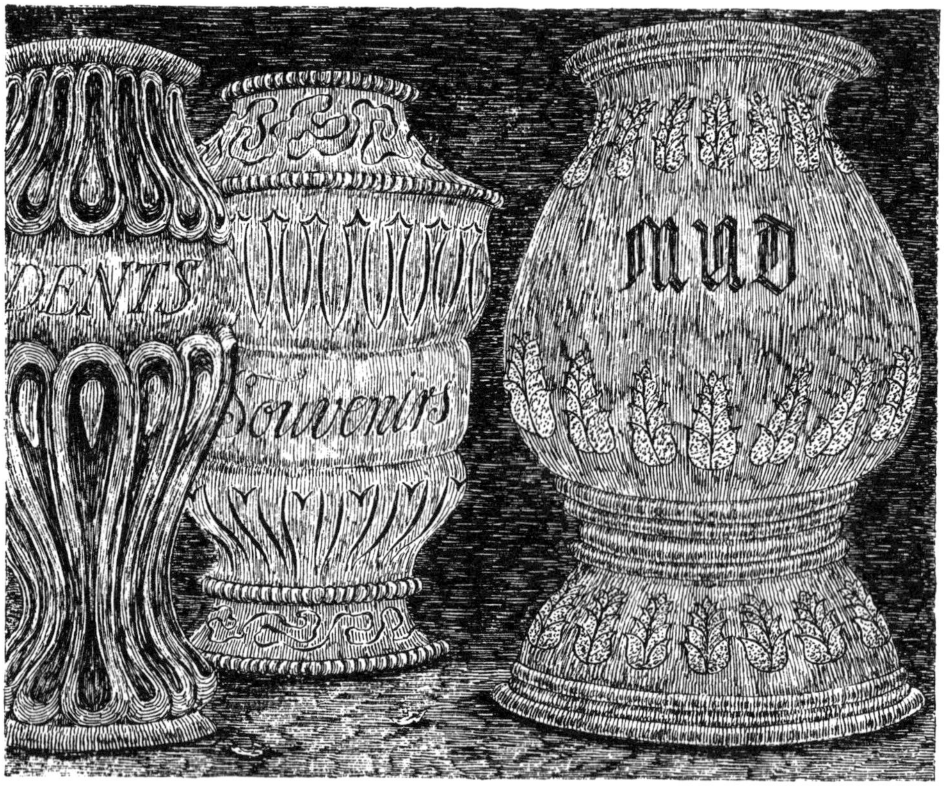
DENTS
Souvenirs
MUD

The Stupid Joke

Edward Gorey

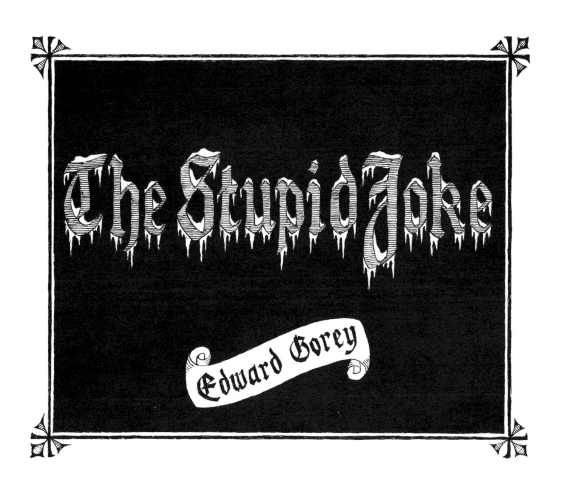

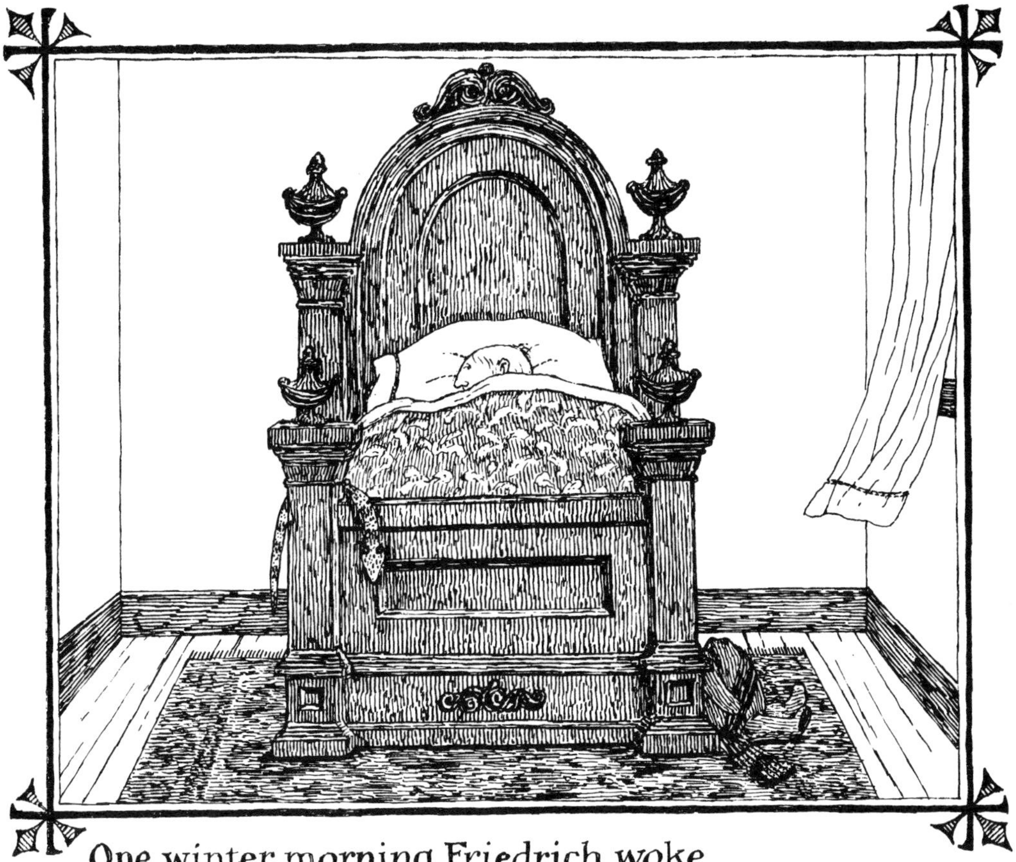

One winter morning Friedrich woke
With an idea for a joke.

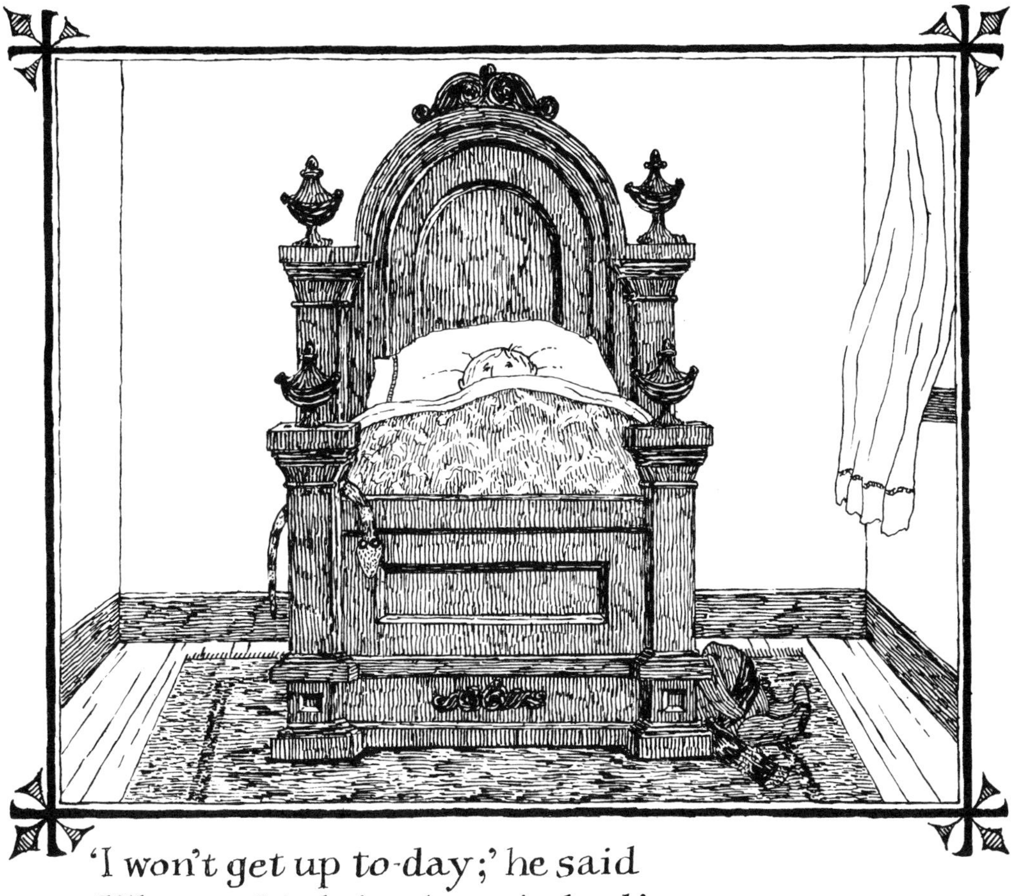

'I won't get up to-day;' he said
'I'll spend it lying here in bed'.

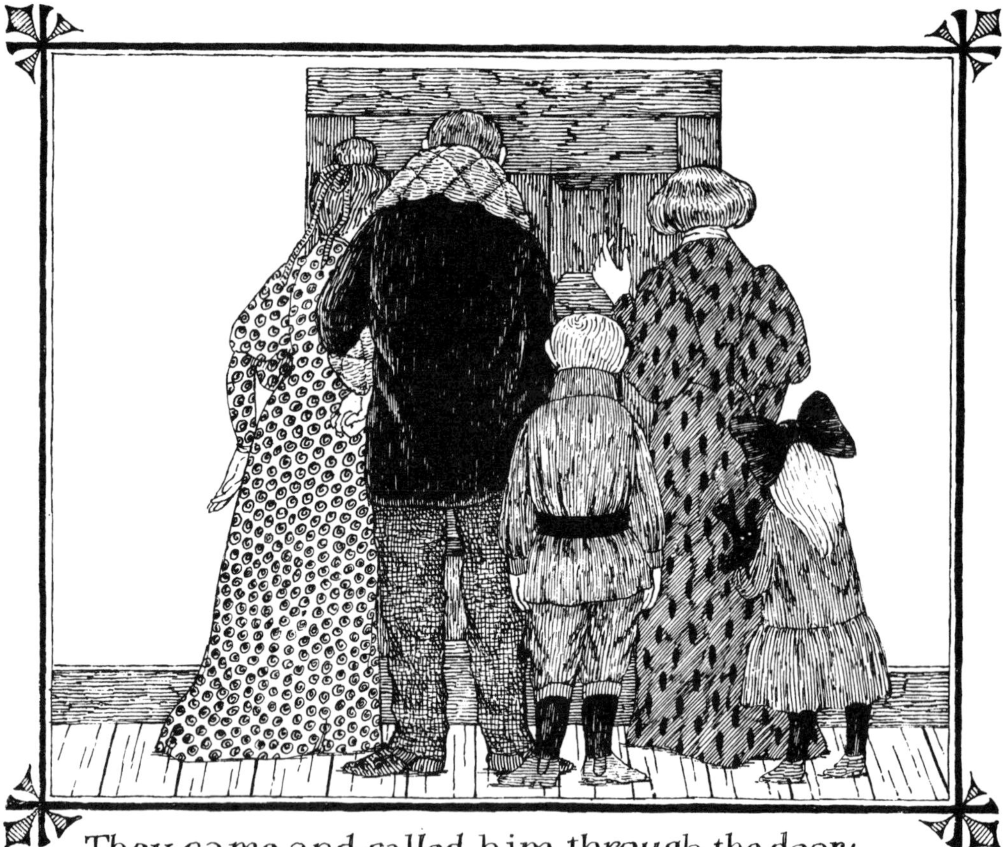

They came and called him through the door;
He only went to *sleep* once more.

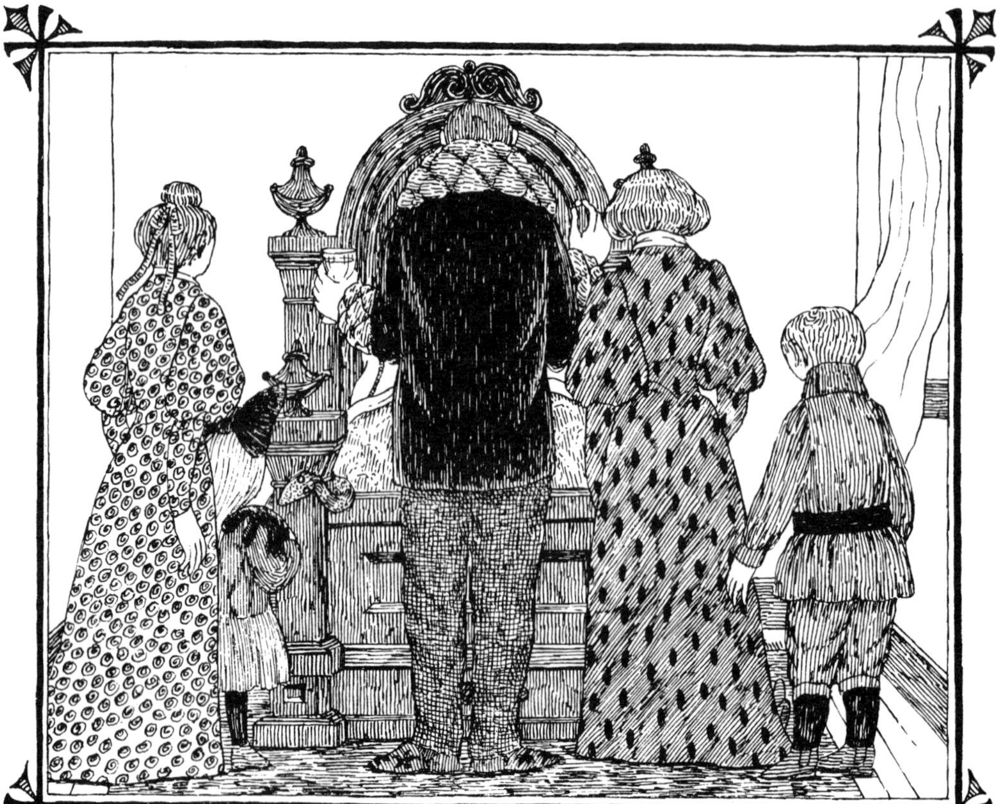

They wondered if he'd fallen ill,
And asked if he would like a pill.

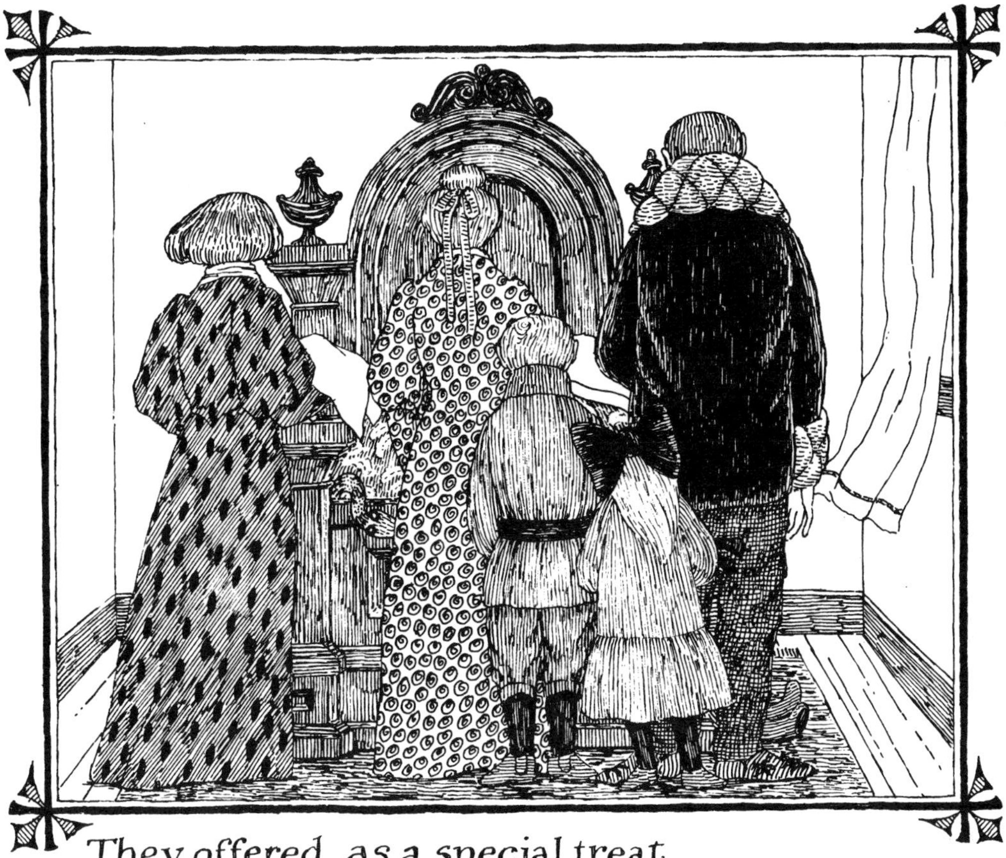

They offered, as a special treat,
To give him anything *to* eat.

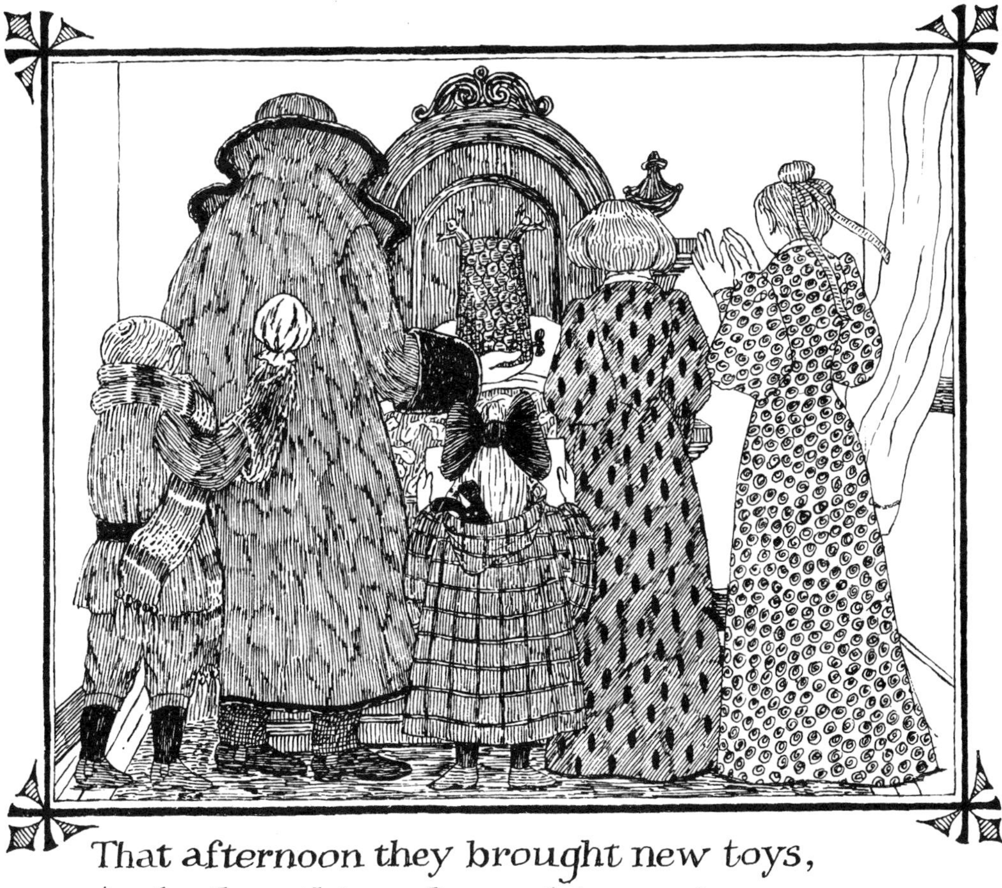

That afternoon they brought new toys,
And other things for making noise.

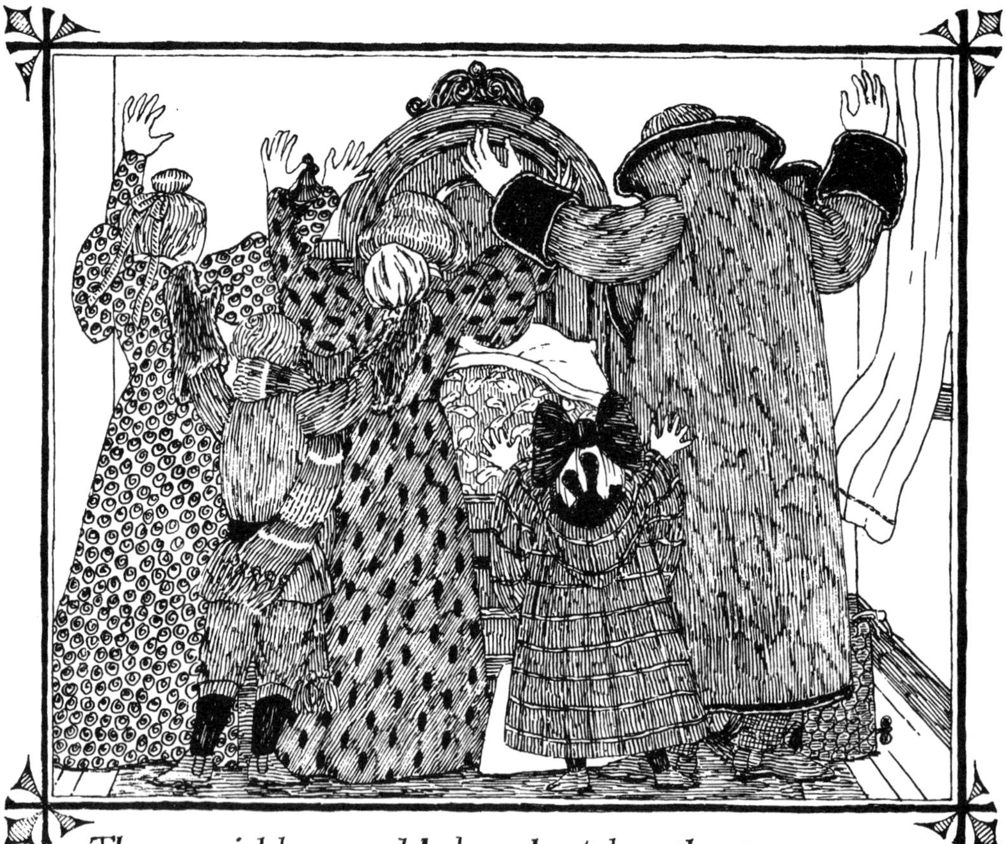

They said he could do what he chose;
He only hid beneath the clothes.

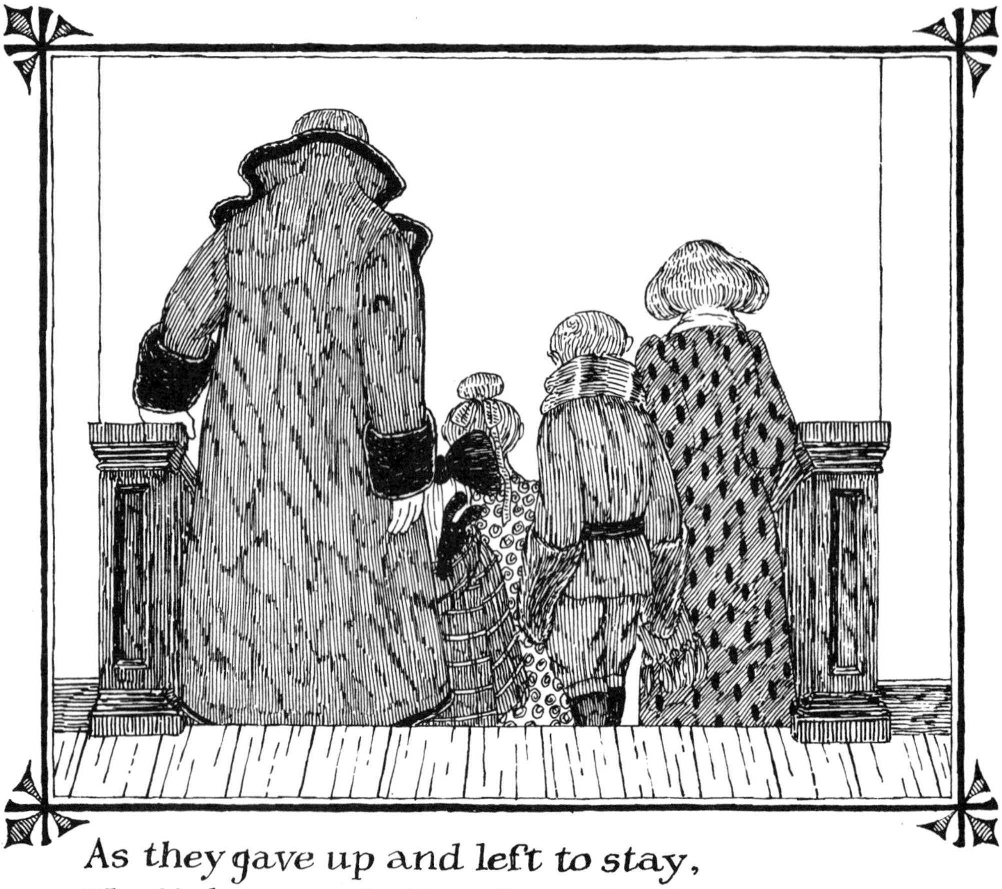

As they gave up and left to stay,
The light was fading from the day.

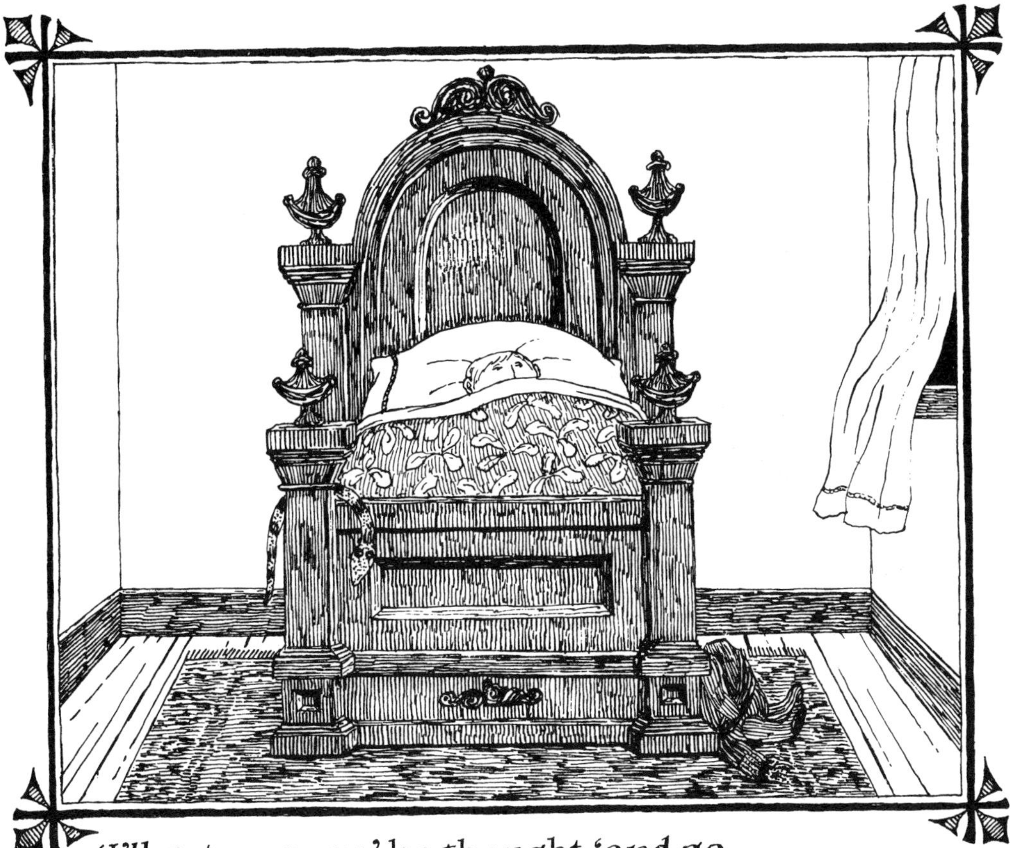

'I'll get up now,' he thought 'and go
And play till supper in the snow'.

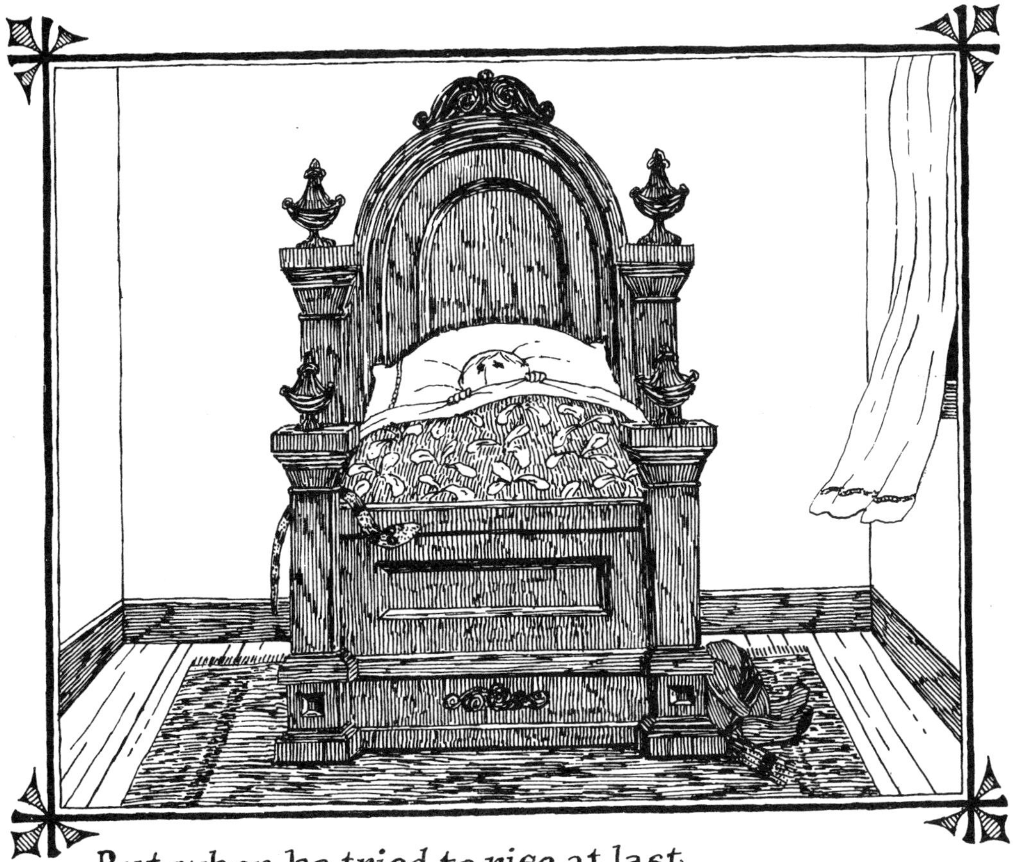

But when he tried to rise at last
The sheets and blankets held him fast.

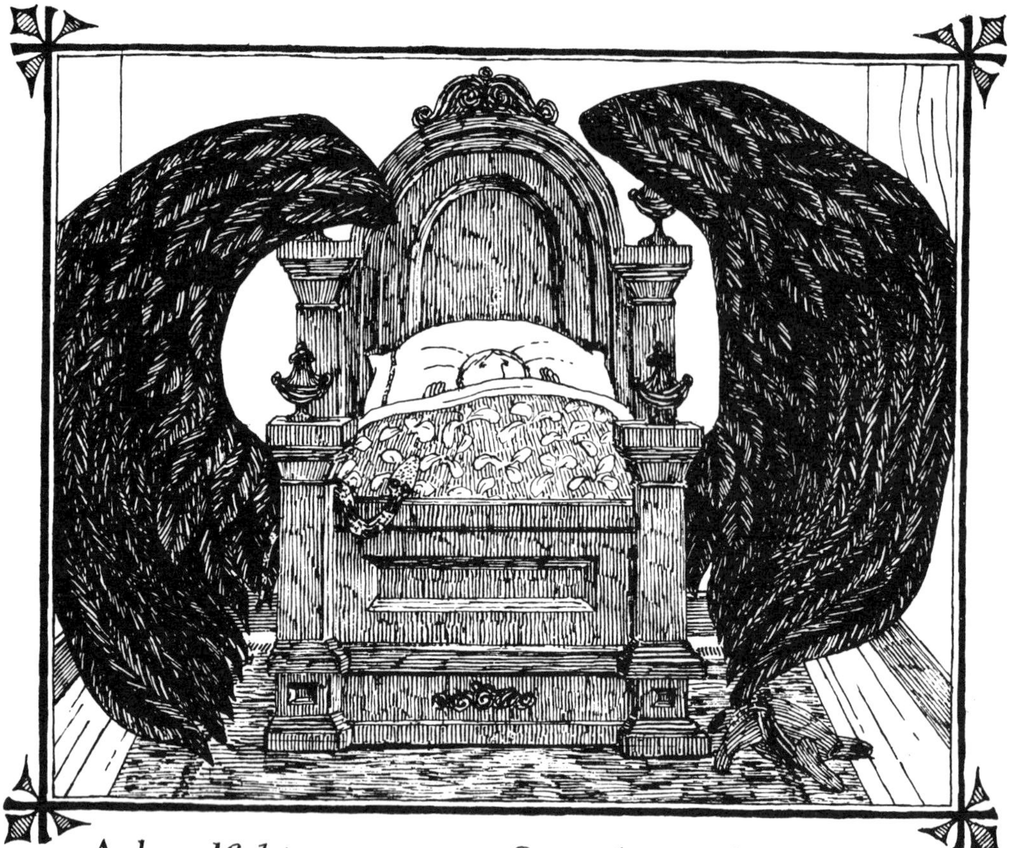

A dreadful twang came from the springs;
The bed unfolded great black wings.

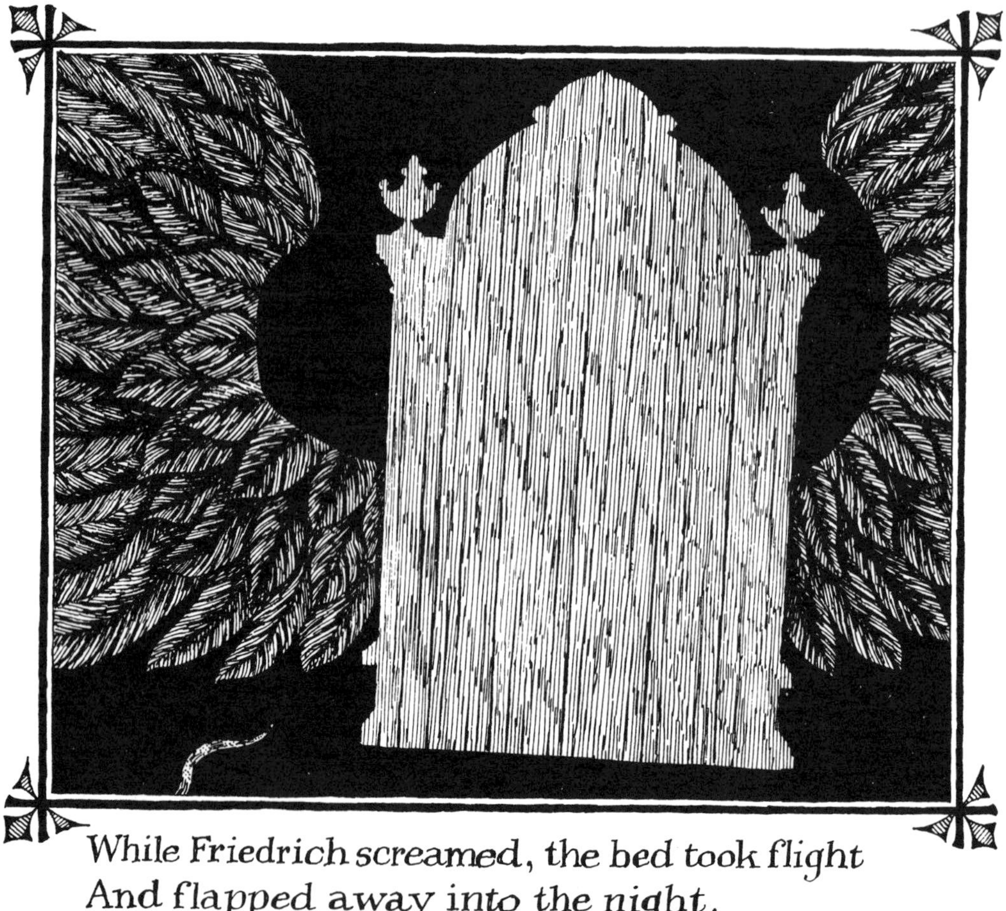

While Friedrich screamed, the bed took flight
And flapped away into the night.

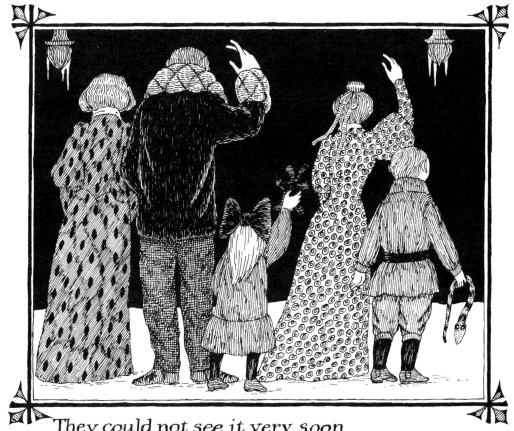

They could not see it very soon
Because there wasn't any moon.

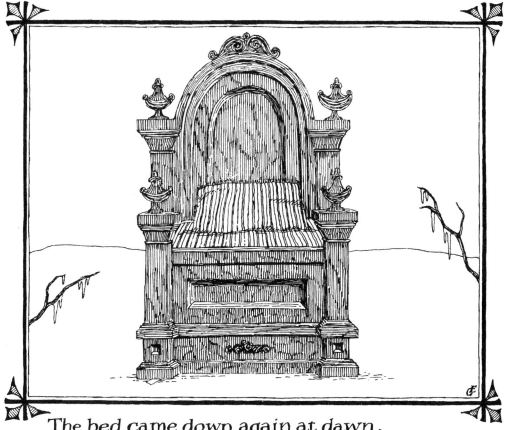

The bed came down again at dawn,
Both Friedrich and the bed-clothes gone.

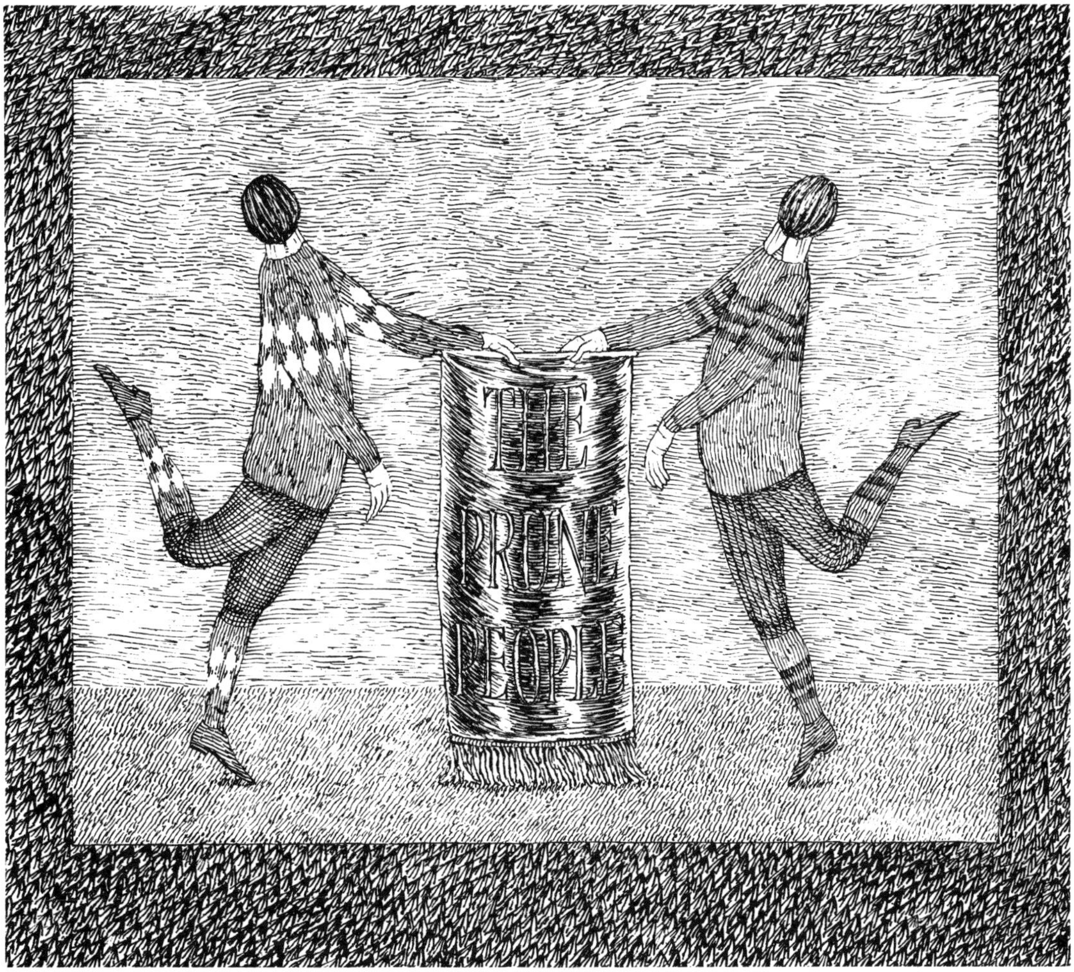
THE
PRUNE
PEOPLE

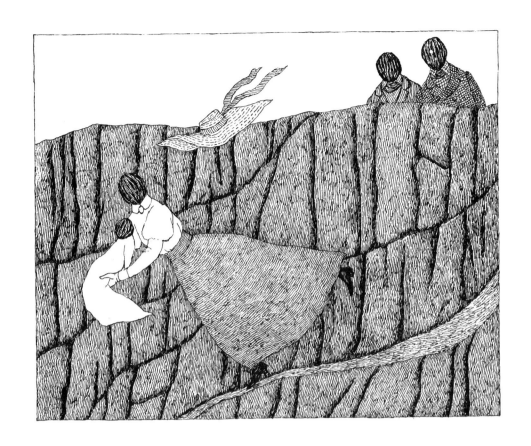

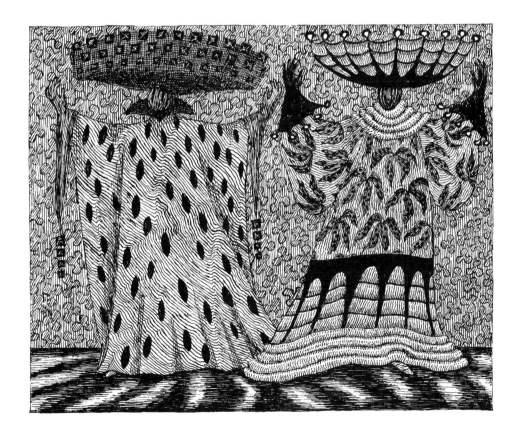

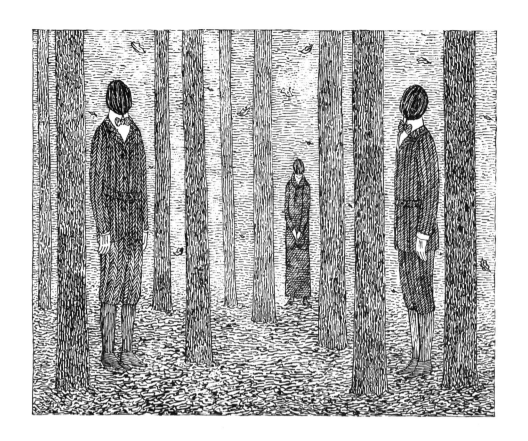

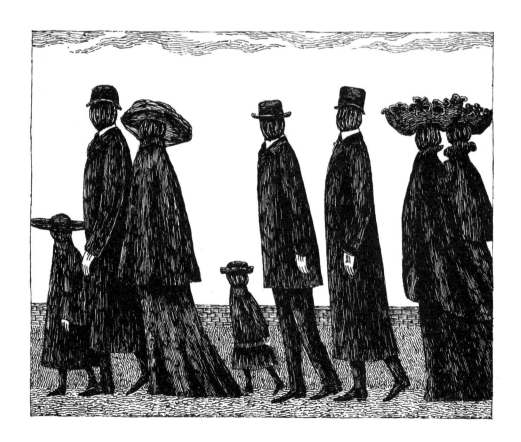

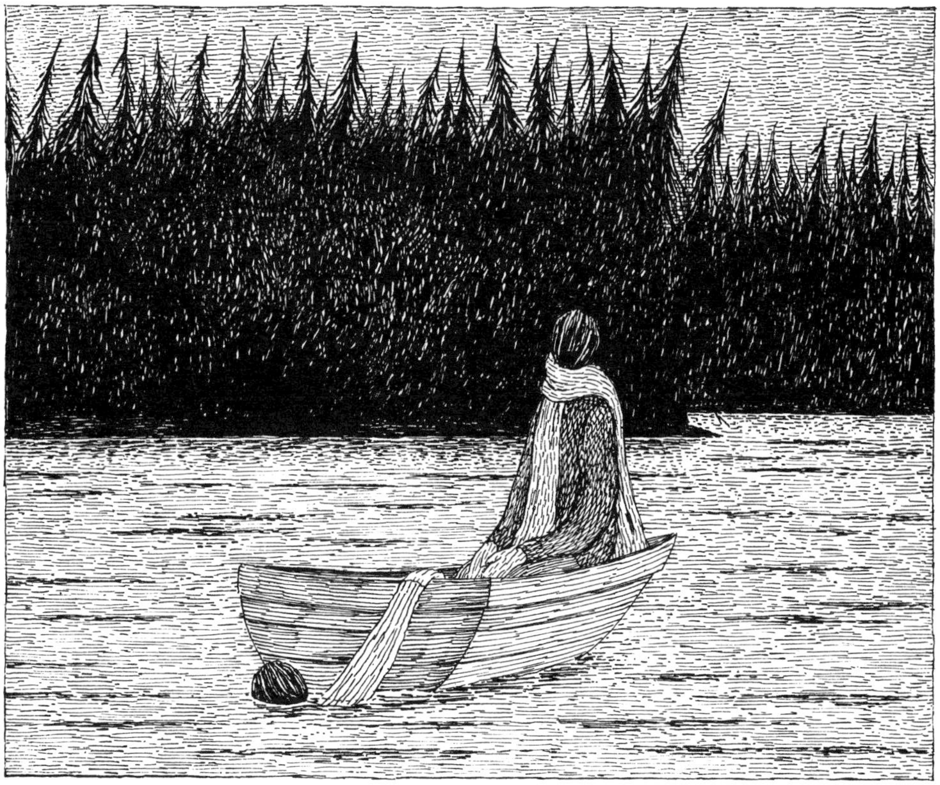

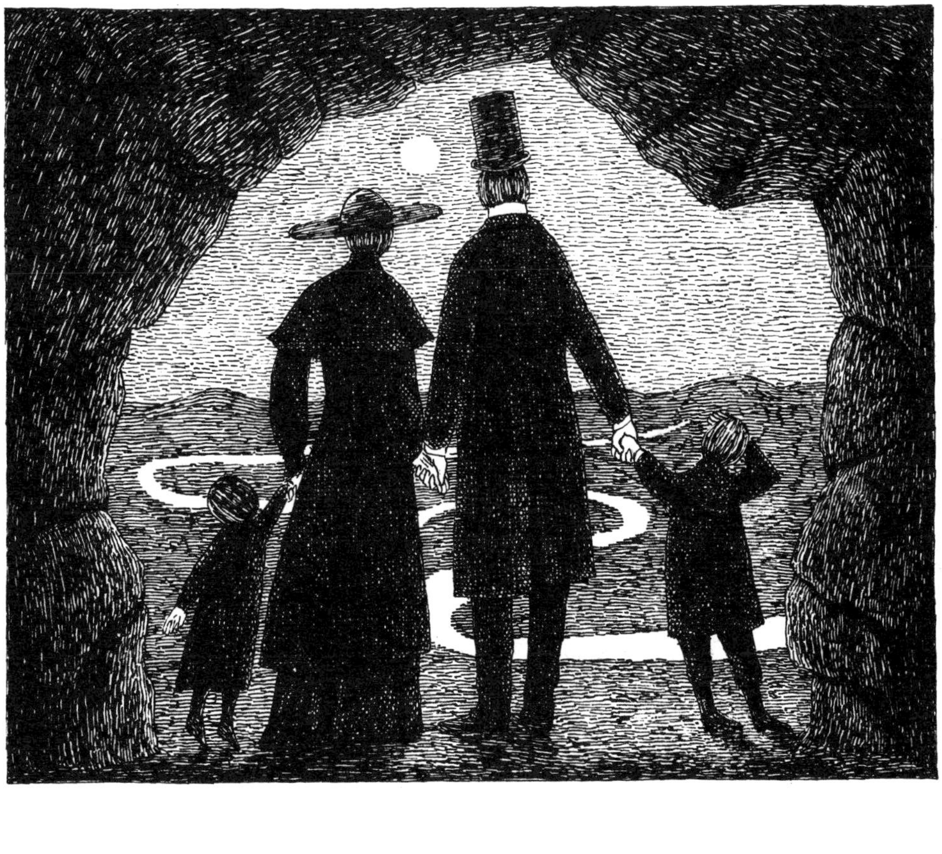

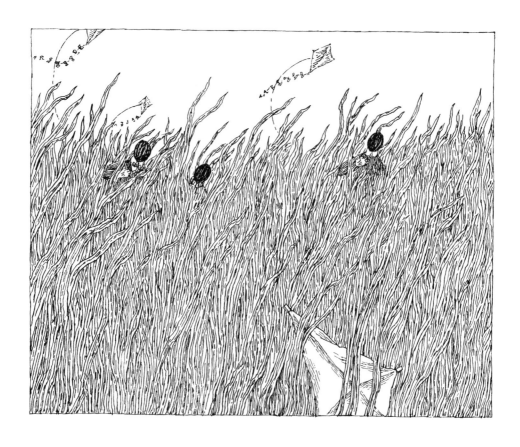

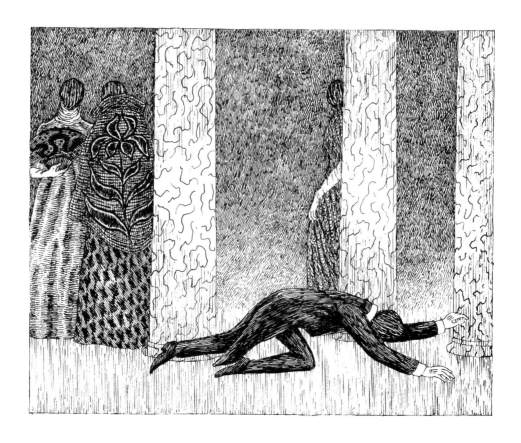

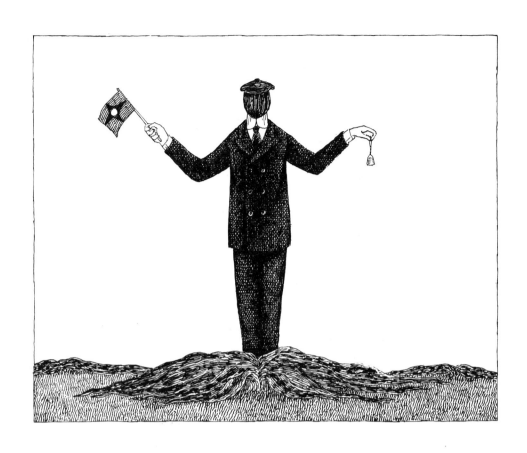

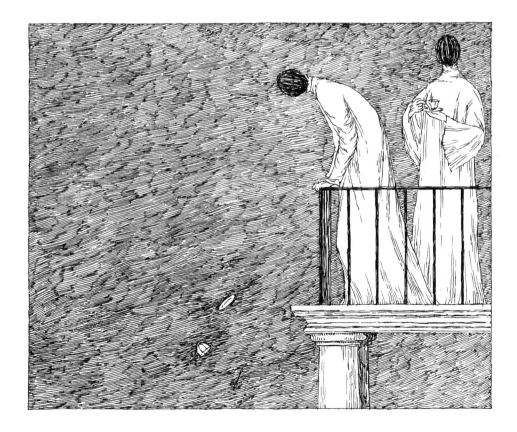

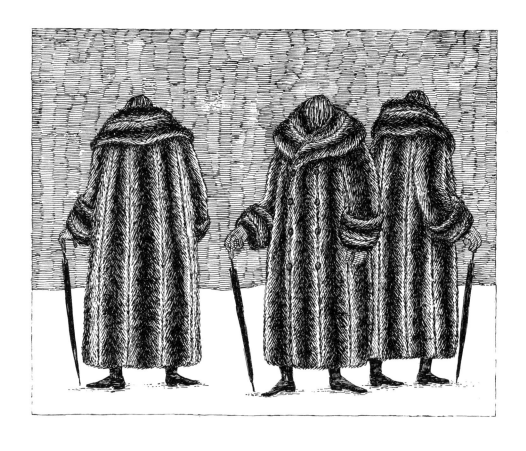

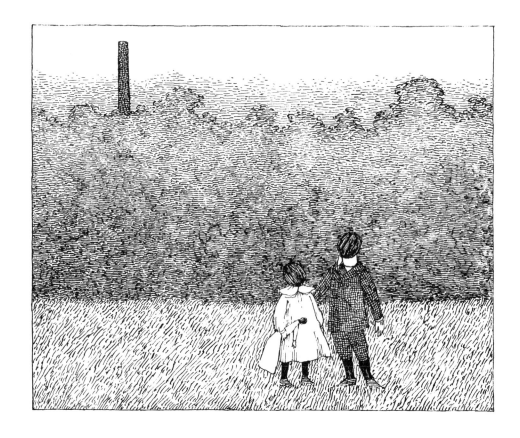

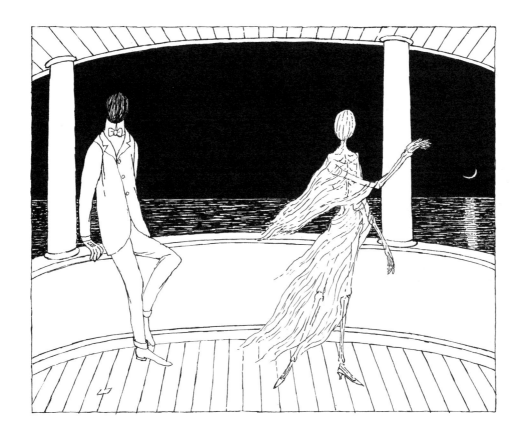

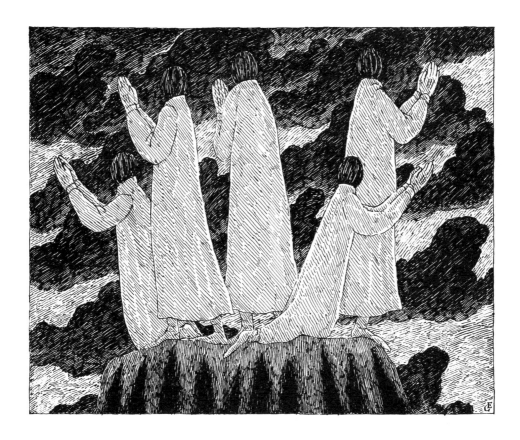

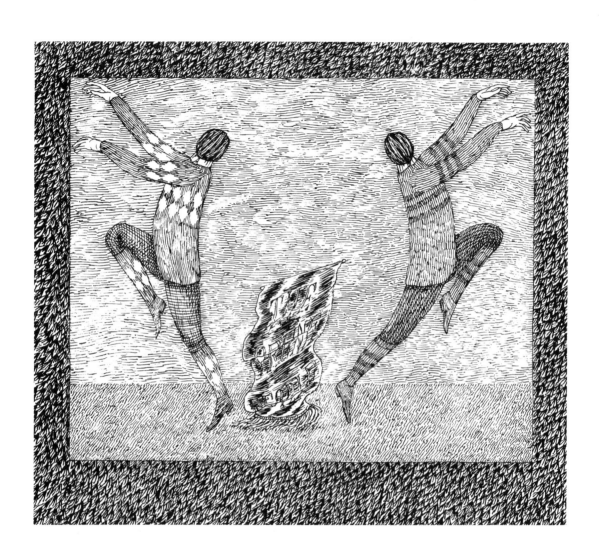

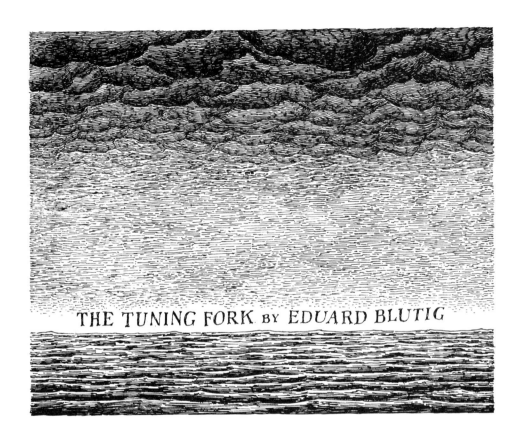

THE TUNING FORK BY EDUARD BLUTIG

Eduard Blutig's D e r Z e i t i r r t h u m
in a translation by Mrs Regera Dowdy
with the original pictures by O. Müde

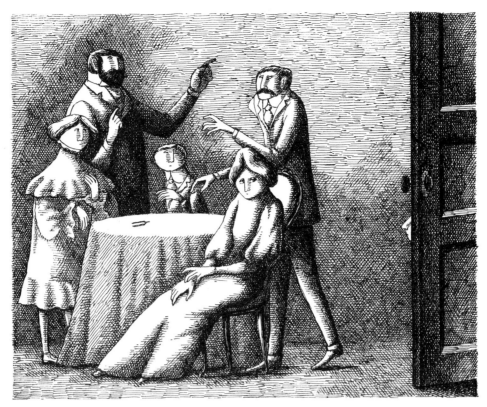

Theoda was a homely child
Whose presence drove her family wild.

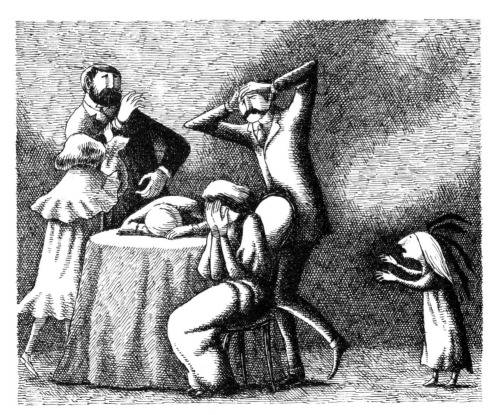

Her conversation and her dress
Alike inspired them with distress.

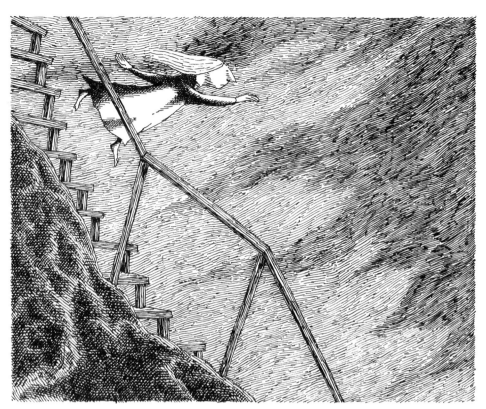

Theoda, bent on suicide,
Rushed down to meet the rising tide.

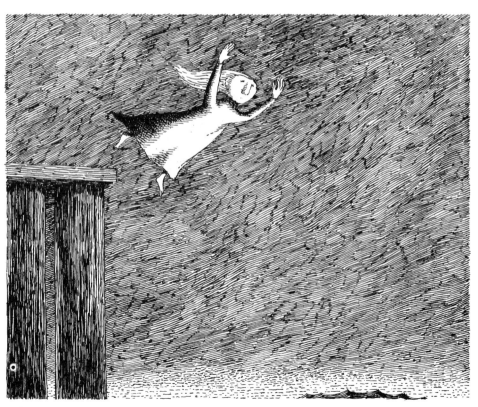

She cried 'Farewell!' to empty air,
And leapt off of the jetty there.

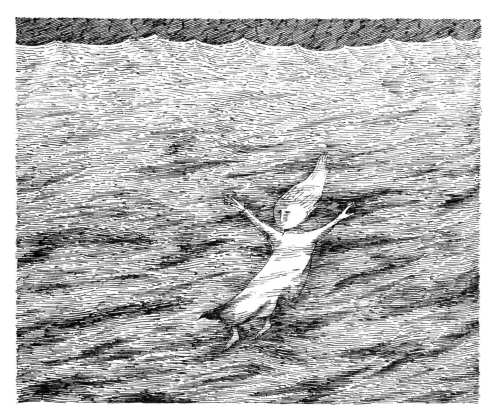

She sank; the water chilled her limbs;
She recollected bits of hymns.

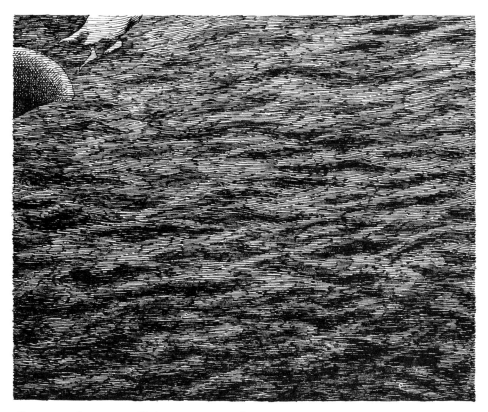

She sank—until her senseless toes
Came into contact with a nose.

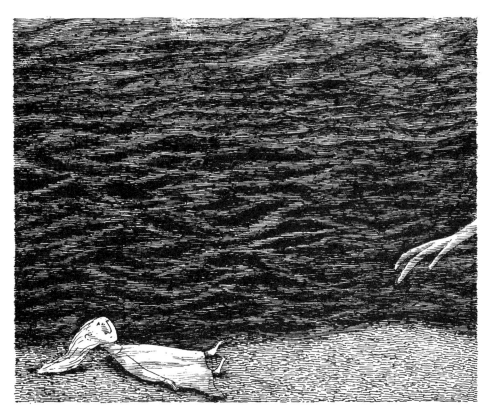

When she revived, she was not dead,
But on the ocean's floor instead.

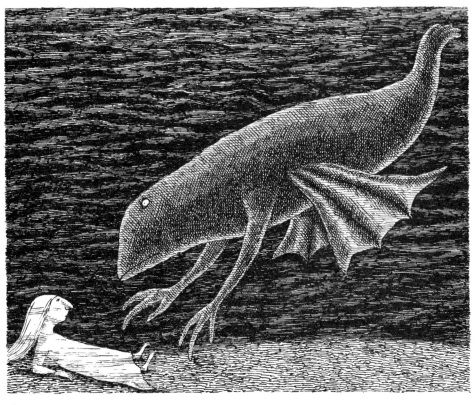

A monster of alarming size
Was peering at her in surprise.

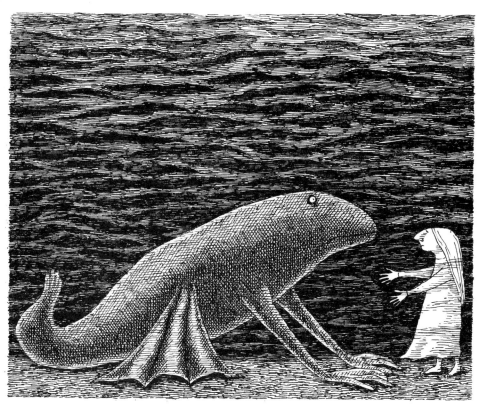

Despite this sudden change of fate,
She soon began to perorate.

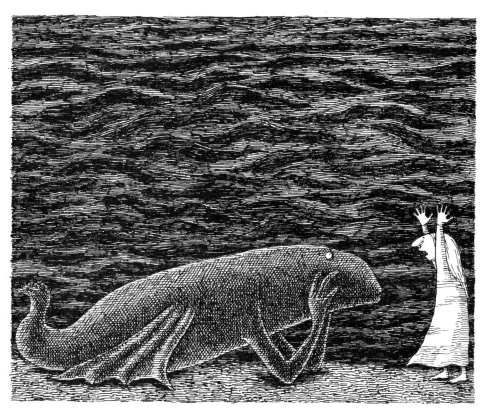

The simple creature was aghast
At hearing of her cruel past.

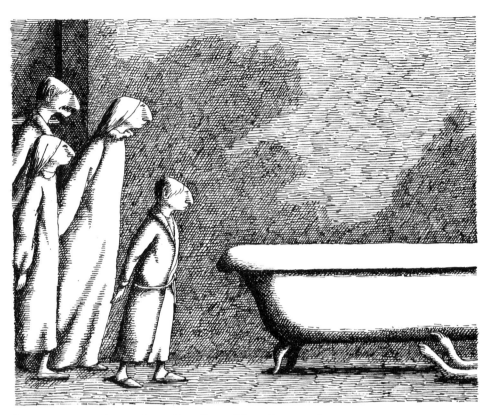

Next day her joyful family found
Her father by the bathtub, drowned.

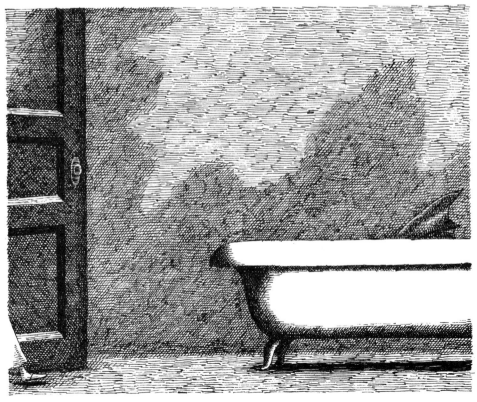

The same thing happened, **one by one**,
To all the rest. How was it done?

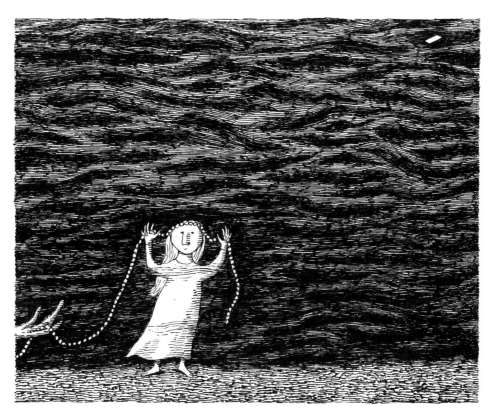

Theoda, having wanted curls,
Now draped her head with ropes of pearls.

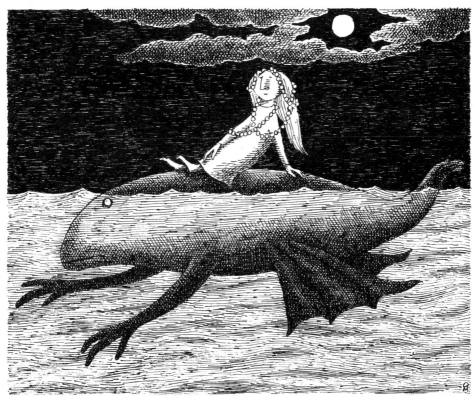

The natives, afterwards, took fright
When she was seen, off shore, at night.

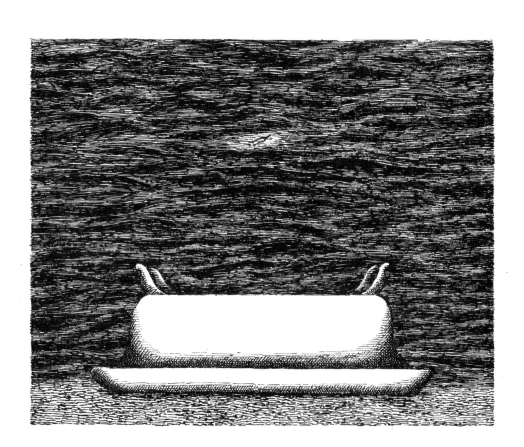

ALSO BY EDWARD GOREY

AMPHIGOREY
The Unstrung Harp
The Listing Attic
The Doubtful Guest
The Object-Lesson
The Bug Book
The Fatal Lozenge
The Hapless Child
The Curious Sofa
The Willowdale Handcar
The Gashlycrumb Tinies
The Insect God
The West Wing
The Wuggly Ump
The Sinking Spell
The Remembered Visit

AMPHIGOREY TOO
The Beastly Baby
The Nursery Frieze
The Pious Infant
The Evil Garden
The Inanimate Tragedy
The Gilded Bat
The Iron Tonic
The Osbick Bird
The Chinese Obelisks (bis)
The Deranged Cousins
The Eleventh Episode
[The Untitled Book]
The Lavender Leotard
The Disrespectful Summons
The Abandoned Sock
The Lost Lions
Story for Sara, ALPHONSE ALLAIS
The Salt Herring, CHARLES CROS
Leaves from a Mislaid Album
A Limerick

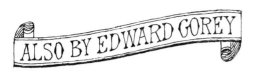

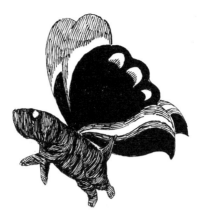

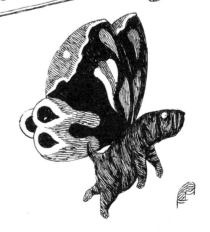

ALSO

The Black Doll

Le Mélange Funeste

The Dwindling Party

The Water Flowers

THE SECRETS

The Other Statue

The Night Bandage et al (in preparation)

MISCELLANEOUS

Category

Dracula: a Toy Theatre

Dogear Wryde Postcards: various series

WITH PETER NEUMEYER

Donald and the ...

Donald Has a Difficulty

Why we have day and night

WITH VICTORIA CHESS

Fletcher and Zenobia

Fletcher and Zenobia Save the Circus

DRAWINGS FOR

The Jumblies, The Dong with a Luminous Nose, EDWARD LEAR

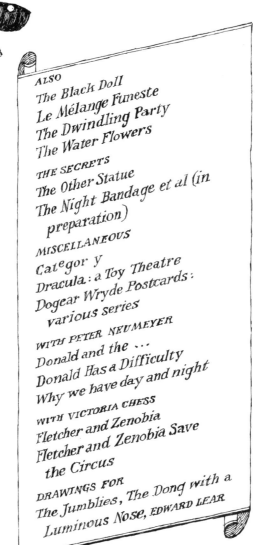

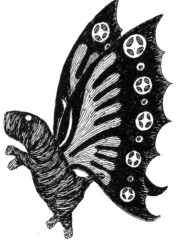

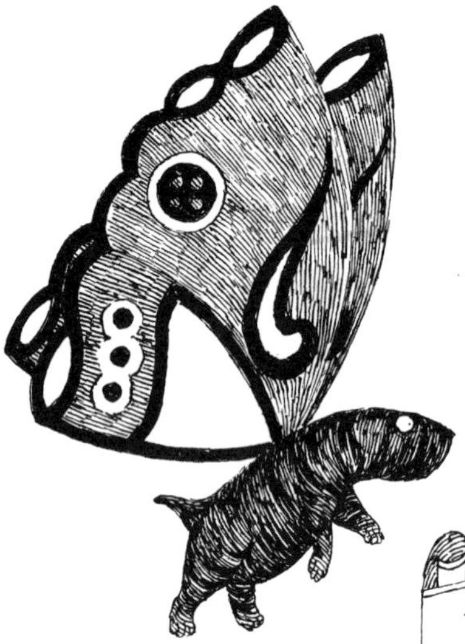